A
GENEVA SERIES
COMMENTARY

1 & 2 TIMOTHY and TITUS

A COMMENTARY ON
1 & 2 TIMOTHY and TITUS

Patrick
Fairbairn

THE BANNER OF TRUTH TRUST

THE BANNER OF TRUTH TRUST
3 Murrayfield Road, Edinburgh EH12 6EL, UK
P. O. Box 621, Carlisle, PA 17013, USA

★

Originally published as *The Pastoral Epistles*
by T. & T. Clark, Edinburgh, 1874

First Banner of Truth Edition 2002
ISBN 0 85151 820 6

★

Printed and bound in Great Britain
by the Bath Press,
Bath.

PREFACE.

THIS expository volume on the Pastoral Epistles had its origin in a department of labour connected with my official duties. Till lately, it was for many years my lot to conduct a class of Pastoral Theology for advanced students preparing for the work of the Christian ministry; and a portion of the time during each session was usually devoted to the exposition and illustration of more or less of those Epistles. Practically, it was found impossible to overtake more, in any particular session, than a comparatively limited portion of them. But as comments on the whole had been prepared, I have thought that the publication of them might be of some advantage to students of Sacred Scripture, especially to those who are either in the position of candidates for the ministry, or without lengthened experience in the discharge of its duties. The requirements and interests of such have been kept specially in view throughout the volume. On that account also, particular respect has been had, both in the course of exposition, and in the introduction and supplementary dissertations, to the objections which have been urged—latterly, indeed, with great boldness and persistency—against the apostolic authorship and divine inspiration of these portions of New Testament Scripture.

The aim of this volume, therefore, will readily be understood to differ considerably from that of Bishop Ellicott's, whose commentary on the Pastoral Epistles bears the designation of "critical and grammatical." The portion of the late Dean Alford's *Commentary on the New Testament* which embraces these Epistles is to a large extent of the same description. Both commentators have very ably accomplished the objects they had more especially in view; and the frequent references I have made to their productions will sufficiently evince how profoundly sensible I am of the services they have rendered to the correct knowledge of the language and import of the Epistles—though on points of some moment I have occasionally felt myself obliged to differ from each of them. While the critical and grammatical have been with me a somewhat less prominent object, neither of them has been overlooked; and wherever the text or the construction is such as to call for special examination or adjustment, this has uniformly received attention, before anything as to doctrine or instruction has been founded on the words. The text of Tischendorf, in his 8th edition, so nearly coincides with what I take to be the correct one, that I have simply adopted it—twice with a measure of hesitation (see pp. 273, 373), and once only with a formal dissent (p. 233). Minor deviations from the Received Text, as in respect to the spelling and order of words, I have consequently deemed it unnecessary to notice; but wherever the sense has been at all affected by any change, the principal grounds have uniformly been adduced on which the text of Tischendorf seems entitled to the preference.

In regard to the translation, my object has been simply

to present the meaning of the original, as I understand it, in the words most nearly equivalent—whether they might accord with those of the Authorized Version or not. This, however, has never been needlessly departed from. With the view of rendering the exposition more extensively useful, I have also, for the most part, translated the quotations taken from the Greek and Latin commentators; but the original has always been given when anything of moment depended upon the precise form of expression. The edition of Winer's *Grammar* referred to is that published by the Messrs. Clark, edited by the Rev. W. F. Moulton.

May the effort here made to explain a portion of the Divine Word, and to vindicate and apply the important lessons of truth and duty therein contained, carry with it the Divine blessing, and prove, in however small a degree, conducive both to the due appreciation of the Word, and to the furtherance of the great ends of the Christian ministry.

P. F.

GLASGOW, *January* 1874.

CONTENTS.

INTRODUCTION—	PAGE
SECTION I.—THE AUTHORSHIP OF THE EPISTLES,	1–19
II.—TIMES AND PLACES OF WRITING,	19–30
III.—NOTICES OF TIMOTHY,	31–34
IV.—NOTICES OF TITUS,	35–36
TEXT AND TRANSLATION OF FIRST TIMOTHY,	38–51
TEXT AND TRANSLATION OF TITUS,	52–57
TEXT AND TRANSLATION OF SECOND TIMOTHY,	58–67
EXPOSITORY NOTES ON FIRST TIMOTHY,	71–254
EXPOSITORY NOTES ON TITUS,	255–305
EXPOSITORY NOTES ON SECOND TIMOTHY,	306–404
APPENDIX A.—THE PECULIAR TESTIMONY FOR GOSPEL TIMES,	405–416
APPENDIX B.—THE MEANING OF THE EXPRESSION, "HUSBAND OF ONE WIFE," IN I TIM. III. 2, ETC.,	416–432
APPENDIX C.—THE TREATMENT OF SLAVERY IN NEW TESTAMENT SCRIPTURE,	432–451
NOTE ON I COR. VII. 21,	448–451

ERRATUM.—Omit "both" in chap. iv. 10, p. 45.

THE PASTORAL EPISTLES.

INTRODUCTION.

SECTION I.—*The Authorship of the Epistles.*

THE designation of *Pastoral Epistles* has been commonly applied to the two Epistles to Timothy and the Epistle to Titus, because alike addressed to persons engaged in pastoral work, and chiefly discoursing of matters relating to such work. They all bear on their front the signature of the Apostle Paul; and never till a comparatively recent period has their connection with his name been called in question by any one having a recognised position in the Christian Church. There *were* parties in ancient times who excluded them from the list of St. Paul's genuine writings; but these were the leaders of Gnosticism, rationalists of a very extreme type, and always regarded by the Fathers as opponents, rather than adherents, of the Christian faith. Speaking of such generally, Clement of Alexandria states that they rejected the Epistles to Timothy (*Strom.* ii. 11); and Marcion, we are told by Tertullian, did the same both with these and with the Epistle to Titus (*Adv. Marc.* v. 21). Jerome, at a later period, repeats the assertion in his Preface to the Epistle to Titus; and referring to Tatian, the disciple of Marcion, mentions that he so far differed from his master as to accept the Epistle to Titus. The conduct of these parties admits of a ready explanation: they found the sentiments contained in the epistles irreconcilable with their speculative tenets and ascetic virtues, and so they discarded the epistles in the interest of their system; as they also, for the same reason, distorted the meaning of many parts of the writings they actually received. The exception made by Tatian in favour of Titus doubtless arose from its less marked contrariety to Gnostic tendencies. But both he and Marcion, and several also who preceded them in the Gnostic schools, are witnesses to the early existence and general acknowledgment of the epistles in question; since otherwise their rejection of these could not have been reported as a noticeable circumstance.

But besides this *incidental* proof, the *direct* evidence of the apostolic authority of the epistles, and of the church's belief in it, is of the most satisfactory kind. The epistles have a place in the most ancient versions, the Peschito and the Italic. They are included in the so-called Canon of Muratori, which, with reference to St. Paul's epistles, mentions *ad Titum una, et ad Timotheum duas*. Irenæus commences his work against heresies with an express quotation from First Timothy, as the words of an apostle suited to the occasion and object of his writings; and in other places he makes direct reference to other passages in the three epistles, always identifying them with the penmanship of the apostle (for example, at iii. 14. 1, iv. 16. 3, i. 16. 3). The same thing is done by Clement of Alexandria (*Strom.* ii. 11, iii. 6, i. 14) and by Tertullian (*De Præscr. Hær.* c. 25, etc.); while by Eusebius the whole three are included among the writings universally acknowledged (*Eccl. Hist.* iii. 25). As a proof, also, of their being in very early and common use, we find expressions and forms of thought peculiar to them appropriated in some of the most ancient Christian writings; for example, in the Epistle of the Roman Clement (as at c. 29, comp. with 1 Tim. ii. 8), the Epistle of Polycarp (c. 4, comp. with 1 Tim. vi. 7, 10), and still more in the writings of Athenagoras, Justin, and Theophilus of Antioch. In short, the historical evidence of the authenticity of the epistles is as full and explicit as could justly be expected, and it were impossible to disparage it in their case without denying its validity in respect to the best accredited books of New Testament Scripture.

Schleiermacher was the first man of note in the church who formally rejected the testimony of antiquity on the subject, and took up a hostile position. His objections, however, were laid only against the First Epistle to Timothy, which he held to be chiefly a compilation out of the second, and the Epistle to Titus. His views were set forth in a letter, published in 1807; but they met with strenuous opposition, even from some who were not remarkable for the strictness of their orthodoxy — in particular, Planck, Bertholdt, Hug, Guericke, Heydenreich. But Schleiermacher had his followers, and followers who, for the most part, did not confine their attacks to the First Epistle to Timothy, but took exception to all the three. So, for example, Eichhorn, Schott, Credner, who regarded them as forgeries done with a good design, probably by Luke, or some other of Paul's disciples. But Baur went further: he thought the work of criticism was imperfectly done till another period altogether than that to which Paul himself belonged was shown to be the one which gave birth to the epistles. And this he thought he found in the times immediately subsequent to the rise of the Marcionite heresy, that is, somewhere about the middle of the second century; when, alarmed at the appearance of this heresy, and anxious to check it, some one bethought himself of a series of letters as the most effectual antidote, written in the name of Paul to two of his well-known companions and fellow-workers. But a date so late, as a basis for such an artificial hypothesis, so palpably conflicts with the historical evidence regarding the epistles, that few beyond the small circle of the Tübingen school have been found ready to accept the solution. De Wette, while he renounced the Pauline authorship of the epistles, was equally opposed to Baur's position, and to the last maintained that the epistles must be ascribed to the closing period of the first century. There are still probably a considerable number of critics in Germany, and a few in our own country, who are inclined to rest in this unsatisfactory conclusion,—a negative one as regards the relation of the epistles to Paul, and, must we not add also, as regards their claim to a place in the canon of New Testament Scripture?

Such is not the inference of the parties themselves. With them the term *canon*, as applied to Scripture, is of somewhat doubtful interpretation, and may include the spurious as well as the genuine, if only written with a good purpose, and in conformity with sound doctrine. So Bleek, for example, in respect to the First Epistle to Timothy (to which he confines his objections, *Introd.* § 186, 187); but Dr. Davidson gives it more roundly in the last form of his Introduction to the New Testament; and with reference to all the Pastoral epistles, he very complacently tells us: "The author chose the name of an apostle to give currency to his sentiments. Being impressed with the idea that a united church with sound doctrine was the best safeguard against heresy [could anybody, we might ask, doubt it?], he chose Timothy and Titus as the superintendents of churches, to whom Paul might address directions about ecclesiastical organization and heretical views. In all this there was no dishonesty, because the intention was good. The device was a harmless one. Though it misled many, the object of the author was gained." Does not this, however, savour of the wily maxim, that the end sanctifies the means? that one may innocently lie, if through the lie the truth of God can anyhow be made to abound more to His glory? St. Paul himself said of all who espoused such a course, that "their damnation was just" (Rom. iii. 7, 8). And beyond doubt it is his verdict, not the loose, easy-going utilitarianism of modern rationalism, that the conscience of Christendom will respond to and ratify. The authority of these epistles for pious uses is gone, if their apostolic authorship cannot be sustained; they must share the fate of all hollow pretensions. But then, how unlike to such is their real character—so simple, so earnest, so elevated in tone, so resolutely contending against every form of corruption, expressly against speaking lies in hypocrisy! How all this, if the writer was conscious to himself of starting with a lie, and lying throughout? For it is not merely that he has at the outset assumed a name not really his own, but has invented a whole series of circumstances and relations which had no foundation in truth; and this, strange to say, in the interest of the truth, and as the best mode of securing its perpetuity in the church! The supposition involves a moral impossibility; for, as has been justly said, "the belief preached by the apostles was not the offspring of the morality, but the morality was the natural fruit of the belief."

It is no small matter, therefore, which is at stake in this controversy; nothing less than the authoritative character and practical value of these Pastoral epistles. Even this consideration should not induce us to play false with any portion of the evidence; but it should certainly dispose us to examine carefully, and with much deliberation weigh, the objections urged against the epistles, before we assent to their validity. Men of the most varied gifts, but of the most approved scholarship and matured judgment, have done so, both in this country and on the Continent, and arrived at the result that there is nothing in the objections to shake their confidence in the genuineness of the writings as the veritable productions of St. Paul. But we shall, for ourselves, consider the more important of them in order.

I. One class of objections is derived from an alleged reference to parties and customs which belong to a later age than the apostle's.

(1.) Of this description is the supposed allusion in several places to Gnosticism of the Marcionite or Valentinian type. There certainly are expressions in the epistles, especially in the First Epistle to Timothy, which can scarcely be understood otherwise than as pointing to the operation of the Gnostic spirit; but still only to this spirit in its incipient state, not in any developed semi-Christian form. Thus, in chap. vi. 20, Timothy is warned to avoid "profane and vain babblings, and oppositions of science falsely so called," or rather "the falsely named gnosis (τῆς ψευδωνύμου γνώσεως)." Nothing is here indicated as to any particular Gnostic theory, which might be rising to the surface in the sphere of Timothy's labours. The expression is quite general, and might have been employed of the Gnostic spirit, as it is known to have manifested itself in the Gospel age, and even prior to it. No one acquainted with the history of the times can doubt that the elements of Gnosticism were then actively at work in many places, and entered deeply into the Alexandrian and Eastern theosophy. But tending, as this always did, to draw the mind into vain and foolish speculations upon subjects which lay beyond the range of human apprehension, it was necessarily characterized by much empty talk, and assumptions of knowledge which had no foundation in realities—soaring idealisms, which might please the imagination or gratify the pride of intellect, but which were of no avail to the higher interests of the soul. Even in Philo there is not a little of this sort of gnosis, although in his writings the tendency exhibited itself in a subdued form as compared with what it did in others.

(2.) Much the same may be said of what is intimated at the beginning of chap. iv., of the apprehended forthputtings of the ascetic spirit—forbidding people to marry, and commanding to abstain from meats, which God made to be received with thanksgiving. Such an intimation is perfectly consistent with the apostolic authorship. For the writer does not say that the teaching in question had already come into operation, and was meeting with acceptance in the church, but that the Spirit gave warnings of its approach; and all that there is any need for supposing is, that tendencies had begun to manifest themselves, which to men of spiritual discernment seemed to point in that direction. But for this there was ample ground in the apostolic age—in the widespread feeling among the better class of theosophists, that the higher degrees of purity were to be attained only through corporeal fastings, and a disentanglement from flesh and blood relations. Such a feeling, with corresponding practices, had been known to exist for generations among the Therapeutæ of Egypt and the Essenes of Judea. And it could scarcely be matter of doubt to thoughtful minds, even without any special revelation from the Spirit of God, that the great facts of Christianity, and the mighty moral impulse that went along with them, would exert a potent influence upon many of the class referred to, and incline them to court an alliance with the church. Indeed, we have evidence from the apostle's own hand, in another and not disputed epistle, that characters of a distinctly marked ascetic type had already been pressing into the Christian fellowship, and in a much less likely quarter than the towns of Asia Minor. It is in chap. xiv. of the Epistle to the Romans where notice is taken, several years before the Pastoral epistles were written, of some who, on religious grounds, would eat nothing but herbs, and abstained from wine; whom the apostle, indeed, characterizes as weak, yet exhorts others to receive and treat as Christian brethren. Even Baur has said of this part of the apostle's writings (*Paulus*, p. 300): "Among the Jewish Christians at Rome there already existed a dualistic view of the world, very closely allied in its root to the Ebionitism of a later age; which is the less to be wondered at, as this dualism in reference to civil life stands in a very natural connection with that view, which sees in the life of nature an impure and demoniacal principle, awakening dislike and abhorrence."

Now this mode of contemplation, and the asceticism naturally springing from it, were not, it must be remembered, indigenous at Rome: their native home was in the East, and they were sure to be met with in greater frequency and fuller efflorescence in the regions where Timothy was fulfilling his commission, than in the western capital of the Empire. The period, also, was more advanced; and it is but natural to suppose, that as elements of that description came to grow and intensify in the church, what might at first be considered merely as a tolerable weakness, should, a little further on, be warned against as a dangerous departing from the simplicity of the gospel.

(3.) There is still another passage in the First Epistle to Timothy, near the commencement, which has been alleged to contain a reference to opinions that were first broached by the Gnostics of the second century. It is at chap. i. 4, where Timothy is exhorted to beware of giving heed to fables ($\mu\tilde{u}\theta o\iota$) and endless genealogies, which served chiefly to minister strife and debate. Apparently, it is things of the same sort which are referred to in Tit. i. 14 under the name of "Jewish fables and commandments of men," and again in chap. iii. 9 as "foolish questions and genealogies, and strifes, and disputations about the law." These genealogies and myths or fables are held by the party of Baur to refer to the fabulous stories of the Gnostics respecting the generation of æons, and in particular to the scheme of Valentinus with its regulated system of 30 æons. It is true that Irenæus, at the beginning of his work on the Gnostic heresies, prefaces what he is going to say on the Valentinian gnosis, by saying certain men had arisen " who set the truth aside, and brought in lying words and vain genealogies, which, as the apostle says, minister questions rather than godly edifying, which is in faith;" but it is merely a passing allusion, and cannot be regarded as more than an accommodation of scriptural words to the subject in hand, whether they might have been originally intended to bear such a reference or not. Tertullian makes a similar use of them, but is more express in connecting that use with their original and proper meaning; for, after noticing the Valentinian fables about the æons, he affirms, " These are the fables and endless genealogies which, while the seeds of them were beginning to bud forth, the spirit of the apostle by anticipation condemned." (*Adv. Valent.* c. iii.). Tertullian so often strains Scripture to make it bear a sense favourable to his own particular views, that no great stress can be laid on his interpretation in the present case. But a considerable number of modern commentators have substantially concurred in that interpretation, such as Grotius, Hammond, Mosheim, Alford, etc. It is open, however, to serious, and indeed fatal objections. First of all, the expressions of the apostle, in their natural and proper sense, refer not to things in heaven, but to things on earth—to the records preserved of personal or family relationships, and tales associated with them. If the writer had actually in view emanations proceeding in the spirit-world, he could with no propriety have presented them under the name of *genealogies*, which are not *emanations*, or even *births* simply, but *birth-registers*—a term inapplicable except by way of figure or accommodation to the heavenly sphere. Besides, in the parallel passages in Titus, the genealogies are connected with contests about the law, and the fables are expressly designated *Jewish;* so that the parties in question must obviously have been viewed as standing on distinctively Jewish ground, and dealing with matters which partook more of a Jewish than a Gnostic complexion. So also, in 1 Tim. i. 7, the persons spoken of as desiring to be teachers of the law are evidently the same with those who a little before are noticed as the broachers of the fables and genealogies warned against. But with matters of law Gnosticism of the fully-fledged kind —the Gnosticism which indulged its fancy in concocting emanation-systems—took little concern; it soared above them. It is a further confirmation of the same view, that Polybius, the only ancient writer out of Scripture who couples together μῦθοι and γενεαλογίαι, does so in precisely the same manner as the apostle: that is, he applies them to the origins of families and nations on earth. He speaks of many having narrated the *genealogies and myths* of nations, their colonies, and kindreds, and foundations (L. ix. c. 2). Schöttgen also has brought forward, on 1 Tim. i. 4, some specimens of Jewish fables respecting genealogies, one of which at least has an important doctrinal bearing; and the whole, whether or not as ancient as the apostle's time, are yet sufficient to show how materials of this description might be made to minister to much fruitless disputation, and even to erroneous teaching. So that we hold—in opposition to a statement made by Alford—they might, and in reality did, touch religious interests quite enough to account for the apostle's strong denunciations of them. We conclude, therefore, that the parties meant by the apostle in this class of references were a sort of pragmatical formalists, if in some sense Christian, or with acknowledged leanings in that direction, yet more Rabbinical than Christian— persons who delighted to talk and wrangle about legal points, who could raise questions and relate stories on the nature and bearings of genealogies, but which were of little moment, however they might be settled; which, for the most part, might be settled anyhow, so far as the great interests of truth and righteousness are concerned. It was every way becoming the aged apostle to warn the youthful evangelist to keep aloof from such a frivolous and fruitless line of things. Indeed, it was just then that such warnings were likely to be needed; as, shortly after the close of the apostolic age, troublers of that description might be said to lose their standing-ground for the Christian church. After that, her chief dangers came from other quarters. This is virtually admitted by Alford, though it seems scarcely to consist with the view he takes of the genealogies and fables. He is satisfied that the false teachers alluded to in the epistles have more of a Judaistic cast about them than could have been the case if full-blown Gnostics had been referred to; that, looked at generally, " they seem to hold a position intermediate to the apostle's former Judaizing adversaries and the subsequent Gnostic heretics—distinct from both, and just at that point in the progress from the one form of error to the other which would suit the period subsequent to the Epistle to the Philippians, and prior to the destruction of Jerusalem. There is therefore nothing in them and their characteristics which can cast a doubt on the genuineness of the epistles" (*Prolog.* p. 77). No, but at the period in question the church had as yet heard nothing of genealogies, in the sense of generations and cycles of æons.

(4.) A class of objections belonging to the same general head of references to things subsequent to the apostolic period, but derived from a different quarter, has respect to the notices contained in the epistles of church order and organization: these seem to betoken too advanced a state of matters for St. Paul's time. So De Wette, as well as Baur and many others, have contended. According to them, the writer gives indication of hierarchical tendencies. If so, they must be allowed to have had little in common with the hierarchical tendencies of a later age. Here we find no bishop, in the modern sense of the term; no priest with strictly sacerdotal functions; no presiding head even of the common council of presbyters, who in a more special manner was charged with the spiritual oversight of the church in each particular place; but an eldership, more or less numerous, sharing in common the spiritual guardianship and edification of the flock. In short, we find only the earliest and simplest form known to us of church order and government, that which had already existed for generations in the Jewish synagogues, and which with little variation was transferred to the newly planted churches of Christian believers. Not only so, but the instructions given through Timothy and Titus to those spiritual overseers are entirely void of hierarchical and ritualistic elements: they press only moral considerations and duties, which had nothing to do with formal distinctions and minutely prescribed observances. In addition to that primitive type of spiritual officers, mention is made only of deacons — the class appointed first, within a few years after the Ascension, in the mother church at Jerusalem, then in the larger churches generally, for administering the pecuniary affairs and charitable offerings of the people. Even these are noticed but once, in connection with Ephesus, not with Crete, where matters were only beginning to take a regulated form when the apostle wrote. All, in a word, as to official organization, is as one might have expected it to be, if anything of this sort was to have been noticed at all; and it is assuredly very different from the kind of references that would have been found, if the epistles had been written after hierarchical principles had developed themselves.

As to what is said about widows, also of marriage-relationships in the case of church officers, there is nothing, when the passages are rightly interpreted, which can be deemed indicative of a state of things alien to the first age of the church. But this can only be exhibited by an analysis of the passages bearing on the subject.

II. We now therefore pass on to another feature in the

epistles, to which exception has been taken; namely, certain peculiarities in the cast of thought and the mode of expression found in these epistles, but not in the genuine writings of Paul. Undoubtedly there are differences of the kind referred to, which cannot well be overlooked. The only question is, Whence did they originate? Are they not explicable by the different circumstances in which the epistles were written, the different topics handled, and the comparatively novel opinions and practices brought into consideration? Beyond doubt, there were very obvious and material differences in these respects. It is nothing to the purpose, therefore, to be told that a great many words occur in these epistles not elsewhere found in the apostle's writings: for, to a certain extent, such are to be found in all his epistles; and here, for the reasons stated, they might be justly expected in greater frequency. The difference is not, after all, very large. Planck has shown that there are 81 words of the kind in question in First Timothy, 63 in Second Timothy, and 44 in Titus. But then in the Epistle to the Philippians there are 54, in Galatians 57, in Ephesians and Colossians together 143. But in these epistles it is the common truths and obligations of the gospel which form the chief subjects of discourse, while the three Pastoral epistles occupy ground in a great degree peculiar to themselves. And when one looks to the varieties produced, and finds among them such examples as the following,—ἔλεος, used in the salutation to Timothy, along with χάρις and εἰρήνη, πιστὸς ὁ λόγος, λόγος ὑγιής, ζητήσεις, μῦθος, σώφρων, εὐσέβεια, βέβηλος,—words which any writer might have used as the particular occasion or the impulse of the moment might have prompted,—one can only wonder at the frivolous ingenuity, which out of things so common could have thought of discovering formidable instances.

The questions which in this respect would really be of a testing kind are such as these: Does any term occur in the Pastoral epistles which was not in use when the apostle lived? Or are words used in senses which were not acquired till a later time? Or, finally, are these turns of thought and expression not appropriate or natural for the apostle to have employed in the position actually occupied by him, and with reference to the ends for which he lived? Such questions would be strictly relevant, and, if capable of being answered in the affirmative, would be fatal to the genuineness of the epistles. But nothing of such a description has been established. There are, indeed, certain forms of expression occurring with some frequency in these epistles, which might, for aught that we can see, have been employed in the other epistles, though in reality they are not: such, for example, as the application of the term *Saviour* specially to God (1 Tim. i. 1, ii. 3, iv. 10; Tit. i. 3); the designation of teaching, according to its quality, as *sound, healthful*, or *unsound, diseased* (1 Tim. i. 10, vi. 3, 4; 2 Tim. i. 13, iv. 3; Tit. i. 9, 13, ii. 1, 8); and the favourite expression of "faithful is the word," or saying (1 Tim. i. 15, iii. 1, iv. 9; 2 Tim. ii. 11; Tit. i. 9). But surely it is quite conceivable that the state of things in the church about the time the epistles were written, especially the kind and tendencies of the errors which had begun to prevail, may have naturally enough led to the employment of such a phraseology. That certain *probable* reasons can be assigned for them, will be shown in the exposition. But is it not also competent to ask, whether it was upon the whole less likely that the apostle would himself resort to such modes of speech in his latter days; or that a mere imitator, counterfeiting his name, would do so? The latter could scarcely afford to venture on a liberty of this description; he would be afraid of his speech betraying him; while Paul himself, writing in the conscious freedom of his own powers and purposes, might readily vary his language, as seemed natural or proper in the circumstances. There is the more force in this consideration, as the general character of the diction is quite Pauline, and in a much greater number of expressions is there a marked resemblance to the other epistles than in those referred to a dissimilarity. On the supposition of our epistles being the production of an artful but well-intentioned imitator, can any reason be conceived why so many delicate and pervading correspondences should have been associated with such marked divergences? Surely he who could catch the one would have taken care to avoid the other.[1]

So far, then, as a change is perceptible in the style, though it is not without a measure of difficulty, it seems most readily accounted for by change of circumstances and lapse of time. "New words very soon are employed, when new ideas arise to require them. The growth of new heresies, the development of church organization, the rapid alteration of circumstances in a great moral revolution, may fitly account for the use of new terms in a new sense. Moreover, the language of letters to individual friends might be expected to differ somewhat from that of public letters to churches" (Conybeare and Howson, ii. 553).

III. A still further source of objections has been found in the contents and structure of the epistles. Of these some are so insignificant and captious, that it is unnecessary to specify them here. Others, also, are so intimately connected with the nature and design of the epistles, that they might equally be urged against any author whatever, as against

[1] Alford has given a pretty long list of the resemblances found in the language of the three epistles with a single one of the undisputed Pauline—that to the Galatians: τοῦ δόντος ἑαυτὸν περί, Gal. i. 4, 1 Tim. ii. 16, Tit. ii. 14; εἰς τοὺς αἰῶνας τῶν αἰώνων, Gal. i. 5, 1 Tim. i. 17; προέκοπτον, Gal. i. 14, 2 Tim. ii. 16, iii. 9; στύλος, Gal. ii. 9, 1 Tim. iii. 15; ἀνόητοι, Gal. iii. 1, 1 Tim. vi. 9, Tit. iii. 3; μεσίτης, Gal. iii. 20, 1 Tim. ii. 5; ἐλπίς objective, Gal. v. 5, Tit. ii. 13; πνεύματι ἄγεσθε, Gal. v. 18, 2 Tim. iii. 6; καιρῷ ἰδίῳ, Gal. vi. 19, 1 Tim. ii. 6, Tit. i. 3. In Rom. xvi. 25, also, there are as many as five verbal correspondences with expressions in the Pastoral epistles.

St. Paul, if not more so. Thus, exception is taken to the constant *moral* reference of what is said in various passages respecting faith, the identifying of sound views of Christian doctrine with a good conscience, and of erroneous doctrine with a bad one. In substance, the same thing is done in other epistles of Paul, only in a more general way (for example, Rom. i. 17, 18, Gal. ii. 17-20, v. 6, etc.). But if what served in good measure to call forth the Pastoral epistles was the growth of a species of heretical doctrine, which tended to sophisticate the conscience, and substitute speculative for saving knowledge, then, whoever the writer might be, he could not have effectually met the evil he sought to correct and guard against, without tracing the evil thus up to its source. The Apostle John does precisely the same thing, when writing with a similar aim, though after his own peculiar style; for example, 1 John i. 6-10, iii. 5-7, 2 John 9-11. "The precepts and directions (says Davidson in his more advanced criticism on these epistles, *Introd.* ii. 169) are ethical and outward, relating to conduct. They touch upon matters of conscience or propriety. The very health of Timothy is attended to. Regulations about churches, their organization, and their office-bearers, are such as might have been left to the judgment of Timothy and Titus themselves." That is to say, everything of such a nature is a matter of perfect indifference as regards the true interests of the church, and may be regulated as seems good to persons of ordinary capacity; although it is notorious from the history of the past, that infinite evil has come into the church from individual caprice in such things, and that if we had wanted this portion of the apostle's writings, we should have been without the best materials we now possess for understanding the original polity and government of the church. Indeed, as Alford has remarked, the opponents of the apostolic authorship of the epistles have most effectually defeated themselves on the aspect of the matter now under consideration. " Schleiermacher, holding First Timothy to be compiled out of the other two, finds it in many respects objectionable and below the mark; Baur will not concede this latter estimate; and De Wette charges Schleiermacher with having failed to penetrate the sense of the writer, and found faults where a more thorough exposition must pronounce a favourable judgment. These differences may well serve to strike out the argument, and indeed all such purely subjective estimates, from the realms of Biblical criticism."

Nor is there any more force in what has been alleged from the structure of the epistles,—those especially to Timothy,—that they want the compactness of Paul's other writings, are somewhat loosely put together, and are occasionally abrupt in their transitions from one topic to another. As if Paul, in writing to a bosom friend and fellow-labourer, should have observed the same regard to method, and pursued a like formal treatment of subjects, as in those epistles which were of the nature of regular discussions! This would have been unnatural; the more so, as the things which fell to be noticed here were of a somewhat varied description, partly relating to Timothy's personal behaviour, and partly to the state of affairs in the church. Accordingly, one of the most striking examples of the unmethodical and abrupt character of the mode of writing characteristic of the epistles — the advice, interjected amid things of higher moment, that Timothy should use a little wine for his stomach's sake and frequent infirmities (1 Tim. v. 23)— is, with his usual discrimination, seized upon by Paley as a convincing proof of verisimilitude and genuineness. " In actual letters (he says), in the negligence of a real correspondence, examples of this kind frequently take place— seldom, I think, in any other production. For the moment a man regards what he writes as a *composition*, which the author of a forgery would of all others be the first to do, notions of order in the management and succession of his thoughts suggest themselves to his judgment, and guide his pen." Thus, what the mere critic, on the outlook for objections, brands with his mark of suspicion, the man of shrewd discernment and practical sagacity, guided mainly by a regard to the habits of actual life, perceived to be one of the surest indications of a genuine frankness and simplicity. Wieseler, I may add, in a recent article in Herzog's *Encyclopædia* (Suppl. iii. p. 296), delivers himself even more strongly, while considering the passage from a slightly different point of view: he conceives the passage, so peculiarly introduced, "to be a striking proof of the genuineness of the epistle, because the deep solicitude manifested in it by Paul for Timothy, not only corresponds with what is known of his loving heart, but appears so individually coloured, and breaks forth so instantaneously, that it could not possibly be counterfeited."

A similar judgment might be pronounced upon a request in 2 Tim. iv. 13, equally homely in its character, and equally abrupt in its manner of introduction. *There* Timothy is desired to bring with him the cloak the apostle had left at Troas, and the books, especially the parchments; quite natural if the apostle himself so wrote, but a most improbable and senseless thing for any one to invent in his name! For "what possible motive there could be for inserting such minute particulars, unexampled in the apostle's other letters, founded on no incident in history, tending to no result, might well baffle the acutest observers of the phenomena of falsification to declare" (Alford).

Without going further into detail here, the conclusion which forces itself upon us from the leading characteristics of the contents and structure of the epistles, is that it was infinitely more likely they should have proceeded from the hand of St. Paul, than from any one falsely assuming his name. There are ample reasons for the one supposition, but none adequate to sustain the other. Had a desire to meet the rising indications of Gnosticism tempted some one to enter the field under false colours, the object would have appeared far more prominent than it actually does, and the epistles would not have presented either the varied or the earnest character which belongs to them. No sinister aim, no predominant idea in the mind of a forger, but only truth and reality, can account for them as they actually exist.

SECTION II.—*Time and Places of Writing.*

A point remains for consideration, and one certainly not unattended with difficulty,—namely, where to find in the history of the apostle a probable or appropriate time and place for the writing of the epistles. It is a difficulty which respects more especially the First Epistle to Timothy. The second epistle bears to have been written in the closing stage of the apostle's career, when the prospect of martyrdom was staring him in the face. Nor is there anything in the known circumstances of the time that can justly be regarded as incompatible with this supposition. The only room for question is, whether it may have been written toward the close of a first or of a second imprisonment. And on this question opposite opinions have been, and probably may still be held; but we shall have occasion to advert to it before we close. As for the Epistle to Titus, since it merely implies a brief connection sometime had by the apostle with Crete,—a connection never touched on in the history of the Acts,—it scarcely admits either of confirmation from circumstantial evidence, or the reverse. It is quite possible, that during the apostle's long sojourn at Corinth, he might have paid a visit to that important island. Or, supposing there was a second imprisonment taking place after a considerable interval from the first, it is perfectly conceivable that opportunity was taken during the interval to visit Crete, leaving Titus behind him to complete the organization of the infant churches. Our chief disadvantage here lies in the scantiness of our materials, the chief historical record having closed some time before the termination of his labours. But, from the striking similarity both in sentiment and modes of expression which the Epistle to Titus presents to the two other Pastoral epistles, it can scarcely be doubted that they belong to much the same period in the apostle's history; and no solution of the question can be deemed quite satisfactory which would place a considerable interval between them.

The historical problem has its chief difficulty, as we have said, in connection with the First Epistle to Timothy. In that epistle no allusion is made to any personal arrest or imprisonment; and for aught that appears, the apostle was quite free when he wrote to regulate his own movements, and discharge his apostolical functions. The most specific historical allusion is at chap. i. 3, where he states that, on setting out for Macedonia, he had besought Timothy to abide still at Ephesus, for the purpose of repressing certain errors in doctrine and corrupt tendencies which had begun to manifest themselves. It is clear from this, and from the whole tenor of the epistle, that the charge devolved on Timothy at Ephesus was one that would require some time for its execution, and that it could not have been St. Paul's intention to assign a very brief limit to it, when, at chap. iii. 14, he expressed a hope of being able to rejoin Timothy shortly (τάχιον). Now there is no period in the history of the apostle, as recorded in the Acts, which exactly meets these conditions, although three several methods have been devised to bring what is recorded into a measure of conformity with them.

1. One, and indeed the readiest to have occurred—adopted by Theodoret, Benson, Michaelis, etc.—was the occasion of the tumult raised in Ephesus by Demetrius and his crafts-

men, which greatly imperilled the life of the apostle, and obliged him to leave the city (Acts xix. 24-xx. 1 ; 2 Cor. i. 8). Paul did then actually go from Ephesus to Macedonia. But a notice in the history shortly before, informs us that he had previously sent Timothy and Erastus away into Macedonia, intending himself presently to follow (xix. 22); the outbreak of Demetrius only served to hasten a little the period of his departure. / But since Timothy had on that occasion been despatched before the apostle, it must plainly have been of some other time that Paul spoke, when he represents himself as having gone to Macedonia, and Timothy as left behind for special work in Ephesus. It is evident also from another consideration, viz. that when he reached Macedonia, he appears either to have rejoined Timothy there, or to have been immediately rejoined by him ; for the Second Epistle to the Corinthians, which was written soon after his going into Macedonia, has the name of Timothy along with his own in the opening salutation. In another epistle also, that to the Romans, which was written only a little later, and after he had proceeded to Corinth, Timothy is mentioned as being at the time with the apostle (xvi. 21). A short period further on, again, his name occurs among several others who left Greece with the apostle, with the view of accompanying him on his last visit to Jerusalem (Acts xx. 4). In such a chain of circumstances, with Timothy always present as a constituent portion, there seems no possibility of getting a situation that corresponds with the opening statement of the epistle.

2. Nor do they suit any better with another mode of explanation,—one adopted by Grotius, Hammond, Bertholdt, etc.,—according to which, while the deputies who accompanied Paul from Greece to Jerusalem went before to Troas, where they waited for the apostle (Acts xx. 5), Timothy, it is supposed, may have proceeded to Ephesus, where he was followed by this epistle, requesting him to

attend to certain matters of importance, and to abide till Paul himself should come. This is altogether improbable, and at variance with the language employed. For, in such a case, it could not with truth have been said that Timothy was besought to abide still at Ephesus (προσμεῖναι) after the apostle had left it. Or, if an earlier period were thought of, as has been done, when Timothy *was* left behind at Ephesus, though he had rejoined the apostle before his work was completed, and again went back from Troas to resume and finish it, the supposition becomes so peculiarly complicated, that it cannot be accepted as a natural explanation of the historical allusion in the epistle. Besides, Paul could not have said at Miletus, a few days after leaving Troas, to the Ephesian elders, that he expected to see their face no more (Acts xx. 25), and yet have written Timothy that he hoped ere long to be with him at Ephesus.

3. A third hypothesis has been formed, and, with several modifications, has met with support from men of thought and learning. Mosheim was the first to propose the solution, according to which there was a temporary visit of Paul to Macedonia, and perhaps to other parts of Greece, some time during his three years' sojourn at Ephesus,—a visit left unnoticed in the history of the Acts. Mosheim thought this view afforded an explanation of an apparent discrepance in the notes of time given in the Acts respecting the duration of the apostle's labours in Ephesus; in one of which, chap. xix. 9, 10, he is said to have first continued for three months, meeting and disputing with the Jews in the synagogue; and in another, that for two whole years he taught in the school of one Tyrannus; while he himself, in addressing the Ephesian elders, reminded them that his labours among them had been protracted to three years (xx. 31). It is supposed that by this expression the apostle may have meant merely that the burden of his time and active agency for that period had been given to Ephesus, while a portion

of it—eight or nine months—may have been spent in Macedonia and elsewhere. And if so, then Timothy may have been left behind at Ephesus to supply the apostle's place, and attend to the matters mentioned in the first epistle. Considered by itself, this supposition is not one that can be designated impossible; and if other things suited, it might (notwithstanding the silence of the writer of the Acts) be accepted as a *probable*, if not quite natural, solution of the difficulty. But it is attended with serious embarrassments, which cannot well be got over; and those who agree in the general about it, fall out among themselves when they go to work out the details. Mosheim placed the supposed visit to Jerusalem early in the three years, without allowing sufficient time for the formation of a church at Ephesus so regularly organized, and the development of tendencies so evidently heretical, as is implied in the epistle. Therefore Schrader and Wieseler have preferred throwing the time back to the latter part of the period in question; but they connect with this tour, besides the visit to Macedonia, a visit also to Achaia and Crete, and even to Cilicia and Antioch.

It seems, however, by no means likely that Paul would have pursued such a lengthened course of ministerial agency in these other places, while matters were plainly emerging at Ephesus which called for delicate and authoritative dealing. Some very urgent reason would have been required to make him do so; of which, however, we know nothing. Then, it is difficult to conceive that at any period during the three years, and while Paul himself was taking the chief charge at Ephesus, the teachers of false doctrine should have begun to assume so dangerous an aspect: their having done so would rather seem to argue his absence for some considerable time, and more favourable circumstances for their mischievous purposes. We may the rather conclude thus, as at a later period still, when addressing at Miletus the elders from Ephesus, it was not yet the actual presence, but only the probable rise, at no distant period, of heretical teachers, respecting which the apostle warned them. Still further, the epistle, in its general character and bearing, seems plainly to point to a much more prolonged and responsible agency on the part of Timothy at Ephesus, than he was at all likely to have had devolved on him if the apostle had only left it for a brief missionary tour. And lastly, we should be obliged, on the hypothesis in question, to separate the First Epistle to Timothy, and also the Epistle to Titus, from the Second Epistle to Timothy, by an interval of several years; while yet the cast of thought and expression in it presents so many resemblances to the two other epistles, and so characteristically differs in that respect from those certainly belonging to an earlier time, that it is difficult to believe there did actually exist such an interval. The whole of the Pastoral epistles must be assigned to much the same period, and *that* later by some years than the other epistles.

This combination of difficulties has been felt by many of the more impartial and considerate investigators to be so serious, that they have renounced as hopeless the attempt to find a place for the Pastoral epistles anywhere within the historical period embraced in the Acts of the Apostles, and have consequently transferred them to a time subsequent to his release from the first imprisonment. So, for example, Paley, Wiesinger, Huther, Conybeare and Howson, Alford, Ellicott. It is no new notion, however; for it was a part of the traditional belief in ancient times concerning the apostle, that the appeal he took at Cæsarea to the Emperor terminated in his favour, and that some years of freedom were granted to him afterwards for the preaching of the gospel. The closing notice in the Acts may itself be taken as proof; for a man who "dwelt two whole years in his own hired house, and received all that came in unto him," could no longer have been looked upon as a culprit: he must either have been acquitted of the charge brought against him, or, as is equally probable, it must have been allowed to drop by the non-appearance of his accusers to support it. They must have seen long before, that in the eye of Roman law they had no proper ground to stand upon. The cause had been heard twice by Roman procurators at Cæsarea, and each time without any legal offence being established against him. Festus even expressed his inability to give formal expression to the charge in a form that could render it properly cognisable in a court of law; and Agrippa, after hearing him, declared his conviction, that but for his own appeal, the prisoner might have been set at liberty (Acts xxv. 27, xxvi. 32). It can scarcely be doubted that lawyers at Rome would come to the same conclusion about it.

This result—namely, that Paul was acquitted and again resumed his labours—is confirmed by various allusions and testimonies. When writing from Rome to the Philippians, some time during his first confinement, he spoke of it as not improbable that he might again be permitted to see them (i. 27). In his Epistle to Philemon also, written probably a little later, he even went further; and as well-nigh certain of being able to revisit his old field of labour in Asia Minor, he requested Philemon to prepare for him a lodging (ver. 22). Then, passing to the Patristic testimonies, the Roman Clement, in his letter to the church at Corinth, represents Paul as having, after being frequently imprisoned and stoned, gone to the extreme west ($\tau\grave{o}$ $\tau\acute{\epsilon}\rho\mu\alpha$ $\tau\hat{\eta}s$ $\delta\acute{v}\sigma\epsilon\omega s$), testifying of the gospel (c. v.), which seems to point to ministrations somewhere farther west than Rome, as the capital of the Empire could scarcely be designated the extremity of the west by any intelligent writer in the Gospel age. Eusebius, giving the common tradition of his time, says that, "after pleading his cause, Paul is reported to have been again sent forth upon the ministry of preaching, and that, on coming a second time to the city, he finished his course with martyrdom" (*Eccl. Hist.* ii. 22). Eusebius connects with this second imprisonment the writing of the Second Epistle to Timothy; and after quoting various passages from it to support the view he takes, he states it as probable that, "since Nero was more disposed to mildness in the beginning of his reign, the apostle's defence of his doctrine would be more willingly received;" but that, as he afterwards advanced to the greatest criminal excesses, the apostles, as well as others, were made to experience the effects. Jerome confirms this testimony in its more essential parts. He says (*Vir. illus.*) that Paul was dismissed by Nero to preach the gospel in the west; and he connects the martyrdom of Paul with the fourteenth year of Nero's reign, probably A.D. 68, *seven* years after Paul first reached Rome, and *five* after the period at which the narrative of the Acts closes.

Holding, then, to the fact of two imprisonments, we may suppose that the apostle, after having regained his liberty from the first, and continued his labours for some time in Rome, went elsewhere to prosecute his apostolic calling. It is possible that he then made good his former purpose of visiting Spain (Rom. xv. 24), though we have no certain evidence of the fact; and the more advanced period of life at which he had now arrived would probably induce him, if not altogether to abandon the design, at least to devote little time to its accomplishment. Hence no particular church in Spain appears to have been able to claim him as its founder. It would naturally seem better for him, a work more in accordance with his declining years, to revisit the scenes of his former labours in Greece and Asia, and give to the churches he had been honoured to plant the benefit of what still remained to him of active service.

He might the more readily be induced to take this course, from the knowledge he had obtained, that during his long confinement, first in Cæsarea and then in Rome, the seeds of error had begun to spring up in several of those churches, and needed to be repressed with a firm yet tender hand. Indications of this are not wanting in some of the epistles he wrote from Rome. But it is impossible for us to trace with any certainty the course he followed. He had expressed a hope of soon being able to see in person his beloved Philippians; and it is quite probable that Philippi and other parts of Greece, being the more easily reached, might be among the first places he revisited. From thence he may have passed over into Asia, spending more or less time at such places as Troas, Laodicea, Colossæ, Ephesus; at which last place, finding matters in a peculiarly critical condition, and requiring prolonged and careful superintendence, he left Timothy behind, himself returning to Macedonia, whence he might find his way back to Ephesus or to the Nicopolis which is mentioned in Tit. iii. 12 as the place where he had resolved to spend a winter. It was most probably the town of that name in Epirus which was meant, but others have thought of Nicopolis in Cilicia. In some one or other of those goings and returnings he most likely took Crete on his way, and, after a short period of labour, left Titus to complete the work.

When the final arrest was laid on the apostle's movements, whether at the instance of some adversaries of the gospel in the regions he was visiting, or by persons in the Roman capital after he had again returned thither, we cannot tell. The ferocious treatment which the Christians in Rome received from Nero in A.D. 64, would naturally embolden the formerly baffled opponents of the apostle to renew their attempts against his life; and, taught by past experience, to do it *now* on more general grounds. The former accusation turned on what might be called distinctively Jewish points; and being laid against one who had the rights of a Roman citizen, the result would necessarily come to be determined by the principles of Roman jurisprudence. But the persecution of Nero had drawn a distinction between Jew and Christian, and had virtually given the adversaries of the gospel a warrant to regard and treat its adherents as in a kind of exceptional position, not entitled to the protection afforded to others by the laws of the Empire. It would therefore be quite easy to get up an accusation against so noted a Christian as Paul, charging him with a violation of the law (for instance) which forbade the introduction of a new and illicit religion (*religio nova et illicita*), or of being a ringleader of the party who had set fire to the city. To be so arraigned was to be placed in a far more perilous position than when charged merely with disrespect as to the punctilios of Jewish religiousness; it was to be brought into conflict with the constitution and safety of the commonwealth, and eyed as a person of dangerous revolutionary principles. On this account, doubtless, it is that we are to explain, not only the different termination of the second impeachment from the first, but also the painfully different behaviour of his friends under it. On the former occasion the apostle seems to have had no reason to complain; he received from them the most gratifying proofs of sympathy and kindness, so that his prison-house became a centre of attraction rather than a ground of repulsion. But during the second trial all seems sadly changed for the worse: at the first hearing of his case, "no man stood by him;" "all forsook him and fled;" and things looked so disastrously, that friend after friend departed, one in this direction, another in that. Onesiphorus is mentioned as singular in having "sought him out, not being ashamed of his chain." Luke alone at last remained with him. All, doubtless, because, from the nature of the accusation, it was to imperil one's life even to appear in a friendly relation to the apostle; his sympathizers might be involved in the same condemnation with himself. It is evident, from the notices in the closing verses of Second Timothy, that Paul very keenly felt the loneliness in which this state of matters left him; but he clung only the more closely to the one all-sufficient Friend, and found the support he needed. As to the kind of death he suffered, Jerome says it was by being beheaded, and the body was buried in the Ostian Way. But these are only later traditions, and no great value can be attached to them.

There is so much of verisimilitude in the general outline just sketched, that it may be acquiesced in as by much the most probable view that can now be entertained of the last days of the apostle. And in addition to the various collateral circumstances already noticed, which speak in favour of it, there are a few allusions of an incidental kind in the Second Epistle to Timothy, which can scarcely be made to consist with anything but a later visit to Greece and Asia, between a first and a second impeachment. Thus, at chap. iv. 13, he requests Timothy to bring with him the cloak and the books he had left at Troas,—a request which can hardly be understood of things left there when the apostle was on his way from Greece to Jerusalem, before his arrest in the temple; since, on any computation, a good many years must have elapsed between that and the writing of the epistle, and many opportunities must meanwhile have occurred to regain possession of the things he had left. Again, it is said in iv. 20, that the apostle had left Trophimus at Miletus sick, which was certainly not the case on the occasion of his going up from Greece to Jerusalem; for not only was Trophimus then with him, but it was his appearance with Paul in the city which afforded the Jews a pretext for charging Paul with defiling the temple, by bringing Greeks into it. Still further, it is said in the same verse that "Erastus abode at Corinth," that is, remained there when Paul left it. But as Timothy himself was with Paul when he left Corinth to proceed to Jerusalem, Timothy could not require to be informed of it; and besides, as years had anyhow elapsed since then, it would have been out of place to notice it as a piece of news *now*. Everything seems to point to a succession of circumstances belonging to a period subsequent to the first imprisonment.

Of the subscriptions to the three Pastoral epistles, the first is manifestly wrong; for it names Laodicea as the place of writing, while in the epistle itself the writer speaks of himself as having left Ephesus for Macedonia: so that Philippi, or some other town in that region, is most naturally thought of as the place from which it proceeded. There is also an error in the subscription to the Epistle to Titus; for it gives the date as from Nicopolis in Macedonia, while no Nicopolis is known to have belonged to that province. Probably Nicopolis in Macedonia was a mistake for Nicopolis in Epirus. But even that had been wrong (see at Tit. iii. 12). So that, out of three subscriptions, two are almost certainly erroneous. And this is but a sample of the subscriptions generally, which are oftener wrong than right; because, as Paley notes, they were founded on loose traditions, or a hasty view of some particular text. Yet, as he justly adds, "if the *epistles* had been forged, the whole must have been made up of the same elements as those of which the subscriptions are composed; and it would have remained to be accounted for, how, whilst so many errors were crowded into the concluding clauses of the letters, so much consistency should be preserved in other parts."

Section III.—*Notices of Timothy.*

The Timothy to whom two of the Pastoral epistles were addressed, was from an early period a close companion and attendant of St. Paul. He is first mentioned in the narrative of Paul's *second* missionary tour through the cities of Asia Minor (Acts xvi. 1 sq.). He was a native of Derbe or Lystra—of which of them cannot be quite certainly determined; but the probability seems to lie on the side of Lystra, as, in a passage where Gaius and Timothy are mentioned together (Acts xx. 4), the epithet Δερβαῖος is applied only to Gaius, as if in that respect to distinguish him from Timothy. His mother and grandmother were exemplary and pious Jewish females (2 Tim. i. 5), but his father was a Greek. That he was converted to the Christian faith through the ministrations of the apostle, and on the occasion of his first visit to Lystra, there can be little doubt, as the apostle designates him his own or his true child in the faith (1 Tim. i. 2); and by the time of the apostle's second visit, he was in good repute among the brethren (Acts xvi. 2). Young as he was, there was something in his spirit and deportment which deeply impressed the apostle with his aptitude for the work of the ministry; and finding that Timothy himself, and those more immediately interested in him, were disposed to comply with St. Paul's wish in the matter, "he took and circumcised him," because the Jews in the neighbourhood knew that his father was a Greek, and would, as a matter of course, have refused to allow Timothy to utter a word in their synagogues, until he had submitted to the initiatory ordinance of the covenant (ver. 3). He was afterwards solemnly destined to the work, by the imposition both of the apostle's hands and of the hands of the presbytery (1 Tim. iv. 14; 2 Tim. i. 6), though the specific time and place are not mentioned.

We have no other instance of such a near, unbroken, and prolonged fellowship in the history of apostolic times, as that which appears to have subsisted between Paul and this youthful disciple; the more remarkable, considering the disparity of their ages. From the period that Timothy entered upon his ministerial discipleship, he seems rarely to have been absent for any length of time from the apostle; and even when not expressly mentioned among his companions, some turn in the affairs, or incidental expression, reveals the presence of the beloved disciple. Thus, in the narrative of the Acts, Paul and Silas are alone mentioned as having come to Philippi, preaching the gospel: yet Timothy, it appears, must also have been with them; for, when Paul was sent away from Beræa to Athens, Silas and Timothy are said to have remained behind (Acts xvii. 14 sq.). His youthful appearance, in all probability, saved him from the violent treatment which Paul and Silas had to endure at Philippi, and the other places they visited in that region. After staying for some time at Beræa, and, at Paul's request, returning again to Thessalonica (1 Thess. ii. 5, iii. 2), he rejoined the apostle at Corinth, along with Silas (1 Thess. iii. 6). He seems to have continued with the apostle during his long stay in that city; and the name of Timothy, as well as that of Silas, is coupled with his own by the apostle in both of the epistles to the Thessalonians, which were sent from Corinth. We next find him with St. Paul at Ephesus (Acts xix. 22), whence he was sent with Erastus to Macedonia and Corinth (1 Cor. iv. 7, xvi. 10). He was again with Paul in Macedonia when the Second Epistle to the Corinthians was written, in which his name has a place in the address, along with Paul's. He was also with Paul at Corinth during the brief sojourn there, when the Epistle to the Romans was written, although his name is not in the address (Rom. xvi. 21); and he was one of those who accompanied the apostle from Greece, when he went towards Jerusalem with the contributions of the churches (Acts xx. 4). But the last notice of him in that connection reaches no further than Troas (chap. xx. 5); and for a period of upwards of two years nothing more is heard of him. We can scarcely doubt, however, that he was chiefly at Cæsarea during Paul's long imprisonment there, ministering as far as possible to his comfort, and in every available way acting for him, and for the interests of the gospel. But the next express mention that is made of him is in some of the epistles written by Paul from Rome; though we are without any information as to the mode of his transference thither—whether by accompanying the apostle (as is most likely) in his perilous voyage, or going by some other route. His name, at any rate, occurs in three of the epistles sent from Rome — those to Philippi, Colossæ, Philemon — following that of Paul in the opening address; and in the Epistle to the Philippians there is a very strong and favourable testimony given respecting Timothy, placing him above all the other fellow-labourers of the apostle for thorough devotedness of spirit and self-sacrificing zeal: " But I trust in the Lord Jesus to send Timothy shortly unto you, that I also may be of good comfort when I know your state. For I have no man like-minded, who will naturally care for your state; for all seek their own, not the things which are Jesus Christ's. But ye know the proof of him, that, as a son with his father, he hath served me in the gospel" (Phil. ii. 19-22).

Whether Timothy was able to fulfil the mission here contemplated cannot be certainly determined; nor do we know much of his future course, except that he appears to have also, like his master, suffered unto bonds (Heb. xiii. 23)—showing that he did not want the martyr spirit; and after having for a time accompanied Paul in his apostolic labours during the period between his first and second imprisonment in Rome, Timothy (as we learn from the two epistles addressed to him) was left at Ephesus for a season, while

Paul went to labour elsewhere. The last request from the apostle to him, of which we have any record, is one entreating him to hasten with all speed to Rome, that Paul might see him again before he suffered. But whether this solace was granted to him or not, remains doubtful. The connection between the two probably lasted from about A.D. 51 to A.D. 67 or 68.

The character of Timothy is chiefly to be inferred from the incidental notices of him which have been alluded to. It speaks much for his stedfast faith, his warm piety, and unflagging zeal, that he should have remained so firm in his attachment to the apostle, sharing with him in all his trials, dangers, and labours; and not less that the apostle should so fondly have clung to him, and so highly appreciated him. Attempts have been made to show that some abatement has to be made in this respect in the later period of their connection; but, I am convinced, entirely without success, as I have endeavoured to prove in the exposition of those passages in the Second Epistle on which the charge has been chiefly grounded. To the last, St. Paul appears to have reposed in Timothy the fullest confidence, and to have made him the object of the fondest solicitude and affection. Important and responsible duties were devolved on him, in the discharge of which his name is associated with no failure or disappointment. And yet he seems to have been fitted for a subordinate rather than a primary place in ministerial agency; and he may have been constitutionally deficient, to some extent, in decision and practical energy. This impression is not unnaturally produced by the very urgent entreaties to watchfulness and fidelity addressed to him in the epistles; and is confirmed by the total absence of any memorials of his agency, except in connection with his spiritual father. No church appears to have claimed him as its founder.

Section iv.—*Notices of Titus.*

Extremely little is known of Titus, either as a man or as an evangelist. The accounts that have reached us about him are quite incidental and fragmentary. His name never occurs in the history of the Acts; which is somewhat strange, as we know from the Epistle to the Galatians that he was with Paul and Barnabas at Antioch, and accompanied them to Jerusalem when they went to have the dispute settled about circumcision (Gal. ii. 1–3). We learn, from the brief notice given us of what took place on that occasion, that Paul sternly refused to have him circumcised, as some of the Jewish Christians wished; because he saw that in *his* case the principle of gospel liberty was at stake, and must at whatever hazard be vindicated. It therefore appears not only that Titus was a Gentile, but that he must have also been employed chiefly in ministering to Gentiles, or to churches in which these formed the predominating element. He appears, at a later period, to have been with Paul and Timothy at Ephesus, doubtless sharing with these in the manifold labours attendant on the planting of the church in that centre of idolatry and corruption. From Ephesus he was sent forth by Paul to Corinth, for the purpose of stimulating the brethren to get forward their contributions for the poor saints at Jerusalem (2 Cor. viii. 6, xii. 18). He rejoined the apostle in Macedonia, and cheered him with the report he brought, not only of the progress of the contributions, but also of the salutary effect produced by the first epistle of Paul to the church at Corinth (vii. 6–15). In the whole of these delicate transactions he appears to have conducted himself with great prudence and fidelity.

The precise period when he went with the apostle to Crete cannot (as already stated) be ascertained. But that the work entrusted to him there bespoke the high confidence placed in him by the apostle, admits of no doubt. And subsequently to this, only one notice more occurs of him; it is in 2 Tim. iv. 10, where he is said to have gone to Dalmatia. The fact alone is mentioned, and we cannot be sure whether it took place before the apostle was again laid under arrest, or previously to it. It served, among other things, to make the apostle feel more lonely and desolate; but we are not thence warranted to infer that any blame on account of it was attributable to Titus.

THE GREEK TEXT OF THE EPISTLES

AND

ENGLISH TRANSLATION.

ΠΡΟΣ ΤΙΜΟΘΕΟΝ Α΄.

I. 1 Παῦλος ἀπόστολος Χριστοῦ Ἰησοῦ κατ' ἐπιταγὴν Θεοῦ σωτῆρος ἡμῶν καὶ Χριστοῦ Ἰησοῦ τῆς ἐλπίδος ἡμῶν 2 Τιμοθέῳ γνησίῳ τέκνῳ ἐν πίστει. χάρις, ἔλεος, εἰρήνη ἀπὸ Θεοῦ πατρὸς καὶ Χριστοῦ Ἰησοῦ τοῦ κυρίου ἡμῶν.

3 Καθὼς παρεκάλεσά σε προσμεῖναι ἐν Ἐφέσῳ, πορευόμενος εἰς Μακεδονίαν, ἵνα παραγγείλῃς τισὶν μὴ ἑτεροδιδασκαλεῖν 4 μηδὲ προσέχειν μύθοις καὶ γενεαλογίαις ἀπεράντοις, αἵτινες ἐκζητήσεις παρέχουσιν μᾶλλον ἢ οἰκονομίαν Θεοῦ τὴν ἐν πίστει· 5 τὸ δὲ τέλος τῆς παραγγελίας ἐστὶν ἀγάπη ἐκ καθαρᾶς καρδίας καὶ συνειδήσεως ἀγαθῆς καὶ πίστεως ἀνυποκρίτου, 6 ὧν τινὲς ἀστοχήσαντες ἐξετράπησαν εἰς ματαιολογίαν, 7 θέλοντες εἶναι νομοδιδάσκαλοι, μὴ νοοῦντες μήτε ἃ λέγουσιν μήτε περὶ τίνων διαβεβαιοῦνται. 8 οἴδαμεν δὲ ὅτι καλὸς ὁ νόμος, ἐάν τις αὐτῷ νομίμως χρῆται, 9 εἰδὼς τοῦτο, ὅτι δικαίῳ νόμος οὐ κεῖται, ἀνόμοις δὲ καὶ ἀνυποτάκτοις, ἀσεβέσι καὶ ἁμαρτωλοῖς, ἀνοσίοις καὶ βεβήλοις, πατρολῴαις καὶ μητρολῴαις, ἀνδροφόνοις, 10 πόρνοις, ἀρσενοκοίταις, ἀνδραποδισταῖς, ψεύσταις, ἐπιόρκοις, καὶ εἴ τι ἕτερον τῇ ὑγιαινούσῃ διδασκαλίᾳ ἀντίκειται, 11 κατὰ τὸ εὐαγγέλιον τῆς δόξης τοῦ μακαρίου Θεοῦ, ὃ ἐπιστεύθην ἐγώ. 12 χάριν ἔχω τῷ ἐνδυναμώσαντί με Χριστῷ Ἰησοῦ τῷ κυρίῳ ἡμῶν, ὅτι πιστόν με ἡγήσατο θέμενος εἰς διακονίαν, 13 τὸ πρότερον ὄντα βλάσφημον καὶ διώκτην καὶ ὑβριστήν· ἀλλὰ ἠλεήθην, ὅτι ἀγνοῶν ἐποίησα ἐν ἀπιστίᾳ, 14 ὑπερεπλεόνασεν δὲ ἡ χάρις τοῦ κυρίου

THE FIRST EPISTLE TO TIMOTHY.

I. 1 Paul, an apostle of Christ Jesus, according to the commandment of God our Saviour, and Christ Jesus our hope; 2 to Timothy, [my] true child in the faith: Grace, mercy, peace from God the Father, and Christ Jesus our Lord. 3 According as I besought thee when setting out for Macedonia, [so I do now], to abide still at Ephesus, in order that thou mightest charge some not to teach any other doctrine; 4 nor to give heed to fables, and endless genealogies, inasmuch as they minister strifes rather than God's dispensation that is in faith. 5 Now the end of the charge is love out of a pure heart, and a good conscience, and faith unfeigned: 6 from which some having swerved, they turned aside into vain talk; 7 desiring to be teachers of the law, without understanding either what things they speak, or concerning what things they affirm. 8 We know, indeed, that the law is good, if one use it lawfully; 9 knowing this, that the law is not made for a righteous person, but for the lawless and unruly, for the ungodly and sinful, the unholy and profane, for smiters of fathers and smiters of mothers, for murderers, 10 for fornicators, abusers of themselves with mankind, men-stealers, liars, perjured persons, and if there be anything else that is contrary to the sound instruction; 11 according to the gospel of the glory of the blessed God, which was committed to my trust. 12 I give thanks to Christ Jesus our Lord, who hath strengthened me, for that he reckoned me faithful, appointing me to the service [of the ministry]; 13 though I was formerly a blasphemer, a persecutor, and outrageous: but I obtained

ἡμῶν μετὰ πίστεως καὶ ἀγάπης τῆς ἐν Χριστῷ Ἰησοῦ. 15 πιστὸς ὁ λόγος καὶ πάσης ἀποδοχῆς ἄξιος, ὅτι Χριστὸς Ἰησοῦς ἦλθεν εἰς τὸν κόσμον ἁμαρτωλοὺς σῶσαι, ὧν πρῶτός εἰμι ἐγώ· 16 ἀλλὰ διὰ τοῦτο ἠλεήθην, ἵνα ἐν ἐμοὶ πρώτῳ ἐνδείξηται Ἰησοῦς Χριστὸς τὴν ἅπασαν μακροθυμίαν, πρὸς ὑποτύπωσιν τῶν μελλόντων πιστεύειν ἐπ᾽ αὐτῷ εἰς ζωὴν αἰώνιον. 17 τῷ δὲ βασιλεῖ τῶν αἰώνων, ἀφθάρτῳ ἀοράτῳ μόνῳ Θεῷ, τιμὴ καὶ δόξα εἰς τοὺς αἰῶνας τῶν αἰώνων· ἀμήν.

18 Ταύτην τὴν παραγγελίαν παρατίθεμαί σοι, τέκνον Τιμόθεε, κατὰ τὰς προαγούσας ἐπὶ σὲ προφητείας, ἵνα στρατεύσῃ ἐν αὐταῖς τὴν καλὴν στρατείαν, 19 ἔχων πίστιν καὶ ἀγαθὴν συνείδησιν, ἥν τινες ἀπωσάμενοι περὶ τὴν πίστιν ἐναυάγησαν· 20 ὧν ἐστιν Ὑμέναιος καὶ Ἀλέξανδρος, οὓς παρέδωκα τῷ σατανᾷ, ἵνα παιδευθῶσιν μὴ βλασφημεῖν.

II. 1 Παρακαλῶ οὖν πρῶτον πάντων ποιεῖσθαι δεήσεις, προσευχάς, ἐντεύξεις, εὐχαριστίας, ὑπὲρ πάντων ἀνθρώπων, 2 ὑπὲρ βασιλέων καὶ πάντων τῶν ἐν ὑπεροχῇ ὄντων, ἵνα ἤρεμον καὶ ἡσύχιον βίον διάγωμεν ἐν πάσῃ εὐσεβείᾳ καὶ σεμνότητι. 3 τοῦτο καλὸν καὶ ἀπόδεκτον ἐνώπιον τοῦ σωτῆρος ἡμῶν Θεοῦ, 4 ὃς πάντας ἀνθρώπους θέλει σωθῆναι καὶ εἰς ἐπίγνωσιν ἀληθείας ἐλθεῖν. 5 εἷς γὰρ Θεός, εἷς καὶ μεσίτης Θεοῦ καὶ ἀνθρώπων, ἄνθρωπος Χριστὸς Ἰησοῦς, 6 ὁ δοὺς ἑαυτὸν ἀντίλυτρον ὑπὲρ πάντων, τὸ μαρτύριον καιροῖς ἰδίοις, 7 εἰς ὃ ἐτέθην ἐγὼ κῆρυξ καὶ ἀπόστολος, ἀλήθειαν λέγω, οὐ ψεύδομαι, διδάσκαλος ἐθνῶν ἐν πίστει καὶ ἀληθείᾳ.

8 Βούλομαι οὖν προσεύχεσθαι τοὺς ἄνδρας ἐν παντὶ τόπῳ ἐπαίροντας ὁσίους χεῖρας χωρὶς ὀργῆς καὶ διαλογισμοῦ· 9 ὡσαύτως καὶ γυναῖκας ἐν καταστολῇ κοσμίῳ, μετὰ αἰδοῦς καὶ σωφροσύνης κοσμεῖν ἑαυτάς, μὴ ἐν πλέγμασιν καὶ χρυσῷ ἢ μαργαρίταις

mercy, because I did it ignorantly in unbelief. 14 But the grace of our Lord superabounded with faith and love that are in Christ Jesus.

15 Faithful is the word, and worthy of all acceptation, that Christ Jesus came into the world to save sinners, of whom I am chief. 16 Howbeit for this cause I obtained mercy, in order that in me first Jesus Christ might show forth all long-suffering, for a pattern to those who are going to believe on him to life everlasting. 17 Now to the King of the ages, the incorruptible, invisible, only God, be honour and glory, for ages of ages (or, for ever and ever). Amen.

18 This charge I commit to thee, child Timothy, according to the prophecies which went before on thee, in order that in them thou mayest war the good warfare; 19 holding faith and a good conscience, which some having thrust away, concerning faith made shipwreck: 20 of whom is Hymenæus and Alexander, whom I delivered over to Satan, that they might learn not to blaspheme.

II. 1 I exhort then, first of all, that petitions, prayers, supplications, thanksgivings, be made for all men; 2 for kings, and all that are in authority; in order that we may pass a quiet and tranquil life in all godliness and gravity. 3 For this is good and acceptable before our Saviour God; 4 Who willeth all men to be saved, and to come to the full knowledge of the truth. 5 For there is one God, one Mediator also of God and men, [a] man Christ Jesus; 6 who gave himself a ransom for all—the testimony for its own seasons. 7 Whereunto I was appointed a herald, and an apostle (I speak the truth, I lie not), a teacher of the Gentiles in faith and truth. 8 I wish, then, that prayer be made in every place by men, lifting up holy hands, without wrath and doubting. 9 Likewise also, that women adorn themselves in orderly apparel, with shamefastness and discretion; not in plaitings, and gold, or pearls, or costly

ἢ ἱματισμῷ πολυτελεῖ, 10 ἀλλ᾽ ὃ πρέπει γυναιξὶν ἐπαγγελλομέναις θεοσέβειαν, δι᾽ ἔργων ἀγαθῶν. 11 Γυνὴ ἐν ἡσυχίᾳ μανθανέτω ἐν πάσῃ ὑποταγῇ· 12 διδάσκειν δὲ γυναικὶ οὐκ ἐπιτρέπω, οὐδὲ αὐθεντεῖν ἀνδρός, ἀλλ᾽ εἶναι ἐν ἡσυχίᾳ. 13 Ἀδὰμ γὰρ πρῶτος ἐπλάσθη, εἶτα Εὔα. 14 καὶ Ἀδὰμ οὐκ ἠπατήθη, ἡ δὲ γυνὴ ἐξαπατηθεῖσα ἐν παραβάσει γέγονεν, 15 σωθήσεται δὲ διὰ τῆς τεκνογονίας, ἐὰν μείνωσιν ἐν πίστει καὶ ἀγάπῃ καὶ ἁγιασμῷ μετὰ σωφροσύνης.

III. 1 Πιστὸς ὁ λόγος· εἴ τις ἐπισκοπῆς ὀρέγεται, καλοῦ ἔργου ἐπιθυμεῖ. 2 δεῖ οὖν τὸν ἐπίσκοπον ἀνεπίλημπτον εἶναι, μιᾶς γυναικὸς ἄνδρα, νηφάλιον, σώφρονα, κόσμιον, φιλόξενον, διδακτικόν, 3 μὴ πάροινον, μὴ πλήκτην, ἀλλὰ ἐπιεικῆ, ἄμαχον, ἀφιλάργυρον, 4 τοῦ ἰδίου οἴκου καλῶς προϊστάμενον, τέκνα ἔχοντα ἐν ὑποταγῇ μετὰ πάσης σεμνότητος, — 5 εἰ δέ τις τοῦ ἰδίου οἴκου προστῆναι οὐκ οἶδεν, πῶς ἐκκλησίας Θεοῦ ἐπιμελήσεται;— 6 μὴ νεόφυτον, ἵνα μὴ τυφωθεὶς εἰς κρίμα ἐμπέσῃ τοῦ διαβόλου. 7 δεῖ δὲ καὶ μαρτυρίαν καλὴν ἔχειν ἀπὸ τῶν ἔξωθεν, ἵνα μὴ εἰς ὀνειδισμὸν ἐμπέσῃ καὶ παγίδα τοῦ διαβόλου. 8 Διακόνους ὡσαύτως σεμνούς, μὴ διλόγους, μὴ οἴνῳ πολλῷ προσέχοντας, μὴ αἰσχροκερδεῖς, 9 ἔχοντας τὸ μυστήριον τῆς πίστεως ἐν καθαρᾷ συνειδήσει. 10 καὶ οὗτοι δὲ δοκιμαζέσθωσαν πρῶτον, εἶτα διακονείτωσαν ἀνέγκλητοι ὄντες. 11 γυναῖκας ὡσαύτως σεμνάς, μὴ διαβόλους, νηφαλίους, πιστὰς ἐν πᾶσιν. 12 διάκονοι ἔστωσαν μιᾶς γυναικὸς ἄνδρες, τέκνων καλῶς προϊστάμενοι καὶ τῶν ἰδίων οἴκων. 13 οἱ γὰρ καλῶς διακονήσαντες βαθμὸν ἑαυτοῖς καλὸν περιποιοῦνται καὶ πολλὴν παρρησίαν ἐν πίστει τῇ ἐν Χριστῷ Ἰησοῦ.

14 Ταῦτά σοι γράφω ἐλπίζων ἐλθεῖν πρὸς σὲ τάχιον· 15 ἐὰν

raiment; 10 but, which becometh women professing godliness, through good works. 11 Let a woman learn in silence, in all subjection. 12 But I permit not a woman to teach, nor to lord it over the man, but to be in silence. 13 For Adam was first formed, then Eve. 14 And Adam was not deceived; but the woman, being wholly deceived, fell into transgression. 15 But she shall be saved through the child-bearing, if they abide in faith, love, and holiness, with discretion.

III. 1 Faithful is the saying, If any one seeketh the office of pastor, he desireth a good work. 2 A pastor, then, ought to be blameless, husband of one wife, sober, discreet, orderly, hospitable, apt to teach; 3 not a brawler, not a striker, but mild, peaceable; not a lover of money; 4 ruling well his own house, having children in subjection with all gravity. 5 But if one knows not how to rule his own house, how shall he take charge of the church of God? 6 Not a novice, lest, being carried with conceit, he should fall into the condemnation of the devil. 7 But he must also have a good testimony from those that are without, lest he fall into reproach and the snare of the devil.

8. In like manner, [ought] the deacons to be grave, not double-tongued, not addicted to much wine, not lovers of base gain; 9 holding the mystery of the faith in a pure conscience. 10 And these, too, let them first be proved; then let them serve as deacons, if they be without blame. 11 Women, in like manner, [it behoves] to be grave, not slanderers, sober, faithful in all things. 12 Let the deacons be husbands of one wife, ruling well their children and their own houses. 13 For those who have done the office of a deacon well obtain for themselves a good degree, and much boldness in the faith which is in Christ Jesus.

14. These things I write to thee, hoping to come to thee shortly. 15 But if I should tarry, in order that thou mayest

δὲ βραδύνω, ἵνα εἰδῇς πῶς δεῖ ἐν οἴκῳ Θεοῦ ἀναστρέφεσθαι, ἥτις ἐστὶν ἐκκλησία Θεοῦ ζῶντος, στῦλος καὶ ἑδραίωμα τῆς ἀληθείας. 16 καὶ ὁμολογουμένως μέγα ἐστὶν τὸ τῆς εὐσεβείας μυστήριον· ὃς ἐφανερώθη ἐν σαρκί, ἐδικαιώθη ἐν πνεύματι, ὤφθη ἀγγέλοις, ἐκηρύχθη ἐν ἔθνεσιν, ἐπιστεύθη ἐν κόσμῳ, ἀνελήμφθη ἐν δόξῃ.

IV. 1 Τὸ δὲ πνεῦμα ῥητῶς λέγει ὅτι ἐν ὑστέροις καιροῖς ἀποστήσονταί τινες τῆς πίστεως, προσέχοντες πνεύμασιν πλάνοις καὶ διδασκαλίαις δαιμονίων, 2 ἐν ὑποκρίσει ψευδολόγων, κεκαυστηριασμένων τὴν ἰδίαν συνείδησιν, 3 κωλυόντων γαμεῖν, ἀπέχεσθαι βρωμάτων, ἃ ὁ Θεὸς ἔκτισεν εἰς μετάλημψιν μετὰ εὐχαριστίας τοῖς πιστοῖς καὶ ἐπεγνωκόσι τὴν ἀλήθειαν. 4 ὅτι πᾶν κτίσμα Θεοῦ καλόν, καὶ οὐδὲν ἀπόβλητον μετὰ εὐχαριστίας λαμβανόμενον· 5 ἁγιάζεται γὰρ διὰ λόγου Θεοῦ καὶ ἐντεύξεως.

6 Ταῦτα ὑποτιθέμενος τοῖς ἀδελφοῖς καλὸς ἔσῃ διάκονος Χριστοῦ Ἰησοῦ, ἐντρεφόμενος τοῖς λόγοις τῆς πίστεως καὶ τῆς καλῆς διδασκαλίας ᾗ παρηκολούθηκας· 7 τοὺς δὲ βεβήλους καὶ γραώδεις μύθους παραιτοῦ. γύμναζε δὲ σεαυτὸν πρὸς εὐσέβειαν. 8 ἡ γὰρ σωματικὴ γυμνασία πρὸς ὀλίγον ἐστὶν ὠφέλιμος· ἡ δὲ εὐσέβεια πρὸς πάντα ὠφέλιμός ἐστιν, ἐπαγγελίαν ἔχουσα ζωῆς τῆς νῦν καὶ τῆς μελλούσης. 9 πιστὸς ὁ λόγος καὶ πάσης ἀποδοχῆς ἄξιος. 10 εἰς τοῦτο γὰρ κοπιῶμεν καὶ ἀγωνιζόμεθα, ὅτι ἠλπίκαμεν ἐπὶ Θεῷ ζῶντι, ὅς ἐστιν σωτὴρ πάντων ἀνθρώπων, μάλιστα πιστῶν.

11 Παράγγελλε ταῦτα καὶ δίδασκε. 12 μηδείς σου τῆς νεότητος καταφρονείτω, ἀλλὰ τύπος γίνου τῶν πιστῶν, ἐν λόγῳ, ἐν ἀναστροφῇ, ἐν ἀγάπῃ, ἐν πίστει, ἐν ἁγνείᾳ. 13 ἕως ἔρχομαι πρόσεχε τῇ ἀναγνώσει, τῇ παρακλήσει, τῇ διδασκαλίᾳ. 14 μὴ ἀμέλει τοῦ ἐν σοὶ χαρίσματος, ὃ ἐδόθη σοι διὰ προφητείας μετὰ

know how thou oughtest to conduct thyself in God's house, which indeed is the church of the living God, the pillar and basement of the truth. 16 And confessedly great is the mystery of godliness, who was manifested in the flesh, was justified in the Spirit, was seen by angels, was preached among the Gentiles, was believed on in the world, was received up into glory.

IV. 1 But the Spirit speaks expressly, that in after times some shall depart from the faith, giving heed to seducing spirits and teachings of demons; 2 in hypocrisy of speakers of lies, who have had their conscience scarred; 3 forbidding to marry, [bidding] to abstain from meats, which God made to be partaken of with thanksgiving by the faithful, and those who have the full knowledge of the truth. 4 For everything made by God is good, and nothing to be rejected, being received with thanksgiving; 5 for it is sanctified through the word of God and prayer. 6 By submitting these things to the brethren, thou shalt be a good servant of Christ Jesus, nourishing thyself up in the words of the faith, and of the good instruction which thou hast diligently followed. 7 But the profane and old-wives' fables avoid; and rather exercise thyself unto godliness. 8 For bodily exercise is profitable unto little; but godliness is profitable unto all things, having promise of the life that now is, and of that which is to come. 9 Faithful is the word, and worthy of all acceptation. 10 For to this [end] we both toil and strive, because we have hoped upon the living God, who is the Saviour of all men, especially of those who believe.—11 Charge these things, and teach. 12 Let no one despise thy youth; but become thou a pattern of the believers, in word, in behaviour, in love, in faith, in purity. 13 Till I come, give attention to the reading, the exhortation, the teaching. 14 Neglect not the gift that is in thee, which was given thee through prophecy, with the laying on

ἐπιθέσεως τῶν χειρῶν τοῦ πρεσβυτερίου. 15 ταῦτα μελέτα, ἐν τούτοις ἴσθι, ἵνα σου ἡ προκοπὴ φανερὰ ᾖ πᾶσιν. 16 ἔπεχε σεαυτῷ καὶ τῇ διδασκαλίᾳ, ἐπίμενε αὐτοῖς· τοῦτο γὰρ ποιῶν καὶ σεαυτὸν σώσεις καὶ τοὺς ἀκούοντάς σου.

V. 1 Πρεσβυτέρῳ μὴ ἐπιπλήξῃς ἀλλὰ παρακάλει ὡς πατέρα, νεωτέρους ὡς ἀδελφούς, 2 πρεσβυτέρας ὡς μητέρας, νεωτέρας ὡς ἀδελφὰς ἐν πάσῃ ἁγνείᾳ. 3 Χήρας τίμα τὰς ὄντως χήρας. 4 εἰ δέ τις χήρα τέκνα ἢ ἔκγονα ἔχει, μανθανέτωσαν πρῶτον τὸν ἴδιον οἶκον εὐσεβεῖν καὶ ἀμοιβὰς ἀποδιδόναι τοῖς προγόνοις· τοῦτο γάρ ἐστιν ἀπόδεκτον ἐνώπιον τοῦ Θεοῦ. 5 ἡ δὲ ὄντως χήρα καὶ μεμονωμένη ἤλπικεν ἐπὶ Θεὸν καὶ προσμένει ταῖς δεήσεσιν καὶ ταῖς προσευχαῖς νυκτὸς καὶ ἡμέρας· 6 ἡ δὲ σπαταλῶσα ζῶσα τέθνηκεν. 7 καὶ ταῦτα παράγγελλε ἵνα ἀνεπίλημπτοι ὦσιν. 8 εἰ δέ τις τῶν ἰδίων καὶ μάλιστα οἰκείων οὐ προνοεῖται, τὴν πίστιν ἤρνηται καὶ ἔστιν ἀπίστου χείρων.

9 Χήρα καταλεγέσθω μὴ ἔλαττον ἐτῶν ἑξήκοντα γεγονυῖα, ἑνὸς ἀνδρὸς γυνή, 10 ἐν ἔργοις καλοῖς μαρτυρουμένη, εἰ ἐτεκνοτρόφησεν, εἰ ἐξενοδόχησεν, εἰ ἁγίων πόδας ἔνιψεν, εἰ θλιβομένοις ἐπήρκεσεν, εἰ παντὶ ἔργῳ ἀγαθῷ ἐπηκολούθησεν. 11 νεωτέρας δὲ χήρας παραιτοῦ· ὅταν γὰρ καταστρηνιάσωσιν τοῦ Χριστοῦ, γαμεῖν θέλουσιν, 12 ἔχουσαι κρίμα ὅτι τὴν πρώτην πίστιν ἠθέτησαν· 13 ἅμα δὲ καὶ ἀργαὶ μανθάνουσιν περιερχόμεναι τὰς οἰκίας, οὐ μόνον δὲ ἀργαὶ ἀλλὰ καὶ φλύαροι καὶ περίεργοι, λαλοῦσαι τὰ μὴ δέοντα. 14 βούλομαι οὖν νεωτέρας γαμεῖν, τεκνογονεῖν, οἰκοδεσποτεῖν, μηδεμίαν ἀφορμὴν διδόναι τῷ ἀντικειμένῳ λοιδορίας χάριν· 15 ἤδη γάρ τινες ἐξετράπησαν ὀπίσω τοῦ σατανᾶ. 16 εἴ τις πιστὴ ἔχει χήρας, ἐπαρκείσθω αὐταῖς, καὶ μὴ βαρείσθω ἡ ἐκκλησία, ἵνα ταῖς ὄντως χήραις ἐπαρκέσῃ.

of the hands of the presbytery. 15 Be mindful of these things; be in them, in order that thy progress may be manifest to all. 16 Give heed to thyself and to the teaching; continue in them; for, by so doing, thou shalt save both thyself and them that hear thee.

V. 1 Reprimand not an elderly person, but exhort him as a father, younger men as brothers; 2 elderly women as mothers; the younger as sisters, with all purity. 3 Honour widows that are widows indeed. 4 If, however, any widow has children or grandchildren, let them first learn to show piety in their own home, and requite their parents, for this is acceptable before God. 5 But she who is a widow indeed, and desolate, has set her hope on God, and abides in supplications and prayers night and day. 6 But she that lives deliciously is dead while she lives. 7 And these things enjoin, in order that they may be without reproach. 8 But if any one provides not for his own, and especially for those of his own house, he has denied the faith, and is worse than an unbeliever.—9 Let a widow be enrolled who has become not less than sixty years old, wife of one man, 10 well reported of in respect to good works; if she brought up children; if she entertained strangers; if she washed the feet of saints; if she relieved the distressed; if she followed after every good work. 11 But younger widows decline: for when they shall become wanton against Christ, they desire to marry; 12 having condemnation, because they made void their first faith. 13 Moreover, they learn also to be idle, going about from house to house; and not only idle, but tattlers also, and busybodies, speaking things which they ought not. 14 I wish, therefore, that the younger [widows] marry, bear children, manage the house, give no occasion for reproach to the adversary. 15 For already some have turned away after Satan. 16 If any woman that believes hath widows, let support be given to them, and let not the

17 Οἱ καλῶς προεστῶτες πρεσβύτεροι διπλῆς τιμῆς ἀξιούσθωσαν, μάλιστα οἱ κοπιῶντες ἐν λόγῳ καὶ διδασκαλίᾳ. 18 λέγει γὰρ ἡ γραφή· βοῦν ἀλοῶντα οὐ φιμώσεις, καί· ἄξιος ὁ ἐργάτης τοῦ μισθοῦ αὐτοῦ. 19 κατὰ πρεσβυτέρου κατηγορίαν μὴ παραδέχου, ἐκτὸς εἰ μὴ ἐπὶ δύο ἢ τριῶν μαρτύρων. 20 Τοὺς ἁμαρτάνοντας ἐνώπιον πάντων ἔλεγχε, ἵνα καὶ οἱ λοιποὶ φόβον ἔχωσιν. 21 Διαμαρτύρομαι ἐνώπιον τοῦ Θεοῦ καὶ Χριστοῦ Ἰησοῦ καὶ τῶν ἐκλεκτῶν ἀγγέλων ἵνα ταῦτα φυλάξῃς χωρὶς προκρίματος, μηδὲν ποιῶν κατὰ πρόσκλισιν. 22 Χεῖρας ταχέως μηδενὶ ἐπιτίθει, μηδὲ κοινώνει ἁμαρτίαις ἀλλοτρίαις. σεαυτὸν ἁγνὸν τήρει. 23 μηκέτι ὑδροπότει, ἀλλὰ οἴνῳ ὀλίγῳ χρῶ διὰ τὸν στόμαχον καὶ τὰς πυκνάς σου ἀσθενείας. 24 Τινῶν ἀνθρώπων αἱ ἁμαρτίαι πρόδηλοί εἰσιν προάγουσαι εἰς κρίσιν, τισὶν δὲ καὶ ἐπακολουθοῦσιν· 25 ὡσαύτως καὶ τὰ ἔργα τὰ καλὰ πρόδηλα, καὶ τὰ ἄλλως ἔχοντα κρυβῆναι οὐ δύνανται.

VI. 1 Ὅσοι εἰσὶν ὑπὸ ζυγὸν δοῦλοι, τοὺς ἰδίους δεσπότας πάσης τιμῆς ἀξίους ἡγείσθωσαν, ἵνα μὴ τὸ ὄνομα τοῦ Θεοῦ καὶ ἡ διδασκαλία βλασφημῆται. 2 οἱ δὲ πιστοὺς ἔχοντες δεσπότας μὴ καταφρονείτωσαν, ὅτι ἀδελφοί εἰσιν, ἀλλὰ μᾶλλον δουλευέτωσαν, ὅτι πιστοί εἰσιν καὶ ἀγαπητοὶ οἱ τῆς εὐεργεσίας ἀντιλαμβανόμενοι.

Ταῦτα δίδασκε καὶ παρακάλει. 3 εἴ τις ἑτεροδιδασκαλεῖ καὶ μὴ προσέχεται ὑγιαίνουσιν λόγοις τοῖς τοῦ κυρίου ἡμῶν Ἰησοῦ Χριστοῦ καὶ τῇ κατ' εὐσέβειαν διδασκαλίᾳ, 4 τετύφωται, μηδὲν ἐπιστάμενος, ἀλλὰ νοσῶν περὶ ζητήσεις καὶ λογομαχίας, ἐξ ὧν γίνεται φθόνος, ἔρις, βλασφημίαι, ὑπόνοιαι πονηραί, 5 διαπαρατριβαὶ διεφθαρμένων ἀνθρώπων τὸν νοῦν καὶ ἀπεστερημένων τῆς ἀληθείας, νομιζόντων πορισμὸν εἶναι τὴν εὐσέβειαν. 6 ἔστιν δὲ πορισμὸς μέγας ἡ εὐσέβεια μετὰ αὐταρκείας. 7 οὐδὲν γὰρ εἰση-

church be burdened, that it may relieve those who are widows indeed. 17 Let the elders who govern well be counted worthy of double honour, especially those who labour in word and teaching. 18 For the Scripture saith, Thou shalt not muzzle an ox while treading out [the corn]; and, The labourer is worthy of his hire. 19 Against an elder receive not an accusation, except it be upon two or three witnesses. 20 Those that sin rebuke before all, in order that the rest also may have fear. 21 I solemnly charge thee before God and Christ Jesus, and the elect angels, that thou keep these things, without prejudging, doing nothing by partiality. 22 Lay hands on no one hastily, neither be partaker in other men's sins. 23 No longer drink water, but use a little wine for thy stomach's sake, and thy frequent ailments. 24 The sins of some men are manifest, going before to judgment; with some, again, they follow after. 25 In like manner also the works that are good are manifest, and those that are otherwise cannot be hid.

VI. 1 Whoever are under the yoke as bond-servants, let them reckon their own masters worthy of all honour, that the name of God and his doctrine may not be blasphemed. 2 But such as have believing masters, let them not despise them, because they are brethren; but the rather serve them, because they who receive the benefit are faithful and beloved. These things teach and exhort. 3 If any one teacheth other doctrine, and does not assent to sound words, those [namely] of our Lord Jesus Christ, and the instruction that is according to godliness; 4 he is carried with conceit, knowing nothing, doting about questions and word-fightings, whence come envy, strife, blasphemies, evil surmisings, 5 settled feuds of men corrupted in their mind and destitute of the truth, who suppose that godliness is gain. 6 But godliness with contentment is great gain. 7

νέγκαμεν εἰς τὸν κόσμον, ὅτι οὐδὲ ἐξενεγκεῖν τι δυνάμεθα· 8 ἔχοντες δὲ διατροφὰς καὶ σκεπάσματα, τούτοις ἀρκεσθησόμεθα. 9 οἱ δὲ βουλόμενοι πλουτεῖν ἐμπίπτουσιν εἰς πειρασμὸν καὶ παγίδα καὶ ἐπιθυμίας πολλὰς ἀνοήτους καὶ βλαβεράς, αἵτινες βυθίζουσιν τοὺς ἀνθρώπους εἰς ὄλεθρον καὶ ἀπώλειαν. 10 ῥίζα γὰρ πάντων τῶν κακῶν ἐστὶν ἡ φιλαργυρία, ἧς τινὲς ὀρεγόμενοι ἀπεπλανήθησαν ἀπὸ τῆς πίστεως καὶ ἑαυτοὺς περιέπειραν ὀδύναις πολλαῖς.

11 Σὺ δέ, ὦ ἄνθρωπε Θεοῦ, ταῦτα φεῦγε· δίωκε δὲ δικαιοσύνην, εὐσέβειαν, πίστιν, ἀγάπην, ὑπομονήν, πραϋπαθίαν. 12 ἀγωνίζου τὸν καλὸν ἀγῶνα τῆς πίστεως, ἐπιλαβοῦ τῆς αἰωνίου ζωῆς, εἰς ἣν ἐκλήθης καὶ ὡμολόγησας τὴν καλὴν ὁμολογίαν ἐνώπιον πολλῶν μαρτύρων. 13 παραγγέλλω ἐνώπιον Θεοῦ τοῦ ζωογονοῦντος τὰ πάντα καὶ Χριστοῦ Ἰησοῦ τοῦ μαρτυρήσαντος ἐπὶ Ποντίου Πειλάτου τὴν καλὴν ὁμολογίαν, 14 τηρῆσαί σε τὴν ἐντολὴν ἄσπιλον ἀνεπίλημπτον μέχρι τῆς ἐπιφανείας τοῦ κυρίου ἡμῶν Ἰησοῦ Χριστοῦ, 15 ἣν καιροῖς ἰδίοις δείξει ὁ μακάριος καὶ μόνος δυνάστης, ὁ βασιλεὺς τῶν βασιλευόντων καὶ κύριος τῶν κυριευόντων, 16 ὁ μόνος ἔχων ἀθανασίαν, φῶς οἰκῶν ἀπρόσιτον, ὃν εἶδεν οὐδεὶς ἀνθρώπων οὐδὲ ἰδεῖν δύναται· ᾧ τιμὴ καὶ κράτος αἰώνιον, ἀμήν.

17 Τοῖς πλουσίοις ἐν τῷ νῦν αἰῶνι παράγγελλε μὴ ὑψηλὰ φρονεῖν, μηδὲ ἠλπικέναι ἐπὶ πλούτου ἀδηλότητι, ἀλλ' ἐπὶ Θεῷ τῷ παρέχοντι ἡμῖν πάντα πλουσίως εἰς ἀπόλαυσιν, 18 ἀγαθοεργεῖν, πλουτεῖν ἐν ἔργοις καλοῖς, εὐμεταδότους εἶναι, κοινωνικούς, 19 ἀποθησαυρίζοντας ἑαυτοῖς θεμέλιον καλὸν εἰς τὸ μέλλον, ἵνα ἐπιλάβωνται τῆς ὄντως ζωῆς.

20 Ὦ Τιμόθεε, τὴν παραθήκην φύλαξον, ἐκτρεπόμενος τὰς βεβήλους κενοφωνίας καὶ ἀντιθέσεις τῆς ψευδωνύμου γνώσεως, 21 ἥν τινες ἐπαγγελλόμενοι περὶ τὴν πίστιν ἠστόχησαν.

Ἡ χάρις μεθ' ὑμῶν.

For we brought nothing into the world, because neither are we able to carry anything out of it. 8 But if we have food and raiment, with these we shall be satisfied. 9 But they who aim at being rich fall into temptation, and a snare, and many foolish and hurtful lusts, such as sink men into destruction and perdition. 10 For a root of all evils is the love of money, which some reaching after, have wandered away from the faith, and pierced themselves through with many pangs.—11 But thou, O man of God, flee these things; and follow after righteousness, godliness, faith, love, patience, meekness of spirit. 12 Maintain the good contest of the faith, lay hold of eternal life, unto which thou wert called, and didst confess the good confession before many witnesses. 13 I charge thee before God, who preserveth alive all things, and Christ Jesus, who before Pontius Pilate witnessed the good confession, 14 that thou keep the commandment spotless and unrebukeable, until the appearance of our Lord Jesus Christ: 15 which in his own seasons he shall show, [who is] the blessed and only Potentate, the King of kings, and Lord of lords; 16 who only has immortality, dwelling in light that is unapproachable; whom no man hath seen, nor can see: to whom be honour and power everlasting. Amen.

17 Charge them that are rich in this world not to be high-minded, nor to set their hopes on the uncertainty of riches, but on God, who ministers to us all things richly for enjoyment; 18 that they do good, that they be rich in excellent deeds, free in distributing, ready to communicate; 19 treasuring up for themselves a good foundation for the future, in order that they may lay hold of what is life indeed.—20 O Timothy, keep the deposit, turning away from the profane babblings, and oppositions of knowledge falsely so called; 21 which some professing, have erred concerning the faith. Grace be with you.

ΠΡΟΣ ΤΙΤΟΝ.

I. 1 Παῦλος δοῦλος Θεοῦ, ἀπόστολος δὲ Ἰησοῦ Χριστοῦ κατὰ πίστιν ἐκλεκτῶν Θεοῦ καὶ ἐπίγνωσιν ἀληθείας τῆς κατ᾽ εὐσέβειαν 2 ἐπ᾽ ἐλπίδι ζωῆς αἰωνίου, ἣν ἐπηγγείλατο ὁ ἀψευδὴς Θεὸς πρὸ χρόνων αἰωνίων, 3 ἐφανέρωσεν δὲ καιροῖς ἰδίοις τὸν λόγον αὐτοῦ ἐν κηρύγματι, ὃ ἐπιστεύθην ἐγὼ κατ᾽ ἐπιταγὴν τοῦ σωτῆρος ἡμῶν Θεοῦ, 4 Τίτῳ γνησίῳ τέκνῳ κατὰ κοινὴν πίστιν. χάρις καὶ εἰρήνη ἀπὸ Θεοῦ πατρὸς καὶ Χριστοῦ Ἰησοῦ τοῦ σωτῆρος ἡμῶν.

5 Τούτου χάριν ἀπέλιπόν σε ἐν Κρήτῃ, ἵνα τὰ λείποντα ἐπιδιορθώσῃ καὶ καταστήσῃς κατὰ πόλιν πρεσβυτέρους, ὡς ἐγώ σοι διεταξάμην, 6 εἴ τις ἐστὶν ἀνέγκλητος, μιᾶς γυναικὸς ἀνήρ, τέκνα ἔχων πιστά, μὴ ἐν κατηγορίᾳ ἀσωτίας ἢ ἀνυπότακτα. 7 δεῖ γὰρ τὸν ἐπίσκοπον ἀνέγκλητον εἶναι ὡς Θεοῦ οἰκονόμον, μὴ αὐθάδη, μὴ ὀργίλον, μὴ πάροινον, μὴ πλήκτην, μὴ αἰσχροκερδῆ, 8 ἀλλὰ φιλόξενον, φιλάγαθον, σώφρονα, δίκαιον, ὅσιον, ἐγκρατῆ, 9 ἀντεχόμενον τοῦ κατὰ τὴν διδαχὴν πιστοῦ λόγου, ἵνα δυνατὸς ᾖ καὶ παρακαλεῖν ἐν τῇ διδασκαλίᾳ τῇ ὑγιαινούσῃ καὶ τοὺς ἀντιλέγοντας ἐλέγχειν. 10 Εἰσὶν γὰρ πολλοὶ ἀνυπότακτοι, ματαιολόγοι καὶ φρεναπάται, μάλιστα οἱ ἐκ τῆς περιτομῆς, 11 οὓς δεῖ ἐπιστομίζειν, οἵτινες ὅλους οἴκους ἀνατρέπουσιν διδάσκοντες ἃ μὴ δεῖ αἰσχροῦ κέρδους χάριν. 12 εἶπέν τις ἐξ αὐτῶν ἴδιος αὐτῶν προφήτης· Κρῆτες ἀεὶ ψεῦσται, κακὰ θηρία, γαστέρες ἀργαί. 13 ἡ μαρτυρία αὕτη ἐστὶν ἀληθής. δι᾽ ἣν αἰτίαν ἔλεγχε αὐτοὺς ἀποτόμως, ἵνα ὑγιαίνωσιν ἐν τῇ πίστει, 14 μὴ προσέχοντες Ἰουδαϊκοῖς μύθοις καὶ ἐντολαῖς ἀνθρώπων ἀποστρεφομένων τὴν ἀλήθειαν. 15 πάντα καθαρὰ τοῖς καθαροῖς· τοῖς δὲ μεμιαμμένοις καὶ ἀπίσ-

THE EPISTLE TO TITUS.

I. 1 Paul, a servant of God, also an apostle of Jesus Christ for the faith of God's elect, and the full knowledge of the truth that is according to godliness; 2 in hope of eternal life, which God, that cannot lie, promised before eternal times; 3 but in its own seasons manifested his word in preaching, which was entrusted to me, according to the commandment of our Saviour God; 4 to Titus, [my] true son in respect to the common faith: Grace and peace from God our Father, and Christ Jesus our Saviour.—5 For this cause I left thee behind in Crete, that thou shouldest further set in order the things which are wanting, and mightest appoint elders in every city, as I directed thee: 6 If any one is blameless, husband of one wife, having faithful children, not accused of profligacy, or unruly. 7 For a pastor must be blameless, as God's steward; not self-willed, not soon angry, not a brawler, not a striker, not greedy of gain; 8 but hospitable, a lover of good, discreet, righteous, holy, temperate; 9 holding fast the faithful word according to the teaching, in order that he may be able both to exhort with the sound doctrine and to convince the gainsayers. 10 For there are many unruly vain-talkers and deceivers, especially they of the circumcision: 11 whose mouths must be stopped; who for the sake of base gain subverted whole houses, teaching things which they ought not. 12 One of them, their own prophet, has said, The Cretans are alway liars, evil beasts, idle bellies. 13 This testimony is true: wherefore reprove them sharply, that they may be sound in the faith; 14 not giving heed to Jewish fables and commandments of men, who turn away from the truth. 15 To the pure all things

τοις οὐδὲν καθαρόν, ἀλλὰ μεμίανται αὐτῶν καὶ ὁ νοῦς καὶ ἡ συνείδησις. 16 Θεὸν ὁμολογοῦσιν εἰδέναι, τοῖς δὲ ἔργοις ἀρνοῦνται, βδελυκτοὶ ὄντες καὶ ἀπειθεῖς καὶ πρὸς πᾶν ἔργον ἀγαθὸν ἀδόκιμοι.

II. 1 Σὺ δὲ λάλει ἃ πρέπει τῇ ὑγιαινούσῃ διδασκαλίᾳ. 2 πρεσβύτας νηφαλίους εἶναι, σεμνούς, σώφρονας, ὑγιαίνοντας τῇ πίστει, τῇ ἀγάπῃ, τῇ ὑπομονῇ· 3 πρεσβύτιδας ὡσαύτως ἐν καταστήματι ἱεροπρεπεῖς, μὴ διαβόλους, μὴ οἴνῳ πολλῷ δεδουλωμένας, καλοδιδασκάλους, 4 ἵνα σωφρονίζουσιν τὰς νέας φιλάνδρους εἶναι, φιλοτέκνους, 5 σώφρονας, ἁγνάς, οἰκουργούς, ἀγαθάς, ὑποτασσομένας τοῖς ἰδίοις ἀνδράσιν, ἵνα μὴ ὁ λόγος τοῦ Θεοῦ βλασφημῆται. 6 Τοὺς νεωτέρους ὡσαύτως παρακάλει σωφρονεῖν, 7 περὶ πάντα σεαυτὸν παρεχόμενος τύπον καλῶν ἔργων, ἐν τῇ διδασκαλίᾳ ἀφθορίαν, σεμνότητα, 8 λόγον ὑγιῆ ἀκατάγνωστον, ἵνα ὁ ἐξ ἐναντίας ἐντραπῇ μηδὲν ἔχων λέγειν περὶ ἡμῶν φαῦλον. 9 Δούλους ἰδίοις δεσπόταις ὑποτάσσεσθαι, ἐν πᾶσιν εὐαρέστους εἶναι, μὴ ἀντιλέγοντας, 10 μὴ νοσφιζομένους, ἀλλὰ πᾶσαν πίστιν ἐνδεικνυμένους ἀγαθήν, ἵνα τὴν διδασκαλίαν τὴν τοῦ σωτῆρος ἡμῶν Θεοῦ κοσμῶσιν ἐν πᾶσιν.

11 Ἐπεφάνη γὰρ ἡ χάρις τοῦ Θεοῦ σωτήριος πᾶσιν ἀνθρώποις, 12 παιδεύουσα ἡμᾶς, ἵνα ἀρνησάμενοι τὴν ἀσέβειαν καὶ τὰς κοσμικὰς ἐπιθυμίας σωφρόνως καὶ δικαίως καὶ εὐσεβῶς ζήσωμεν ἐν τῷ νῦν αἰῶνι, 13 προσδεχόμενοι τὴν μακαρίαν ἐλπίδα καὶ ἐπιφάνειαν τῆς δόξης τοῦ μεγάλου Θεοῦ καὶ σωτῆρος ἡμῶν Χριστοῦ Ἰησοῦ, 14 ὃς ἔδωκεν ἑαυτὸν ὑπὲρ ἡμῶν ἵνα λυτρώσηται ἡμᾶς ἀπὸ πάσης ἀνομίας καὶ καθαρίσῃ ἑαυτῷ λαὸν περιούσιον, ζηλωτὴν καλῶν ἔργων.

15 Ταῦτα λάλει καὶ παρακάλει καὶ ἔλεγχε μετὰ πάσης ἐπιταγῆς· μηδείς σου περιφρονείτω.

are pure : but to them that are defiled and unbelieving is nothing pure ; but both their mind and conscience are defiled. 16 They profess that they know God ; but in works they deny [him], being abominable, and disobedient, and unto every good work reprobate.

II. 1 But speak thou the things which become the sound instruction [of the gospel] : 2 that the aged men be sober, grave, discreet, sound in faith, in love, in patience. 3 In like manner the aged women, that they demean themselves as becomes holiness, not slanderers, not enslaved to much wine, teachers of what is good ; 4 that they school the young women to be lovers of their husbands, lovers of their children, 5 discreet, chaste, workers at home, good, submitting themselves to their own husbands, that the word of God may not be blasphemed. 6 The younger men, in like manner, exhort to be sober-minded. 7 In all things showing thyself a pattern of good works : in thy teaching [showing] incorruption, gravity, 8 sound discourse that cannot be condemned ; in order that he who is of the contrary part may be ashamed, having no evil thing to say of us. 9 Bondmen [exhort to be] in subjection to their own masters, in all things to be well-pleasing ; not gainsaying ; 10 not purloining, but showing all good fidelity ; in order that in all things they may adorn the doctrine of our Saviour God.—11 For the grace of God, having salvation for all men, was manifested ; 12 disciplining us to the end that, denying ungodliness and worldly lusts, we might live soberly, justly, and godlily in this present world ; 13 looking for the blessed hope and appearing of the glory of the great God, and of our Saviour Jesus Christ ; 14 who gave himself for us, in order that he might redeem us from all iniquity, and purify to himself a peculiar people, zealous of good works. 15 These things speak, and exhort, and reprove with all authority. Let no one despise thee.

III. 1 Ὑπομίμνησκε αὐτοὺς ἀρχαῖς ἐξουσίαις ὑποτάσσεσθαι, πειθαρχεῖν, πρὸς πᾶν ἔργον ἀγαθὸν ἑτοίμους εἶναι, 2 μηδένα βλασφημεῖν, ἀμάχους εἶναι, ἐπιεικεῖς, πᾶσαν ἐνδεικνυμένους πραΰτητα πρὸς πάντας ἀνθρώπους. 3 ἦμεν γάρ ποτε καὶ ἡμεῖς ἀνόητοι, ἀπειθεῖς, πλανώμενοι, δουλεύοντες ἐπιθυμίαις καὶ ἡδοναῖς ποικίλαις, ἐν κακίᾳ καὶ φθόνῳ διάγοντες, στυγητοί, μισοῦντες ἀλλήλους· 4 ὅτε δὲ ἡ χρηστότης καὶ ἡ φιλανθρωπία ἐπεφάνη τοῦ σωτῆρος ἡμῶν Θεοῦ, 5 οὐκ ἐξ ἔργων τῶν ἐν δικαιοσύνῃ ἃ ἐποιήσαμεν ἡμεῖς, ἀλλὰ κατὰ τὸ αὐτοῦ ἔλεος ἔσωσεν ἡμᾶς διὰ λουτροῦ παλινγενεσίας καὶ ἀνακαινώσεως πνεύματος ἁγίου, 6 οὗ ἐξέχεεν ἐφ᾽ ἡμᾶς πλουσίως διὰ Ἰησοῦ Χριστοῦ τοῦ σωτῆρος ἡμῶν, 7 ἵνα δικαιωθέντες τῇ ἐκείνου χάριτι κληρονόμοι γενηθῶμεν κατ᾽ ἐλπίδα ζωῆς αἰωνίου. 8 πιστὸς ὁ λόγος, καὶ περὶ τούτων βούλομαί σε διαβεβαιοῦσθαι, ἵνα φροντίζωσιν καλῶν ἔργων προΐστασθαι οἱ πεπιστευκότες Θεῷ. ταῦτά ἐστιν καλὰ καὶ ὠφέλιμα τοῖς ἀνθρώποις· 9 μωρὰς δὲ ζητήσεις καὶ γενεαλογίας καὶ ἔριν καὶ μάχας νομικὰς περιΐστασο· εἰσὶν γὰρ ἀνωφελεῖς καὶ μάταιοι. 10 αἱρετικὸν ἄνθρωπον μετὰ μίαν καὶ δευτέραν νουθεσίαν παραιτοῦ, 11 εἰδὼς ὅτι ἐξέστραπται ὁ τοιοῦτος καὶ ἁμαρτάνει ὢν αὐτοκατάκριτος.

12 Ὅταν πέμψω Ἀρτεμᾶν πρὸς σὲ ἢ Τυχικόν, σπούδασον ἐλθεῖν πρός με εἰς Νικόπολιν· ἐκεῖ γὰρ κέκρικα παραχειμάσαι. 13 Ζηνᾶν τὸν νομικὸν καὶ Ἀπολλὼν σπουδαίως πρόπεμψον, ἵνα μηδὲν αὐτοῖς λίπῃ. 14 μανθανέτωσαν δὲ καὶ οἱ ἡμέτεροι καλῶν ἔργων προΐστασθαι εἰς τὰς ἀναγκαίας χρείας, ἵνα μὴ ὦσιν ἄκαρποι.

15 Ἀσπάζονταί σε οἱ μετ᾽ ἐμοῦ πάντες. ἄσπασαι τοὺς φιλοῦντας ἡμᾶς ἐν πίστει.

Ἡ χάρις μετὰ πάντων ὑμῶν.

III. 1 Put them in mind to submit themselves to magistrates, to authorities, to obey rulers, to be ready to every good work, 2 to revile no man, to be no brawlers, forbearing, showing all meekness unto all men. 3 For we also were once foolish, disobedient, going astray, serving divers lusts and pleasures, living in malice and envy, hateful, and hating one another. 4 But when the kindness and the love toward man of our Saviour God was manifested, 5 not of works—works in righteousness—which we did, but according to his mercy he saved us, through the laver of regeneration, and [through] renewing of the Holy Ghost; 6 which he poured out on us richly through Jesus Christ our Saviour; 7 in order that, being justified by his grace, we might become heirs according to the hope of eternal life. 8 Faithful is the saying, and concerning these things I would have thee strenuously affirm, to the end that they who have believed God may be careful to practise good works. These things are good and profitable to men. 9 But foolish questionings, and genealogies, and strifes, and contentions about the law, avoid; for they are unprofitable and vain. 10 A heretical man, after one and a second admonition, shun; 11 knowing that such an one is perverted and sinneth, being self-condemned. 12 When I shall send Artemas to thee, or Tychicus, make haste to come to me to Nicopolis; for I have determined to spend the winter there. 13 Zealously forward on their journey Zenas the lawyer and Apollos, that nothing may be wanting to them. 14 But let ours also learn to practise good deeds for necessary uses, in order that they may not be unfruitful. 15 All that are with me salute thee. Salute those that love us in the faith. The grace [of God] be with you all.

ΠΡΟΣ ΤΙΜΟΘΕΟΝ Β'.

I. 1 Παῦλος ἀπόστολος Χριστοῦ Ἰησοῦ διὰ θελήματος Θεοῦ κατ' ἐπαγγελίαν ζωῆς τῆς ἐν Χριστῷ Ἰησοῦ 2 Τιμοθέῳ ἀγαπητῷ τέκνῳ. χάρις, ἔλεος, εἰρήνη ἀπὸ Θεοῦ πατρὸς καὶ Χριστοῦ Ἰησοῦ τοῦ κυρίου ἡμῶν.

3 Χάριν ἔχω τῷ Θεῷ, ᾧ λατρεύω ἀπὸ προγόνων ἐν καθαρᾷ συνειδήσει, ὡς ἀδιάλειπτον ἔχω τὴν περὶ σοῦ μνείαν ἐν ταῖς δεήσεσίν μου νυκτὸς καὶ ἡμέρας, 4 ἐπιποθῶν σε ἰδεῖν, μεμνημένος σου τῶν δακρύων ἵνα χαρᾶς πληρωθῶ, 5 ὑπόμνησιν λαβὼν τῆς ἐν σοὶ ἀνυποκρίτου πίστεως, ἥτις ἐνῴκησεν πρῶτον ἐν τῇ μάμμῃ σου Λωΐδι καὶ τῇ μητρί σου Εὐνίκῃ, πέπεισμαι δὲ ὅτι καὶ ἐν σοί. 6 Δι' ἣν αἰτίαν ἀναμιμνήσκω σε ἀναζωπυρεῖν τὸ χάρισμα τοῦ Θεοῦ, ὅ ἐστιν ἐν σοὶ διὰ τῆς ἐπιθέσεως τῶν χειρῶν μου. 7 οὐ γὰρ ἔδωκεν ἡμῖν ὁ Θεὸς πνεῦμα δειλίας, ἀλλὰ δυνάμεως καὶ ἀγάπης καὶ σωφρονισμοῦ. 8 μὴ οὖν ἐπαισχυνθῇς τὸ μαρτύριον τοῦ κυρίου ἡμῶν μηδὲ ἐμὲ τὸν δέσμιον αὐτοῦ, ἀλλὰ συνκακοπάθησον τῷ εὐαγγελίῳ κατὰ δύναμιν Θεοῦ, 9 τοῦ σώσαντος ἡμᾶς καὶ καλέσαντος κλήσει ἁγίᾳ, οὐ κατὰ τὰ ἔργα ἡμῶν ἀλλὰ κατὰ ἰδίαν πρόθεσιν καὶ χάριν τὴν δοθεῖσαν ἡμῖν ἐν Χριστῷ Ἰησοῦ πρὸ χρόνων αἰωνίων, 10 φανερωθεῖσαν δὲ νῦν διὰ τῆς ἐπιφανείας τοῦ σωτῆρος ἡμῶν Χριστοῦ Ἰησοῦ, καταργήσαντος μὲν τὸν θάνατον, φωτίσαντος δὲ ζωὴν καὶ ἀφθαρσίαν διὰ τοῦ εὐαγγελίου, 11 εἰς ὃ ἐτέθην ἐγὼ κήρυξ καὶ ἀπόστολος καὶ διδάσκαλος· 12 δι' ἣν αἰτίαν καὶ ταῦτα πάσχω, ἀλλ' οὐκ ἐπαισχύνομαι· οἶδα γὰρ ᾧ πεπίστευκα, καὶ πέπεισμαι ὅτι δυνατός ἐστιν τὴν παραθήκην μου φυλάξαι εἰς ἐκείνην τὴν ἡμέραν. 13 ὑποτύπωσιν ἔχε ὑγιαινόντων λόγων ὧν παρ' ἐμοῦ ἤκουσας ἐν πίστει καὶ ἀγάπῃ τῇ ἐν Χριστῷ Ἰησοῦ·

THE SECOND EPISTLE TO TIMOTHY.

I. 1 Paul, an apostle of Christ Jesus by the will of God, according to the promise of life which is in Christ Jesus, 2 to Timothy, [my] beloved child : Grace, mercy, peace, from God the Father, and Christ Jesus our Lord.—3 I give thanks to God, whom I serve from my forefathers in a pure conscience, how unceasing remembrance I have of thee in my prayers night and day ; 4 longing to see thee, mindful of thy tears, that I may be filled with joy; 5 recollecting the unfeigned faith [that is] in thee, which dwelt first in thy grandmother Lois, and thy mother Eunice ; but I am persuaded that in thee also. 6 For which cause I remind thee to stir up the gift of God, which is in thee through the laying on of my hands. 7 For God gave us not the spirit of cowardice, but of power, and love, and correction. 8 Be not thou therefore ashamed of the testimony of our Lord, nor of me his prisoner : but suffer hardship with me, according to the power of God ; 9 Who saved us, and called us with an holy calling, not according to our works, but according to his own purpose, and the grace which was given us in Christ Jesus before eternal times ; 10 but manifested now by the appearing of our Saviour Jesus Christ, who abolished death, indeed, but brought life and immortality to light : 11 for which I was appointed a herald, and apostle, and teacher of the Gentiles. 12 For which cause also I suffer these things : but I am not ashamed ; for I know whom I have trusted, and am persuaded that he is able to keep my deposit against that day. 13 Have (possess) the pattern of sound words, which thou heardest

14 τὴν καλὴν παραθήκην φύλαξον διὰ πνεύματος ἁγίου τοῦ ἐνοικοῦντος ἐν ἡμῖν.

15 Οἶδας τοῦτο, ὅτι ἀπεστράφησάν με πάντες οἱ ἐν τῇ Ἀσίᾳ, ὧν ἐστὶν Φύγελος καὶ Ἑρμογένης. 16 δῴη ἔλεος ὁ κύριος τῷ Ὀνησιφόρου οἴκῳ, ὅτι πολλάκις με ἀνέψυξεν καὶ τὴν ἅλυσίν μου οὐκ ἐπαισχύνθη, 17 ἀλλὰ γενόμενος ἐν Ῥώμῃ σπουδαίως ἐζήτησέν με καὶ εὗρεν. 18 δῴη αὐτῷ ὁ κύριος εὑρεῖν ἔλεος παρὰ κυρίου ἐν ἐκείνῃ τῇ ἡμέρᾳ. καὶ ὅσα ἐν Ἐφέσῳ διηκόνησεν, βέλτιον σὺ γινώσκεις.

II. 1 Σὺ οὖν, τέκνον μου, ἐνδυναμοῦ ἐν τῇ χάριτι τῇ ἐν Χριστῷ Ἰησοῦ, 2 καὶ ἃ ἤκουσας παρ' ἐμοῦ διὰ πολλῶν μαρτύρων, ταῦτα παράθου πιστοῖς ἀνθρώποις, οἵτινες ἱκανοὶ ἔσονται καὶ ἑτέρους διδάξαι. 3 συνκακοπάθησον ὡς καλὸς στρατιώτης Χριστοῦ Ἰησοῦ. 4 οὐδεὶς στρατευόμενος ἐμπλέκεται ταῖς τοῦ βίου πραγματίαις, ἵνα τῷ στρατολογήσαντι ἀρέσῃ. 5 ἐὰν δὲ καὶ ἀθλῇ τις, οὐ στεφανοῦται ἐὰν μὴ νομίμως ἀθλήσῃ. 6 τὸν κοπιῶντα γεωργὸν δεῖ πρῶτον τῶν καρπῶν μεταλαμβάνειν. 7 νόει ὃ λέγω· δώσει γάρ σοι ὁ κύριος σύνεσιν ἐν πᾶσιν. 8 Μνημόνευε Ἰησοῦν Χριστὸν ἐγηγερμένον ἐκ νεκρῶν, ἐκ σπέρματος Δαυείδ, κατὰ τὸ εὐαγγέλιόν μου, 9 ἐν ᾧ κακοπαθῶ μέχρι δεσμῶν ὡς κακοῦργος, ἀλλὰ ὁ λόγος τοῦ Θεοῦ οὐ δέδεται. 10 διὰ τοῦτο πάντα ὑπομένω διὰ τοὺς ἐκλεκτούς, ἵνα καὶ αὐτοὶ σωτηρίας τύχωσιν τῆς ἐν Χριστῷ Ἰησοῦ μετὰ δόξης αἰωνίου. 11 Πιστὸς ὁ λόγος· εἰ γὰρ συναπεθάνομεν, καὶ συνζήσομεν· 12 εἰ ὑπομένομεν, καὶ συνβασιλεύσομεν· εἰ ἀρνησόμεθα, κἀκεῖνος ἀρνήσεται ἡμᾶς· 13 εἰ ἀπιστοῦμεν, ἐκεῖνος πιστὸς μένει, ἀρνήσασθαι γὰρ ἑαυτὸν οὐ δύναται.

14 Ταῦτα ὑπομίμνησκε, διαμαρτυρόμενος ἐνώπιον τοῦ Θεοῦ μὴ λογομαχεῖν, ἐπ' οὐδὲν χρήσιμον, ἐπὶ καταστροφῇ τῶν ἀκουόντων. 15 σπούδασον σεαυτὸν δόκιμον παραστῆσαι τῷ Θεῷ, ἐργά-

of me, in faith and love which are in Christ Jesus. 14 The goodly deposit keep through the Holy Ghost that dwelleth in us. 15 Thou knowest, that all who are in Asia turned away from me; of whom are Phygellus and Hermogenes. 16 The Lord give mercy to the house of Onesiphorus, because he ofttimes refreshed me, and was not ashamed of my chain; 17 but (on the contrary), when he arrived in Rome, he sought me out with greater diligence, and found me. 18 May the Lord grant to him that he may find mercy from the Lord in that day. And how many things he ministered at Ephesus, thou knowest very well.

II. 1 Thou therefore, my child, be strengthened in the grace that is in Christ Jesus. 2 And the things which thou hast heard from me with many witnesses, these commit to faithful men, such as shall be able to teach others also. 3 Suffer hardship with me, as a good soldier of Jesus Christ. 4 No one serving as a soldier entangles himself in the businesses of life, in order that he may please him who has called him to be a soldier. 5 But if any one also strive in the games, he is not crowned, unless he have striven lawfully. 6 The toiling husbandman must first partake of the fruits. 7 Understand what I say; for the Lord will give thee discernment in all things. 8 Remember Jesus Christ as having been raised from the dead, of the seed of David, according to my gospel: 9 in which I suffer hardship up to bonds, as a malefactor; but the word of God is not bound. 10 For this reason I endure all things for the sake of the elect, in order that they also may obtain the salvation that is in Christ Jesus with eternal glory. 11 Faithful is the saying: For if we died with him, we shall also live with him; 12 if we endure, we shall also reign with him; if we shall deny him, he also will deny us; 13 if we are unbelieving, he abideth faithful: he cannot deny himself.—14 Put them in mind of these things, solemnly charging them before God

την ανεπαίσχυντον, ορθοτομούντα τον λόγον της αληθείας. 16 τας δε βεβήλους κενοφωνίας περιίστασο· επι πλείον γαρ προκόψουσιν ασεβείας, 17 και ο λόγος αυτών ως γάγγραινα νομήν έξει. ων εστιν Ύμέναιος και Φιλητός, 18 οίτινες περι την αλήθειαν ηστόχησαν, λέγοντες ανάστασιν ήδη γεγονέναι, και ανατρέπουσιν τήν τινων πίστιν. 19 ο μέντοι στερεος θεμέλιος του Θεού έστηκεν, έχων την σφραγίδα ταύτην· έγνω κύριος τους όντας αυτού, και· αποστήτω από αδικίας πας ο ονομάζων το όνομα κυρίου. 20 εν μεγάλη δε οικία ουκ έστιν μόνον σκεύη χρυσα και αργυρά, αλλα και ξύλινα και οστράκινα, και α μεν εις τιμήν α δε εις ατιμίαν· 21 εαν ουν τις εκκαθάρη εαυτον από τούτων, έσται σκεύος εις τιμήν, ηγιασμένον, εύχρηστον τω δεσπότη, εις παν έργον αγαθον ητοιμασμένον. 22 τας δε νεωτερικας επιθυμίας φεύγε, δίωκε δε δικαιοσύνην, πίστιν, αγάπην, ειρήνην μετα των επικαλουμένων τον κύριον εκ καθαράς καρδίας. 23 τας δε μωρας και απαιδεύτους ζητήσεις παραιτού, ειδως ότι γεννώσιν μάχας· 24 δούλον δε κυρίου ου δεί μάχεσθαι αλλα ήπιον είναι προς πάντας, διδακτικόν, ανεξίκακον, 25 εν πραΰτητι παιδεύοντα τους αντιδιατιθεμένους, μήποτε δώη αυτοίς ο Θεος μετάνοιαν εις επίγνωσιν αληθείας, 26 και ανανήψωσιν εκ της του διαβόλου παγίδος, εζωγρημένοι υπ' αυτού εις το εκείνου θέλημα.

III. 1 Τούτο δε γίνωσκε, ότι εν εσχάταις ημέραις ενστήσονται καιροι χαλεποί. 2 έσονται γαρ οι άνθρωποι φίλαυτοι, φιλάργυροι, αλαζόνες, υπερήφανοι, βλάσφημοι, γονεύσιν απειθείς, αχάριστοι, ανόσιοι, 3 άστοργοι, άσπονδοι, διάβολοι, ακρατείς, ανήμεροι, αφιλάγαθοι, 4 προδόται, προπετείς, τετυφωμένοι, φι-

not to wrangle about words profitable for nothing, to the subversion of them that hear.

15 Give diligence to present thyself to God approved, a workman not ashamed, rightly handling the word of truth. 16 But profane babblings shun, for they will advance to more of ungodliness. 17 And their word will eat as a gangrene: of whom is Hymenæus and Philetus; 18 men who concerning the truth swerved, saying that the resurrection has already taken place, and overthrow the faith of some. 19 Nevertheless the firm foundation of God stands, having this seal, "The Lord knoweth them that are his." And, Let every one that nameth the name of the Lord depart from iniquity. 20 But in a great house there are not only vessels of gold and of silver, but also of wood and of earth; and some to honour, others to dishonour. 21 If any one, then, shall have purged himself from these, he shall be a vessel for honour, sanctified, serviceable to the Master, prepared for every good work. 22 But flee youthful lusts; but follow after righteousness, faith, love, peace with them that call upon the Lord out of a pure heart. 23 But foolish and ignorant questions avoid, knowing that they do gender strifes. 24 But the servant of the Lord must not strive, but be gentle toward all, apt to teach, patient of wrong; 25 in meekness correcting those who oppose themselves, if peradventure God may give them repentance unto the full knowledge of the truth; 26 and that they may return to soberness out of the snare of the devil, having been taken captive by him, according to the will of him (God).

III. 1 This know, however, that in the last days grievous times shall set in: 2 for men shall be selfish, covetous, boastful, haughty, censorious, disobedient to parents, unthankful, unholy, 3 without natural affection, implacable, false accusers, incontinent, fierce, haters of good, 4 betrayers, headlong, carried with conceit, lovers of pleasure rather than

λήδονοι μᾶλλον ἢ φιλόθεοι, 5 ἔχοντες μόρφωσιν εὐσεβείας τὴν δὲ δύναμιν αὐτῆς ἠρνημένοι· καὶ τούτους ἀποτρέπου. 6 ἐκ τούτων γάρ εἰσιν οἱ ἐνδύνοντες εἰς τὰς οἰκίας καὶ αἰχμαλωτίζοντες γυναικάρια σεσωρευμένα ἁμαρτίαις, ἀγόμενα ἐπιθυμίαις ποικίλαις, 7 πάντοτε μανθάνοντα καὶ μηδέποτε εἰς ἐπίγνωσιν ἀληθείας ἐλθεῖν δυνάμενα. 8 ὃν τρόπον δὲ Ἰαννῆς καὶ Ἰαμβρῆς ἀντέστησαν Μωϋσεῖ, οὕτως καὶ οὗτοι ἀνθίστανται τῇ ἀληθείᾳ, ἄνθρωποι κατεφθαρμένοι τὸν νοῦν, ἀδόκιμοι περὶ τὴν πίστιν. 9 ἀλλ' οὐ προκόψουσιν ἐπὶ πλεῖον· ἡ γὰρ ἄνοια αὐτῶν ἔκδηλος ἔσται πᾶσιν, ὡς καὶ ἡ ἐκείνων ἐγένετο. 10 Σὺ δὲ παρηκολούθησάς μου τῇ διδασκαλίᾳ, τῇ ἀγωγῇ, τῇ προθέσει, τῇ πίστει, τῇ μακροθυμίᾳ, τῇ ἀγάπῃ, τῇ ὑπομονῇ, 11 τοῖς διωγμοῖς, τοῖς παθήμασιν, οἷά μοι ἐγένετο ἐν Ἀντιοχείᾳ, ἐν Ἰκονίῳ, ἐν Λύστροις· οἵους διωγμοὺς ὑπήνεγκα, καὶ ἐκ πάντων με ἐρύσατο ὁ κύριος. 12 καὶ πάντες δὲ οἱ θέλοντες ζῆν εὐσεβῶς ἐν Χριστῷ Ἰησοῦ διωχθήσονται. 13 Πονηροὶ δὲ ἄνθρωποι καὶ γόητες προκόψουσιν ἐπὶ τὸ χεῖρον, πλανῶντες καὶ πλανώμενοι. 14 σὺ δὲ μένε ἐν οἷς ἔμαθες καὶ ἐπιστώθης, εἰδὼς παρὰ τίνων ἔμαθες, 15 καὶ ὅτι ἀπὸ βρέφους ἱερὰ γράμματα οἶδας τὰ δυνάμενά σε σοφίσαι εἰς σωτηρίαν διὰ πίστεως τῆς ἐν Χριστῷ Ἰησοῦ. 16 πᾶσα γραφὴ θεόπνευστος καὶ ὠφέλιμος πρὸς διδασκαλίαν, πρὸς ἐλεγμόν, πρὸς ἐπανόρθωσιν, πρὸς παιδίαν τὴν ἐν δικαιοσύνῃ, 17 ἵνα ἄρτιος ᾖ ὁ τοῦ Θεοῦ ἄνθρωπος, πρὸς πᾶν ἔργον ἀγαθὸν ἐξηρτισμένος.

IV. 1 Διαμαρτύρομαι ἐνώπιον τοῦ Θεοῦ καὶ Χριστοῦ Ἰησοῦ τοῦ μέλλοντος κρίνειν ζῶντας καὶ νεκρούς, καὶ τὴν ἐπιφάνειαν αὐτοῦ καὶ τὴν βασιλείαν αὐτοῦ, 2 κήρυξον τὸν λόγον, ἐπίστηθι εὐκαίρως ἀκαίρως, ἔλεγξον, παρακάλεσον, ἐπιτίμησον, ἐν πάσῃ μακροθυμίᾳ καὶ διδαχῇ. 3 ἔσται γὰρ καιρὸς ὅτε τῆς ὑγιαινούσης διδασκαλίας οὐκ ἀνέξονται, ἀλλὰ κατὰ τὰς ἰδίας ἐπιθυμίας ἑαυτοῖς

lovers of God; 5 having a form of godliness, but denying the power thereof. From such turn away. 6 For of these are they who creep into houses, and take captive silly women laden with sins, led away by divers lusts; 7 ever learning, and never able to come to the full knowledge of the truth. 8 Now in the same manner that Jannes and Jambres withstood Moses, so do these also withstand the truth: men corrupted in their mind, reprobate concerning the faith. 9 But they shall not make progress; for their folly shall become manifest to all, as *theirs* also came to be.

10 Thou, however, hast closely followed my instruction, my manner of life, my purpose, my faith, my long-suffering, my love, my patience, 11 my persecutions, my sufferings, such as befell me in Antioch, in Iconium, in Lystra; such persecutions as I endured: and out of them all the Lord delivered me. 12 Yea, and all who are minded to live piously in Christ Jesus shall be persecuted. 13 But evil men and deceivers shall grow worse and worse, deceiving, and being deceived. 14 But do thou continue in the things which thou didst learn, and wert assured of, knowing of whom thou didst learn them; 15 and that from a very child thou knowest the holy Scriptures, which are able to make thee wise unto salvation, through faith which is in Christ Jesus. 16 Every scripture [is] given by inspiration of God, and [is] profitable for instruction, for conviction, for correction, for discipline in righteousness; 17 in order that the man of God may be perfect, thoroughly furnished for every good work.

IV. 1 I solemnly charge thee before God, and Christ Jesus, who is going to judge living and dead, and by his appearance and his kingdom: 2 preach the word; be instant in season, out of season; reprove, exhort, rebuke, in all long-suffering and teaching. 3 For there shall be a time when they will not endure the healthy instruction; but after their own lusts will heap up to themselves teachers, having

ἐπισωρεύσουσιν διδασκάλους κνηθόμενοι τὴν ἀκοήν, 4 καὶ ἀπὸ μὲν τῆς ἀληθείας τὴν ἀκοὴν ἀποστρέψουσιν, ἐπὶ δὲ τοὺς μύθους ἐκτραπήσονται. 5 σὺ δὲ νῆφε ἐν πᾶσιν, κακοπάθησον, ἔργον ποίησον εὐαγγελιστοῦ, τὴν διακονίαν σου πληροφόρησον. 6 Ἐγὼ γὰρ ἤδη σπένδομαι, καὶ ὁ καιρὸς τῆς ἀναλύσεώς μου ἐφέστηκεν. 7 τὸν καλὸν ἀγῶνα ἠγώνισμαι, τὸν δρόμον τετέλεκα, τὴν πίστιν τετήρηκα· 8 λοιπὸν ἀπόκειταί μοι ὁ τῆς δικαιοσύνης στέφανος, ὃν ἀποδώσει μοι ὁ κύριος ἐν ἐκείνῃ τῇ ἡμέρᾳ, ὁ δίκαιος κριτής, οὐ μόνον δὲ ἐμοὶ ἀλλὰ καὶ πᾶσι τοῖς ἠγαπηκόσι τὴν ἐπιφάνειαν αὐτοῦ.

9 Σπούδασον ἐλθεῖν πρός με ταχέως. 10 Δημᾶς γάρ με ἐγκατέλιπεν ἀγαπήσας τὸν νῦν αἰῶνα, καὶ ἐπορεύθη εἰς Θεσσαλονίκην, Κρήσκης εἰς Γαλλίαν, Τίτος εἰς Δαλματίαν· 11 Λουκᾶς ἐστὶν μόνος μετ' ἐμοῦ. Μάρκον ἀναλαβὼν ἄγε μετὰ σεαυτοῦ· ἔστιν γάρ μοι εὔχρηστος εἰς διακονίαν. 12 Τυχικὸν δὲ ἀπέστειλα εἰς Ἔφεσον. 13 τὸν φελόνην, ὃν ἀπέλιπον ἐν Τρῳάδι παρὰ Κάρπῳ, ἐρχόμενος φέρε, καὶ τὰ βιβλία, μάλιστα τὰς μεμβράνας. 14 Ἀλέξανδρος ὁ χαλκεὺς πολλά μοι κακὰ ἐνεδείξατο· ἀποδώσει αὐτῷ ὁ κύριος κατὰ τὰ ἔργα αὐτοῦ. 15 ὃν καὶ σὺ φυλάσσου· λίαν γὰρ ἀντέστη τοῖς ἡμετέροις λόγοις. 16 ἐν τῇ πρώτῃ μου ἀπολογίᾳ οὐδείς μοι παρεγένετο, ἀλλὰ πάντες με ἐγκατέλιπον· μὴ αὐτοῖς λογισθείη· 17 ὁ δὲ κύριός μοι παρέστη καὶ ἐνεδυνάμωσέν με, ἵνα δι' ἐμοῦ τὸ κήρυγμα πληροφορηθῇ καὶ ἀκούσωσιν πάντα τὰ ἔθνη, καὶ ἐρύσθην ἐκ στόματος λέοντος. 18 ῥύσεταί με ὁ κύριος ἀπὸ παντὸς ἔργου πονηροῦ καὶ σώσει εἰς τὴν βασιλείαν αὐτοῦ τὴν ἐπουράνιον· ᾧ ἡ δόξα εἰς τοὺς αἰῶνας τῶν αἰώνων, ἀμήν.

19 Ἄσπασαι Πρίσκαν καὶ Ἀκύλαν καὶ τὸν Ὀνησιφόρου οἶκον. 20 Ἔραστος ἔμεινεν ἐν Κορίνθῳ, Τρόφιμον δὲ ἀπέλιπον ἐν Μιλήτῳ ἀσθενοῦντα. 21 σπούδασον πρὸ χειμῶνος ἐλθεῖν. ἀσπάζεταί σε Εὔβουλος καὶ Πούδης καὶ Λίνος καὶ Κλαυδία καὶ οἱ ἀδελφοὶ πάντες.

22 Ὁ κύριος μετὰ τοῦ πνεύματός σου. ἡ χάρις μεθ' ὑμῶν.

itching ears; 4 and they will turn away their ears from the truth, and be turned aside to fables. 5 But watch thou in all things; endure hardship; do the work of an evangelist; fully accomplish thy ministry. 6 For I am already being offered, and the time of my departure is at hand. 7 I have fought the good fight, I have finished the course, I have kept the faith. 8 Henceforth there is laid up for me the crown of righteousness, which the Lord, the righteous Judge, shall award to me in that day; and not to me only, but to all them that love his appearing.

9 Do thy endeavour to come to me quickly. 10 For Demas forsook me, having loved this present world, and is gone to Thessalonica; Crescens to Gaul, Titus to Dalmatia. 11 Luke alone is with me. Mark take up, and bring with thee, for he is serviceable to me for the ministry. 12 But Tychicus I sent to Ephesus. 13 The cloak which I left at Troas with Carpus, bring when thou comest, and the books, especially the parchments. 14 Alexander the coppersmith did me much evil. The Lord will requite him according to his works. 15 Of whom be thou also on thy guard, for he exceedingly withstood our words. 16 In my first defence no man stood forward with me, but all forsook me. May it not be laid to their charge. 17 But the Lord stood by me, and strengthened me, in order that through me the preaching [of the gospel] might be fully accomplished, and that all the Gentiles might hear; and he delivered me out of the mouth of the lion. 18 The Lord will deliver me from every evil work, and preserve me to his heavenly kingdom: to whom be glory for ever and ever. Amen.

19 Salute Prisca and Aquila, and the household of Onesiphorus. 20 Erastus abode at Corinth; but Trophimus I left at Miletus sick. 21 Do thy endeavour to come before winter. Eubulus saluteth thee, and Pudens, and Linus, and Claudia, and all the brethren.

22 The Lord be with thy spirit; grace be with you.

THE

FIRST EPISTLE TO TIMOTHY.

CHAPTER I.

Vers. 1, 2. *Paul, an apostle of Christ Jesus according to the commandment of God our Saviour, and Christ Jesus our hope; to Timothy, [my] true child in the faith: Grace, mercy, peace, from God the Father, and Christ Jesus our Lord.*

If this had been simply a private letter, having for its object the expression merely of kindly feelings, or the communication of prudent advice as from one friend to another, it would certainly have been unnatural in the apostle (as some have objected) to begin in so formal a manner, and to give such prominence at the outset to his divine call to the apostleship, with which Timothy was doubtless perfectly familiar. But the letter plainly bears an official character; and while partaking of the graceful and affectionate freedom which fitly arose from the intimate relations of the parties, it was designed to carry with it an authoritative value—to convey instructions respecting church order and Christian work, which called for implicit obedience. Timothy, the youthful companion, was now coming in a measure to take the place of the apostle in ministerial agency; and he must have both the nature of the work, and the warrant on which he was to proceed with it, distinctly laid upon his conscience. He might possibly need such an authoritative commission to bear him up against others in the discharge of his delegated function; and therefore I would not exclude (with Ellicott) a regard to the due maintenance of his authority. He might have at times to exhibit, or even press, the grounds on which he spake and acted as he did. But for himself also it was needful. For it was evidently an irksome and delicate task which was assigned him at Ephesus, with so many germs of error sprouting, and headstrong, conceited men bent on carrying matters their own way. If himself, as would appear, of a meek, amiable disposition, and accustomed hitherto to be led rather than to lead, he might in some things be tempted to give way to the will or resistance of others. It was right, therefore, he should feel that necessity was laid upon him; that the voice which speaks to him is that not merely of a revered instructor or a spiritual father, but of a Heaven-commissioned ambassador, who has a right to declare the divine will and rule with authority in the Christian church. So Bengel: *Hic titulus facit ad confirmandum Timotheum; familiaritas seponenda est, ubi causa Dei agitur.*

St. Paul's mode of expressing his divine relation to the apostleship here is somewhat peculiar: he is an apostle of Christ Jesus, not, as he sometimes puts it, from being called thereto (Rom. i. 1; 1 Cor. i. 1), or as having received his destination to it through the will of God (1 Cor. i. 1; 2 Cor. i. 1; also in Ephesians, Colossians, 2 Timothy), but *according to God's commandment* (κατ' ἐπιταγὴν Θεοῦ), or by God's appointment (as κατὰ τύχην, by chance, κατ' εὔνοιαν, by good-will). His apostolic calling is thus brought into connection with the direct ordering of Heaven—the active carrying out or result of the divine will. If it is asked, How or when was the commandment issued? we may point, with Chrysostom, to Acts xiii. 2, where the Holy Ghost is related to have said by certain prophets in the church at Antioch: "Separate me Barnabas and Saul for the work whereunto I have called them;" only, this command of the Spirit was but the echo, as indeed it professes to be, of a prior command or vocation given from above, which therefore was the fundamental thing. And so Chrysostom himself felt, for he presently refers the matter to that original source; stating, that while it was the glorified Redeemer from whom the command was directly received, it was not the less from God: for the things of the Father are the Son's, as those again of the Son are the Spirit's. So that whether we look to the Spirit's injunction to the church at Antioch, or to Christ's charge to the apostle himself on the road to Damascus, we see in each the expression of the Father's will and appointment. In two other passages—Rom. xvi. 26, Tit. i. 3—the apostle has used the same expression of "God's commandment;" in the former case generally, with respect to the ministration of the gospel, in the latter specially, with respect to his own commission.

It is another peculiarity here that God is called *our Saviour*, a designation applied to God with great frequency in the Pastoral epistles (not only here, but at 1 Tim. ii. 3, iv. 10, Tit. i. 3, ii. 10, iii. 4), and occurs elsewhere only in Luke i. 47, and Jude, ver. 25. It is impossible to deny, however, that the idea involved in the designation is common to all the epistles of Paul; in some of the others, also, salvation is expressly and formally coupled with God (as in 2 Thess. ii. 12, 1 Cor. i. 21). So that it is merely the employment of *Saviour* as a personal designation of God in Christ which is peculiar to the Pastoral epistles. Why the apostle should in these have not only adopted, but evinced a special fondness for such a designation, can only be proximately determined. But it may not improbably have presented itself to his mind, as a kind of counteractive to the false teaching which in his latter days was beginning to corrupt the truth. In that presumptuous, self-willed spirit, which was striving to hew out new paths for itself, and aiming at heights of knowledge and virtue beyond those which were accessible to ordinary believers in Christ, the apostle could not fail to see what tended to separate between God and salvation; in fact, to change altogether the idea of salvation as a work originating in the purpose, and carried into effect by the agency, of God. Christianity would come to be viewed only as a higher sort of school instruction and spiritual discipline, which might be ever so much remodelled and improved upon by the efforts of successive theosophists. To associate salvation, therefore, not simply with Christ (which, however, is also done by the apostle, 1 Tim. i. 14, Tit. i. 4, ii. 13, iii. 6), but directly and prominently with God, might seem a fitting mode of testifying against the false tendency of the times. It would certainly have been to believers a preservative against much of the evil then emerging, if they kept firm hold of the truth that salvation is of God; for thus would all arbitrariness in speculation and undue licence in practice be repressed.

With God as *our Saviour* the apostle couples Christ Jesus as *our hope*, precisely as in Eph. ii. 14 he calls Him *our peace;* and, with a still nearer resemblance to the present passage, in Col. i. 27, *the hope of glory* in believers. He is so called, not merely because the reception of His gospel lights up the hope of blessing and glory in the heart, but because all that is hoped for is so indissolubly linked to Christ Himself, that our relation to Him carries also our relation to it. *In eo solo tota salutis nostræ materia* (Calvin).

To Timothy, [*my*] *true child in the faith.* The rendering in the Authorized Version, "mine own son," is not altogether correct, γνήσιος being true, in opposition to false or spurious; hence genuine, real. Had it been used of a relation in the natural sphere, *own* might have been taken as the proper equivalent: one's own child, as contradistinguished from another's, from a supposititious offspring. But it is otherwise in the spiritual; for Timothy might have been a genuine child of the divine kingdom, though brought into it through the instrumentality of another than the apostle. But as having been so brought,—brought as a mere youth, and almost from the date of his conversion kept in constant attendance upon the apostle,—it was natural for the latter to use the term *child* rather than *son* to express the relation, even now when Timothy was in the ripeness and vigour of manhood; it was more distinctly indicative of tenderness and affection. The other would have been more natural to an imitator. The addition, *in faith*, or, in *the* faith,—for there can be no doubt that it refers to the specific faith of the gospel,—is made to prevent mistake, by defining the sphere to which the filial relationship belonged. So also, in 1 Cor. iv. 17, Timothy is described by the apostle as "his beloved child, and faithful in the Lord." The endearing spiritual relationship subsisting between them had on Timothy's part been properly maintained.

Grace, mercy, and peace, from God the Father, and Christ Jesus our Lord. The only thing calling for special notice here is the insertion of ἔλεος, *mercy*, between *grace* and *peace*. In all the rest of Paul's epistles, except the Second to Timothy (in Titus the word, though in the received text, should likewise be omitted), *mercy* is not found in the salutation, but only grace and peace. It seems, however, a strange mode of reasoning to press this as an argument against the genuineness of the two epistles; for the very uniformity of the apostle's style in his earlier epistles would have been sure to catch the eye of a forger, and in a manner constrained him to adopt the same. It was not for him at the very outset to deviate from the beaten track; least of all to do so by such an addition to the two regular epithets as *mercy*, which has respect to sin and misery in the object of it. Grace and peace might fitly enough be sought for Timothy as an honoured member of the church of Christ, and more especially as one called to the discharge of an onerous and responsible commission in it; but who, save such a man as Paul, could have thought of mercy? If even in the case of the erring Galatians and the backsliding Corinthians, mercy was omitted from the apostolic saluta- tion, was it for an unknown, a lying imitator, to conceive of Paul's dear child of faith, his substitute in the performance of what was properly apostolic work, as a subject for mercy? This, surely, was a very unlikely thing to come from such a quarter; and it may therefore be regarded as the apostle's own signature—the impress of his peculiarly thoughtful and deeply exercised heart. He knew how much he needed mercy for himself, not merely at the outset of his spiritual career, when he was rescued as a brand from the burning, but also when engaged in his work as an ambassador of Christ. He knew that, even when he was outwardly doing all, he was still spiritually coming short; that evil was more or less present with him, when seeking to do what was good; therefore he must ever feel himself a debtor to mercy. And could he wish his dear child and deputy to feel other- wise? Would he not rather be disposed to consider it essential to Timothy's safety and success to live in the exercise of such a spirit? It came well from so richly en- dowed a workman, and so experienced a saint, to convey to his youthful disciple the important instruction couched under this word—from him alone could it have so come; and it embodies a lesson for all future ministers of the gospel, which it well becomes them to ponder. While they are ambassadors of mercy to others, let them never forget that they need to be themselves partakers of mercy—never more so than when they are engaged in the higher duties, and pressing the more sacred interests of the gospel. If they know aright what they are, and what they should be, they will be ever throwing themselves on God's mercy, and also looking for the glorious issue as the consummating display of that same mercy toward them in Christ Jesus unto eternal life (Jude 25).

The proof should not be overlooked which this impetration of grace, mercy, and peace for Timothy affords of the essential divinity of Christ; since He is coupled with God the Father as alike concerned in the bestowal of strictly divine gifts. Had our Lord possessed only a creature's place and prerogatives, even though it were the highest in creation, it had been impossible for a truly pious mind to have presented Him, without further explanation, in this apparently co-equal fellowship with the Father; such a mind would have instinctively shrunk from so unseemly a conjunction. We can only, therefore, regard the place given to Christ here as a virtual declaration of the apostle's belief in the truth enunciated by Christ Himself, " All things that the Father hath are mine," and again, when He affirmed that the Son hath life in Himself, even as the Father hath life in Himself (Matt. xi. 27 ; John xvi. 15, v. 26).

Vers. 3, 4. *According as I besought thee when setting out for Macedonia, [so I do now], to abide still at Ephesus, in order that thou mightest charge some not to teach any other doctrine, nor to give heed to fables and endless genealogies, inasmuch as they minister strifes rather than God's dispensation in faith.* The sentence is elliptical in the earlier part, to be explained, with Winer (*Gr.* § 64), by the rapidity of the apostle's style, throwing into the protasis what should have been expressed in an apodosis, such as οὕτω καὶ νῦν παρακαλῶ: As before I besought, so now also I beseech. Our translators, after Erasmus (*ita facito*), have supplied, at the end of the entire sentence, *so do*—which makes the sense plain enough ; but it seems better to introduce the supplement a little earlier. The verb expressive of Timothy's continued residence at Ephesus, which as to the sense betokens a kind of prolonged present, is put in the aorist ($\pi\rho o\sigma\mu\epsilon\hat{\iota}\nu\alpha\iota$), because dependent on an aorist which precedes, according to the principle of the parity of tenses, which the Greeks particularly regarded (Winer, § 45, 8). The preceding verb itself —$\pi\alpha\rho\epsilon\kappa\acute{\alpha}\lambda\epsilon\sigma\alpha$, *I besought*—was viewed by Chrysostom as indicative of the apostle's gentleness and affection toward Timothy: he would not authoritatively enjoin his prolonged stay at Ephesus, but would only give an earnest expression of his desire regarding it, as in a matter that deeply concerned the interests of the church. There appears ground for the remark; and Tit. i. 5, where a stronger word is used in regard to the evangelistic labours of Titus in Crete—" as I appointed," or ordered thee ($\delta\iota\epsilon\tau\alpha\xi\acute{\alpha}\mu\eta\nu$)—is no argument to the contrary, for the cases were not strictly similar. Titus stood in a somewhat different relation to Paul from Timothy. The latter, like a beloved son and bosom companion, had his appropriate place beside the apostle; and any arrangement which involved a departure from this rule, was rather a subject for mutual consent, or at the most for earnest entreaty on the one side, and submissive compliance on the other, than for express command. Titus, however, was simply one of various fellow-labourers in the gospel, and by the nature of his office stood under the authority and direction of the apostle. So that, viewed with respect to the relative position of the parties, there was a fitness and delicacy in the choice of the words applied to each, such as might quite naturally present itself to the mind of the apostle, though by no means likely to occur to another person. The difficulties connected with the apostle's going into Macedonia, and leaving Timothy to tarry on at Ephesus, in a historical point of view, have already been considered in the Introduction.

The more special and immediate object of Timothy's continued residence at Ephesus, was *that he might charge some not to teach any other doctrine*—ἑτεροδιδασκαλεῖν. By ἕτερος is meant *other*, or *different*, in the sense of *diverse*, or of another kind; so that the teaching meant was teaching after a different type of doctrine from that which bore on it the sanction of apostolic authority. This, it is implied, was the standard; all right teaching must conform to it; what did not do so was an unwarranted deviation—*a heterodoxy*. So, at an earlier period, the apostle had designated the Jewish leaven introduced into the churches of Galatia; it was another gospel (ἕτερον εὐαγγέλιον, i. 6) which they had received, and the persons who had pressed it on their acceptance were false teachers. But in neither case might there be any formal abjuration of the essential facts of the gospel, such as to constitute them heretics in the modern sense; the error lay rather in superinducing thereupon foreign elements, and giving way to considerations and practices which were at variance with the proper genius of the gospel, and inevitably tended to corrupt its character and mar its design. Here, the false admixtures are described as *fables and endless genealogies*. The application which began to be made at an early period of these words to the generations of æons in the Gnostic systems of the second century, has already been noticed in the Introduction: it was an accommodation, as there stated, rather than a just and proper interpretation; both because the term *genealogies* could not, except in a kind of secondary and figurative sense, be understood of such ethereal fancies; and also because alike here and in Titus they are connected directly with Jewish perversions and misuses of the law.

We have undoubted evidence, that about, and even previous to, the gospel era, the minds of a certain portion of the Jewish dispersion took a set in that direction, and from a strange, incongruous combination of their own religion with the spirit of heathen philosophy, formed a sort of Cabalistic system, made up of allegory, fable, mystic notions, and legal technicalities. Philo partly reflected and partly also aided this false tendency, though with him it was kept free from many of the extravagances which discovered themselves among the inferior class of Jews, who often sought through such things to secure their own carnal and selfish ends. But with whatever view prosecuted, as they were in their nature entirely speculative and fanciful, they necessarily tended, as the apostle says, to give occasion to questions and strifes which admitted of no proper settlement, and yielded no real profit: αἵτινες ζητήσεις παρέχουσιν, being such as do so, having that for their natural consequence.

The converse of this has unhappily been obscured by a corruption in the received text. Following this, the A. V. reads, "rather than godly edifying," a fair enough rendering of οἰκοδομίαν Θεοῦ. But it should undoubtedly be οἰκονομίαν Θεοῦ, which is the reading of all the older MSS.; and this can only mean *God's dispensation*, or economy—His specific plan or arrangement for the administration of His kingdom. So it is plainly used by St. Paul in other parts of his writings, as at 1 Cor. ix. 17, Eph. i. 10, iii. 9. The method of salvation by Jesus Christ unfolded in the gospel is God's dispensation, as connected with the fulness of the times (Eph. i. 10); and as an apostle of Christ, Paul had this dispensation entrusted to him; as a steward, he was put in charge, to a certain extent, with the direction of its affairs (1 Cor. iv. 1, ix. 17). The idea, it is true, does not exactly suit the verb in the preceding clause (παρέχουσιν); as one can scarcely say, "do not minister God's dispensation;" and hence, no doubt, the tendency in the later copyists and the versions to substitute *edification* for *dispensation*. But it is merely an example of what is of frequent occurrence in Greek—of construction by zeugma, which requires that a verb, when coupled with words too diversified in import to be strictly applicable to each, be taken in a looser sense with its more remote than with its more immediate object. Here, the apostle chose a verb that was quite appropriate to the things which were foremost in his regard—namely, the frivolous disputations which the fondness for fables and genealogies naturally generated; and he left it to the good sense of his reader to make the requisite adaptation of the import to the matter subsequently presented: they minister questions rather than subserve what belongs to God's dispensation. And he indicates the reason, when he adds τὴν ἐν πίστει, *that is in faith*, has its sphere therein, or stands vitally related to that humble, confiding principle in the soul, as the bond more especially which connects men with it, and the avenue through which it developes spiritual life and hope in their experience. But fables and genealogies of whatsoever sort belonged to a different category; they did not address themselves to the principle of faith; they merely exercised the fancy and the intellect, and did so in a manner fitted rather to create a distaste for the proper objects of faith. The more one might give himself to such a line of things, the more would he find himself carried away from the sphere of God's merciful economy for the salvation of sinners.

Ver. 5. *Now the end of the charge is love out of a pure heart, and a good conscience, and faith unfeigned.* The *charge* (παραγγελίας) here meant cannot be the law strictly so called —as if παραγ. were all one with νόμος or ἐντολή—for the word is never so used; but it indicates the charge lying upon those who have a part to do in connection with God's dispensation—the obligation they have to fulfil in order to carry out its design. They are emphatically persons under charge (ὑπὸ παραγγελίας), being put in trust with the scheme of God for the wellbeing of men, and so having love for its grand aim (τέλος)—love in the fullest sense—love to God, the author of the dispensation, and love to mankind as the objects whose present and eternal good it contemplates. The possession and exercise of such love may be taken as the measure of one's sympathy with the spirit of the dispensation, and preparedness for executing the charge which comes along with the knowledge and belief of its realities, and which rests especially upon those who are called to act as its more select instruments of working. — [The word παραγ. was probably suggested in this connection by the παραγγείλῃς in ver. 3, and only makes general what was there given with a special application. Timothy was to charge the teachers in the church at Ephesus, who seemed in danger of turning aside from the right path, to beware of giving heed to things which were quite alien to the proper aim and calling of the evangelical office. And proceeding now from the particular to the general, the apostle briefly describes the nature of the charge which lies upon all true evangelists—what, from the very nature of the gospel, is and must be the heart and spirit of their calling. Comp. also ver. 18, iv. 11, v. 7, vi. 13, 1 Thess. iv. 2.]

But as the apostle has indicated the relation of the gospel charge to love, so, lest the nature of love itself might be mistaken, he shows its connection with the internal state and condition of the regenerated man: it is love out of *a pure heart*, hence incapable of working to ignoble ends, or the gratification of corrupt desires, but issuing like crystal streams from a pure fountain; also out of a *good conscience*, properly responsive to the claims of moral obligation, honestly bent on following out its convictions of truth and duty; finally, out of *faith unfeigned* (ἀνυποκρίτου),—a term frequently used to characterize the graces of the Christian character—love (Rom. xii. 9; 2 Cor. vi. 6), brotherly kindness (1 Pet. i. 22), spiritual wisdom (Jas. iii. 17); but when applied to faith, serving to indicate its reality and power as an internal principle, its living apprehension and firm grasp of the things presented to its view; hence widely different from that lazy assent to the doctrines of the gospel, that merely formal profession of adherence to them, which often goes by the name of faith. In specifying so many sources of Christian love, the apostle is not to be understood as giving a theoretical exposition of the matter, or presenting in strict philosophical order the relation of love to the heart, conscience, and faith respectively, or of these to each other. He is contemplating the subject in a practical point of view, and simply unfolding, in the order that seemed natural to him at the time, the several elements which must conspire to the production and exercise of genuine Christian love. In the order of nature, the unfeigned faith must undoubtedly be placed first; for in fallen men, laden with guilt and alienated from the life of God, there is no way of attaining to real purity of heart and a purged conscience but through faith in Christ. When through this faith entering, however, the soul is brought into fellowship with the realities of salvation, the bonds of its captivity are broken; it becomes re-united to the one source of life and blessing, and at once experiences and reciprocates a love which prompts it to a life of beneficence and worth. But considered with respect to practical working, the order adopted by the apostle is quite natural : furthest in, as the deep fountainhead of all the outgoings of Christian love, there is the purified heart; then, to regulate the actings of love, and determine their course and measure, there is the good conscience; and finally, to sustain and animate the soul in the varied works and labours proper to love, there is the faith unfeigned, embracing the glorious promises of God, and ministering strength from the things therein contained to its vital energy. Such, probably, is the order and relation in which these spiritual characteristics presented themselves to the mind of the apostle; and in the concurrent action and due subordination of them to each other will ever be found to consist the stability and progress of the Christian life.

Ver. 6. *From which*—namely, the several moral qualities just mentioned—*some having swerved*, ἀστοχήσαντες (found only besides in chap. vi. 20, 2 Tim. ii. 18, where it is coupled with περί,—" said in regard to those who do not reach whither they are tending—do not attain their aim" (Bengel) : failing, either because they did not set the aim properly before them, or did not prosecute it in a manner fitted to accomplish what was sought. They wanted, in short, the requisite moral bent and energy of soul; and so *they turned aside into vain talk*—the preposition in the verb (ἐξετράπησαν) having respect to the path or direction which *should* have been followed, but from which the parties in question deviated. They had not the root of the matter in them; and having thus no heart for the great things of the gospel, they naturally fell to discoursing about vain questions, the debateable and speculative points about which they *could* find themselves at home. The secret undoubtedly lies here of much unsatisfactory and unprofitable preaching. If the heart is not *in* the great things of the gospel, if it is out of accord with their deep spiritual tone, it cannot delight to speak of them, and will be only too glad to turn aside to inferior topics.

Ver. 7. The parties warned against are further characterized as *desiring* (θέλοντες, *wishing*) *to be teachers of the law;* implying that it was but a wish, a bootless aiming at what, in its proper reality, lay far from them, as is afterwards more distinctly brought out. The interpretation of Baur, which was demanded by his hypothesis, would find in this description not law *teachers*, but law *opposers*, Antinomians of the Marcionite school; but the view is so arbitrary, and so much at variance with the natural import of the words, that it has met with almost universal rejection. The apostle is evidently speaking of men who by no means disparaged the law as vile, or at least as too low and carnal for persons aspiring to perfection, but rather had high notions of the law, and set themselves up as its more advanced and enlightened advocates, though utterly disqualified for the office they assumed. It is also evident, from the concession made in regard to their pretensions in ver. 8, "We know, indeed, that the law is good;" so far there is no dispute between us. It was an admission to the parties against whom he was contending, in favour of that which they so zealously lauded, in case the apostle's own position regarding it might be perverted or misunderstood. The false teachers, then, were in *some* sense legalists; the question is, in what sense? In what form, or with what intent, did they press the claims of law? Not, we have good reason to believe, after the manner of the Jewish Christians, who first disturbed the church—zealous for the maintenance of the ancient customs; for the way in which the apostle meets them (as noticed by all the recent better commentators) is quite different from what we find in the Epistles to the Romans, Galatians, and Colossians. Here he charges the parties in question, not with bringing in legal observances out of their proper place, but with utter ignorance and misapprehension as to the real nature and design of the law: μὴ νοοῦντες μήτε ἃ λέγουσιν, μήτε περὶ τίνων διαβεβαιοῦνται—*not understanding neither*, or, as suits our idiom better, *without understanding either what things they speak, or concerning what things they affirm.* They spoke, it would seem, dogmatically enough; for the verb (διαβεβαιοῦσθαι) means to make asseveration, or give forth one's view in a firm, dogmatic tone. But in doing so, the apostle declares they went beyond their depth; they merely displayed their own ignorance, and *that* in two respects—both as regards the things they said, and the topics concerning which they uttered their sentiments. The language is such as might very readily be applied to persons of a dreamy and speculative mood, disposed to take things otherwise than in their plain natural sense; attempting, as men of a higher order of thought, to refine and soar, and lose themselves in mystic reveries or fanciful allegorizings. And this, as already stated, is precisely the form of evil which we are led to understand then began to develope itself. It was a compound of Gnostic and Judaic elements. The persons who advocated it would keep the law—they would even make more of it than the apostle did; but then, the law not according to the letter—the law sublimated by the speculative reason, and explained in accordance with the theosophy of the East. A dangerous spirit this in which to meddle with the law! Even as applied by the thoughtful, discreet, Platonic mind of Philo, it served in good measure to evacuate the *moral* element in the old revelation, and sought to explain by the help of a mistaken physics many things that should have been viewed with a direct reference to the heart and conscience. But in the hands of inferior men—especially men of a sophistical cast of mind, who wished to employ religion to their own sinister purposes—both the fancifulness of the explanations given of the law, and its misapplication to other than its legitimate and proper ends, may justly be supposed to have been of a much more marked and conspicuous kind. There would now, probably, be frivolous distinctions, wild extravagance, possibly licentious freedom cloaked under high-sounding professions, a hunting after everything but that which should have been most especially regarded. And so, indeed, the corresponding passage in Titus distinctly tells us, chap. i. 10 sq., "There are many unruly and vain talkers and deceivers, specially they of the circumcision, whose mouths must be stopped, who subvert whole houses, teaching things which they ought not, for filthy lucre's sake." Then he refers to the Jewish fables and commandments of men that turn from the truth, and speaks of those who set them forth as unbelieving, and in their very conscience defiled. Their dreamy refinements and speculations on the law not only led them into practical neglect of its profoundly ethical spirit, but left them in a manner incapable of perceiving it—deadened their whole moral nature. And in the writings of St. John, so far as they bore respect to the state of things existing at a later period, and existing in that very region in which Timothy now laboured, we perceive indications of the same spirit, only in a more advanced stage of development. They make mention of "the blasphemy of those which say they are Jews and are not, but are of the synagogue of Satan" (Rev. ii. 9); of persons "teaching the doctrine of Balaam," practising the seductions of Jezebel, and knowing the depths of Satan (chap. ii. 14, 20, 24); in short, of men who had so sophisticated their own minds, and tried so to sophisticate the minds of others, that the apostle had to warn the disciples to remember that "he who doeth righteousness is righteous, and that he who committeth sin is of the devil;" that "no lie is of the truth;" that for one to say he has fellowship with God, while he walks in darkness, is practically to lie (1 John iii. 7, ii. 21, i. 6). The state of things had come to be such, that it was found necessary to recall them to first principles, and teach them, as it were, the A B C of Christian truth and morality.

[Mark here the progression of error in false teaching. What in its first movements may be but a deflection in a single line, may in course of time lead to a general depravation; for example, ritualism in the early church. Mark, too, what is the result of that knowledge and teaching which would soar above the simplicity of the gospel: it ends in licence and corruption—becomes dazzled in the clearer light it affects to live in, and stumbles as in gross darkness.]

Ver. 8. The apostle turns here from the false to the true, gives his own view of the nature of the law, and of the right use of it, as contradistinguished from that which he had condemned in others. *We know, indeed* (so δέ here may be best rendered), *that the law is good:* our quarrel, therefore, with those pretentious law-teachers is not about the quality of the instrument they profess to handle, but only about their manner of handling it; we know it to be like Him from whom it proceeds—good. The theme, in this point of view, had been already discussed at considerable length in other parts of the apostle's writings, especially in his Epistle to the Romans. Here, as what he says is of the nature of an admission, he merely asserts it; and then brings in a regulating principle as to that respecting which there *was* a difference betwixt him and the false teachers at Ephesus,—namely, as to the use or application to be made of the law. The principle is, *if one use it lawfully;* that is, in accordance with its proper nature and design. For, if a man mistakes regarding this, he cannot possibly handle the law rightly; he necessarily turns it into a wrong direction, and loses at least the spirit, if not also the substance, of its teaching.

Vers. 9, 10. The specific application is here given of the general principle just announced—not, of course, the only application which it admitted of, but the one which was of importance for the present time: *knowing this* (holding it as a settled point regarding the proper design of the law), *that the law is not made for a righteous person.* Although νόμος is here without the article, there seems no reason why it should not be understood of the law of God as revealed in Old Testament Scripture, rather than, with some, of law generally. For parallel passages, see Rom. ii. 25, iii. 30, vii. 1; Gal. ii. 19, vi. 13, etc.[1] Middleton would take an intermediate view; he would understand *law* in the general sense, but take it as inclusive of the law of Moses. It is, however, of this law, specially and peculiarly, that the

---

[1] See Winer, *Gr.* § 19. 1. He brings the usage under the general rule, that appellatives often want the article, when they are such that only one of the kind exists, or are so used that there can be no reasonable doubt as to what object is intended. Besides νόμος, such words as δικαιοσύνη, ἀγάπη, and others, are similarly used.

apostle is evidently speaking: for the persons against whom he is directing his remarks assumed to be teachers of law only in this speeific sense; and we have no reason for supposing that the subject of law was in any other respect before the mind of the apostle. But law so considered, unless the context plainly determines otherwise, always bears pointed reference to the decalogue; for this was the law in the more emphatic sense—the heart and essence of the whole economy of law; hence alone deposited in the ark of the covenant. And that this here also is more especially in the eye of the apostle, is evident from the different sorts of character presently after mentioned as intended to be checked and restrained by the law: they admit of being all ranged under the precepts of the two tables. Now this law *is not made* (οὐ κεῖται, the appropriate expression for the introduction or enactment of a law; whence οἱ νόμοι οἱ κείμενοι is equivalent to our phrase, "the established laws") *for the righteous* (δικαίῳ). By the latter expression is to be understood, not one who in a worldly sense is just or upright (for the apostle is not here speaking of such), but who in the stricter sense is such,—one who, whether by nature or by grace, has the position and character of a righteous man. Why is the law not made for such? It can only be because he is of himself inclined to act in conformity with its requirements. If Adam had continued in such a state of righteousness, he would not have needed any objective revelation of law; the *spirit* of the law in his bosom would spontaneously have prompted him to all that is pure and good. And of justified believers now the apostle elsewhere says: "They are not under law, but under grace;" yet so under grace that sin cannot have dominion over them, and their walk is not after the flesh, but after the Spirit (Rom. vi. 14, viii. 4). It is thus they have found whatever goodness belongs to them, and thus also that they are to go on to perfection—not by serving themselves of the law, or using it as the ladder for reaching to higher attainments in goodness, but by laying hold of, or apprehending, that for which they are apprehended of Christ; drinking more deeply into the spirit of His gospel, and receiving into their souls fuller impressions of the great realities and hopes it presents to their acceptance. But this bespeaks nothing as to imperfection in the law itself, or the possibility of attaining to a height of excellence beyond its requirements. What is said has respect, not to the kind or measure of goodness men are called to aspire after, but to the way and means necessary to reach it; and when the law is represented as the antithesis of moral evil, in its various forms of irreligious and wicked behaviour, it is manifestly implied that the spirit and aim of the law itself is the perfection of moral excellence.

In regard to those for whom, he says, the law *is* made,—those, that is, who need the check and restraint of its discipline,—the apostle gives first a general description: they are *the lawless and unruly*, or disobedient, the self-willed, fiery and arrogant spirits that would fain spurn from them all surveillance and control. Then he branches out into particulars, the earlier portion of which have respect to offences against God, the later to offences against one's fellow-men: *for the ungodly and sinful* (ἀσεβέσιν καὶ ἁμαρτωλοῖς, both words occurring in 1 Pet. iv. 18), *the unholy and profane* (ἀνοσίοις καὶ βεβήλοις), differing from the preceding pair only in pointing more distinctly to certain manifestations of the ungodly spirit, in irreverent and contemptuous behaviour toward the things more peculiarly associated with the name of God. What follows has respect to human relations: *for smiters of fathers and smiters of mothers*—πατρολῴαις καὶ μητρολῴαις—such is the proper import of the terms, rather than *murderers* of fathers and mothers; for the verb (ἀλόαω or ἀλοίαω) which forms the root of the second part of the compound expressions signifies merely to *thresh, smite,* or *beat down;* and so the smiting of father and mother, in itself a most unnatural and shameful violation of the honour due to them, whether or not it might issue in fatal consequences, was in the Old Testament legislation reckoned so heinous a transgression of the fifth command, that the penalty of death was attached to it (Ex. xxi. 15). Then come the violators of the sixth command, *murderers;* those of the seventh, *fornicators, abusers of themselves with mankind* (ἀρσενοκοίταις, a term for which fortunately our language has no proper equivalent); those of the eighth, the most repulsive and inhuman class of them, *men-stealers,* kidnapping and making merchandise of their fellow-creatures; finally, those of the ninth commandment, *liars, perjured persons.* But as in this enumeration the apostle had mentioned only the more flagrant forms of transgression, and had no intention of furnishing a complete list of lawless characters, he winds up the description with a comprehensive form of expression, which includes whatever besides that can be reckoned evil: *and if there be anything else that is contrary to the sound instruction* (τῇ ὑγιαινούσῃ διδασκαλίᾳ),—that sort of instruction, namely, which was exemplified in the teaching of our Lord and His apostles. Why such teaching should be characterized as sound or healthful—why, at least, it should be so characterized here, and often besides in the Pastoral epistles (as at 1 Tim. vi. 3; 2 Tim. i. 13, iv. 3; Tit. i. 9, ii. 1), but not in Paul's other writings, we may be but imperfectly competent to say. But neither can others be entitled to deny that the circumstances of the time were of a kind to render such an expression natural to Paul—natural for him *now,* as contradistinguished from a preceding time. And the simple fact of its absence from the earlier epistles of Paul was almost certain to have deterred a forger of Paul's name to have used it, at least with such marked frequency. The apostle himself, however, might well enough do it, if the erring tendencies against which he warned and wrote in the closing period of his ministry differed materially from those which had manifested themselves previously, and, in a moral respect, were of a sickly and distempered nature. Such appears to have been actually the case. It was no longer the avowed adversaries of the gospel that the apostle had to meet, nor its mistaken and bigoted corrupters of the pharisaical type, but a class of sophistical, dreamy, self-sufficient theosophists, who, without directly opposing or disparaging the gospel, sought to introduce a fine-spun but sickly sentimentalism, —teaching abstinence from things in themselves proper and lawful, as if incompatible with the higher attainments of the divine life, and refining upon the law so as to derive from it an instruction it could not yield in its direct and natural import. This was essentially a morbid, an unhealthful sort of teaching, to which the apostle fitly opposed the sound and robust character of his own teaching and that of the other apostles. It was therefore the altered circumstances of the times which gave rise to this change in the language of the apostle; and it is absurd to urge the phraseology employed as an argument against the apostolic origin of the epistles, unless one could disprove the previous alteration in the circumstances—which has certainly not yet been done.

Ver. 11. *According to the gospel of the glory of the blessed God, which was committed to my trust*—not *the glorious gospel*, taking τῆς δόξης as a qualitative genitive, equivalent to ἔνδοξος (see Winer, *Gr.* § 34. 6). The gospel of God's glory is the gospel which peculiarly displays His glory,— unfolds this to the view of men by showing the moral character and perfections of God exhibited as they are nowhere else in the person and the work of Christ. Quite similarly, the apostle speaks in 2 Cor. iv. 4 of "the gospel of the glory of Christ, who is the image of God;" and elsewhere of "the riches of God's glory toward the vessels of mercy," or of the power which He gives them, "according to the riches of His glory" (Rom. ix. 23; Eph. iii. 16). By presenting the gospel thus as the manifestation of God's glory, and the God from whom it comes as the *blessed* God, the apostle evidently intends to make it known as adequate to all the wants of men's spiritual natures, and the purposes of their salvation. But while the meaning of the words is thus clear, what precisely is the nature of the connection between them and the preceding context? What does the apostle mean to tell us is according to his gospel? Is it simply the sound doctrine spoken of immediately before? So some have thought (as Theophylact, Bengel); but in that case there must have been required a connecting link with the διδασκαλίᾳ, such as τῇ κατὰ τὸ εὐαγ. (as is done in D; and Theophylact has the gloss, τῇ οὔσῃ κατὰ τὸ εὐαγ.). But there being no such connecting particle, we are obliged to refer this concluding statement to the whole of the preceding passage; and so the meaning comes to be, that the assertion about the law being made rather for restraining the wicked, than for establishing and perfecting the righteous, is according to the gospel of the grace of God with which the apostle was entrusted.

Ver. 12. The thought of such a gospel having been committed to him—one so unworthy in himself of having *any* treasure of God entrusted to him—leads the apostle to recall with adoring gratitude the treatment he had received from God *his* Saviour. In doing so, he in one sense breaks off the thread of his former discourse,—leaving, as he does, for a time the false teachers, against whom he had been cautioning Timothy; but, in another, he is still prosecuting his design: for undoubtedly his main object was to inspire Timothy with right views of the nature of the gospel, and of the course it behoved him to follow in teaching and enforcing its lessons. The reference to false teachers was itself subordinate to this design; so that the occasion now taken to discourse of his own case as a singular exemplification of the gospel of God's glory, is not of the nature of a digression, but is in perfect keeping with the general drift and aim of his instructions. It is also such an experimental record as might well come from the pen of the apostle himself, though we can scarcely conceive any one presuming to indite it in his behalf, far less to palm it on the church in his name. Ellicott, who vindicates the entire suitableness of the passage to the purpose of the apostle, justly says of it: "Thus, without seeking to pursue the subject in the form of a studied contrast between the law and the gospel (he was not now writing against *direct* Judaizers), or of a declaration how the transgressors of the law were to attain righteousness, he more than implies it all in the history of his own case. In a word, the law was for the *condemnation* of sinners, the gospel of Jesus Christ was for the *saving* of sinners and the ministration of forgiveness; verily, it was *a gospel of the glory of the blessed God.*"

Χάριν ἔχω — *I give thanks.* This is not the apostle's usual mode of expressing thanks: he generally uses the single verb εὐχαριστῶ; but χάριν ἔχειν also occurs in 2 Tim. i. 3, in Heb. xii. 28, Luke xvii. 9; and χάρις itself in the sense of *thanks* frequently by our apostle, Rom. vi. 17; 1 Cor. xv. 57; 2 Cor. ii. 14, etc. The apostle gives thanks *to Christ Jesus our Lord, who had given him power*, or *strengthened* him — ἐνδυναμώσαντι — namely, to receive such a commission or charge as had been entrusted to him. He has respect to the work of an apostle, in relation to the gospel of Christ's glory, as at once a very arduous and a very responsible undertaking, which, however honourable, would have oppressed and crushed him, but for the strengthening and sustaining grace which he received from above. This endowment of grace is undoubtedly to be connected with the whole work of his apostleship; not merely, as some, with the performance of miracles, or, as others, with the patient endurance of trial and suffering: for, while supernatural power was needed for these, they still formed an incidental and subsidiary, not the primary, object of the apostolic calling. The great end for which he received this calling, as Paul himself elsewhere testifies, was to preach the unsearchable riches of Christ, and thereby win men to the love and service of God, and form them into communities of believing Christians. And as this was emphatically a divine work, in which, if left to himself, he should have laboured in vain, the same gracious Lord who gave him the call to the work, gave him also the aid necessary to its successful prosecution.

With thanks for the power conferred on him, however, the apostle couples the acknowledgment of his own deep unworthiness: he had been counted worthy to be put in trust with the weightiest charge, and furnished with the noblest gifts for its execution, though in himself he had been an offender of the deepest dye. The Lord, he says, *reckoned me faithful,* or trustworthy ($\pi\iota\sigma\tau\acute{o}\nu$); adding the proof in a participial clause, *appointing me for service*—εἰς διακονίαν—for ministerial employ. Such employ necessarily requires fidelity in the person appointed to discharge it; and on this account, no doubt, the apostle chose the humbler and more general term of service, rather than apostleship, to designate his office, because viewing it here with reference to the work he had to do, not to the prerogatives given him to exercise. He thus also, for practical purposes, brought his case down to a level with Timothy's, or that of any other servant of Christ. Whatever specific office they may hold, it is essentially a service they have to render; and the higher the office, the more onerous and important also the service: so that every one bearing office in the church of Christ is here admonished, by the example of the apostle, to regard himself as appointed to a duty of service, and to see in that a proof of the trust reposed in him by the great Head of the church; therefore also a call to fidelity in the work given him to do.

Ver. 13. Then comes the contrast between the present and the past, enhancing in the apostle's esteem the mercy and loving-kindness he had experienced: *though I formerly was* (τὸ πρότερον ὄντα, the participle of concession, or limitation, Jelf, § 697, *c*) *a blasphemer*—one, that is to say, who was wont to speak evil of the name of Jesus, and compel others to do the same (Acts xxvi. 11)—*a persecutor, and outrageous.* Our English version is here too weak, translating ὑβριστὴν by "injurious;" for the word signifies a doer of violence and outrage. "The ὑβριστής is contumelious; his insolence and contempt of others break forth in *acts* of wantonness and outrage" (Trench, *Syn.*). Such, certainly, was Paul's behaviour toward the Christian party before his conversion, and such also too commonly was the behaviour of his countrymen towards him after it (1 Thess. ii. 2, where the verb ὑβρισθείς is used with reference to his treatment at Philippi). *But I obtained mercy,* the apostle continues: great as his wickedness and guilt were, he yet became a subject of divine compassion; *because* (he adds) *I did it ignorantly in unbelief:* not meaning thereby to lessen the enormity of his guilt; for his very ignorance was culpable, having within his reach the means of correcting it, if he had been seriously minded to arrive at the truth. What he intends by the statement is, that his outrageous and violent procedure, however inexcusable in itself, was still not of such a kind as placed him beyond the pale of mercy; since he had not, like the worse part of the blaspheming and persecuting Pharisees, sinned against his better convictions (Mark iii. 28-30); he had not deliberately set at nought the counsel of God, and defied Heaven to its face. He stood, therefore, substantially on a footing with the Jerusalem sinners who, on and after the day of Pentecost, were charged by St. Peter with the awful crime of having crucified the

Lord of glory, yet with the qualifying circumstance of having done it in ignorance (Acts iii. 17). In both cases alike the sin was of the deepest dye, only not unpardonable; it still lay within the sphere of redeeming grace—but of grace in its more rare, one might even say, its exceptional exercise. This the apostle virtually admits in the words that follow.

Ver. 14. *But the grace of our Lord superabounded*—ὑπερ-πλεόνασεν—not merely manifested itself in an act of mercy, and exhibition of undeserved goodness, as in the case of ordinary sinners, but overflowed, in a manner, its wonted channels, and like a mighty flood poured its gifts of love into his bosom. And with the wonderful grace received, the apostle couples the frame of mind awakened by it: *with faith and love that are in Christ Jesus*—the fruit, certainly, of the grace bestowed, yet, as De Wette justly notes, not indicated here precisely as the fruit, but rather as the concomitants of grace—the subjective side of a work of grace. While he continued a stranger to the grace of Christ, he was also without faith, in unbelief; and so far from being animated by a spirit of love, he pursued a course of blasphemy, persecution, and outrage. But with grace came also faith and love, because by grace he was brought into living fellowship with Christ, the causal source and nourisher of both. There is a singular pregnancy in the passage, and also a profound Christian feeling pervading it, which leads the apostle to find all his springs in Christ, and in Christ as at once the embodiment of sovereign redeeming mercy, and the grand medium of its communication to the soul. In the strongest possible form he here again utters the confession, "By the grace of God I am what I am" (1 Cor. xv. 10; Eph. iii. 8).

Ver. 15. Now follows a general announcement respecting this grace, grounded on the apostle's own experience, and exemplified by it. *Faithful is the word, and worthy of all acceptation*, etc. The expression at the commencement, introducing the great truth which follows, *Faithful is the word* (πίστος ὁ λόγος), is one of those peculiar to the Pastoral epistles, occurring in these no fewer than five times (besides here, 1 Tim. iii. 1, iv. 9 ; 2 Tim. ii. 11 ; Tit. iii. 8), but occurring nowhere else,—a proof, therefore, that it had somehow passed into a kind of proverbial utterance with the apostle in the later period of his ministry, and a proof also that those epistles belonged to about the same period. If we have nothing exactly parallel to this in Paul's other epistles, we have at least what approaches it, in his marked predilection for particular words and modes of thought. By designating the word he is going to enunciate as *faithful*, he presents it to our view as perfectly reliable, entitled to implicit credit ; and the additional characteristic, *worthy of all acceptation* (that is, of every sort and manner of it, πάσης being without the article), commends it to us as deserving not only of being rested on with confidence, but of being received with every mark of inward affection and regard. It should be everywhere hailed by men, and embraced with the full accord of their soul, because of the benign aspect it carries towards them, and the blissful effect it is fitted to produce on their condition and destiny. The word is, *that Christ Jesus came into the world to save sinners*—the whole gospel in a sentence—and, indeed, but a slightly modified form of the original announcement made to Joseph, "Thou shalt call His name JESUS, for He shall save His people from their sins" (Matt. i. 21). Only here, along with the fact of the salvation of sinners as the one and all, in a manner, of Christ's undertaking, He is represented as coming into the world to accomplish it, which implies His pre-existence in a higher condition, and His descent from that into this lower world for the execution of the task He had previously undertaken. So also in John i. 9, xvi. 28.

But the apostle is not satisfied with expressing the

general object of Christ's mission; he must also indicate his own specific relation to it, or to the class whose good it contemplates. And this is the more remarkable part of the statement, as he places himself in the foremost rank of sinners: *of whom I am chief* (or first, ὧν πρῶτός εἰμι ἐγώ —first in the sense of greatest, as at Mark xii. 28, 29). Commentators have often sought to qualify the strength of the expression by confining the reference to converts from Judaism, and understanding the apostle merely to mean, that he had gone further in a sinful antagonism to the claims of Jesus than his believing countrymen generally, or that he held a leading place among such. But there is no warrant for any limitation of this sort. It accorded with the deep practical insight which St. Paul had through the Spirit obtained into his own case, that he should set his guilt in the foremost place: to his own eye it bulked more than all; as, indeed, for direct and palpable hostility to the cause of Jesus, it could scarcely be exceeded. It is not surely for *us* to extenuate what he has himself so broadly marked—the less so, as in this very depth and intensity of feeling respecting his sinfulness we recognise the essential element of his spiritual greatness, according to our Lord's declaration, that he who humbles himself most shall be greatest in the kingdom of heaven (Matt. xviii. 4).

Ver. 16. *Howbeit* (so the A. V. well, giving full expression to the contrast indicated by the ἀλλά between the apostle's behaviour toward Christ, and Christ's procedure toward him), *for this cause I obtained mercy, in order that in me first Christ Jesus might show forth all long-suffering, for a pattern to those who are going to believe on Him to life eternal.* The former reason assigned by the apostle for his obtaining mercy had respect to his personal relation to the principles of the divine government, as one little entitled to expect any manifestation of mercy, yet not placed beyond the sphere of its exercise. But the reason here adduced points to the economical design of God in selecting such a sinner to be a vessel of mercy: it was that he might be a living exemplar or pattern, as well as herald, of the wonderful grace exhibited in the gospel ; so that from what had been wrought in him others might take courage, and repair to Christ for the pardon of sin and life eternal, —might, as it is put by Bengel, conform themselves to the pattern, and say to themselves, If thou believest as Paul, thou shalt be saved as Paul. Such is the general import, and the particular words and phrases involve no special difficulty. There is a difference in the reading in one part; the received text having τὴν πᾶσαν μακροθυμίαν, while Lach. and Tisch. prefer τὴν ἅπασαν μακ. This last is certainly somewhat better supported, being found in ℵ, A, F, G, while the other has only D, I, K. But the difference in meaning is not material. If we adopt ἅπασαν, it merely renders the entireness or fulness of the long-suffering manifested toward the apostle more distinctly pronounced : *the whole of His long-suffering*, all that He had to show of it. But the other reading (πᾶσαν) also includes all ; for πᾶς, when standing between the article and the noun, according to the rule, marks the noun as an abstract, and indicates that it is to be taken in its entirety, without respect to individual members or component parts (Winer, *Gr.* § 17, 10 ; Green, *Gr.* p. 194). So that τὴν πᾶσαν μακ. denotes all that can be comprised in the term *long-suffering*—this in its totality. And so Chrysostom explains, though the reading he followed was that of the received text : " As if he said, In none more than in me has He need to show long-suffering ; nor can He find one who has been so much a sinner, needing all His mercy, all His long-suffering, not a part merely, as they who have sinned in part." He could not have said more, if he had read ἅπασαν. The word for *pattern*, ὑποτύπωσις, which is found only here and in 2 Tim. i. 13, does not materially differ from τύπος, the term commonly used by Paul (Rom. v. 14; 1 Cor. x. 6, 11, etc.); but is of more active import—expresses not so properly the inanimate form as the living exemplification, the personified action of the long-suffering referred to. And being coupled with the genitive of possession—τῶν μελλόντων πιστεύειν—it is represented as in some sense belonging to these future believers—called into existence and set forth for their special behoof. In St. Paul *first*—first in the sense of chief, or foremost exemplification—had the attribute of mercy been displayed, that they might be the more distinctly assured of the divine purpose to extend its manifestation to themselves. And being described as going to believe on Christ to life eternal, these future believers, who would take the benefit of the apostle's marvellous experience, have presented to them at once the high destiny to which they should be called, and the ground on which their hope of it must rest—faith in the person and work of Christ.

[The question here naturally suggests itself, how far Christian ministers should in their preaching disclose their more marked personal experiences, or should interweave references to their spiritual history with their manifestations of divine truth to their fellow-men. But it were unwise to lay down any precise rule in the matter, or prescribe one method for all. That there may occasionally be made such personal references, and with advantage to the hearers, the example of the apostle is itself a sufficient proof. Not only here, but in several other parts of his epistles, he brings prominently forward what had befallen or had been done by himself; and these are universally felt to be among the most interesting and instructive portions of his writings. And so will it ever be with men of like minds, men of ardent temperaments, vivid imaginations, and energetic wills, in whom everything in experience and behaviour naturally assumes a distinctly personal, characteristic impress. It will be natural for such persons to reveal themselves at times in their discourses, whether by direct reference to the past workings of their own mind, and God's dealings with them, or by subjective exhibitions of Christian truth and duty, raised on the background of their own experience. When fitly and discreetly done, it may throw a peculiar charm and glow over the preacher's discourse. But very great caution is needed in the use of such an element, lest it should degenerate into egotism, or become merely a display of individual singularity and importance. Deep sincerity—the impulse of strong feeling—a conviction of its fitness to subserve some spiritual end, should ever go along with, and condition, any personal references one may make in public discourse. And if some men of note have dealt much in them, and by doing so have lent an attractive power to their mode of address, such as Luther, Bunyan, Irving, Guthrie; others, again, of the very highest mark as public speakers,—for example, Leighton, R. Hall, Chalmers,—have studiously avoided it: their individuality has discovered itself only in the distinctive character and spirit of their discourse.]

Ver. 17. *Now, to the King of the ages, the incorruptible, invisible, only God, be honour and glory for ages of ages* (or, for ever and ever). *Amen.* The language in this doxology is somewhat peculiar, and has no exact parallel in New Testament Scripture. In a very few passages is the epithet *King* applied to God, as in Matt. v. 35, "the great King;" 1 Tim. vi. 15, "King of kings;" Rev. xv. 3, "King of nations" (according to the correct reading), but here only *King of the ages.* Our translators have softened and generalized the expression, by rendering "the King eternal." It is better, however, to adhere to the proper import of the word. Αἰών, from ἀίω, ἄημι, to *breathe* (Hom. *Il.* xv. 252), means (1) lifetime, life; (2) long period of time, perpetuity = Lat. *ævum;* and in this latter sense various shades of meaning quite naturally arise according to the connection: in particular, (*a*) *past time*, from of old, or since time began (Luke i. 70; Acts iii. 21; Col. i. 26); (*b*) the *present epoch of passing time*, the age in which one lives, or the existing world (Matt. xiii. 22; Luke xvi. 8; Rom. xii. 2, etc.); (*c*) *the successive stages or epochs of the world's history*, dispensational time (Matt. xxiv. 3; Heb. ix. 26; 1 Cor. x. 11),—the termination of the æons or ages being in this case coincident with the end of the world. But as the indefinite extension of such successive periods may readily enter into our conceptions of the future as well as of the past, so there naturally came, (*d*) by a reduplication of the word, the idea of eternity—*ages of ages*, dispensational epochs of indefinite number = eternity. So here, for example, at the close of the doxology, εἰς τοὺς αἰῶνας τῶν αἰώνων, *for ever and ever;* and in other passages, the word, sometimes in the singular, sometimes in the plural, stands simply for eternity, whether as before or as after the periods we designate by the general name of *time*, as in Eph. iii. 11, 21; 1 Pet. i. 25; 2 Pet. iii. 18; Mark iii. 29, xi. 14, etc. There is no difficulty in understanding the import of the expression as connected with God; and it is best, as we have said, to retain it in its simplicity. When He is spoken of as King of the ages, He is presented to our view as supreme Lord and Director of the successive cycles or stages of development through which this world, or creation at large, was destined to pass—the Sovereign Epoch-maker, who arranges everything pertaining to them beforehand, according to the counsel of His own will, and controls whatever takes place, so as to subordinate it to His design. The idea is presented in many other parts of Scripture, in the Old Testament as well as in the New; and in Ps. cxlv. 13, the kingdom of God is in the Septuagint described as βασιλεία πάντων τῶν αἰώνων, a kingdom of all the ages. In the apocryphal books the expression *King of ages* is distinctly applied to God (Ecclus. xxxvi. 17 (22);

Tob. xiii. 6).—The epithets which follow, ἀφθάρτῳ, ἀοράτῳ, μόνῳ (the received text has also σοφῷ, but against the best authorities), are to be coupled with the Θεῷ which follows, —the whole specifying and characterizing the Being designated as King of the ages; He is *the incorruptible, invisible, sole God.* To Him alone belong honour and glory, and to Him they belong to all eternity. The same expressions are together applied to God in Rev. iv. 9, 11, and to the glorified Christ in Heb. ii. 9, Rev. v. 13.

As to the reason for introducing here such an ascription of praise to God, no other can be assigned than the devout and grateful emotions of the apostle's heart; nor is any other needed. The train of reflection into which he had been led, naturally brought the thought of God very prominently before him; of God as the free and sovereign dispenser of the grace which he had received, and which had changed the whole state of his condition and prospects. And penetrated with a sense of the infinite greatness and overruling wisdom, power, and goodness of God as manifested in his own singular history, he rises from the particular to the general, and winds up this touching and personal interlude in his discourse by a devout acknowledgment of God as the Lord of the universe,—of all its ages, and the issues therewith connected,—and glorifying Him as such.

Vers. 18–20. In these verses the apostle again returns to his proper theme—that, namely, of giving specific counsels and directions to Timothy. *This charge I commit to thee, child Timothy.* What charge? Referring back to ver. 3, we find the apostle charging Timothy (ἵνα παραγγείλῃς) respecting those who were acting as teachers at Ephesus, that they should be urged to avoid teaching after a certain manner; and at ver. 5 he had spoken generally of what he held to be the end of the gospel charge (παραγγελία), for all who might assume the office of Christian instructors. Several commentators have consequently brought the charge mentioned here into direct connection with those earlier passages, as Theodoret, Mack, and some others. It is a serious objection, however, to such a view, that the preceding references to a charge lie so remote from the one before us; and the subject, also, as here introduced, has the appearance of being in itself both special and complete. Most recent commentators, therefore, justly conceive that nothing more than perhaps an indirect allusion can be supposed to exist here to the charges or commands mentioned previously, and that the more direct and immediate object of the present charge is expressed in the ἵνα στρατεύῃ which follows. The apostle, in short, has passed from his own peculiar calling, and the trust therewith connected, to the inferior yet still very important office and trust now committed to Timothy, and lays on him the command to do in regard to it the part of a good soldier of Christ, that he might wage successfully the conflict with evil. The more remarkable part of the passage is the reference it contains to certain prophecies which had been uttered concerning Timothy, and which the apostle introduces as a kind of justification of the command he is going to lay on his disciple: *according to the prophecies that went before on thee*, or that were at an early period pronounced over thee. When precisely these prophecies were uttered, we are nowhere informed; but the probability is that they belong to the period of Timothy's special designation to Christian work under the authority and guidance of the apostle, given then for the purpose of encouraging the church to make the designation, and disposing Timothy to accede to it. His extreme youth, and possibly also slender frame, might render such intimations of the Divine mind respecting the future course of Timothy in a sense necessary at the commencement of his official connection with St. Paul. And it may be inferred, from the allusion to them here, that they contained indications both of the arduous nature of the work which he was called to do, and of the divine aid that should be given him to discharge it. On this account the apostle speaks of them, not simply as having been given at a definite period in the past, but as being still in a manner operative: *in order that in them thou mayest war the good warfare;* in them (ἐν αὐτοῖς), not simply, according to them (Huther), but as being, so to speak, encompassed by them, and finding in them whatever thou needest to stimulate and encourage thee amid the perils and difficulties which thou hast to encounter. The apostle thus had, in the prophecies in question, a specific occasion for the charge he was going to deliver; and the object of both was, that the early promise made to Timothy of a successful career in the cause of the gospel might be realized. The image employed to describe Timothy's course of Christian activity— that of a warfare—was quite familiar to the apostle. In other passages he uses it of believers generally, Eph. vi. 12; of himself as an apostle, 2 Cor. x. 3, 4; and of Timothy again in the second epistle, chap. ii. 3.

Ver. 19. Here follows an instruction as to the more essential qualifications for prevailing in such a spiritual warfare: *having* (or holding, ἔχων) *faith and a good conscience;* possessing these moral elements as indispensable prerequisites, or accompaniments of the work. Faith fitly goes first; for it is this which provides the Christian combatant with his only valid standing-ground for the conflict, and supplies him with the weapons which alone can enable him to repel the assaults of the adversary, and counterwork his devices. But a good conscience is here faith's necessary handmaid; for the contest is in the strictest sense a moral one, and a depravation of the conscience is a virtual abandonment of the struggle: it is yielding to the adversary an entrenchment in the citadel. A single flaw even in the conscience is fatal to the believer's security, and his heartiness in the work; nor can it be permitted to exist without gnawing like a worm at the root of faith itself. The man who would do battle for the truth of God must be responsive in his inmost soul to the claims of divine truth, and render it clear as day that he identifies himself with its interests—is ready, in a manner, to live and die in its behalf. The two, therefore, must go together as inseparable companions: the good conscience can no more be dispensed with than the living faith; and much must ever depend on the healthful, harmonious, and concurrent action of the two for the result that is attained in the Christian warfare.

Sacred history presents too many instances of the disastrous effects of holding these qualifications apart — the faith without a good conscience, as, in Old Testament times, Balaam, Saul; in New, Judas, Demas. And here the apostle points to several in the region of Timothy's labours, though he only specifies two by name: *which some having thrust away* (ἀπωσάμενοι), *concerning faith made shipwreck.* The relative (ἥν) can only refer to the second of the two qualifications previously mentioned, the good conscience; and the manner of dealing with it affirmed of certain parties, can only be understood of violent overbearing suppression: they resolutely stifled its monitions, or drove from them whatever it suggested in the way of moral suasion to restrain them in the course they were pursuing. They thus, in the first instance, proved false to the convictions of their better nature; and this, by a natural process of reaction, led them to make shipwreck of faith itself. For faith, having failed to influence their practice, turned as a matter of course into a speculation: their views of divine truth became dim and wavering; they began first to undervalue, then to disrelish what should have been prized as their necessary food, until at last faith lost its hold altogether of the foundations, and as an anchorless vessel drifted among the rocks of scepticism.

A melancholy history, of which no age of the church has been without its memorable examples!

Ver. 20. *Of whom* (the apostle adds) *is Hymenæus and Alexander.* Both these names occur again in an unfavourable connection (Hymenæus in 2 Tim. ii. 17, and Alexander in 2 Tim. iv. 14); and it is a question among commentators, whether the same persons are in each case denoted by them. In regard to Hymenæus, there seems no proper reason for doubting the identity. For the name was by no means a common one; and that it should have been borne by two different persons, both in the same locality, and both exhibiting heretical tendencies, so near the beginning of the church, is against all probability. It has been alleged against this view (by Mosheim and others), that the Hymenæus in the second epistle is spoken of in milder terms than the one here—in the later reference only as a dangerous errorist to be shunned, in the earlier as one cast out like " an abominable branch " from the communion of the faithful. But the different aspects under which the subject is contemplated in the two places, sufficiently account for the different sort of representation employed in each. In the second reference it is his erroneous teaching which is brought into prominence, and which is characterized as a denying of the doctrine of the resurrection, and a consequent overthrowing of the faith of those who listened to it,—in that point of view, surely, a strong enough statement, since it denounces Hymenæus as erring in regard to one of the cardinal doctrines of Christianity, and thereby undermining what he should have striven to establish. Here, however, it is the diseased moral state of the man himself, and the disciplinary treatment which it called for, if there was to be any chance of arresting its progress, and saving him from perdition. But this representation concerning the person is no way incompatible with what is afterwards said respecting the doctrine. Both notices are brief; they give us only the more prominent features; but the probability is, from what we otherwise know, that the denial *doctrinally* of the literal resurrection was far from standing alone,—that it was simply an indication of that pretentious spiritualistic Gnosticism, which had its worst effect in the moral sophistication it wrought in the heart—distorting men's views of the divine life, and blunting their consciences as to the essential distinctions between right and wrong, holiness and sin.—The Alexander who is here coupled with Hymenæus may or may not be the same person who is mentioned in Second Timothy, designated there as the coppersmith, and a personal enemy of the apostle, "who did him much harm." The name was a very common one, and may have belonged to several persons in the same church or neighbourhood at the period the apostle wrote. It tells also somewhat against the identification, that while both Hymenæus and Alexander reappear in the second epistle as the names of false disciples, they are no longer connected together. Philetus is there associated with Hymenæus; and Alexander is mentioned alone, and apparently as a worker of evil, not at Ephesus, but in Rome, though it is possible enough he may have belonged to the region of Asia. Our materials are too scanty to enable us to draw more definite conclusions.

How had the apostle dealt with such offenders? *Whom* (says he) *I delivered over to Satan, that they might be disciplined* (or taught by chastisement) *not to blaspheme*. The verb παιδεύω, though its primary meaning was to educate or train up, and it is sometimes so used in the New Testament (as in Acts vii. 22), yet usually bears, both in the Sept. and in the New Testament, the sense of scourging, correcting, or chastising with a view to reformation and improvement (Luke xxiii. 16, 22; Heb. xii. 6, 7; 1 Cor. xi. 32; 2 Cor. vi. 9, etc.). A severe schooling of some sort is therefore meant here—a subduing and corrective discipline, having for its object the recovery of the persons subjected to it from their grievous backsliding, and being made to cease from blaspheming, that is, misrepresenting and calumniating the truth of God. But what is to be understood of the kind of discipline itself, expressed in the very solemn and peculiar phraseology of delivering them over to Satan? It might seem as if this, were it really effected, must have precluded all hope of a better future, and was like consigning the parties concerned to utter perdition. So doubtless it would, if, according to the doctrine of Scripture and the truth of things, Satan were an absolutely independent as well as hostile power, who had an indefeasible right to retain whatever was given as a prey into his hand. But such is by no means the case. Satan is but a creature and an instrument — one who has a definite sphere to occupy and a power to exercise, in relation to the purposes of God's moral government, but still only of a subordinate and ministerial kind. Thus, in Old Testament times, Job was for a season left to be bruised and afflicted by Satan; only, however, for a season, and in order that he might through the fiery ordeal be raised to a higher purity and a more serene bliss. David, also, in a time of carnal pride and security, was allowed to be tempted by Satan, so as to be thereby drawn into the vortex of severe retributory judgments, yet with the ultimate design of having the flesh destroyed and the spirit raised to a nobler elevation (1 Chron. xxi. 1; Ps. xxx.). In New Testament Scripture we are met with the numerous demoniacs on whom our Lord so frequently exercised His healing power; cases, indeed, respecting which as a whole we have very imperfect information, while yet we have no reason to doubt that in most, if not all of them, the demoniacal agency was of the nature of a chastisement, and was rendered subservient to great moral purposes for the individuals affected by it (see Matt. xii. 43-45). Still more nearly allied, perhaps, to the point in hand, was the giving up of Peter and his fellow-disciples to Satan for a season, that they might, for their obstinate blindness and corruption, be sifted as wheat (Luke xxii. 31, 32). It was doubtless on the basis of such considerations and examples that St. Paul acted here, as previously, in a somewhat parallel case, at Corinth (1 Cor. v. 5). In respect to that earlier occasion he told the Corinthians, since they had failed in their duty concerning it, that " in the name of the Lord Jesus he had adjudged the offending person to Satan for the destruction of the flesh:" he had done it by virtue of his apostolic function, yet so that the church might bring it home to the party concerned; as in this case also the church at Ephesus would certainly have to indorse and act upon the apostle's judgment. The infliction in both cases is purposely left general; its *object* rather than its *nature* is indicated: it was for the destruction of the flesh. But this might partly be accomplished by the shame and mortification of a formal removal from the flock and guardianship of Christ to the desert world, partly by inward remorse and sorrow on account of the guilt incurred, by the sense of forlornness and desolation produced, and possibly also by some outward tribulations—sickness of body, or calamities of life—as salutary warnings and preludes of coming wrath. For the working of such bitter experiences Satan was the proper instrument—the antinomy, indeed, in his aim and immediate action of the Spirit of God, whose presence ever makes itself felt in all peace, and joy, and blessing; yet an antinomy which is capable of being turned by the benignant will and controlling agency of God into an ultimate harmony; since the destruction of the flesh effected by the one class of operations might through the other become a fit preparation for awakening in the soul convictions of sin and longings for salvation. So that the delivering to Satan was in the apostle's intention and desire only an expedient for accomplishing a spiritual cure. It was the most solemn form of excommunication, and betokened that those against whom it was employed were in a most perilous condition—trembling on the brink of final impenitence, and if capable of being saved at all, saved only as by fire. The form, indeed, was such that it seems to have been regarded as fit for none but an apostle to use, as if he alone had the spiritual discernment to perceive when it should be done, or the authority requisite for doing it with effect. Hence, however common excommunication was in the ancient church, the authorities did not presume to give it this form, not even in the case of the greatest offenders (see Bingham, *Ant.* B. xvi. c. 2). At the same time, there can be no doubt that the apostolic practice in this respect tended materially to sustain the ancient church in enforcing that stringent discipline by which she was so long distinguished, but which was ultimately carried to an excess that ministered to prevailing errors.

CHAPTER II.

Ver. 1. *I exhort then, first of all, that petitions, prayers, supplications, thanksgivings, be made for all men.* The connection marked here by the οὖν with what precedes cannot be designated very close, and our *then* may more fitly be taken to represent the illative particle than the *therefore* of the Authorized Version. But it is absurd to deny, with some German critics (Schleiermacher, De Wette), that there is any logical connection whatever. The apostle had immediately before been charging Timothy and others situated like him to take heed to fulfil with all good fidelity the gospel charge, so that they might be able to war a good warfare, and escape the dangers amid which others had made shipwreck. What could be more natural, after this, than to exhort to the presentation of constant prayers in behalf generally of men, and especially of kings and rulers, that by the proper exercise of their authority these might restrain the evils of the time, and make it possible for God-fearing men to lead quiet and peaceable lives? The multiplication of terms for this intercessory function is somewhat remarkable: *petitions* (δεήσεις, the simple expression of want or need), *prayers* (προσευχάς), *supplications* (ἐντεύξεις, the same as the preceding, with the subordinate idea of closer dealing, *entreaties*, or earnest pleadings). The distinction between them cannot be very sharply drawn; for in several passages certain of them are used where we might rather have expected others, if respect were had to the distinctive shade of meaning suggested by the etymology (as in chap. iv. 5, where ἐντεύξεις is used of ordinary prayer for the divine blessing, and Eph. vi. 18, where supplications of the most earnest kind are intended, and yet only the two first of the words found here are employed). The variety of expression is perhaps chiefly to be regarded as indicating the large place the subject of intercessory prayer had in the apostle's mind, and the diverse forms he thought should be given to it, according to the circumstances in which, relatively to others, the people of God might be placed. Hence, *thanksgivings* were to be added, when the conduct of the parties in question was such as to favour the cause of righteousness and truth,—a fit occasion being thereby presented for grateful acknowledgments to God, who had so inclined their hearts. And when it is said, that *first of all* such thanksgivings and supplications should be offered, if the expression is coupled with the acts of devotion referred to, it can only mean that they should have a prominent place in worship, should on no account be overlooked or treated as of little moment, not that they should actually have the precedence of all others. But the expression is most naturally coupled with the apostle's request on the subject; he first of all entreats that this be done; it is his foremost advice that people should deal with God in the matter, as the most effectual safeguard.

Ver. 2. By mentioning *all men* as the object of their prayers and thanksgivings, the apostle undoubtedly meant to teach Christians to cherish wide and generous sympathies, and to identify their own happiness and wellbeing with those of their fellow-men. But he specially associates the duty with those on whose spirit and behaviour the peace and good order of society more directly depended —*kings* (quite generally, as in the address of our Lord to His disciples, Matt. x. 18; also Rom. xiii. 1; 1 Pet. ii. 13; hence affording no ground to the supposition of Baur, that the emperor and his co-regents in the time of the Antonines were meant by the expression), and *all that are in authority* (ὑπεροχῇ, strictly *eminence*, but here, as elsewhere, the eminence of social position—a place of authority). Then follows the more immediate end, as regards the praying persons themselves: *in order that we may pass a quiet and tranquil life, in all godliness and gravity;* that is, may be allowed freely to enjoy our privileges, and maintain the pious and orderly course which becomes us as Christians, without the molestation, the troubles, and the unseemly shifts which are the natural consequence of inequitable government and abused power. The last epithet, *gravity,* σεμνότητι, is quite in its proper place; for though it has respect to deportment rather than to Christian principle or duty, it is very closely allied to this, and is such a respectable and decorous bearing as is appropriate to those who live under the felt apprehension of the great realities of the gospel. The term *honesty* in the A. V. is quite unsuitable, in the now received sense of that word.

Vers. 3, 4. *For this*—namely, to make intercession to God in behalf of kings, of rulers generally, and of men of all sorts—*is good and acceptable before our Saviour God*,—a thing which in His reckoning is good, and is sure of meeting with His approval: for there seems no need for confining the *before God* to the latter epithet alone; it should be connected as well with what is good as what is acceptable, though things really and properly good are such also apart from Him. But by placing both epithets in connection with God, it is more distinctly implied that they are to be taken in their fullest import. (Ἀποδεκτός found in New Testament only here and at chap. vi. 4.) Then follows the reason why such conduct meets with God's approval as right and proper: *who willeth all men to be saved, and to come to the full knowledge of the truth*—ἐπίγνωσιν, knowledge in the fuller sense, knowledge that reaches its end, *saving knowledge;* and the governing verb, it will be observed, is θέλει, not the stronger βούλεται, which would have expressed *will* with an implied purpose or intent (see at ver. 8). Nothing can be better than the comment of Chrysostom here: "Imitate God. If He is willing that all men should be saved, it is meet to pray for all. If He willed that all should be saved, do thou also will it; but if thou willest, pray; for it is the part of such to pray. . . . But if God wills it, you will say, what need is there for my prayers? This is of great benefit both for you and for them: it draws *them* to love; thyself, again, it prevents from being treated as a wild beast; and such things are fitted to allure them to faith." There seems no need for going beyond this practical aspect of the matter; and either to press the passage on the one side, with some, to universalism,—as if it bespoke the comprehension of all within God's purpose of salvation,—or, on the other, to limit it, so as to make, not strictly all men, but only all sorts of men (with Calvin and others), the object of the good contemplated, is equally to strain the natural import of the words. It seems to me unnatural to understand the *all men,* twice so distinctly and emphatically expressed, as indicative of anything but mankind generally—men not merely without distinction of class or nation, but men at large, who certainly, as such, are to be prayed for. As the objects of the church's intercessions, there can be no difference drawn between one portion and another; and we are expressly taught to plead for all, because it is the will of God that they should be saved —σωθῆναι: not His will absolutely to save them, as if the word had been σῶσαι; but that they may be brought through the knowledge and belief of the truth into the state of the saved. And the whole character of the gospel of Christ, with its universal call to repent, its indiscriminate offers of pardon to the penitent, and urgent entreaties to lay hold of the hope set before them, is framed on very purpose to give expression to that will; for, surely, in pressing such things on men's acceptance, yea, and holding them disobedient to His holy will, and liable to aggravated condemnation, if they should *refuse* to accept, God cannot intend to mock them with a mere show and appearance of some great reality being brought near to them. No; there is the manifestation of a benevolent desire that they should not die in sin, but should come to inherit salvation (as at Ezek. xxxiii. 11), if only they will do it in the way that alone is consistent with the principles of His moral government and the nature of Christ's mediation. This, necessarily, is implied; and it is the part of the church, by her faithful exhibition of the truth in Christ, by her personal strivings with the souls of men, and earnest prayers in their behalf, to give practical effect to this message of goodwill from Heaven to men, and to do it in the spirit of tenderness and affection which itself breathes.

Such appears to be the fair and natural interpretation of the apostle's declaration, and the whole that it properly calls us to intermeddle with. It is true that all whom God wills to be thus entreated and prayed for shall not actually be saved—not even many who have enjoyed in the highest degree the means and opportunities of such dealing. And seeing, as God does, the end from the beginning, knowing perfectly beforehand whom He has, and whom He has not destined to salvation, grave questions are ready to arise as to whether the work of Christ can be really sufficient to meet the emergency occasioned by the ruin of sin, or whether God be sincere in seeking through His church the salvation of all,—questions which touch upon the deep things of God, and which it is impossible for us, with the materials we now possess, to answer satisfactorily to the speculative reason. Knowing who and what He is with whom in such things we have to do, we should rest assured that His procedure will be in truth and uprightness; and that the mysteries which meanwhile appear to hang around it will be solved to the conviction of every reasonable mind, when the proper time for doing so shall have arrived. But enough is known for present duty. God has unfolded for one and all alike the terms of reconciliation: He is willing, nay desirous, for His own glory's sake, that men should everywhere embrace them; and for this end has committed to His church the ministry of reconciliation, charging it upon the conscience of her members to strive and pray that all without exception be brought to the saving knowledge of the truth. What more can be required for faith to rest on, and for the intercessions and labours of an earnest ministry?

Vers. 5, 6. *For there is one God, one Mediator also of God and men.* The connective particle (γὰρ) presents what is here stated as an adequate ground, more immediately for the statement in the preceding verse, that God would have all men to be saved, and to come to the knowledge of the truth; but also, more remotely, for the call to prayer in behalf of all men, that so the benevolent desires of God toward them may come into effect. For in the mind of the apostle the two are essentially connected together; and what affords a valid reason for the one, provides it also for the other. What, then, is the reason? It is, that all stand related to one and the same God, also to one and the same Mediator; for mankind generally there is but one Dispenser of life and blessing, and one medium through which the dispensation flows; and in the invitations and precepts of the gospel all are put on a footing in regard to them: there is no respect of persons, or formal preference of some over others. Substantially the same thought is exhibited in the Epistles to the Romans (iii. 30) and the Galatians (iii. 20); *there*, as grounding the universality of the gospel offer, as *here* the universality of the goodwill, which the provisions of the gospel on God's part, and the prayers of His people on theirs, are ever breathing toward men. The oneness of the Mediator is followed by a declaration respecting His person and work: *man Christ Jesus, who gave Himself a ransom for all.* The want of the article before ἄνθρωπος is noticeable; not *the* man as contradistinguished from some others, but *man*, one possessing the nature, and in His work manifesting the attributes, of humanity. Not, however, as if this were all; for the very fact of Christ's mediating between God and men implies that He was Himself something that other men were not: they men, indeed, but in a state that men should not occupy toward God (hence requiring a Mediator); He, man in the ideal or proper sense, true image and representative of God, and as such capable of restoring the relations which had been disturbed by sin, between Creator and creature, and rendering earth, as it was designed to be, the reflex of heaven. *Man*, therefore, is used here much in the same emphatic manner that *Son of man* was by Daniel in his prophetic vision (vii. 13), and by our Lord Himself in His public ministry; man as ordained by God to hold the lordship of this lower world, to hold it for God, and therefore to establish truth and righteousness through all its borders (Heb. ii. 6–18). He who should be this is the true Head as well as pattern of humanity—the *New Man*, and at the same time "the Lord from heaven," because only as related to that higher sphere, and having at command powers essentially divine, could He either be or do what such an exalted position indispensably requires. So that the use made of this passage by Unitarians is without any just foundation.

Christ Jesus, who gave Himself a ransom for all—ὁ δοὺς ἑαυτὸν ἀντίλυτρον ὑπὲρ πάντων ; a participial clause indicating how especially Christ did the part of Mediator = Christ Jesus—He who, as Mediator, gave Himself, etc. The expression plainly involves the idea of substitution, an exchange of forfeits, one in the room of all, and for their deliverance. The words are, with a slight variation, an adoption of our Lord's own, who said that He came to give His life λύτρον ἀντὶ πολλῶν (Matt. xx. 28). For that in both passages it is mainly the death of Christ by which the ransom was paid *for*, or in exchange of, the persons indicated by the *many* in the one place, and by the *all* in the other, can admit of no reasonable doubt. And as the apostle is here contemplating Christ as the Messiah that had been promised, and now come for mankind at large, it is perhaps most natural to understand the language here with reference to those prophetical passages which represent the Messiah as obtaining from the Father the heritage of all families or nations of the earth; not the preserved of Israel alone, nor a few scattered members besides of other nations, but also the fulness of the Gentiles (Ps. ii. 8, xxii. 27; Isa. xlix. 6; Luke xxi. 24). So Cocceius, who remarks: "When it is said that Christ *gave a ransom price for all*, it is also signified that Christ of His own right demands all for His inheritance and possession. This, therefore, is a sure foundation for our prayers, that those whom the Father gave for an inheritance to the Son, we should ask may become the Son's possession; and since we know that all are given to the Son, we should pray for all, because we know not at what time God may be going to give this rich inheritance to the Son, and who may belong to the inheritance of Christ, who not; yet we do know, that if we ask all, we shall imitate the love of the Son."

The testimony—that which is to be testified or set forth—*for its own seasons:* a pregnant clause standing in apposition not to the immediately preceding term *ransom*, but to the whole participial clause, which declares Christ to have given Himself a ransom for all. "I understand it to mean," says Scholfield (*Hints for Imp. Version*), "that the great fact of Christ's having given Himself a ransom for all is that which is to be testified by His servants *in His times;* that is, in the times of the gospel: it is to be the great subject of their preaching." (Καιροῖς ἰδίοις, the dative of time, the temporal sphere or space within which the action takes place; Winer, *Gr.* § 31. 9; Fritzsche on Rom. xii. 1, note. The *own*, however, is more appropriately coupled with the testimony than with Christ: comp. Gal. vi. 9; here, vi. 15; Tit. i. 3.) The matter in question being primarily a fact—the death of Christ—but that fact in its doctrinal bearing as a ransom for the sins of men, it is here and in other places presented under the aspect of a testimony. It was above all other things the subject to which the apostles had to bear testimony, since it was through Christ's name, as that of the crucified, atoning Saviour, that they proclaimed the pardon of sin and eternal life to the penitent. And *its* times—the times specially appropriate for the bearing of such a testimony, and the witnessing of its results—are those which follow the great event itself, and reach onward to the second advent. All was but preparatory before; it was the time only for the anticipations of hope respecting it, or the longings of spiritual desire. But with the introduction of the reality, there came also the period destined for its full and proper exhibition, that through belief of the testimony its merciful design might be realized.[1]

Ver. 7. The apostle here introduces his own relation to this testimony-bearing: *Whereunto I was appointed a herald and an apostle (I speak the truth,[2] I lie not), a teacher of the Gentiles in faith and truth.* This personal asseveration, which seems at first thought peculiarly strong for the occasion, especially in an epistle addressed to his bosom companion and associate Timothy, we must remember, is brought in as an important part of the evidence which existed for the universal aspect and bearing of the gospel, in its character as a remedial scheme for the salvation of all who were willing to accept it. The position and calling he had received in the church of Christ had nothing partial, nothing exclusive about it. More even than any or all the original delegates of Christ, he was a witness to the universality of Christ's overtures of mercy, having been appointed a *herald* to proclaim everywhere the glad tidings; a herald even of the highest rank—*an apostle* (however some of a grudging or contentious spirit might dispute his authority, *he* at least will hold fast to it, as a fact written in the depths of his spiritual consciousness, and will have Timothy also to assert it); and as an apostle, *a teacher of the Gentiles in faith and truth.* In this his declaration respecting himself reaches its proper climax, announcing as it does his destination to labour among the Gentiles—the far off, the aliens—as the more special objects of his apostolic agency, and signalizing faith and truth as the elements in which it was to move, the prominent characteristics of

---

[1] See Appendix A.
[2] The received text has ἐν Χριστῷ, but it is wanting in the best MSS., A, D, F, G, also It. Vulg. Syr. Cop. versions, and is therefore justly omitted by Tisch. and others.

the spirit in which he was to teach, and the subjects he was to handle. If emphatically faithful and true in the testimony he was called to give concerning God, how could he be otherwise in what he delivered concerning himself? Self, however, was not an object of concern with him, except in so far as it bore on the nature of the mission he was appointed to fulfil, and the gloriously free and world-embracing character of the interests it sought to promote. But both were of a piece; the one was the proper image and reflex of the other. In principle, we have the same mode of representation at 2 Cor. i. 18–20. Taking this view of the passage, I would discard as very needless questions, whether the expressions *faith* and *truth* are to be taken both objectively, or the former only (with Huther and Ellicott) objectively, and the latter subjectively. In an experimental utterance of this kind, in which the internal and the external necessarily go together, it is hypercritical, and can serve no good purpose, to draw such distinctions.

Ver. 8. *I wish, then* (the οὖν at once resuming the subject of prayer, with an exhortation to which in a particular direction this part of the epistle commenced, and pressing as a conclusion from the views more recently advanced—I wish, then), *that prayer be made in every place by men, lifting up holy hands, without wrath and doubting.* In the verb βούλομαι the active wish is expressed, as of one who, having a right to speak in the name of Christ, should in expressing a wish be regarded as virtually uttering a command. If it had been ἐθέλω, the apostle would merely have said he was willing that the thing in question should be done; but in using βούλομαι he indicates his desire or wish that such a course should be pursued. (See Donaldson, *Cratylus*, § 463, for the clear exhibition and proof of this distinction.[1]) In respect to the object of his wish, the

---

[1] Donaldson has gone into the discussion of this point at great length, refuting an opposite view which had been advanced by Buttmann in his

point of greatest prominence undoubtedly is the praying—hence the προσεύχεσθαι stands first: it is the immediate object of the desire he was breathing in connection with the proper place and responsibilities of believers. But as these are contemplated with reference to the public worship of God, so a certain degree of prominence is also given to the men to whom it properly belongs to manage and direct such worship; while for women, who are presently after mentioned, duties of a more retired and quiet kind are assigned. It seems, however, an awkward way of indicating this subordinate distinction, which is but allusively introduced, to translate with Alford, "that *the men* pray," which is formally correct, no doubt, as the article is found in the original (τοὺς ἄνδρας), but gives a sense which to English readers must appear abrupt and unnatural. Indeed, Alford himself seems partly conscious of this, since he admits that the distinction in respect to men cannot be regarded as the apostle's main object in this verse, and that their relation to public prayer is taken for granted. If so, the kind of double end aimed at in the passage is better gained by such a rendering as we have adopted, giving the act of prayer the chief prominence, but giving the subject, *men*, also a sort of prominent position by throwing it a little

Lexilogus. As regards Biblical usage, the respective meanings of the two verbs are correctly and succinctly stated by Mr Webster, *Syntax and Synonyms of the Greek Testament*, p. 197: "βούλομαι expresses a wish, intention, purpose, formed after deliberation, and upon considering all the circumstances of the case; θέλω denotes a natural impulse or desire, the ground of which is generally obvious, or for which it is unnecessary to assign a reason. Matt. i. 19, μὴ θέλων, being reluctant, as was naturally the case; ἐβουλήθη, 'was minded,' deliberately purposed, intended after careful consideration." He refers to the contrary view of Buttmann, that βούλεσθαι indicates mere inclination, passive desire; but points to Jas. iv. 4, also to 1 Tim. vi. 9, in both of which cases he justly says θέλειν would be altogether out of place. On the contrary, in 1 Tim. v. 11, where the impulse of natural desire is in question, θέλειν is the proper word, and βούλομαι would be unsuitable.

forward, and thus also rendering the transition easy and natural from the male to the female section of believers: *that prayer be made in every place, by men lifting up*, etc.; *likewise also that women* . . . In mentioning *every place* in connection with the offering of prayer, the apostle is not to be regarded, with some, as indicating any contrast with the temple, the synagogue, or other conspicuous places of worship, but merely as giving expression to the universal nature of the duty; so that *wherever* the assemblies of Christian worshippers might meet, *there* prayer should be offered. And with the duty he couples a brief description of the spirit and manner in which it should be done by the persons who conduct it: *lifting up holy hands, without wrath or doubting* (ὁσίους, a masculine termination joined to the feminine χεῖρας, as οὐρανίου at Luke ii. 13, and ὅμοιος in Rev. iv. 3). The lifting up of the hands in their more formal exercises of devotion appears to have been common among the nations of antiquity, Jew as well as Gentile (Gen. xiv. 22; Ps. xxviii. 2, lxiii. 4, cxxxiv. 2; Virgil, *Æn.* i. 92); and from the Jewish it naturally passed into the Christian assemblies. Here it is referred to without explanation, as a thing familiarly known; so also by the Roman Clement in his letter to the Corinthians, c. 29, where, with evident respect to the words of the apostle, he says: " Let us come near to Him in holiness of soul (ἐν ὁσιότητι ψυχῆς), raising pure and undefiled hands toward Him."[1] The hands so employed might fitly be regarded as bearing the petitions of the suppliants heavenwards, and, in

[1] In this primary stage the lifting of the hands in public prayer is spoken of as a mere usage or custom, which was deemed suitable and appropriate. But by and by, like other things of a like kind, it was turned into a piece of sacred pantomime or symbolism, and to make it more expressive the stretched-out hands and arms were thrown into the figure of the cross. See quotations to this effect in Bingham, B. xiii. 10, from Tertullian, Minutius, and many others.

accordance with the action, should themselves possess a character of holiness; in other words, should be the hands of those who are not pursuing courses of iniquity, but are lovers of what is pure and good. All spiritual excellence is necessarily implied in this; yet the apostle adds the further qualifications, *without wrath and doubting:* without wrath, to which especially, in their relation to the heathen, the early Christians were often under great provocation, and might consequently be disposed to offer up imprecations rather than supplications in regard to them. What, however, is meant precisely by the other term ($\delta\iota\alpha\lambda o\gamma\iota\sigma\mu o\hat{u}$) —whether it is to be understood of disputation in the ordinary sense, contendings with others, or disputation in one's own mind, thought contending with thought, doubting —interpreters are not agreed. As the word may be understood either way, we are thrown upon the connection for something to determine our judgment; and in this point of view the second of the two senses indicated seems plainly the most natural and fitting: for the indispensable condition of acceptable prayer is faith; and therefore doubting, which is the mark of a wavering spirit, the conflict between faith and unbelief, must, so far as it prevails, be a hindrance to success. Prayer offered without wrath and doubting is simply prayer animated by a spirit of meek, generous loving-kindness in respect to those for whom it is presented, and by a spirit of faith or assured confidence in Him whom we supplicate in their behalf. This is intelligible, and perfectly cognate to the subject; but not so the reference supposed by some to personal disputations among the parties concerned in the exercise of devotion. Nothing had been said or implied which might seem to call for any particular reference to this.

Vers. 9, 10. *Likewise also, that women adorn themselves in orderly apparel, with shamefastness and discretion.* The passage is obviously elliptical; and the connection with what precedes, indicated by ὡσαύτως (*likewise*), cannot be very close. Looking to the apostle's use of it elsewhere (for example, at Tit. ii. 3, Rom. viii. 26), we must regard it as intended simply to couple the women with the men in having equally with them a relation to duty, bound to a becoming line of conduct in their own particular sphere. Having expressed his wish in respect to the one class, the apostle now turns to the other, and wishes (βούλομαι again understood) that they too, on their part, would adorn themselves in seemly apparel, or in seemly apparel would adorn themselves with shamefastness and discretion. The adorning, from the structure of the sentence, seems more directly connected with the two latter epithets, pointing to qualities of mind and behaviour, while the sort of apparel proper to them is implied as a thing that should certainly be possessed, only not of itself sufficient without the other, the adornments of the spirit. That καταστολή is properly taken in the sense of *apparel*, and not, as Ellicott would understand it, *deportment*,—including look and manner as well as dress,—there seems no just reason to doubt. It points by its etymology (from καταστέλλω) to the letting down of things about one's person, adjusting or arranging them, then the apparel as so arranged (see Alford). The apostle does not further characterize it than that it should be of a becoming or seemly nature (κόσμιος), as contradistinguished from gaudy and extravagant as well as slovenly attire. And with this he couples the inward feelings, which should accompany and give adequate expression to this modest apparel—with *shamefastness* (not shamefacedness, as in the Authorized Version, which is a corruption) *and discretion*. The correct import and mutual relation of the two words here employed (αἰδώς and σωφροσύνη) have been, with his usual discrimination and accuracy, exhibited by Trench (*Syn.* § 20), and applied thus to the explication of our verse : " If αἰδώς is that shamefastness or pudency which shrinks from overpassing the limits of womanly reserve and modesty, as well as from the dishonour which would justly attach thereto, σωφροσύνη is that habitual inner self-government, with its constant rein on all the passions and desires, which would hinder the temptation to this from arising, or at all events from arising in such strength as should overbear the checks and barriers which αἰδώς opposed to it." We have no English word that exactly corresponds to the latter of the two terms; but sober-mindedness or discretion substantially coincides with it, though self-control, perhaps, might more closely approach the original.

In the remaining part of the verse we have a further delineation, in a negative form, of the modest or seemly attire which was noticed in the earlier: *not in plaitings*, —namely, of the hair, but obviously meaning excessive refinements in this line, the meretricious plaitings, and modes of dressing up the hair in nicely adjusted tresses, which Clement of Alexandria, for example, condemns as unsuitable to Christians (*Paid.* iii. 11), condemned also by St. Peter in very similar language to that employed here (1 Pet. iii. 3). *And gold* (in rings, bracelets, etc.), *or pearls, or costly raiment.* These are not to be understood as any further prohibited than they are inconsistent with the seemly apparel previously recommended; only, if used at all, it should manifestly be with moderation, and so as not to befit the impression that they are displayed as the most precious personal adornments. For such the truly Christian mind will look in another direction, and lay the chief stress upon the spiritual and moral qualities, which are the noblest distinctions of rational beings, the only things which are of value in the sight of God. This, therefore, is what the apostle puts in contrast to the worldly equipments of rich jewellery and costly dress: *But, which becomes women professing godliness, through good works*—not (with Theodoret,

Œcum., Luther, Calvin, Huther, and many others), *but in that which*, or *according to that which* (taking ὅ as = ἐν τούτῳ ὅ, or καθ' ὅ, referring back to the ἐν καταστολῇ κοσμίῳ) *becomes women professing godliness, by means of good works.* For this has against it both an artificial construction, which should only be resorted to if absolutely necessary, and the coupling of good works with a godly profession in a way which is not usual,—as if godliness were a kind of art which Christian women were to show their skill or proficiency in by their works of faith and love. This cannot be called a natural style of representation, and it is certainly nowhere else found in St. Paul's writings. The expression ἐπαγγελομέναις must be taken here in the ordinary sense of *professing*,—a sense it unquestionably bears again at chap. vi. 21; while the verb is used in Tit. i. 2, with reference to God, in the cognate sense of *promising*, or giving open exhibition of. By the women in question must be understood those who make profession of godliness (θεοσέβειαν only used here, but substantially equivalent to εὐσέβειαν), in the ordinary way such profession was made,—by taking up the Christian name, submitting to Christian teaching and ordinances, and mingling in the assemblies of Christian worshippers. And as making this profession, the apostle would have them to understand, first, that the kind of dress which becomes them is of a neat and plain as contradistinguished from a luxurious or costly one; and second, that the distinction which women of gay and worldly dispositions seek to acquire by their splendid ornaments and fine apparel, they should endeavour to reach through their good works, —a distinction of a far nobler kind, and the only one that fitly accords with their calling. Such seems to be the most natural and appropriate import of the passage,—only, in connection with the latter point, the apostle varies the construction, so as the better to suit the change involved in the subject itself: he does not say *with* (ἐν) *good works*, as he could say both in regard to the apparel itself, and the outward ornaments on which vain and worldly-minded females prided themselves; but *through* or *by means of* (διά) *good works*, since it was not so properly the works themselves which invested true Christian females with their distinctive honour or adornment, as rather the reflex operation of these,—the consideration and regard, the spiritual halo, as it were, which the performance of such works threw around those who abounded in them.

Vers. 11, 12. The apostle proceeds now to give prescriptions of a more general kind respecting the proper sphere and behaviour of women. *Let a woman learn in silence in all subjection*—spoken primarily and mainly with reference to the public assemblies of the church, and only an abbreviated reinforcement of the instruction previously issued to the church at Corinth (1 Cor. xiv. 34): "Let your women keep silence in the churches; for it is not permitted unto them to speak, but to be under obedience, as also saith the law." The *all subjection*, however, can only be understood to reach as far as the authoritative teaching is of the right stamp. Woman does not lose her rational power of thought and responsibility by abiding in the place assigned her by the gospel; and she also has a right to prove all things— only in a manner suited to her position—in order that she may hold fast that which is good, and reject what is otherwise. *But to teach* (the best authorities place διδάσκειν first) *I permit not a woman*—namely, in public: she is not to act the part of a teacher in the meetings of the faithful; *nor to lord it over the man, but to be in silence.* The verb αὐθεντεῖν scarcely means to *usurp* authority, the sense ascribed to it in the Authorized Version, but only to exercise it in an imperious manner. Leo (as quoted by Huther): "αὐθεντεῖν et αὐθέντης apud seriores tantum scriptores ita occurrit, ut *dominii* notionem involvat; melioribus scriptoribus est αὐθέντης idem quod αὐτόχειρ." Here it is plainly the *later* use that must be adopted; and what is forbidden by it to woman is, that she is not to assume the part of ruling or domineering over man. When she attempts this she goes out of her proper place, and ventures upon a line of things which is not compatible either with her natural constitution or with her distinctive vocation. And in proof of this, the apostle appeals to the original order and course of things as marking out the great landmarks for all time.

Ver. 13. *For Adam was first formed* (ἐπλάσθη taken from the Sept. version of Gen. ii. 7; ἐκτίσθη is used in the corresponding passage at 1 Cor. xi. 9), *then Eve;* the precedence in time implying superiority in place and power. The relation in this respect is still more strongly marked in the Epistle to the Corinthians: "For the man is not of the woman, but the woman of the man; for also the man was not made for the sake of the woman, but the woman for the sake of the man." Thus did God in the method of creation give clear testimony to the headship of man—to his right, and also his obligation, to hold directly of God, and stand under law only to Him; while woman, being formed for his helpmate and partner, stands under law to her husband, and is called to act for God in him. And simply by inverting this relative position and calling—the helpmate assuming the place of the head or guide, and the head facilely yielding to her governance—was the happy constitution of paradise overthrown, and everything involved in disorder and evil.

Ver. 14. From this sinful violation of the primeval order, with its disastrous results, the apostle fetches his second reason for fixing in the manner he does the social position of woman: *And Adam was not deceived; but the woman, being altogether deceived,*[1] *fell into transgression:* literally,

---

[1] The best reading is ἐξαπατηθεῖσα, a stronger form of the verb, in order to emphasize the deception in Eve's case.

became in; but the expression γίγνεσθαι ἐν is always used of entering or falling into a particular state (Luke xxii. 44; Acts xxii. 17; 2 Cor. iii. 7; Phil. ii. 7). This explanatory statement has often been deemed strange, or partially misapprehended, from not sufficiently regarding the precise light in which the matter is contemplated by the apostle, and the purpose for which it is here brought into consideration. As already indicated, the case is referred to as a grand though mournful example, at the commencement of the world's history, of the evil sure to arise if in the general management of affairs woman should quit her proper position as the handmaid of man, and man should concede to her the ascendency. She wants, by the very constitution of nature, the qualities necessary for such a task—in particular, the equability of temper, the practical shrewdness and discernment, the firm, independent, regulative judgment, which are required to carry the leaders of important interests above first impressions and outside appearances, to resist solicitations, and amid subtle entanglements and fierce conflicts to cleave unswervingly to the right. Her very excellences in other respects — excellences connected with the finer sensibilities and stronger impulses of her emotional and loving nature—tend in a measure to disqualify her here. With man, on the other hand, in accordance with his original destination, the balance as between the intellectual and the emotional, the susceptible and the governing powers, inclines as a rule in the opposite direction. Hence, in the great trial to which the parents of the human family were subjected as the test of their allegiance, it was Adam who was mainly charged with the responsibility, and who *should* have been, in everything relating to it, the prime agent. But Eve, affecting to play the master, and to decide the question for herself and her husband, soon gave proof of her incompetency; she was overreached by a subtler intellect than her own, and induced, under specious pretexts, to prefer an apparent to the real good. "The serpent beguiled (or deceived) me, and I did eat" (Gen. iii. 13), was her confession before the Judge, thereby in effect acknowledging her weakness and folly in taking her impressions from such a quarter, and acting independently of her appointed head. But Adam, says the apostle, was not deceived, although the representation of Eve may, in point of fact, have wrought like a deception on his mind. That, however, was not exactly the point of weakness in his case, nor is anything said of it in the original account. "The woman whom Thou gavest to be with me," was *his* confession to the Lord, "she gave me of the tree, and I did eat" (Gen. iii. 12). Yes, but God had given her, not for authority and rule, but for kindly ministrations; to be a helpmate by his side, not a directress to control his judgment or determine for him the course of life. And in allowing her to become this, in what touched the very heart of his calling, whether it might be in the way of deception, by the constraint of love, or by threats of evil, it booted not; anyhow, Adam showed that he had fallen from his true position, and ceased to rule, as he *should* have done, with God. This aspect of the matter, however, it was not necessary for the apostle's purpose to bring out. As his theme was the place and calling of females in respect to things of public moment, he contents himself with pointing to that part of the transactions connected with the fall which more directly concerned Eve, and presents it as a beacon to future generations, in particular to the female members of Christian congregations, lest, amid the greater liberty of gospel times, they might be tempted to assume functions which they were not qualified or called in providence to fill.

Ver. 15. *But she shall be saved through the child-bearing, if they abide in faith, and love, and holiness, with discretion.* It is clear from the structure of the passage, that while Eve was formally before the eye of the apostle, it was she as the representative of her sex, womankind : hence, she *shall be*, not she *has been* saved ; and to render still more plain how the general was contemplated in the particular, it is added, if *they* abide. Viewing womankind as personated in Eve, the apostle had shown how, through one grievous mistake, leading to a departure from her proper place and calling, not a rise, as had been imagined, but a fall, had taken place,—a fall involving in its consequences her partner, along with herself, in present ruin, which also, but for the interposition of divine mercy, would have been irremediable. By reason of this interposition, however, a way of escape was opened to her, in connection, too, with that part of her destination which was in an especial manner to bear the impress of the fatal step which she had taken. She was still, in pursuance of her original appointment, to give birth to offspring—to be the mother, indeed, of all living ; but trouble was henceforth to weigh heavily upon this portion of her lot : in travail she was to bring forth children ; yet at the same time in hope, for it was precisely through the seed thus to be given her that the lost ground was to be recovered, that the doom of evil should be reversed, and the serpent's head, in relation to humanity, should be bruised. It is this complex destination as to child-bearing pronounced over woman at the fall—mournful enough in one respect, but fraught with consolation and hope in another—to which the apostle here briefly alludes. Salvation lay for her through this one channel ; and if it was her condemnation to have been so directly concerned in the guilt which required its appointment, and the pains and perils through which it must be made good, it should also be her peculiar honour, even through such a troubled experience, to be the more immediate instrument of accomplishing for herself and others the destined good. Do we, then, say that the child-bearing here spoken of has direct respect to the birth of Christ, through whom the work of salvation was really secured? We are certainly not inclined, with some commentators (Hammond, for instance), to fix the meaning down simply and exclusively to that. Undoubtedly it is the prime and essential thing,—*that* without which the woman's child-bearing could have wrought no deliverance, and the prospect of which was like the hidden germ which from the first lay enfolded in the promise of a seed of blessing,—yet not without regard, at the same time, to the collective seed associated in the divine purpose with the One. The apostle, in his brief allusion, abstains from details; he merely points to the original word, and the prominent place assigned to woman in connection with its fulfilment, as indicating her proper glory in relation to the plan of salvation. Let her be content, he virtually says, with this, that through her as the mother of a seed, given by the God of grace and blessing, she herself, as well as others, are to find salvation. But lest women should imagine that, by their participation in the simply natural part of the process, they should attain also to the higher good in question, he couples certain spiritual qualifications as indispensable to the result: *if they abide in faith, and love, and holiness, with discretion* (or sober-mindedness). In short, they must fall in here (as Eve *should* have done in Paradise, but did not) with the spiritual provisions and requirements of the plan of God: in *faith*, implicitly resting upon God's word of promise; in *love*, yielding themselves heartily to the duties of their special calling, as well as consenting to live and act within its appointed limits; in *holiness*, wakeful, and striving against occasions of sin; and all tempered and controlled by that spirit of meek and wise *discretion* which instinctively shrinks from whatever is unbecoming, heady, or high-minded.

The view now given, it is scarcely necessary to add, implies that women, as a rule, though admitting of occasional exceptions, should keep within their proper sphere, and give themselves to the family and domestic affairs especially connected with it—which is all that some would find in the passage; but it includes also a great deal more. Alford, who appears to think he had discovered the only tenable interpretation, represents the τεκνογονία as that in which the curse finds its operation (an extravagant statement to begin with, since *death* was plainly set forth as for both man and woman the proper embodiment of the curse), then that she was to be exempted from this curse in its worst and heaviest effects (of which, however, nothing is said in the original word), and that, besides, she should be saved *through*—that is, passing through the curse of her child-bearing trials—saved, notwithstanding the danger and distress connected with these! Surely a most unnatural and forced explanation, and ending in a very lame and impotent conclusion! The peculiar passage of 1 Cor. iii. 16, where the apostle speaks of certain parties being saved, yet so as through fire, which is chiefly leant upon, cannot be fairly applied here: for fire is there figuratively represented as the saving element, since it is that which tests every one; and the parties in question, who had along with the sterling gold at bottom many combustible materials about them, were just saved, and nothing more—escaped, as it were, only with their lives. There is no proper parallel between such a style of representation and the one before us. Ellicott, though very brief, and adhering perhaps somewhat too closely to Hammond, comes nearer the point, and justly lays stress on "the high probability that the apostle, in speaking of woman's transgression, would not fail to specify the sustaining prophecy which even preceded her sentence," also "the satisfactory meaning which the preposition (διά) thus bears," "the uncircumscribed reference of the σωθήσεται, and the force of the article [τῆς τεκνογ., *the* child-bearing,—that, namely, so prominently exhibited from the first]." Indeed, it seems only necessary to present the view which takes all these into account in a judicious manner, not pressing it too much in one direction or another, to commend it to general acceptance.

CHAPTER III.

The apostle here continues his special instructions to Timothy, but directs them to another topic, and one of still greater moment to the right order and government of the church; namely, to the calling and qualifications of its official representatives and guides. The subject, however, is very briefly handled, and with reference chiefly to the personal characteristics which ought to distinguish those who might hold office in the church. Nothing is said about the original institution of the offices themselves; nothing about their distinctive spheres of operation; nothing even respecting the numbers that should fill them, relatively to the membership of the particular church with which they might be associated. It is simply what sort of persons, how qualified and endowed, in whom the rights and responsibilities should be invested.

Ver. 1. *Faithful is the saying, If any one seeketh the office of pastor* (lit. *overseership*), *he desireth a good work.* The saying or word here designated faithful is to be understood of what follows respecting the episcopal or pastoral office, not, with Chrysostom, Theophylact, and some moderns, of the statement made in the preceding context. In designating the office itself, the nearest equivalent in our language now to the original ($\dot{\epsilon}\pi\iota\sigma\kappa o\pi\hat{\eta}s$) is undoubtedly that of pastor. The term *bishop*, which originally bore the same import, has acquired in modern times a different meaning. Alford adopts the literal rendering *overseership*, justly remarking that "we thus avoid any chance of identifying it with a present and different office, and take refuge in the meaning of the word itself, which at the same time bears an important testimony to the duties of the post." It labours, however, under the disadvantage of novelty, as a term applied to a sacred function; and as *pastorate* is substantially equivalent, involving the same general idea of watchful and responsible oversight (hence the epithet *Pastoral* applied by general consent to these Epistles), it is plainly entitled to the preference. By comparing what is written here with the passage in Tit. i. 5–7, it is clear that St. Paul uses the terms ἐπίσκοπος and πρεσβύτερος of the same office: for in Titus the words are interchanged, as of one import; and here much the same description is given of the ἐπίσκοπος which we find given there of the πρεσβύτερος. While, therefore, there were two designations, there was but one office; and the designations were two, because they were derived from two different quarters. *Presbyteros* was of Jewish origin, and was undoubtedly the earlier of the two, having been in use as a term of office in the synagogue for generations before the Christian era, whence it passed over, with little variation, into the Christian church. The term originally had doubtless some respect to the age of the persons who were called to preside over the religious community; they were its seniors, its more experienced and venerated members; but in course of time the etymological was lost sight of in the current official meaning, and the presbyters (זְקֵנִים, elders), whatever might be their relative age, were simply the presiding heads of the synagogal communities in the first instance, and then of the Christian church. Partaking, however, as it did so distinctly, of a Jewish impress, it was natural that, in the churches where the Greek or Gentile element predominated, a properly Greek word, of equivalent import as a designation of office, should come into use. Such a term was ἐπίσκοπος, overseer, the specific or official designation among the Athenians of those whom they sent forth to take the oversight of their subject cities (Suidas on ἐπισ. ; Dion. Hal. *Ant.* ii. 76) ; so that, by an easy transference from the civil to the spiritual sphere, the *episcopoi* of the church were those who had the pastoral oversight of the several churches. Quite naturally, therefore, it is the term employed here, where immediate respect is had to Ephesus, and such like churches in Asia Minor, which were largely made up of converted Greeks ; but even in such churches at an earlier stage, when the primary nucleus consisted mainly of converts from Judaism, the name *presbyters* took precedence of it. So we find this the term employed in respect to the officers set by St. Paul over the churches in his first missionary tour through portions of Asia Minor (Acts xiv. 23) ; and in the infant churches of Crete, which probably partook as much of the Jewish as the Greek element, the one term was used along with the other.

The sentiment here expressed, then, is, that one who seeks (ὀρέγεται, stretches forth towards, longs after) the pastoral office, desires to be engaged in what is emphatically a good work. It is not merely a post of honour, or a position of influence ; not that primarily at least, or in its more direct aspect, but a work of active service, and one that from its very nature brings one into living fellowship with the pure and good. The seeking here intended, therefore, after such an office, must be of the proper kind, not the prompting of a carnal ambition, but the aspiration of a heart which has itself experienced the grace of God, and which longs to see others coming to participate in the heavenly gift. Other objects of a subordinate or collateral kind may not be unlawful, and may justly enough be allowed a certain share in the motives which draw men to the pastoral office ; but if the heart is right with God, and takes anything like a correct estimate of the work of the ministry, it will be that work itself, considered with respect to its own excellent nature, and the blessed fruits that may be expected to spring from it, which ought more especially to awaken the desire and determine the choice. Hence the prominence given in the directions that follow to qualifications of a spiritual and moral kind, in order to its efficient discharge; introduced also by an οὖν, *therefore*, as much as to say: The work being so good, there is of necessity required in him who would enter on its functions a corresponding character of goodness.

Ver. 2. *A pastor, therefore, ought to be blameless* (ἀνεπίλημπτον, irreproachable), *husband of one wife, sober, discreet, orderly, hospitable, apt to teach*. With one exception, all these qualifications are so easily understood, and so obviously becoming in a Christian pastor, that they scarcely call for any remark. The epithet *sober* (νηφάλιον), while it necessarily includes moderation in the use of intoxicating liquors, freedom from intemperance, has also a wider meaning, and denotes a wakeful, vigilant habit, opposed to all kinds of excess. *Hospitable*, also, though simple enough in import, denoted what was relatively of greater moment in apostolic times than it usually is now. For there were not the same conveniences for travellers in those times that almost everywhere exist in the present day; and the loose, ungodly manners which prevailed in all places of public resort, rendered it of especial importance that Christian strangers should know where to find a kindly reception and a proper fellowship. The last of the epithets in the verse, διδακτικός, *having the teaching gift, apt* or *skilled in teaching*, is remarkable as the only one, either here or in the corresponding passage in Titus, which directly bears on the discharge of ministerial functions. In Titus it is more fully expressed: "that he may be able by sound doctrine both to exhort and to convince the gainsayers." The place given to the qualification in both passages is a clear proof of the importance attached by the apostle to the teaching gift in relation to the pastoral office. But even this, possessed too in no ordinary measure, will prove of little avail for the great practical ends of the ministry, unless it is accompanied with not only the sobriety which shuns all lawless excess, but also the *discreet* and *orderly* or becoming deportment which instinctively shrinks from needless occasions of offence, and indicates a temper and habits under due management and control. Both for the comfort and the success of pastoral work, a great deal depends upon the possession of such qualities. How often do ministers, otherwise highly endowed, lose well-nigh the fruit of all their gifts and labours, by marked failings and imperfections here! It is not obvious unfaithfulness in duty; not slothfulness of spirit; not deficiency of life and power in pulpit ministrations, or anything distinctly criminal in behaviour: in these and other respects a man may stand clear from any charge of blame or palpable shortcoming, and yet, by ever recurring exhibitions of ungoverned temper, or specific acts of indiscretion, may as thoroughly defeat the ends of his high calling as if he were living in a course of worldliness and indifference. There is but one safeguard against the evil—the possession of what may be called *sanctified common sense;* and for this the godly pastor should earnestly strive and pray, under the conviction that for him, not open transgression merely, but imprudence also, indiscretion, is sin, since it throws a stumbling-block in the way of his usefulness, and in a manner robs him of his talents and opportunities.

One part, however, of the apostle's description has given rise to difference of opinion, and calls for more consideration. It is that in which he says the pastor ought to be *husband of one wife.* Does this mean that he must never have been more than once married? Or simply, that he must not stand related to more than one living woman as his wife? On this point interpreters have been from early times, and still are, divided; though, if one were to have respect merely to the words themselves employed by the apostle, there might seem no reason, and even no propriety, in looking beyond an existing relationship. For it is of what the individual pastor is or has, at any particular period during his pastorate, that the apostle is speaking, not of this along with what he may have previously had or been. If he should, after having been deprived of a wife by death, become married to another, he still is the man of but one wife; for the previous relationship no longer exists, it was dissolved by death—dissolved absolutely and for ever, since in the life to come the flesh and blood relations of this life are unknown. So that re-marriage cannot with justice be said to constitute him more than the husband of one wife. And, as justly remarked by Harless (*Christian Ethics*, § 52), since the not being husband of one wife is mentioned as a reproach, and a reproach placed on the same line with gluttony and covetousness and the like, the immediate context should alone have guarded us from understanding by the expression "husband of one wife," one that had only once been married. But so many incidental considerations have been imported into the discussion of the subject, and so much can be said that is plausible on the other side, that the full examination of it must be reserved for separate treatment.[1]

The qualification, however, if applied only, as I believe it should be, to an existing relationship, must be taken chiefly in a restrictive meaning, not as prescribing what must invariably be found. From the prominence given to it, indeed, and the stress presently afterwards laid upon the pastor's proper management of his family, we may certainly infer that the pastoral relation was viewed by the apostle as one that would usually be filled by married persons—and should be so. Still, the language employed cannot justly be

[1] See Appendix B.

understood as implying more than that the pastor must not have more than one wife, not that he must absolutely and in every case have a wife. This last is the view taken of the prescription by the Greek Church, which ordains to the oversight of parishes only those who have been once married, and yet, with a kind of stupid inconsistency, the result of ascetic influences early begun and still continued, excludes all married persons from the higher offices of the church: monkish cœlibates, themselves without pastoral experience, ruling over and controlling a married clergy! Bengel's note on the prescription is: "The apostle does not exclude cœlibates from the sacred office, while yet he presupposes that the head of a family would be somewhat fitter for the office; and of two candidates, if other things were equal, that he who has a wife and a well-ordered family should be preferred to a bachelor, who has less of testimony in his behalf from the circumstances of actual life." In some remarks contained in his Life by Burk, he carries the matter rather further,—a little, indeed, too far,—but presenting, at the same time, some excellent remarks on the general subject: "The married state is usually that in which we can best surmount hardships, and attain the happy end of life, with many refreshments by the way. He, therefore, who has no particular calling or occasion forbidding his entrance into this condition, ought to marry. God often teaches us more by our domestic experiences, family illnesses, deaths of children, and the like, than we can learn by any independent speculations, however spiritual these may seem. It is in the married life that I have had my most serious afflictions, but with them my strongest consolations. Therefore I consider it more than a mere permission that a pastor should be 'the husband of one wife,'—to me it seems all but a matter of necessity. And yet so serious a concern is marriage, that if we consider all its bearings on time and eternity, we cannot wonder that some anxious persons are never able to resolve upon it; or that, having a special delight in spiritual things, they should be the more disinclined to become instruments of perpetuating our sinful race: nevertheless, marriage is an ordinance of the good and benevolent Creator" (p. 386).

Ver. 3. The apostle proceeds with the enumeration of qualities that ought to meet in the pastor: μὴ πάροινον, which the Authorized Version renders, "not given to much wine," but it is rather *not a brawler*, or *of vinous temperament*, not given to such impetuous and violent behaviour as is wont to be exhibited by persons under their cups. Hence it is followed by μὴ πλήκτην, *not a striker*, which is in the same line, pointing to the natural outbursts of the kind of temper indicated in the preceding epithet. (The μὴ αἰσχροκερδῆ, which follows in the received text, has no support but from some of the later, the cursive MSS.) Then in two other epithets we have the converse of those negative qualities: *but mild* (ἐπιεικῆ, the equitable, beseeming, as opposed to what is intemperate or boisterous), *peaceable*, averse to fighting (ἄμαχον). A quite different characteristic follows, which has no immediate connection with those just given, and is therefore not to be viewed as dependent on the *but* (ἀλλά) a little before: *not a lover of money*, or avaricious. This points to another very important quality in a minister of the gospel. Few things, indeed, are more certainly fatal to the position he ought to occupy in men's regard, and the spiritual ends he should aim at accomplishing, than a perceptible fondness for worldly treasure. He must be known to love his work for its own sake, not for the incidental earthly benefits that may or may not come in its train. What has been said of genius and wisdom of every kind, may yet more emphatically be said of the spirit that should actuate the true minister of the gospel. "It must learn that its kingdom is not of this world. It must learn to know this, and to be content that this should be so; to be content with the thought of a kingdom in a higher, less transitory region. Then, peradventure, may the saying be fulfilled with regard to it, that he who is ready to lose his life shall save it" (Hare). Striving to awaken generous thoughts and lofty aspirations in the minds of others, the pastor may come in a measure to reap material benefits from the operation of these; but if his own soul is grovelling in the dust, and the love of worldly pelf holds him captive, both himself and his mission are sure to be despised.

Ver. 4. The proper pastor is further described as *ruling well his own house*—his own (ἰδίου) as contradistinguished from God's, the relatively little, and more easily managed; *having children in subjection with all gravity*, or decency of deportment; having, in short, a well-ordered and properly trained household. And the special reason follows, introduced by the adversative particle δέ, which no more in such a connection than any other can be strictly rendered *for* (Winer, *Gr.* § 53, 2, *b*), since it introduces parenthetically a statement which forms an antithesis to the one immediately preceding, yet an antithesis which at the same time constitutes a reason: *But if one knows not how to rule his own house, how shall he take charge of the church of God?*—if within the narrower sphere, and with all the advantage which a parent's position and influence naturally secure for him, he should prove deficient in the proper governing authority, how certainly may he be expected to fail in the efficient management and control of things pertaining to the church of God! The future here (ἐπιμελήσεται), as frequently elsewhere, especially in interrogative sentences, involves the idea of possibility (Winer, *Gr.* xl. 6); and so Chrysostom expressly puts it: "He, then, who does not rightly administer these [smaller] things, how shall he be able (πῶς δυνήσεται) to administer the affairs of the church?"

Ver. 6. A further qualification: *not a novice*, or *recent convert* (νεόφυτον, literally, newly planted). Of course such a qualification must be understood relatively—in some a less, in others a longer period of probation being required, according to circumstances. In quite recently planted churches, such as those of Crete mentioned in Titus, it would not be possible to obtain persons for the presbyterate who had been long established in the Christian faith, though even there also differences in this respect would be found to exist. But in Ephesus, and various other churches in that locality, where for probably not less than twelve or fifteen years there had been Christian communities, there was ample room for the prescription in question; hence it has a place here, while quite naturally it is not found in the instructions given to Titus. And as at Ephesus there were not only numerous adversaries outside the church, but adherents of error also beginning to ply their wiles within, it was of the more importance that those invested with the oversight of the community should be persons of some experience in the divine life—men whose intelligence and solidity of character had been already proved, lest, amid the fermenting of false opinions and the craft of designing hypocrites, they might be betrayed into evil. The specific ground assigned by the apostle is: *lest, being carried with conceit, he should fall into the condemnation of the devil.* The Authorized Version for τυφωθείς has "lifted up with pride," but this scarcely hits the exact shade of meaning. The verb (from τῦφος, smoke, mist, cloud) denotes not simply the self-elating spirit which would raise one as to the clouds, but also the senseless, stupid character of such a spirit; its confusing, mystifying tendency acting like a lure to the emotions, and a cloud to the reason. What the apostle feared was, that the too sudden elevation to office might carry the individual off his feet, as it were, and render him an easy prey to the arts of plausible and designing men. The very probable result he expresses by a reference to the fall of the great adversary, as if this in such a case would be repeated afresh; for there can be little doubt that the condemnation spoken of—judgment in the sense of condemnation—is the genitive of object: the judgment passed upon the devil. The supposed neophyte, through his inexperience and undue elation of spirit, first falls into the sin of the old aspiring apostate, and then shares in his condemnation, passing from the sphere of a minister of light into the doomed condition of an instrument of darkness. The lesson, with its attendant warning, is for all times. It tells the church, that as there are temptations and perils peculiar to the ministerial office, so men should not be in haste to enter it, nor should others seek to push them prematurely forward. At the same time, the matter is wisely left in a certain indefiniteness; no precise age or specific term of probation is fixed in Scripture.

Ver. 7. *But he must also have a good testimony from those that are without.* Here, too, we have something that is not only additional, and to be connected with the preceding by a *moreover*, but this coupled with a sort of counter element, and fitly introduced by the adversative δέ: the person chosen to the pastorate must not be a neophyte, lest he prove unequal to the difficulties and dangers connected with the office; *but*, more than that, he must be well reported of by those who stand *without* the pale of the religious community, as well as known to be of approved Christian worth by those who are *within*. The one cannot be dispensed with, though he should have the other. The expression *those without* (οἱ ἔξωθεν or ἔξω, often used, as at 1 Cor. v. 12, 19; Col. iv. 5; 1 Thess. iv. 12) is a natural mode of designating such as, in regard to the church of God, are *extra fores*, not of the household of faith. Directly, persons of this description have no right to interfere with the appointment of a Christian pastor; but it is of importance that they have nothing to object—that the person raised to such an office be in good repute even among them, so that no occasion may be given them by his appointment to think lightly of the Christian church, or to encourage them in the hope of marring the success of his ministry. Where the minister of the gospel does not enjoy the esteem of the world, it becomes comparatively easy for the instruments of the wicked one to stir up prejudices against him, and involve him in trouble. This seems to be what is meant in the reason assigned by the apostle for the requirement—*lest he fall into reproach and the snare of the devil.* It is disputed whether only *snare* here should be coupled with the devil, or *reproach* also should be included. The question is scarcely worth raising. The devil, as the general head and representative of all evil agencies, may well enough be associated with any mischief or disaster befalling a servant of God—reproach as well as anything else. But in the usual style of Scripture, it is with crafty wiles and moral embroilments that his agency is more commonly connected, rather than outward obloquy or shame; and the related passage in 2 Tim. ii. 26, where snare alone is mentioned, still further favours this view. The most natural explanation, then, of the apostle's fear regarding the appointment of pastors who were not in good repute with the world, is that they would in such a case be exposed to the taunts of ungodly men, disparaged as unworthy of their position, and, conscious of this, would probably be tempted to do things which would entangle them in Satan's net of unseemly wranglings or dangerous relationships. No one who has much experience in life can be at a loss for examples of this nature.

Thus ends the apostle's list of qualifications, which he desired to see meeting in every one who might be placed in the responsible position of an overseer of Christ's flock. They are, as already stated, predominantly moral, and consist of attributes of character rather than of gifts and endowments of mind. The latter also to some extent are included, in so far especially as they might be required to form clear perceptions of truth and duty, to distinguish between things that differ, and in difficult or perplexing circumstances to discern the right, and know how to maintain and vindicate it. Yet, withal, it is the characteristics which go to constitute the living, practical Christian, which together make the man of God, that in this delineation of pastoral equipments are alone brought prominently into view. And whatever else the church may, in the changeful circumstances of her position and history, find it necessary to add to the number, in order to render her responsible heads fit for the varied work and service to which they are called, the grand moral characteristics here specified must still be regarded as the primary and more essential elements in the qualifications of a true spiritual overseer.

Vers. 8, 9. *In like manner that the deacons be grave.*—The likeness indicated here has respect to the qualifications being substantially of the same kind as those connected with the higher office of the pastorate: it is necessary that the deacons, too, have a measure of such characteristics. Two things specially call for notice in this transition to the deacons. One is, that the apostle plainly knew nothing of an intermediate class of officers between those he had designated *episcopoi*, and those he now calls *deacons*. Chrysostom's reason for the omission—namely, of the presbyters as a distinct order—can satisfy no unbiassed interpreter. He thinks it was done because " there is no great difference between them and bishops; for presbyters also have received the right of teaching and the presidency of the church; and the things which he had said of the bishops are applicable also to the presbyters. For in ordination alone are they superior, and in this only do they appear to surpass the presbyters." Jerome, on the corresponding passage in Titus, gives the only tenable explanation:

"Presbyter, therefore, is the same with him who is bishop; and before that through the prompting of the devil ambitious strivings entered into religion, and it was said among the people, 'I am of Paul, and I of Apollos, and I of Christ,' churches were governed by the common council of presbyters," etc. The other thing to be noticed is, that while deacons are named here as a class of officers familiarly known, requiring no description as to their distinctive place and duties, no mention is made of them in the Epistle to Titus. Had the inverse order been adopted, the matter would have been inexplicable; but as it is, the difference may justly be regarded as an evidence of genuineness and of mutual independence. It naturally arose out of the diverse position and circumstances of the churches in the regions respectively of Crete and Ephesus. Crete, where Titus had been left to complete the arrangements originated by the apostle, appears to have been but recently visited by the gospel, and in ecclesiastical matters everything was as yet in comparative infancy. In Christian communities so small, the simplest possible organization would be sufficient; in most cases, indeed, all that was practicable. A beginning must be made, as elsewhere (Acts xiv. 23), with a few respectable elders in each. At Ephesus, however, and in the larger towns of Asia Minor, the churches had already grown into large communities, and inferior as well as superior officers were required (as previously in the church at Jerusalem) for the proper distribution and management of its affairs. The distinct place, therefore, assigned to deacons here is perfectly in keeping with the historical circumstances of the time. It is the only occasion on which they are formally discoursed of in St. Paul's writings; but in epistles of considerably earlier date, they are incidentally noticed as an existing order, more generally in Rom. xii. 7, 1 Cor. xii. 28; and more specifically in Phil. i. 1, also Rom. xvi. 1, where Phœbe is designated a deaconess of the church at Cenchreæ.

It is not necessary to dwell at any length on the several qualifications mentioned by the apostle; they are for the most part such as were needed to beget in the members of the church a feeling of respect and confidence towards them. They must be *grave*, of serious deportment, as opposed to unbecoming levity; *not double-tongued* (διλόγους), prevaricating in their speech, and so giving rise to misunderstandings and differences; *not addicted to much wine; not lovers of base gain* (αἰσχροκερδεῖς), the *base* qualifying the gain, as a thing which becomes base when it is taken as the leading aim and object of persons filling a sacred office (comp. Tit. i. 11; 1 Pet. v. 2),—"greedy of filthy lucre," A.V., "greedy of base gain," Ellicott, seem both rather too strong; *holding* (ἔχοντας, having or possessing) *the mystery of the faith in a pure conscience.* Faith might here be taken either objectively—what the parties apprehended and believed; or subjectively—the apprehensive and believing principle itself,—but more naturally the former: and what is meant by the *mystery* of it is the once secret or hidden nature of the things about which the distinctively gospel faith is conversant, now brought to light by the revelation of Jesus Christ. Reuss (in his *Histoire de la Theol. Chrétienne*, vol. ii. p. 88) has given a good explanation of this peculiar phraseology. After referring to the partial revelations made through the prophets, he says: "The plan of God could not be understood so long as the manifestation of Him who was to accomplish it had yet to be made good. It continued to be a mystery—a matter concealed, not comprehended, and only ceased to be such by the fact of the definitive revelation (ἀποκάλυψις) of Christ (Rom. xvi. 26; 1 Cor. ii. 7; Gal. iii. 23; Eph. iii. 3, etc.). We ought to draw attention to the difference which subsists between the notion of μυστήριον with Paul, and that of a mystery in the scholastic sense; that is, of an incomprehensible dogma. In all the passages just referred to, as in some others, Paul *opposes* to mystery the revelation which puts an end to it; whereas in the scholastic sense it is with the revelation that the mystery commences. The apostle qualifies the plan of God's salvation sometimes as *the mystery of God* (Col. ii. 2; 1 Cor. iv. 1, ii. 1), with reference to its Author, and more completely as *the mystery of the will of God* (Eph. i. 9); sometimes as *the mystery of Christ* (Eph. iii. 4; Col. iv. 3), with respect to its Mediator or executor: besides, as *the mystery of faith* (1 Tim. iii. 9), or *of godliness* (iii. 16), with respect to its practical condition; in fine, as *the mystery of the gospel* (Eph. vi. 19), inasmuch as it is the object of apostolic preaching."

Ver. 10. *But these also*, or, *And these too, let them first be proved*—καὶ οὗτοι δέ: not enough that they seem to have all the qualifications previously mentioned, *but* let this further precaution be taken, let them be first proved; *then let them serve as deacons, if* (namely, after being proved) *they are without blame*—ὄντες ἀνέγκλητοι, being without charge of blame, the period of probation having passed, and no accusation preferred against them.

Ver. 11. There is a difference of opinion among commentators how this verse should be understood: whether of women in the sense of wives—the wives of the deacons mentioned immediately before; or of women holding much the same relative position in the church as deacons—women called to do active service for the community. Our translators have adopted the former view, rendering, " Even so must their wives be grave,"—the wives, namely, of the deacons; and in this they have the support of such men as Bengel, Beza (who, however, would extend the reference to bishops as well as deacons, against the connection), the modern Greek commentator Coray, Conybeare, also Huther, who conceives the wives of deacons to be here mentioned, because in certain parts of their office, especially in ministering to the poor and the sick, their wives would naturally co-operate with them, and often do a considerable part of the work. Whence, quite naturally, the wives of deacons might be noticed with a view to their proper qualifications, while nothing was said of the wives of the bishops or pastors, because the latter could not participate in the official service of their husbands. All this may fairly be alleged in favour of that interpretation, and also the circumstance that, as the apostle returns in the next verse to the deacons, it would seem upon the whole more natural, that what he inserts about women in the middle of his instructions regarding deacons should refer to such women as were in a manner part of themselves, than to others occupying a quite separate position. On the other hand, the mode of expression employed in introducing the women, γυναῖκας ὡσαύτως, apparently marking a transition to another class (as at ver. 8, ii. 9; Tit. ii. 3, 6); also the absence of either the article (τὰς) or the pronoun (αὐτῶν) to connect the women with the men spoken of before; and further, the mention only of such qualifications in respect to the women as might fit them for confidential employment in deacon-work, while nothing is said of those more directly bearing on domestic duties;—these considerations seem very much to favour the view adopted already by Chrysostom,—adopted as too obvious to require any explanation (γυναῖκας διακόνους φησί),—and followed by Theophylact, Grotius, De Wette, Ellicott, Alford, etc.: that not deacons' wives, but female deacons, are meant. It still is somewhat strange, however, that the general term *women* (γυναῖκας) is employed, and not the specific *deaconesses* (τὰς διακόνους), which would have excluded all uncertainty as to the meaning. Possibly the matter was so put as intentionally to include women of both classes; at once wives to the deacons who occasionally shared with their husbands in diaconal ministrations, and women who were themselves charged by the church with such ministrations. Anyhow, it ought to be understood of women who, in the one character or the other, were actively engaged in the kind of work which was proper to deacons. And considering the greater separation which then existed between the sexes, and the extreme jealousy which guarded the approaches to female society, it was in a manner indispensable that women, with some sort of delegated authority, should often be entrusted with various kinds of diaconal service. For those so entrusted, the following simple requisites are mentioned: that they be *grave, not slanderers, sober, faithful in all things;* the same substantially as those required of the deacons, only delivered with more brevity.

Ver. 12. The apostle, returning again to the deacons for the purpose of supplementing what he had previously said, adds concerning them: *Let the deacons be husbands of one wife, ruling well their children and their own houses;* the same qualifications precisely which had been required of the higher officers in respect to family and domestic relations. See at ver. 4, and Appendix B.

Ver. 13. Here follows a reason for exacting such qualifications of deacons, as requisite for the safe and efficient discharge of the trust committed to them; the γάρ, *for*, coupling this to the whole of the preceding instructions on the subject: *for those who have done the work of a deacon well obtain for themselves a good degree, and much boldness in the faith which is in Christ Jesus* (ἐν πίστει τῇ ἐν X. Ἰησοῦ, lit. in faith, that which is in Christ Jesus: fide, eâque in Ch. J. collocatâ—Fritzsche on Rom. iii. 25). There is a certain indefiniteness in the apostle's language here, which has given occasion to a considerable variety in the interpretations that have been adopted. The step or degree (βαθμόν) mentioned has by some been understood of ecclesiastical advancement—the higher office of the pastorate; by others, of the consideration and honour awarded by the members of the church to such as have faithfully acquitted themselves of any sacred trust devolved on them; by others, again, of a subjective elevation—the rise made in faith and the several graces of a Christian life, as the result of continuous and active employment in the divine service; by others, still again, of the place of honour and distinction that will accrue in the great day of final reckoning to those who have served the Lord diligently in His church on earth—their own measure of fidelity and love here shall be meted back to them by the great householder—"a measure full and running over." It is this last reference which is now most commonly adopted by the better class of commentators, and is undoubtedly the one that should mainly be pressed, although I see no reason why at least the two immediately preceding it should not also be included. There can be no doubt that the faithful discharge of the duties of the diaconal office would tend to secure for the individuals giving it a growth in the attainments and virtues of a Christian life,—grace properly used leading to larger endowments of grace; and, as a matter of course, they would at the close of their service occupy a higher place in the esteem and confidence of their brethren than they could possibly do at the commencement. But such things, however true and good, are still inadequate; they fall greatly short of what we may justly conceive the apostle to have had mainly in view, and can only be regarded as among the incidental and temporary grounds of encouragement, which may be looked for by the true servant of the Lord: *the* degree by way of eminence, the grand stage of honour and enlargement which lies before him, is the recompense of glory which shall be conferred on him at that day by the exalted Redeemer. It is surely but natural to suppose that the apostle, when pointing to only one ground of encouragement for fidelity in diaconal work, wishing to fix the eye on a specific prospect of future advancement, would shoot beyond the earthly sphere, and make special account of that which in its worth immensely overshadows all. It also accords best with what immediately follows,—namely, great boldness in the faith which is in Christ Jesus, as conscious, from what is granted to him by the Master Himself, that he does really stand in the faith, and cannot need to be ashamed. It may be added, as a still further confirmation of this view, that the word designating the diaconal service (διακονήσαντες) is in the indefinite past, and appears to contemplate the work as a finished totality. No doubt this might be done in respect to an *immediate* past, as contrasted with a future still in this life, to which it formed the introduction (so that the use of the aorist cannot of itself, with Alford, be held to be conclusive evidence of a regard simply to the day of judgment). Still, it may most fitly be taken to contemplate the diaconate as a thing lying altogether in the past, with the one great future of the day of recompense before it. It is scarcely necessary to add that the doctrine of rewards implied in this view of the passage is in perfect accordance with what is stated on the subject in other parts of Scripture; in our Lord's parables, for instance, of the pounds, the talents, and the judgment day, Matt. xxv., Luke xix. 11-27; and in the apostle's own writings, as at Rom. ii. 6-10, 2 Cor. iv. 10, 2 Tim. iv. 7, 8. But see at chap. vi. 19.

Ver. 14. *These things I write to thee, hoping to come to thee shortly:* τάχιον, literally, more quickly—sooner, that is, than I at one time thought, or than would seem to call for more detailed communications.

Ver. 15. *But if I should tarry,* [the things have been written] *in order that thou mayest know how thou oughtest to conduct thyself in God's house, which indeed is the church of the living God, the pillar and basement of the truth.* The expression rendered, *how thou oughtest to conduct thyself* (δεῖ ἀναστρέφεσθαι), has sometimes been taken in a more general sense: how men ought to conduct themselves, such as have to do generally with the management of God's house (so, for example, Huther). It might, no doubt, be understood in this manner; but it seems better to retain the special reference to Timothy: for, while many of the things written in the preceding portions of the epistle had respect to the conduct which men generally, especially men holding office in the Christian church, ought to maintain, their more immediate object was to instruct Timothy how *he* should himself act in the delicate and responsible position he was for the time called to fulfil at Ephesus. But even on the understanding that the special reference is to Timothy, such a rendering as this might fitly enough be given: how one ought to conduct oneself; but the other is simpler, and is to be preferred.

God's house, which indeed is the church of the living God—οἴκῳ Θεοῦ, ἥτις ἐστὶν ἐκκλησία Θ. ζῶντος; the latter clause epexegetical of the former, defining more exactly what is meant by God's house. The indefinite relative ἥτις is in such a connection stronger than the simple relative, being employed "to introduce an especial attribute belonging to the nature of the object, its real and peculiar property, or *differentia*" (Jelf, *Gr.* § 816, 7; Ellicott on Gal. iv. 24): the house of God, namely that which is—or, which indeed is—the church of the living God. There was a necessity for this definition, as in former times the expression "house of God" had been much associated with the material fabric of the temple, which was, in a sense that nothing of like sort could be in the gospel dispensation, the habitation or dwelling-place of Deity (2 Chron. v. 14; Isa. lvi. 7; Matt. xxi. 13). But even in Old Testament times, the more enlightened believers understood that the temple, with its sacred furniture and services, was an emblem of God's fellowship with His people, who therefore were then, as now, the only proper habitation of God on earth: hence such passages as Num. xii. 7, Isa. lxvi. 2; and those in which habitual communion with God is identified with dwelling in His house, Ps. xxiii. 6, xxvii. 4; or having God Himself for a sanctuary and dwelling-place, Ps. xc. 1, Ezek. xi. 16. There was a mutual indwelling—they in God, and God in them. But, in accordance with the spiritual character of the new dispensation, this truth is brought out more distinctly now, and that, too, in earlier parts of Scripture than in the passage before us. Thus, in Eph. ii. 20–22, the church, as composed of believing Jews and Gentiles, is represented as a glorious building, raised on Christ as the foundation: an holy temple in the Lord, or habitation of God through the Spirit. A quite similar representation is given in 1 Pet. ii. 5, iv. 17, and again in Heb. iii. 6, where, with reference to Christ as a Son in His own house, it is added: " Whose house are we, if we hold fast the confidence and the rejoicing of the hope firm unto the end." In these passages, the house, temple, or habitation of God is plainly associated with individuals, the individuals addressed by the apostle, contemplated as in living union with Christ; and in the strict sense it can only be predicated of such that they are God's house; for in their case alone is there the real link that connects the human with the divine—the spiritual habitation with the glorious inhabitant. It is the church as the *ecclesia* of God, His elect, whom He has called out of the world and gathered into His fold, that He may sustain and keep them unto life eternal. But here, as in many other passages, the apostle does not use the word in this absolute sense; he uses it of the outstanding, organized communities of believers, viewed as the concrete realization, in this or that particular locality, of the spiritual or ideal body. This is what every one of such communities is called to be, though in reality it might be so but in part. He holds it, as it were, to its idea: if it was worthy of the name, it was God's house, a living community of saints pervaded by the presence of the living God; and hence, *the pillar and basement of the truth* (στύλος καὶ ἑδραίωμα τῆς ἀληθείας): for, as so connected with God, it necessarily holds and bears up in the world, that with which His name and glory are peculiarly identified—the truth as it is in Jesus.

Some have sought to connect these last words, not with what precedes, but with what follows—with the mystery of godliness (so Episcopius, Mosheim, Bengel, Rosenmüller, and others, chiefly rationalistic expositors of more recent times). This, however, is against all probability, and is rejected by the great body of interpreters. It would form a most abrupt and artificial commencement were the terms *pillar* and *basement* made to begin a fresh sentence: "Pillar and basement of the truth, and confessedly great is the mystery of godliness!" Not only so, but to couple such specific terms first with a quite general epithet, *great*, and then with an object, mystery of godliness, which does not properly suit them (for with what propriety could a mystery be called a pillar?), would only be justifiable if it were impossible to find a more appropriate connection. But so far is that from being the case, that to regard them as a description of the church in her destination to maintain and exhibit before the world the testimony of divine truth committed to her keeping, is in itself a perfectly natural representation, and in accordance with what we elsewhere read of the calling of the church. Was it not the special calling of Christ Himself to bear witness to the truth, and by doing so to become the Light of the world? But in this Christ was only in a pre-eminent degree what in a measure His people, individually and collectively, should also be found. They should be, and they are, while stedfast to their profession, a basement whereon the truth may securely rest amid all the fluctuations of the world, and a pillar to bear it aloft, that all may know and consider it.

There has been a disinclination in certain quarters to acquiesce in this mode of interpretation, because of its supposed tendency to play into the hands of the Church of Rome. It is, no doubt, one of the passages on which Rome seeks to ground her claim to universal homage as the one church of Christ; but it is no more suitable to her purpose than the promise to St. Peter in Matt. xvi. 18; only by arbitrary distinctions and vain assumptions can either the one passage or the other be made to favour her pretensions. Here, in particular, where the church is set forth as the pillar and basement of the truth, it is a test we have to deal with, as well as a claim to consider. For the truth is not of the church's making, but of God's revealing: she has it, not as of her own, but from above; and has it not to alter or modify at her own will, but to keep as a sacred treasure for the glory of God and the good of men. And if she should anyhow corrupt or lose hold of this truth, she so far ceases to be the house of God; for she now does that part to the devil's lie, which ought to have been done exclusively for the sure word of God. Nor is it too much to suppose such a thing possible with a considerable portion of the professing church. It was so, we know, with by much the most pretentious section of the Jewish community before the time of Christ; and the apostle has elsewhere informed us, that in the Christian church also there was to be a great apostasy, a mystery of iniquity working under the cloak of a Christian profession, in consequence of which many should be given up to believe a lie (2 Thess. ii. 3–11). Rightly understood, therefore, this passage determines nothing for Rome, or for any church which rests its claim to apostolicity on historical descent. The grand test is, does she hold by the truth of God? Is she in her belief and practice a witness for this? Or does she gainsay and pervert it?

It is rather strange that Chrysostom, while he applies the description to the church, inverts the order of the relation it indicates between the truth and the church: the church of the New Testament, he says, "is that which possesses in itself the faith and preaching, for the truth is both the pillar and the basement of the church (ἡ γὰρ ἀλήθεια ἐστι τῆς ἐκκλησίας καὶ στῦλος καὶ ἑδραίωμα)." Theodoret is better, for he expressly calls the company of the faithful who compose the church the pillar and basement of the truth: "for they continue stayed and settled upon the rock, and by active operations (διὰ τῶν πραγμάτων) preach the truth of the doctrines." Not a few of the Fathers, however (see in Suicer at στῦλος), referred the passage to Timothy, misled by other passages in which the designation of *pillars* is applied to persons occupying prominent positions in the church: so also, in recent times, Conybeare, and Stanley (*Apostolic Age*, p. 121). According to this view, the whole sentence would run thus: "That thou mightest know how thou oughtest to conduct thyself in the house of God, [so as to be therein] a pillar and basement of the truth." No grammatical objection can be made to this construction; only, for so specific a meaning the sentence is too indefinitely expressed. We should certainly have expected, as urged by Alford, the personal pronoun after δεῖ (δεῖ σε), and also the article with στῦλος, so as to make: how *thou* oughtest to conduct thyself, who art the pillar, etc. Besides, while the term *pillar* might fitly enough be applied to Timothy, as it is to other individuals (Gal. ii. 9; Rev. iii. 12), the other term, *basement*, is not elsewhere so applied, nor was it strictly applicable to such a person as Timothy,— an evangelist appointed for a short period to execute a definite commission for the churches in and around Ephesus. It were to say more of him, indeed, than is said of Peter and the other apostles, who are simply represented as foundation-stones of the visible church. For in this case the church presents itself as an organized institution, rising up to view in the world, and obtaining an outstanding existence, through the faith and labours of the apostles, who therefore stand to it in the relation of founders. But the truth itself, to which that church owes its distinctive character, and which it is called to preserve and manifest, cannot justly be said to have any individual basement, save in Him who is the very truth in everlasting and embodied fulness. It is quite improbable that the apostle should have designated his "child Timothy" by what is so peculiarly characteristic only of Christ. As to Stanley's objection to the other and more common interpretation, that " it is against the whole tenor of the passage to describe the same object first as a building, and then as a part of that building," this arises from the complex nature of the object represented, as requiring to be contemplated sometimes in a collective, sometimes in an individual aspect; and the same sort of interchange between the one and the other occurs in other passages, as at 1 Pet. ii. 4, 5, where believers are at once regarded as living stones of the spiritual house, then the house itself, and again as a holy priesthood offering up sacrifices within it.

We hold, then, that the description here given with reference to the truth is to be understood of the church—of the church primarily in the higher sense, the church of the redeemed, and of particular communities only in so far as they possess the more essential characteristics of the other. The church in that respect is God's instrument of working. He does not (to use the words of Calvin) "personally descend from heaven to us, nor does He daily send angels for the purpose of promulgating the truth; but He uses the ministry of pastors, to whom for this very end He has granted ordination. To express myself more strongly: Is not the church the mother of all saints?—regenerating them by the word of God, rearing and training them throughout their whole life, establishing and carrying them onward, even to their proper maturity? And for the same reason also she is designated a pillar of the truth, since the office of imparting spiritual instruction which God has committed to her is the sole provision for preserving the truth, so that it do not perish from the minds of men. Therefore this eulogium is to be referred to the ministry of the Word, which, being taken away, would leave the word of God to fall,—not as if it were in itself infirm, and needed to be borne up on the shoulders of men, as the Papists impiously talk; but on this account only, because if the doctrine of the gospel were not continually sounded forth, if there were no godly ministers who by their preaching kept the truth from falling into oblivion, lies, errors, impostures, superstitions, and all forms of corruption, would forthwith usurp the kingdom."

It were wrong to quit the subject without noticing, however briefly, the elevated view which the passage under consideration presents of every church that properly deserves the name: "*The* house of the living God! The pillar and basement of the truth!" When one really takes in this sublime conception of the church of God, how little can anything of a merely adventitious or carnal nature add to its greatness! Let it be admitted that the friendly co-operation or temporal support of worldly powers might, within certain limits, enable her more promptly and successfully to work out the ends of her appointment; yet to raise her to a nobler position and enhance her real glory, this is not theirs to give. The palace differs from other dwellings in the land, and ranks proudly above them all; not, it may be, on account of its finer structure and more beautiful surroundings, but simply as being the seat and habitation of royalty. And such precisely is the distinguishing characteristic of the church of Christ, wherever situated, and whatever its external accompaniments: it is the palace of the Great King, where He is ever graciously present, and dispenses life and blessing to the members of His spiritual household. How careful, therefore, should these members be to maintain its proper character! How careful, especially, to stand in the truth, which alone makes the church what it is as a region of light and blessing!

Three things are essentially necessary to this. 1. That those who bear rule in the church possess only ministerial, not absolute authority — serve while they rule. 2. That God's word be taken as their one grand directory of faith and practice in God's house. God's word must reign paramount: it is the statute book of the kingdom. 3. And then, lastly, the pervading character of all pertaining to it must be holiness; for holiness is the sum of God's moral perfections, "therefore holiness becometh His house for ever."

Ver. 16. The more immediate reason, obviously, which led the apostle to bring so prominently out the spiritual and elevated idea he had just presented of the church of Christ, was to impress upon the mind of Timothy the gravity and importance of the charge devolved on him, and the imperative duty of all who are called to fill in it offices of trust, acting in harmony with its sacred character; especially handling with a profound seriousness the testimony lodged with it concerning truth. For "how dreadful must be their condemnation, if by any fault of theirs that truth, which is the image of the divine glory, the light of the world, and the salvation of men, should go down! This condemnation may well, indeed, strike terror into ministers, not so as to dispirit them, but to quicken them to greater vigilance" (Calvin). And with the view of still further deepening this impression, the apostle goes on now to exhibit the glorious reality, about which both the church herself and the truth committed to her keeping, is chiefly conversant: *And confessedly great is the mystery of godliness: who was manifested in the flesh, was justified in the Spirit, appeared to angels, was preached among the Gentiles, was believed on in the world, was received up in glory.* The controversy so long waged about the correct text in this passage, whether after the mystery of godliness we should read Θεός, or ὅς, or ὅ, may now be regarded as virtually settled in favour of ὅς.[1] It is, indeed, when closely considered, the fittest, indicating Him who in His person and work is the disclosing of that mystery, respecting the divine life in man, which had hitherto been hid in God. "This mystery of the life of God in man (as Alford well remarks) is, in fact, the unfolding of Christ to and in him; the key-text to our passage being Col. i. 27, where God is said to have made known 'what is the wealth of the glory τοῦ μυστηρίου τούτου ἐν τοῖς ἔθνεσιν, ὅς ἐστιν Χριστὸς ἐν ὑμῖν, ἡ ἐλπὶς τῆς δόξης.' This was the thought in St. Paul's mind, that the great revelation of the religious life is *Christ*. And in accordance with his practice in these epistles,—written, as I believe, far on his course, and after the figures and results of deep spiritual thoughts had been long familiar to him,— he at once, without explanation or apology, as beforetime

---

[1] The greatest critical authorities are agreed in this, Lachmann, Tischendorf, Tregelles ; also the more careful and exact commentators, Huther, Alford, Ellicott. It has decidedly the strongest support from ancient authorities—A (such, at least, seems the most probable view of its primary reading, the strokes converting oc into ΘC, being apparently from a later hand; see Ellicott's testimony in his note, also Alford's to the same effect), C, F, G, ℵ ; while for Θεός there are only two uncials, I, K, at first hand, though most of the later MSS. have this reading, and it is that also of Chrysostom, Theod., Euthalius, Damasc., Theophyl., and Œcum. One uncial MS., D, has ὅ at first hand; and both the Latin versions, and nearly all the Latin Fathers, have the corresponding *quod*. But this, as Ellicott notes, was only a Latinizing variation of ὅς ; and as the Coptic, Sahidic, Gothic, as well as Syriac versions all represent ὅς, and the ancient Latin versions and Fathers at least a *relative*, ὅς must undoubtedly be regarded as the more probable reading. Internal considerations also favour it, as will be seen in the exposition.

in Col. i. 27, or expression of the Χριστός justifying the change of gender in the relative, joins the deep and latent thought with the superficial and obvious one, and without saying that the mystery is *in fact* Christ, passes from the mystery to the person of Christ, as being one and the same. Then, thus passing, he is naturally led to a summary of those particulars wherein Christ has been revealed as a ground for the godliness of His church. And the idea of μυστήριον being prominent before him, he selects especially those events in and by which Christ was manifested forth—came forth from that secrecy in which He had beforetime been hidden in the counsels of God, and shone out to men and angels as the Lord of life and glory."

I have no doubt this is the correct explanation; it quite naturally accounts for the substitution of ὅς for the Χριστός. There are not wanting even more abrupt and striking substitutions of a like kind in Scripture. Thus, Ps. lxxxvii. begins with, "His foundation is in the holy mountains." Whose foundation? The Psalmist's mind being full of his subject, he does not expressly name this, but proceeds at once to declare what he knew and thought concerning it. So also 3 John 7, speaking of the believing strangers, represents them as (according to the proper text) "having for *the name* gone forth." What name? This it was needless further to particularize. The ὅς here should therefore be taken simply as the relative, the proper antecedent being omitted, but easily supplied. Ellicott does well in rejecting other modes of explanation; such as considering it at once as demonstrative and relative, "He who," or making it equivalent to *ecce est qui*. But I see no reason for supposing, with him, Huther, and others, that the passage introduced by the relative is part of an ancient hymn or confession adopted by the apostle. The natural supposition, I agree with Alford in thinking, would appear rather to lie the other way. It was more likely that such a passage — a passage so singularly profound and pregnant in meaning—should have been first penned by the apostle, and then possibly passed into some kind of hymnal or liturgical use (though of this we have no certain information), than that, from having been so used, it should have been caught up by the apostle, and woven into his discourse. Its parallelistic structure is no argument against this; for in other parts of the apostle's writings we find him, in his fervent utterances, falling into the same kind of parallelism—Rom. viii. 38, 39, xi. 33–36; 1 Cor. xv. 55–57.

The substitution of ὅς for Θεός as the proper reading, by no means destroys the bearing of the passage on the divinity of Christ; for this is clearly implied in what follows—is, indeed, the ground-element of the whole series of declarations. There had been no proper mystery in the matter, unless the divine here mingled with the human. The first announcement alone may be held to be conclusive on the subject: *was manifested in the flesh;* for who would have dreamt of speaking thus of a simple man? It plainly implies that the person spoken of was something before, something so much greater and higher than man, that it was like the disclosure of a great secret when He manifested Himself in mortal flesh. It is the fact of the incarnation merely which is here mentioned; but this contemplated as embracing not simply the birth, but the whole of our Lord's earthly existence and sojourn. The nearest parallel passages are John i. 14, 1 John i. 1. The next expression is not quite so patent in meaning: *was justified in spirit* (ἐδικαιώθη ἐν πνεύματι). For the question naturally presents itself—What spirit? Is it the Holy Spirit? Or, the spirit in Christ's person, viewed as a kind of antithesis to His flesh? According as the one or the other view of this is adopted, a corresponding difference will arise in the sense we necessarily put on the *justifying.* But as the whole discourse here is of Christ Himself, in His personal properties and marvellous history, the most natural light in which to view *spirit* must be to understand it of Christ's spiritual nature, the seat of His divine life; and, as such, the counterpart of the flesh mentioned in the immediately preceding clause, which together made up His appearance and life among men. It is of that, also, we can best understand the *justifying*, which must be taken here, as elsewhere in St. Paul's writings, in the sense of judged or approved as righteous. Christ was thus justified in spirit, because in His career on earth, from first to last, He fulfilled all righteousness, and once and again was proclaimed to be the Father's beloved Son, in whom He was well pleased. There is, when so explained, both a contrast and a correspondence in the two predicates: manifested in flesh, justified in spirit;—flesh and spirit natural opposites, but the manifesting in the one corresponding to the justifying in the other; *that* indicating His real humanity, *this* His true holiness; on the one side actual manhood, on the other spiritual perfection.

There is the same sort of contrast and correspondence in the two succeeding pairs. And it is this, too much overlooked by commentators, which most readily helps us to the right exhibition of the meaning. *Appeared* — (ὤφθη, rather *appeared* than was seen; it is made Himself seen, for the verb is commonly used in the sense of self-exhibition, Acts vii. 26, xxvi. 16, etc.)—*appeared to angels, was preached among the Gentiles:* angels and Gentiles, again natural opposites—the one the blessed occupants of a higher sphere, the other the more corrupt and debased inhabitants of this lower world. To the former, therefore, He appears as He is; they observe His progress, bring occasional supply to His wants, herald His resurrection, attend Him as guardian hosts to heaven, thereafter minister and serve before Him: to the latter, the Gentiles, He cannot thus render Himself manifest and familiar; but, what in a sense was better, He is preached among them for their salvation, so that through Him they may be raised out of their prostrate condition, and become allied to nobler spirits, even to "the innumerable company of angels and the church of the first-born, whose names are written in heaven." Finally, *Believed on in the world, received up in glory:* the world and glory, how far asunder, and in a sense antagonistic!—the one above, the other beneath; the one suggesting thoughts only of celestial brightness and purity, the other replete with numberless forms and appearances of evil—the region of sin, disease, and death. In this, therefore, Christ, as the perfected Redeemer, was incapable of residing, yet is spiritually present and believed on to the temporal and eternal good of His people; while Himself, as the fit inhabitant of a better region, received up in glory—the glory which He had with the Father before the world was. Thus not merely at the commencement, but throughout the series, there is the evolution of a mystery; an exhibition of contrasts, yet at the same time a preservation of what is fit and becoming in the several relations; a carrying out of what, in its diversified bearings, the scheme of God indispensably required. But I can see no advantage to the meaning, or even suitableness, in endeavouring, with Alford, to make the clauses consecutive—each as it follows taking up the history where the immediately preceding one had left it. It is impossible to work out a natural exposition on this plan; some of the expressions must have a measure of constraint or violence put upon them.

CHAPTER IV.

Ver. 1. *But the Spirit speaks expressly,* etc. The description given toward the close of the preceding chapter of the church as the pillar and basement of divine truth, and of the grand mystery which finds its evolution in connection with the interests and hopes of the church, might well have seemed to bespeak for her future condition a secure and continuous prosperity. There was, however, a shady side to the picture; and it was right that Timothy, and those who might follow after in the ministry of the word, should have timely warning of it. Here, therefore, the apostle proceeds to give some leading characteristics of this darker future, indicating by the connecting particle (the adversative δέ) that the things he was going to utter should form an unhappy contrast to what had been already said: Τὸ δὲ Πνεῦμα ῥητῶς λέγει. By the Spirit is undoubtedly to be understood the Holy Spirit, the immediate source of all prophetic insight into the coming dispensations of Providence, and the history of the church. And when this Spirit is affirmed to have spoken *expressly* (ῥητῶς, used in this sense by Polybius, iii. 23. 5, and some later Greek writers; see in Wetstein) as to the sad declensions that were in prospect, respect is obviously had to the explicit, unambiguous character of the announcements. If it is asked, however, when or by whom the announcements were made, no very definite reply can be given. There may have been, and very probably were, intimations of the coming evil given to the apostle himself, of which no record exists beyond the brief outline contained in the passage before us. But if there were such, we may naturally suppose they would be in the same line with those which have been recorded — further, and probably more specific, developments of the features indicated in them. Even in Old Testament Scripture there are not wanting prophetic glimpses which seem to point in this direction; in particular what is said in Daniel, chap. vii. 25, viii. 23–25, of a dark, subtle, and corrupt power which was destined apparently to arise and work with disastrous energy in Messiah's kingdom, after this kingdom should have been formally set up. More certainly, however, may be taken into account some of our Lord's announcements respecting the future of His church, such as the parable of the tares and the wheat, and the mention of false Christs and false prophets, who should deceive many, in His discourse of the last days (Matt. xxiv. 11 ss.). More especially still may be included Paul's own statements in one of his earliest epistles concerning a great apostasy which was to take place in the Christian church (2 Thess. ii.); also what he said in his address to the elders of Ephesus about persons going to arise within the church who should do the part of wolves to the flock, teaching perverse things (Acts xx. 29, 30); and still again, the pointed reference he made in his Epistle to the Colossians to the depravations of Christian doctrine and worship, which he descried as already beginning to take shape, through the combined influence of ascetic and ritualistic tendencies (chap. ii.). These were all prior in point of time to the passage now under consideration, and were of a kindred nature to it, though none of them speak so expressly of the corruptions now more particularly in the eye of the apostle as he does in this warning to Timothy. We may therefore justly infer, that the explicitness of the Spirit's utterances here given through the apostle really form an advance on the revelations hitherto communicated to the church in this particular line, one required by the circumstances of the time.

The express utterances of the Spirit were to the effect that *in after times some shall depart from the faith.* As to the period indicated, the expression of the apostle is somewhat indefinite; for the ἐν ὑστέροις καιροῖς may be understood of any age or time subsequent to the apostle's own: it was merely the times which, in respect to the persons who then lived, lay somewhere in the future. The expression in 2 Tim. iii. 1, *the last days,* and St. John's, *the last hour,* or season (ἐσχάτη ὥρα, 1 John ii. 18), appear of themselves to point to a yet more remote future—to what was contemplated as a closing period. But, from the habit of Jewish writers to view Messiah's times generally as the later times of the world's history, we cannot, perhaps, draw very sharply the distinction between these forms of expression and the one used in the passage before us. By this the apostle plainly means to denote, in a somewhat general way, the later age of the world; not absolutely its very last or closing period, but stretching, perhaps, over extensive tracks of time. The evil, indeed, was already germinating; and it was to grow into what the apostle calls a departure or apostasy from the faith—*faith* taken objectively, as often elsewhere (Acts vi. 7; Jude 3, etc.), for the truths or doctrines embraced by faith. Men were going to corrupt the simplicity of these by mixing with them errors and traditions of their own. Then follow indications of the erring course.

Giving heed to seducing spirits and teachings of demons. The seducing spirits here referred to evidently stand in contrast to *the Spirit* mentioned immediately before—that Spirit who is to the church of Christ the source of all truth and holiness. Instead of following His guidance, the parties in question were to give way to spirits of error, seducing spirits ($\pi\nu\epsilon\acute{\nu}\mu\alpha\sigma\iota\nu$ $\pi\lambda\acute{\alpha}\nu o\iota\varsigma$), and teachings of demons—that is, teachings which drew their inspiration from demoniacal agencies. For there can be no doubt that the genitive here ($\delta\alpha\iota\mu o\nu\acute{\iota}\omega\nu$) is the genitive of the subject (Winer, § 30), and not, as Mede laboured with great earnestness and industry to show, that of the object—teachings or doctrines concerning demons—demonolatry. Ample proof, indeed, exists, and was produced by Mede (*Works*, p. 623), of the extensive prevalence of demonolatry in apostolic times outside the Christian church, and of the footing it ere long got within the church, under the forms of saint and martyr worship, exorcisms, incantations, and superstitious wrestlings with particular representatives of the demon world. But there is no evidence of that specific form of corruption being here in the eye of the apostle. The particular kinds of evil mentioned by him have no proper affinity with it; they belong to the sphere of ordinary life, and were such as spring from a false but aspiring asceticism, aiming at higher degrees of mortification and self-denial than consisted with the principles of the gospel. To represent teaching of this sort as the offspring of corrupt and misleading spirits—the spirits that rule in the darkness of this world, and strive to keep it in alienation from the life of God—was not to dissociate it from the efforts of a human instrumentality (it is presently, indeed, connected therewith), but to stamp the instrumentality as essentially evil, working under the influence, and for the interest, of the adversary of souls. Some have supposed the instrumental agents themselves to be designated seductive spirits and demoniacal teachers; but this is contrary to the usage of Scripture, and also to the connection here. It is the unseen prime movers of the mischief in the spirit-world, not the instruments employed by them, that are so characterized by the apostle.

Ver. 2. Ἐν ὑποκρίσει ψευδολόγων—not, as in the Authorized Version, "speaking lies in hypocrisy," which would take ψευδολόγων as in apposition with the δαιμονίων of the preceding clause, and so would identify the demons with the instrumental agents—but *in hypocrisy of speakers of lies:* a prepositional clause, defining the manner in which the giving heed to seducing spirits and teachings of demons was to make way, consequently describing the spirit and character of the human agents. The false teaching in question being, as to its origin, from the father of lies, the parties who were to be chiefly instrumental in insinuating its poison into the church were to be the fit representatives and agents of such a cause; not sincere, straightforward, truth-loving men, but persons living in hypocrisy as their natural element, speaking lies as their proper vocation,—men, in short, of subtle and sophistical minds, who had no relish for the pure gospel, and assumed the profession of a regard to it only that they might the more advantageously propagate their transcendental views and practices. Such appears to be the natural import and bearing of the clause; it brings prominently out that dangerous characteristic in the immediate instruments of the false teaching referred to, by means of which the spirit of evil that wrought in them was to acquire ascendency in the church.

The moral condition of these corrupt teachers is further described as that of persons *who have had their conscience scarred* (κεκαυστηριασμένων,[1] cauterized), that is, branded as with a καυτήρ, a marking instrument of hot iron. The application of such an instrument to any part of the human body certainly has a hardening effect—renders the part so branded comparatively insensible to the touch. And this is the figurative meaning not unfrequently attached to the expression here; as in our common version, "seared as with a hot iron;" so, too, Theodoret, who founds his explanation on the physical fact, that "the part cauterized is deadened, and deprived of its former sensibility." But this is probably laying too much stress on an incidental effect of the action, while the action itself affords both a more direct and a quite appropriate sense. Understanding it so, the persons in the eye of the apostle are represented as corrupt at the core; their conscience so far from bearing the impress of moral purity—blurred and spotted, as it were, with the foul prints of former iniquities, and consequently incapable of relishing, or responding aright to, the holy doctrines of the gospel. There is a point, as well as severe emphasis, in the language: *their own conscience* (τὴν ἰδίαν

---

[1] This is the form of the word given in ℵ, A, C, and being the rarer form, is preferred by Tisch.; the greater number of MSS. and the received text have κεκαυτηριασμένων.

συνείδησιν) is affirmed to be in this corrupt state; and if themselves such in their inner being, how unfit to assume the part of teachers to others! how utterly incapable of leading them on to the heights of real purity and bliss! They professed to be guides of this description, to go even beyond the requirements of the gospel in their zeal for a self-denying and mortified life. But their zeal in this direction could not possibly spring from an unfeigned love of the pure and good; carnal self was really the mainspring of their aspirations, though clothing itself in the appearance of an angel of light.

Ver. 3. Here the apostle descends to particulars, indicating in one or two leading points the directions this false pietism was going to assume: *forbidding to marry,* [bidding[1]] *to abstain from meats* (or kinds of food) *which God made for being received with thanksgiving by the faithful, and those who have the full knowledge of the truth.* The prohibition of marriage, and of the use of certain kinds of food, by which more especially animal food must be understood, was among the commoner forms of that ascetic tendency which had already taken root in the East, and, the apostle foresaw, was presently going to win for itself a place within the pale of the Christian church. The Therapeutæ of Egypt, and the Essenes in the south of Palestine, were examples of the tendency in question; since not only at the gospel era, but for generations before it, they had in considerable numbers been systematically carrying out their ascetic principles in the manner indicated by the apostle. They confined themselves to the simplest diet, altogether abstaining from flesh and wine; and, without absolutely forbidding marriage, they still practically condemned and eschewed it, as inconsistent with the higher degrees of excellence in the spiritual life. If the prevalence of the Gnostic spirit had led to such

---

[1] Construction by zeugma, requiring κελευόντων to be supplied to make out the sense (Winer, § 66, 1, *e*).

ascetic developments even under Judaism (for that the parties in question were mainly, if not quite exclusively Jews, admits of no doubt), it was to be expected that the immense impulse given to spiritual thought and contemplation by the great facts of Christianity, would yet more become to many the occasion of aspiring after perfection by the same mistaken course. How far this tendency made way in the church before the rise of the more formally developed Gnostic systems, we have not the means of definitely ascertaining; but shortly after the commencement of the second century, and as the result of Gnostic teaching (more especially under Saturninus, Marcion, Tatian), parties assuming the Christian name, but known by the distinctive appellation of Encratites or Purists, openly preached against marriage, and insisted on abstinence from animal food; thereby (as Irenæus says, i. 28) "indirectly accusing God, who made male and female for the propagation of mankind, and proving themselves ungrateful to Him who made all things."[1] It is plain, therefore, that these early heresiarchs erred on the very points specified by the apostle; and as some of them—in particular, Marcion and Tatian—had been reared in the bosom of the church, and afterwards separated themselves from it by thus departing from the faith, it was a perfectly legitimate application of the passage to turn it, as many of the Fathers did, against their extreme positions. Yet not a few of those Fathers themselves fell in a measure under the same misguiding influence. For they so extolled virginity, as virtually to disparage the married state: the one was with them the ideally perfect, the other the relatively defective and impure form of the Christian life; and it was only by abstinence from marriage, and by frequent fastings, always attended by the disuse of animal food, and by other ascetic exercises, that it was thought possible to become pattern

---

[1] See Dissertation on chap. iii. 2, App. B.

saints, or to *be religious* in the stricter sense. But if it be wrong to forbid marriage as unholy, and proscribe the use of food which God has ordained for man's use; if this be virtually to impeach the wisdom of the Creator, and to impute a character of evil to the bounties of His providence, then assuredly to turn those kinds of abstinence into a ground of pre-eminent virtue, and assign to the persons who practised them a place of surpassing honour, was in a most real sense to depart from the faith of the gospel, since it assumed another rule and standard of worth than what is propounded there. It had, as the apostle elsewhere said, "a show of humility, and neglecting of the body, not in any honour to the satisfying of the flesh" (Col. ii. 23); but was not the less calculated to feed the pride and self-sufficiency of nature, and mar the healthfulness and simplicity of a genuine faith.

Scripture, indeed, does not deny that a person may occasionally abstain from certain meats or from marriage, with advantage to his own spiritual life or the good of the kingdom of God (Matt. vi. 16, 17, xvii. 21, xix. 12; 1 Cor. vii. 32–37). But in such cases the alternative is not put as between a relatively pure and perfect state by the one course, and an impure or defective one by the other; but the one is presented merely as affording opportunities or helps for prosecuting more freely and unreservedly the work of faith than can well be done in the other. If temporary fasting should dispose and enable one to fight more successfully against the lusts of the flesh, or if by abstaining from marriage one could, in particular spheres of labour, or in certain conjunctures of the church's history, more effectually serve the interests of the gospel than otherwise, then the higher principles of that gospel, the nobler ends of a Christian calling, will undoubtedly justify the restraint or the sacrifice. But to do this is only to subordinate a less to a greater good: it creates no factitious distinctions in respect to the allowable or forbidden, holy or unholy, in the ordinary relationships and circumstances of life; and calls for a rejection of the natural good in these only when it may be conducive as means to a definite spiritual end. This is an entirely different thing from that morbid and mawkish asceticism, which, in attempting to soar above the divinely appointed order and constitution of things, imputes a character of evil to what is in itself good, and hence withdraws men from those social environments which, as a rule, are necessary to the well-being of society, and to the full-orbed completeness of the Christian character.

When the apostle speaks, in the latter part of this verse, of the common articles of food as having been made by God,—*for being received with thanksgiving by the faithful, and those who have the full knowledge of the truth* (τοῖς πιστοῖς καὶ ἐπεγνωκόσιν τὴν ἀλήθειαν),—the most natural meaning seems to be: received thus by such persons as well as others: their faith and knowledge in the things of God had no way interfered with their relation to the common bounties of God's providence, and ought to be coupled with a thankful, not with a fearful or doubting, spirit. The expressions might, with Ellicott and others, be taken in the sense of the *dative of interest*—"for the faithful," etc.; but it is more fitting to regard them as ablatives (the ablative of the agent, considered as the instrument whereby anything is done; Jelf, § 611). For it could not but appear somewhat strange, to say that God made the several kinds of food specifically for the possessors of true knowledge and faith in Christ. The teaching of Scripture on the subject rather is, that being natural gifts, they are made for the use of men simply as possessing the properties of human nature; and all that needs to be said of those who rise to a higher position in the divine kingdom is, that, as recipients of God's grace, and heirs of His eternal glory, nothing is withdrawn from them as to the original appointments of God in things pertaining to men's physical and social well-being. On the contrary, these now also rise into the religious sphere; they become associated with the work of grace in the experience of believers, and have a place—though only an inferior place—among the things which may be called theirs (1 Cor. iii. 21). This, indeed, is distinctly indicated in what follows.

Ver. 4. *Because everything made by God* (this is better than *every creature of God*, as *creature* seems to point too definitely to animated being, while by κτίσμα creation in all its parts is meant, whatever has received its being from the Creator, though the apostle's usual term for this is κτίσις, Rom. i. 25, viii. 39, Col. i. 15) *is good*. It necessarily is such as His workmanship, and was so pronounced by God Himself at the moment of creation. The rejection of anything so made and destined for man's use, as in itself evil, involves a Manichæan element. Therefore the apostle adds, *and nothing to be rejected, being received with thanksgiving*—that is, on the supposition of its being so received, but a supposition, as a matter of course, verified in the case of all true believers. What was in itself pure, might (as noted by De Wette) become impure by being received in an ungodly frame of mind. And the apostle means to say, that when the frame of mind is one of thankfulness, then in the manner also of their reception the things are pure and good.

The reason follows in ver. 5: *for it is sanctified through God's word and prayer*—God's word to man warranting him to use the creation gift, and man's word to God acknowledging the gift, and asking His blessing on it. So I understand the import of the expression; and I cannot see the propriety of identifying (with De Wette, Wiesinger, Ellicott, Alford) the word of God with the prayer or thanksgiving— so that this should be no further contemplated than as it embodies the word of God. There appears no reason why the word of God should be taken in so exclusive a sense. It is more natural to regard it as the original utterance of God's mind regarding the productions which are adapted to man's use and comfort—recognised, indeed, but not necessarily embraced in our address to God. The apostle had plainly, in the preceding verse, referred to the divine testimony recorded in the history of creation respecting the goodness of all that God had created and made, coupled also with the express and authoritative permission granted to man there, and still more fully at Gen. ix. 3, 4, freely to use whatever was fit for food in the vegetable and animal kingdoms. The word of God in those passages for ever sanctified all for man's use ; and if man on *his* part, taking God's word for his warrant, gratefully acknowledges God's hand in the gifts bestowed, and entreats His blessing on them, the sanctification is complete both ways—objectively by the word of God, subjectively by prayer ; by the word for all men (if they will but wisely appropriate it), by prayer for the believer. On ἐντευξις, see at chap. ii. 1.

The manner in which the apostle couples the destination of created things for man's use with the spirit of believing prayer and thanksgiving—as if the two must go together to constitute a proper title or warrant to the good—is certainly very striking. It is "as if those that wanted faith and saving knowledge" (to use the exposition of Bishop Sanderson) "did but *usurp* the bread they eat. And indeed it is certain that the wicked have no right to the creatures of God in such ample sort as the godly have. A *kind* of right they have—and we may not deny it to them—given by God's unchangeable ordinance at the creation, which being a branch of that part of God's image in man which was of natural and not of supernatural grace, might be and was foully defaced by sin ; but was not, neither could be, wholly lost. A right, then, they have, but such a right as, reaching barely to the use, cannot afford unto the user true comfort or sound peace of conscience in such use of the creatures; for though nothing be in and of itself unclean, yet to them that are unclean every creature is unclean and polluted, because it is not thus sanctified by the word [and by prayer]. And the very true cause of all this is the impurity of their hearts by reason of unbelief" (*Sermon V. ad Populum*).

Ver. 6. *By submitting these things to the brethren, thou shalt be a good servant of Christ Jesus, nourishing thyself up in the words of the faith, and of the good instruction which thou hast diligently followed.* Chrysostom draws attention to the mildness expressed in the governing word here (ὑποθέμενος): "not ordaining, nor commanding, did he say it, but as one giving counsel let him present these things," with the collateral idea, perhaps, of imparting also suitable advice respecting them. The rendering of the Authorized Version, "putting them in mind," is not absolutely wrong, but too readily suggests the notion of a rehearsing or bringing back what had already been more or less under the consideration of the brethren. This is not implied in the apostle's expression: it simply denotes a presentation of the things in question to the minds of the disciples, with the view of conveying suitable impressions respecting them. And his doing so would be a proof of Timothy's acquitting himself as a good servant of Christ—a proof that he was not unmindful of his proper work, but nourishing himself up (the present participle denoting continuous action) in the words of faith; that is, in the faith considered as embodied in the words of Scripture; and of the good instruction—that, namely, derived from the divinely commissioned servants of Christ, which he had diligently followed. His own faithful teaching after the manner enjoined by the apostle was to be the evidence how far he had profited by the peculiar advantages he had himself enjoyed. The "whereunto thou hast attained" of the English version points more than the original word (παρακολούθηκας) to the result which should have grown out of the course of instruction pursued by Timothy; it is the close and persevering manner in which he had followed that course which alone is indicated. But such following could not, in his case, be without its proper fruit.

Ver. 7. *But* (expressive of a contrast to the things just mentioned and proper to be done) *the profane and old wives' fables avoid*—παραιτοῦ, turn aside from, shun. He gives no further description of them, nor indicates why he reckoned them profane, and such as were hatched in the brains of old wives, rather than of some other classes that might be thought of. But the use of the article seems to imply that he referred to things familiarly known, or perhaps to things noticed near the beginning of the epistle (i. 4), under the name of "fables and endless genealogies." We can scarcely doubt, indeed, that the fables spoken of were the same in both passages, especially as in the earlier passage they are represented as being at the time so much in vogue, that Timothy required to be on his guard against them. They were, as formerly noted, chiefly Jewish fables, but not improbably mixed with certain things also of Gentile origin, or such as were at least in spirit more allied to heathen than to properly Jewish teaching. The epithets *profane* and *anile* (old-wifish) designate them as in their character or tendency frivolous, foolish, and even ungodly; hence quite undeserving of the time and labour which some appear to have bestowed upon them.

And rather exercise thyself unto godliness. The δέ may fitly enough be rendered by *and rather*, marking at once a connection and a contrast with the preceding; so that the *rather* should be printed as part of the proper text. The verb (γύμναζε) pointing to the athletic exercises so common in ancient times, especially among the Greeks, implies that the εὐσέβεια, the work of practical piety or godliness, requires, when properly cultivated, the full bent and strenuous application of the mind. It was that Timothy might be able to give this to what was really worthy of it, and could not be adequately promoted without it, that the apostle urged him to discard the senseless and disputatious fables which were likely to solicit his attention. It is needless to say that there are many things still, different indeed in form, but essentially alike in nature and tendency, which are ever apt to draw off the regard, especially of the youthful pastor, from what ought to be his main business. The spirit of Paul himself—the spirit of concentrated, earnest striving in the work of the Lord—is the right one, and that which alone can achieve great results : " This one thing I do."

Ver. 8. The reason follows : *for bodily exercise is profitable unto little, but godliness is profitable unto all things.* Commentators have long been, and still are, divided as to what should be understood by the bodily exercise (σωματικὴ γυμνασία) : whether of such exercise as pertains to the health and vigour of the bodily frame, more particularly the gymnastics of the athlete ; or of the ascetic discipline spoken of before in connection with the banning of marriage and abstinence from certain kinds of food—bodily restraints, but with a view to spiritual results. In this latter sense it was taken by Ambrose, many Catholic interpreters, also by Calvin, Grotius, latterly by Wiesinger and Ellicott. Two considerations especially are urged in support of it (for example by Ellicott) : first, that the connection seems to demand that the contrast should lie between external observances and inward holiness; and second, that ascetic practices formed a very distinctive feature of that current Jewish theosophy which is specially alluded to in this part of the epistle. The considerations, however, are by no means decisive ; and, indeed, the latter seems rather to point in the opposite direction: for, just because the ascetic practices in question had obtained such a place in the prevalent false religionism of the time, and were threatening to usurp a yet larger one in the future, we might expect the apostle to be chary of meting to them even the smallest commendation. He had already characterized things of this description as doctrines of demons, propagated by hypocrisy, and inimical to the true faith of the gospel; and could he now consistently turn round, and say that they were not altogether worthless—that they did bring a little profit? The tendency of his preceding statements was to separate between ascetic notions of excellence and those of genuine Christianity—to show that the one is rather the subtle counterfeit than the proper exhibition and development of the other. Besides, bodily exercise is not the natural or fitting expression for such things, at least in the incipient stage at which the apostle appears to be contemplating them. It might suit well enough for the more advanced stages—pilgrimages, flagellations, laborious vigils, or the constrained positions of pillar saints; but not for the disuse of certain kinds of food, or abstinence from marriage as a relatively impure condition of life. This is too negative and quiescent a species of asceticism to be appropriately designated a corporeal gymnastics. The literal sense of the expression, therefore, seems plainly entitled to the preference, which also has the support of the three ancient Greek expositors, Chrysostom, Theodoret, and Theophylact, and among the moderns, besides many others, of Bengel, De Wette, Huther, and Alford. The athletic mode of expression which had just been employed by the apostle to characterize the earnest application that should be made to a life of godliness ($\gamma\acute{\nu}\mu\nu\alpha\zeta\epsilon$), called up to his mind the gymnastic training which consumed so much time and energy among the ancient Greeks; and he takes occasion from the allusion to commend that higher kind of energetic striving which became the spiritual athletes of the gospel. The one had a measure of good attending it; it was profitable within a certain limited sphere, since it contributed to the healthfulness and agility of the bodily frame, and brought its successful cultivator a present recompense of honour or reward. But the sincere and strenuous cultivation of vital godliness rises immensely above this; it carries in its train the highest good of which man is capable, and *that* not merely for a few fleeting seasons of time, but throughout the ages of eternity. For such is the explanation the apostle himself gives in the words that follow of the *all things* unto which godliness is profitable.

Having promise of the life that now is, and of that which is to come. By *life* is evidently meant one's proper being and well-being, whatever goes to make up a well-conditioned and happy state of existence. Life in this higher sense is inseparably connected with godliness. The possession of it was originally suspended on the actual and unfailing exercise of godliness; and now, since the original title to the possession has been forfeited by sin, the *promise* of regaining what has been lost, though it cannot indeed be meritoriously secured by any amount of personal goodness, yet neither can it be realized otherwise than in connection with this; for only as men become established in the love and practice of goodness, do they become qualified for the possession and enjoyment of life. Interest in Christ goes first, then likeness to Christ; and as this grows, their meetness also increases for an inheritance in His blessedness and glory. A stimulating thought surely for the people of Christ generally, but especially for such as devote themselves to active work in His spiritual vineyard! It is work emphatically which is twice blessed: they reap even while they are sowing; lay up treasures for themselves while they are spending for the good of others; do best for themselves when they do most for God.

Ver. 9. *Faithful is the word, and worthy of all acceptation.* This form of expression, peculiar to the Pastoral epistles, has already occurred in another connection, chap. i. 15.

Here it is applied to the promise of life now and hereafter, as connected with the earnest pursuit of holiness, which the apostle not only sets forth, but commends as entitled to implicit confidence, and worthy of cordial acceptance. He proceeds also to confirm what he thus says of it by a reference to his own aim in the work of the ministry, and that of his fellow-labourers in the gospel.

Ver. 10. *For to this* (εἰς τοῦτο, with a view to it, in order that we may in our own case realize the good contained in the promise) *we toil* (κοπιῶμεν, which is somewhat stronger than ἐργάζομεν, labour) *and strive* (ἀγωνιζόμεθα),[1] *because we have hoped upon the living God, who is the Saviour of all men, especially of those who believe.* This statement being presented as a reason or ground of procedure in respect to the promise of life mentioned immediately before, clearly enough shows in what sense the apostle understood the life; for, so far from aiming at mere animal existence or corporeal satisfaction and repose, as if this were the *summum bonum* of life, he and his fellow-labourers readily parted with the things pertaining to that lower sphere, cheerfully encountered hardships, and persevered in a great life-conflict, that they might become partakers of life in that higher and nobler sense which the grace of God in Christ had rendered it possible for them to attain. They felt, in short, that their grand interest, alike for time and eternity, lay in the service and blessing of God; and without disparaging anything naturally pleasant or advantageous which the course of divine providence might place within

---

[1] This is undoubtedly the best supported reading, being that of ℵ, A, C, F, G, K, while the ὀνειδιζόμεθα of the received text is found in only three uncials at first hand, D, L, P, though it has the support of the Vulg., Greek, Syr., Cop., Arm., and Ethiop. versions. The unanimity of the versions is certainly entitled to weight, yet is scarcely sufficient to counterbalance the evidence of so many of the most important MSS. The omission of the first καί has the support of all the versions, and that also of ℵ, A, C, D, P.

their reach, or shunning as unclean what God had given to be used, they still showed that they were prepared to undergo any sacrifice of fleshly ease or worldly honour that might be required by their devotion to the cause of Christ, assured that thereby they gained more than they lost—that they advanced their interest in what alone is of supreme and imperishable moment. The ground of this assurance is made to rest in God: it was because they had hoped upon the living God (the ἐπὶ, with the dative, indicative of the solid basis they had obtained for their expectations), that they could so confidently reckon on an endless heritage of peaceful and blessed life, and so willingly submit to all privations and toils that might meet them in the pursuit of it; for He who is Himself the living One, having the very fountain of life in perpetual freshness and inexhaustible sufficiency, is in this case the surety and the promiser. Such a hope, therefore, must be one that shall not make ashamed.

In this direction also points the further description given of God: *who is the Saviour of all men, especially of those who believe.* The term Saviour (σωτήρ) represents Him as the deliverer and preserver of life; but in what sense, or to what effects, must be inferred from the connection. As the living God, He may be said to be the Saviour of all men, since by His watchful and beneficent providence they are constantly delivered from destruction and preserved in being. Actually He is not more to all men, although more in manifestations of goodwill and acts tending toward salvation, since He sets before men generally, and often even presses on their acceptance, the benefits of a work of reconciliation, which, from its essential nature, is perfectly sufficient to meet the necessities of all, and recover them to life and blessing. As it is in the character of a Saviour-God that He does this, there seems no valid reason why it should not be comprised in the sense we put upon the apostle's language. Yet, as the language indicates rather what God actually is to men, what they actually receive from Him, than what He reveals Himself as ready and willing to give them, we are led by the natural and unconstrained import of the words to think mainly of the relation in which God stands to men indiscriminately as the Author and Preserver of their present life. And from this as the less, the apostle rises to the greater. From what God is and does in behalf of such as are dependent on Him for the common bounties of providence, he proceeds to indicate what God is and does besides, in respect to those who are related to Him as His redeemed in Christ—*the Saviour, especially of those who believe:* in them the character of God as Saviour reaches its proper culmination. Put in the form of an argument, the idea might be thus expressed : If in that character God does so much for sinful and unbelieving men, how much may He not be justly expected to do for His own chosen people, who are partakers of His grace, and have trusted in His word! In *their* case there is nothing to hinder the outgoings of His loving-kindness, or to restrain the riches of His beneficence, but everything rather to encourage them to expect all from His hand. Expressing the Father's mind towards them in this respect, our Lord said, "I have come that they might have life, and that they might have it more abundantly" (John x. 10).

Ver. 11. From the beginning of this new section to the end of the chapter, we have a series of practical exhortations to Timothy respecting his personal bearing and character : *Charge these things, and teach;* the things, namely, which had been mentioned in the immediately preceding verses, and which concerned the whole church of Christ—involving serious dangers to be guarded against, and lines of duty to be resolutely pursued. On Timothy's part, therefore, there were both charges to be given respecting them, and principles as to truth and error to be taught.

Ver. 12. *Let no one despise thy youth.* This is, doubtless, the proper rendering, although the position of the pronoun is somewhat peculiar, σου τῆς νεότητος καταφρονείτω; but it again occurs in ver. 15, where also the governing substantive follows. The sense plainly is, "Let no one despise thee on account of thy youth," as Chrysostom expressly puts it. The youth of Timothy, as mentioned in the Introduction, must be understood relatively: though a person in the full vigour of manhood, he still was young for such a charge as had been devolved on him—much younger, in all probability, than some on whom he had to exercise disciplinary treatment; and if the apostle himself, who was not only considerably older than Timothy, but invested also with higher official dignity, found it difficult at times to maintain his authority in the face of the aspiring and disputatious spirits that sought to have pre-eminence in the church, we can easily understand how persons of that description would be ready to take advantage of Timothy's comparative youth. The natural disposition of Timothy, also, formed rather for helping and obeying than commanding, could scarcely fail to aggravate the danger; so that against this, as a weak point in his position, he was fitly called by the apostle to guard. Respect for the sacred interests entrusted to him, required that he should be manly and firm.

But become thou a pattern of the believers in word, in behaviour, in love,[1] *in faith, in purity.* A sort of counteractive to the danger indicated in the preceding clause; as much as to say, If thou wouldst properly retain thy place, and overcome the disadvantage connected with thy youth, take heed that thou be such an exemplar of Christian excellence and worth, that all true believers will be disposed to esteem and love thee. The specific points, though not mentioned in any logical order, comprise all the leading

[1] The ἐν πνεύματι after this in the received text is wanting in the best authorities.

characteristics that should distinguish a Christian minister: in *word*,—careful of what he might say, whether in the assemblies of the faithful or in his private intercourse with individuals,—in *behaviour* equally careful as to what he might do in the general course and tenor of his life; in *love*, in *faith*,—showing that, with the form, he also knew and exercised the two grand motive powers of a Christian life; finally, in *purity* (ἁγνείᾳ),—such in his bearing toward the female portion of society, as to prevent even the suspicion from entering that he was otherwise than scrupulously observant of the rules of chastity. It is of incalculable importance for the youthful minister that he establish for himself a character in these respects; a palpable failure in any one of them will be fatal to his success.

Ver. 13. *Till I come* (the present, ἔρχομαι, probably to express the purpose of an early return to Ephesus), *give attention to the reading, the exhortation, the teaching*. The definiteness indicated respecting these things by the use of the article, seems to point to them as well known: stated employments connected with ministerial agency. The reading, therefore, will most naturally be taken for that kind of reading which formed part of the public service of the church,—namely, the reading of Scripture, chiefly as yet, if not entirely, Old Testament Scripture. Chrysostom appears to have thought of Scripture, and nothing else, as indicated by the expression (πρόσεχε τῇ ἀναγνώσει, τῇ τῶν θείων γραφῶν); and so, undoubtedly, the expression is used at Acts xiii. 15, also 2 Cor. iii. 14, with reference to the regular reading of the Old Testament Scriptures in the Jewish synagogues. The *exhortation* and the *teaching* are understood by Chrysostom, the former of social or mutual interchange of sentiments with a view to edification, the other of public discourse. We should rather, perhaps, suppose the apostle to be referring throughout to the service of the sanctuary; so that he shall here be advising Timothy in regard to the things which belonged to his ministrations in public, as he had previously counselled him regarding his more strictly personal character and deportment. But to try to distinguish exactly between the exhortation and the teaching is superfluous, except that, from the import of the terms, the one may be supposed to have had respect more especially to practice, and the other to instruction.

Ver. 14. *Neglect not the gift* (the charism) *that is in thee, which was given thee through* (or by means of) *prophecy, with laying on of the hands of the presbytery.* There can be no reasonable doubt that this is the correct rendering, and that the attempts which have at various times been made to give another sense to the preposition (διά) than that of expressing the medium or instrumental cause, have entirely failed. Prophecy and imposition of hands by the presbytery are represented as the concurrent means through which the gift in question came to Timothy: prophecy the first and highest—hence having the preposition of the instrument coupled with it; imposition of hands by the presbytery the secondary or subordinate—hence presented as an accompaniment of the other. But what is to be understood by the gift itself, which thus came to Timothy's possession? The word χάρισμα, which occurs altogether fourteen times in the writings of St. Paul, but nowhere else in the New Testament, except in 1 Pet. iv. 10, always means an endowment or gift of grace, bestowed by the Holy Spirit for some special ministration or official service. Timothy had in tender youth been destined to peculiar evangelistic work under the direction and oversight of St. Paul, and he had received from above a measure of grace proportioned to his calling and responsibilities. This qualifying grace had somehow been indicated through the spirit of prophecy as a gift destined for him, authoritatively certified to be awaiting him—therefore in a sense conferred through that; and then, acting on this divine certification or assurance, the presbytery gave him the imposition of hands,—an act which always formed "an appropriation of the gift of the Spirit in prayer through the instrumentality of others for a definite object" (Wiesinger). The prophecy, therefore, is to be viewed as the distinct enunciation of God's will in respect to Timothy's qualifications—his spiritual as well as natural qualifications for the evangelistic office; and the formal designation of him by the presbytery was the church's response to the declared mind of God, and appropriate action to carry it into effect. The *presbytery* is to be taken in the natural and obvious sense, for the body of presbyters or elders in the particular place where Timothy was set apart to the work of the Lord. It means *bishops* here, says Chrysostom, since only such could ordain by imposition of hands: true in one sense, but not certainly in that meant by Chrysostom; that is, not as denoting the presence and co-operation of officers of a higher grade than presbyters. The language of the apostle, neither here nor elsewhere, furnishes any warrant for such a supposition. Bengel's explanation is still more arbitrary; he would couple προφητείας with πρεσβυτερίου, and throw the intervening words into a parenthesis—thus: "which was given thee through the prophecy of the presbytery, with the laying on of hands." And the hands laid on he would understand to be those of the apostle's, on the supposed ground that imposition of hands was the act of one person, and that a person of higher dignity than he on whom the act was performed. Such, however, was not the case at Antioch, when Paul and Barnabas were by imposition of hands designated to special ministerial work (Acts xiii. 1); nor have we any reason to think it was necessarily or even ordinarily so, except when the gift conferred had respect to the exhibition of miraculous agency. The conferring of this gift by imposition of hands belonged exclusively to an apostle. But in appointments to ministerial employ it was otherwise; and when, in another place (2 Tim. i. 6), the apostle speaks of this same gift having come to Timothy through the laying on of *his* hands, this no way prejudices the supposition of a more general concurrence in the act. The part taken by the apostle in the matter could not but be the most assuring circumstance to Timothy of an external kind, and a very special consideration prompting him to the exercise of the gift; but it did not preclude the official action of the presbytery, nor render this unimportant in its own place.

Ver. 15. *Be mindful of these things* (μελέτα, found only here and at Acts iv. 25, but signifying to *care for, attend to*, or *be mindful of*): let them have their proper place in the regard and application of thy soul. *Be in them;* have your very life, as it were, in such things. On which Bengel remarks: "He who *is* in them will be less in worldly companies, in other kinds of pursuits, in collecting books, shells, coins, in which many pastors unconsciously spend a great part of their life." *In order that thy progress may be manifest to all:* implying, first, that a perceptible advance in the things which constitute a faithful and effective ministry is what may justly be expected even in the most qualified servant of God; and then, that the way to effect this is by a sincere and devoted application to the work itself. Here also it is the hand of the diligent which maketh rich—though only, of course, when the hand is the instrument of an earnest and willing mind.

Ver. 16. *Give heed to thyself, and to the teaching:* not precisely *doctrine*, though doubtless including what is understood by that, but the whole matter of teaching in relation to Christianity; hence, in the first place, making due preparation for the work of public discourse, and then, when actually employed in it, seeing that it be of the right sort, that it embrace the great principles of truth and duty as unfolded in the gospel, and press these in the proper manner and spirit. *Continue in them;* that is, in the various parts of evangelistic and pastoral duty enjoined in the preceding sentences: let there be, not a fitful, but a steady and persevering application to them. Then follows the twofold blessed result: *for by so doing thou shalt save both thyself and them that hear thee.* The direct object of the ministry of the gospel is the salvation of those who come within the circle of its operations; but along with this the apostle happily combines another, the saving of one's own soul. Nothing is so well fitted for bringing us safely to heaven as engaging in good earnest to be instruments in God's hand of bringing others thither. For, as an old and, in the best sense, spiritual writer has excellently noted on the words, " the work of Christianity is woven in with the right discharge of the office of the ministry. Many ministers can say, that if they had not been ministers they had in all appearance lost their souls. The subject of the minister's work is the same with that of a Christian's; and above all men should he be careful of his heart and intentions, that all be pure and spiritual. No man is under so strict a necessity of dependence on the influence and assistance of the Holy Ghost, both for gifts and grace. And are not all these great helps to one's own salvation?" (Sermon by Robert Traill.)

CHAPTER V.

From matters relating to the strictly personal state and behaviour of Timothy, the apostle now proceeds to give a series of directions in respect to the proper method of dealing with persons differently situated as to age and position in life. *Reprimand not an elderly person, but exhort him as a brother.* That the term πρεσβυτέρῳ here has respect simply to the relative age, not to the official standing, of individuals, seems plain from the connection; younger men being presently mentioned as another class, and afterwards females, first of a more advanced, and then of a younger period of life. This view was taken by Chrysostom, and is now generally followed, although the other was once the more common, and is that also expressed in the Authorized Version. A man full of years should not, the apostle says, be sharply rebuked, or reprimanded; for such undoubtedly is the force of the verb (ἐπιπλήσσω): it is originally to *strike*, to *beat*, and when used of words spoken to any one, indicates reproof of the severer kind—chiding in a rough or acrimonious manner. There was a special propriety in the observance of such a direction by Timothy, being himself still comparatively young, and having consequently to take heed lest his bearing toward his seniors should in any way prejudice his calling (iv. 12). But the exhortation is doubtless to be applied generally; it virtually prescribes a rule of procedure for all Christian pastors. They should, even when called to administer reproof to aged offenders, bear in mind that a measure of respect is due to them on account of their age, and in a tender, subdued tone perform the duty imposed on them. Nor should something of this spirit be wanting in respect also to others; for as the elderly were to be exhorted as fathers, so, the apostle adds, should *the younger men as brothers*, that is, with kindness and affection, though not unmingled, perhaps, at times with severity; for while the *exhorting*, as the nearer verb, must be chiefly thought of, we are not altogether to lose sight of the *reprimanding*, which undoubtedly indicates that there might be room at least for earnest and faithful admonition—exhorting of such a nature as bespoke cause for censure or regret.

Ver. 2. *Elderly women as mothers, the younger as sisters with all purity,*—the same advice tendered in respect to the female members of the Christian community as had just been given regarding the male, with a marked qualification as to the moral danger incident to work among this portion of the flock : *in all purity*—so as even to avoid the appearance of anything unbecoming or improper. A most necessary caution for all times !

Ver. 3. *Honour widows that are widows indeed.* It is questioned whether the honouring here enjoined is to be understood in the general sense of showing deference and respect to one, or in the more specific sense of ministering support, relieving and raising one's condition : a very needless question, as appears to me. The general, and what is also the usual import of the expression, is perfectly sufficient. The widows who are such in reality,—those, namely, who are in a truly widowed and forlorn condition, and have a state of mind and behaviour suited to their circumstances, —are the proper subjects of respectful and considerate treatment; but the particular direction this should take, the substantial acts in which it should manifest itself, will naturally be determined by the circumstances in which the individuals are placed : if destitute in a pecuniary respect, then of course chiefly in furnishing them with the means of material comfort; but if otherwise, with suitable manifestations of sympathy and regard. Ministrations of the former kind are afterwards specifically noticed (ver. 8); but it by no means follows from this (as is supposed by De Wette, Wiesinger, Alford, Ellicott, etc.), that such alone were here in the eye of the apostle : for neither might these be always the chief, nor in any case, indeed, could they be the only marks of honourable treatment which a Christian community should give to persons in that state of bereavement. It seems best, therefore, to take the brief exhortation at the outset as indicating generally the *kind* of behaviour that should be exhibited toward them; and to see in the directions which follow detailed instructions as to the proper mode of applying it to particular cases.

Ver. 4. *If, however, any widow has children or grandchildren* (ἔκγονα, *offspring;* but remoter than *children*, τέκνα τέκνων, Hesych.—*grandchildren*, which was once also the meaning of our *nephews*), *let them first learn to show piety at home* (or toward their own house), *and requite their parents:* πρόγονοις, *forbears*, a Scottish term, exactly corresponds; and so formally does *progenitors* in English, only this is now commonly used of relatives in the direct line further off than those meant by the apostle. Is is best, therefore, to retain *parents*, but understanding by it grandparents as well. A widow in the circumstances here supposed occupies a position considerably different from the *widow indeed* of the preceding verse, having persons residing with her to whom, as her own children, or her children's children, she is entitled to look for every becoming mark of honour and affection. It primarily belonged to these to do what in them lay to relieve the wants and cheer the loneliness of her widowhood; and for the most part, if that were properly done, no special oversight of the matter would need to be taken by the authorities of the church. Such appears to be by much the most natural interpretation of the passage; so that the children and grandchildren are regarded as the subjects of the learning: "let *them* learn," not the *any widow* (as most of the ancient, and some also of the modern commentators take it, considering the τις χήρα as equivalent to χῆραι). Were this latter construction adopted, the *showing piety* and *rendering requitals* (ἀμοιβὰς ἀποδιδόναι) would necessarily lose their proper force. *Filial* piety and *filial* requitals are perfectly natural; for they correspond to the honour due from children to parents, are but different modes of expressing this; but understood of parents with reference to the conduct they should exhibit toward their children, if they can be made at all to bear such a sense, they are certainly not the forms of expression one would have looked for. What chiefly, perhaps, led to the interpretation in question, is a feeling that if widows were not the subject of the verb, there would fail to what goes before the proper apodosis; since *there* it is what pertains to the widows that is made prominent, while here it is what pertains to the children. In reality, however, there is no ground for such a feeling; for the instruction given is not directly addressed to the parties mentioned, but to Timothy. It is he who is charged to see to it, that matters were rightly ordered in the households of believing widows, and especially that the young should be taught to manifest respect and gratitude toward the mother that bore them, and watched over their infant years. The expression, to *show piety* (εὐσεβεῖν) to such, points back to the fifth commandment, in which the honouring of parents is placed in immediate connection with the reverence and homage due to God, and the things which most nearly concern His glory: *that* in youthful bosoms is the germ of fealty to God, and so its becoming exercise is reckoned a department of piety. To do this *first*, therefore, *toward their own house*, as having a prior claim even in comparison of what is due to the church or house of God, and to do it in the way of substantial ministrations of relief, which in such a case are but returns for similar ministrations formerly received (Matt. xv. 4-6), *is acceptable before God;* He regards it in a manner as done to Himself, and sees in it the earnest of future worth. The homes in which such reverential feelings are cherished, and such acts of lovingkindness are reciprocated, are the best nurseries of the church—churches themselves, indeed, in embryo, because the homes of Christian tenderness, holy affection, self-denying love, and fruitfulness in well-doing.

Ver. 5. Turning, then, from such widows and their families to those whom he wished more particularly to press on the notice of Timothy and the officers of the church, the apostle says: *But she who is a widow indeed* (a widow in the full and proper sense), *and desolate, has set her hope on God, and abides in supplications and prayers night and day:* she has lost, in a manner, all she had on earth, and now she seeks all from above. The Anna who is mentioned at the threshold of gospel history may be taken as one of the better types of the class, since it is written of her that "she departed not from the temple, but served God with fastings and prayers night and day." It is not to be supposed, of course, that in every case of this description the entire life was to be devoted to prayer and other religious exercises; for this would commonly be impossible, and even where possible would not be the most profitable course. To preserve the healthfulness of its tone, and its capacity for efficient service, the mind requires variety of employment; and in all ordinary cases, the discharge of relative duties amid the affairs and occupations of life not only may, but should, be ever interchanging with acts of piety. Hence, it will be observed, the temporal expressions are in the genitive (νυκτὸς καὶ ἡμέρας), indicative of the *when* rather than the *how long;* not *throughout* night and day, but *by* night as well as *by* day —a steady and regular habit of devotion. The *supplications* and *prayers* (δεήσεσιν, προσευχαίς) are not to be sharply distinguished from each other.

Ver. 6. *But she that lives deliciously* (or wantonly; σπαταλῶσα occurs only again in Jas. v. 5), *is dead while she lives:* the reverse of the true widow, who was represented as comparatively dead to the world, and alive to God, this person appears to have a relish only for the world and its pleasures, and to be dead to what is of God. The description substantially coincides with that given of the church of Sardis in Rev. iii. 1, "Thou hast a name that thou livest, and art dead." Only here the living has respect not so much to a profession of godliness as to the world's idea of life—an unreserved surrender to present objects and entertainments. Such life in the lower sphere involves death in the higher. And though the apostle does not expressly state it, yet it is plainly implied in what he says, that widows living after such a fashion were to be regarded as cut off from the sympathy and oversight extended to true Christian widows.

Ver. 7. *And these things enjoin, in order that they may be without reproach*—namely, the parties referred to in the preceding statements — widows more particularly, but along with them also the families which belonged to some of them. They are consequently supposed to be connected with the Christian community, and to be ready to listen to sound instruction. In the next verse, however, a class of characters is noticed that are expressly declared to be unworthy of the Christian name.

Ver. 8. *But if any one provides not for his own* (that is, his near relatives), *and especially for those of his own house, he has denied the faith, and is worse than an unbeliever.* Special respect is probably had in this strong declaration to a class of relatives previously mentioned—the children and grandchildren of widows; but there is no reason for confining it to such. The declaration itself is quite general, and comprehends other cases as well. It asserts in the most emphatic manner the obligations springing out of family relationships, as grounded in the constitution of nature, and, so far from being annulled or relaxed by the gospel, only thereby rendered the more sacred and imperatively binding. The parent who refuses (if he is able) to support his children while from youth or infirmity they are dependent on his care and help, or the children who refuse to minister to the sustenance and comfort of aged parents, both alike act an unfeeling and unnatural part: they are not true to the moral instincts of their own nature, and fall beneath the standard which has been recognised and acted on by the better class of heathens. For one, therefore, bearing the Christian name to disregard such claims, is utterly inexcusable; it is not simply dishonouring to Christ, it is to bring reproach on our common humanity.

Vers. 9, 10. Very few parts of this epistle have given rise to greater diversity of opinion than the instruction contained in these verses; and from the scantiness of our information respecting the domestic economy of the churches in the earliest times, it may be difficult to present a view of the passage which shall appear free from all appearance of strangeness or uncertainty. It is the more important, however, that we adhere strictly to the natural meaning of the words, and refrain from attempting, as has too often been done, to impose on them a sense derived from what belonged, or is supposed to have belonged, to a much later period. *Let a widow be enrolled*—so the verb καταλέγειν properly signifies: put on the list or register. The question is, what list? and for what specific purpose were names inserted in it? Was the list simply a catalogue of those who were formally recognised as widows of the church, and, as such, were held entitled to special oversight and support? Or was it as widows qualified and admitted to a kind of official position and service in the church?

These questions have been differently answered; and not a few, judging chiefly from the specifications afterwards given by the apostle as to age and character, have supposed that the list in question was composed of persons designated to a place of honour and responsibility—either that of deaconesses, or of trusted female ministrants, who were charged with much the same kind of oversight in respect to children and the members of their own sex, that was exercised by the elders over other portions of the community. This view has been held in its stronger form by the opponents of the genuineness of the epistle (Schleiermacher, De Wette, Baur, etc.), who would find here a class of female ecclesiastics of whom some partial and obscure notices occur in the third and fourth centuries,[1] but a class (the writers conceive) of too artificial a nature and too much associated with ascetic notions of excellence to have had a place in the apostolic church. There are others who reject the idea in this form, yet so far adopt it, that they regard the widows spoken of by the apostle as even in his time formed into a kind of distinct order, with the view of performing certain ministrations for the good of the church; so, for example, Mosheim, Wieseler, Conybeare and Howson, Huther, Alford, Ellicott. We may take as a specimen of this mode of representation the note of Conybeare and Howson, one of the most temperate of its kind: "We suppose that the *list* here mentioned was that of all the widows who were officially recognised as supported by the church; but was not confined to such persons, but included also richer widows, who were willing to devote themselves to the offices assigned to the proper widows. It has been argued that we cannot suppose that needy widows who did not satisfy the conditions of ver. 9 would be excluded from the benefit of the fund; nor need we suppose this. But since all could scarcely be supported, certain conditions were prescribed which must be satisfied before any one could be considered as officially entitled to a place on the list. From the class of widows thus formed the

[1] Tertullian, *de Vel. Virg.* c. 9 : "Ad quam sedem [viduarum] præter annos LX. non tantum univiræ, *i.e.* nuptæ aliquando, eliguntur, sed et matres et quidem educatores filiorum." Laodic. Concil. can. xi. : "Mulieres quæ apud Græcos presbyteræ appellantur, apud nos autem viduæ seniores, univiræ, et matriculariæ nominantur, in ecclesia tanquam ordinatos constitui non debere." Epiphanius, *adv. Hær.* L. iii. c. 79, § 4 : Παρατηρητέον δέ, ὅτι ἄχρι διακονισσῶν τὸ ἐκκλησιαστικὸν ἐπεδεήθη τάγμα, χήρας τε ὠνόμαζε, καὶ τούτων τὰς ἔτι γραοτέρας πρεσβύτιδας,— spoken, however, simply of deaconesses, some of whom were sometimes called *widows*, whether they really were such or not. Chrysostom, vol. iii. p. 273, Paris, ed. Gaume, speaks of there being anciently bands of widows, χηρῶν χοροί, as latterly of virgins; but he says nothing of consecration to office, or official work in the church.

subsequent order of widows (τάγμα χηρῶν) would naturally result."

It is guardedly put, and yet in one leading point it seems to go beyond what there is any distinct warrant for in the passage itself; namely, in its speaking of "the offices assigned to the proper widows." Of such offices the text makes no mention; and the existence of them can only be regarded as matter of more or less probable presumption and inference, from the conditions attached to the reception of individuals into the widow list. Yet a conclusion drawn from such premises must obviously be very uncertain, especially if the requisite characteristics be only such as respectable elderly females in a Christian community might be expected generally to possess. For, in that case, why might they not have been prescribed as a necessary safeguard against the abuse of the church's benefactions?—a security that those whom it sought to embrace and cherish as its peculiar charge from the Lord, were really worthy of the honour? And nothing more than this apparently is either indicated in the apostle's language, or needed to explicate its meaning. It is certain, first of all, that here, and in all he says respecting widows, such as he calls widows indeed, it is simply what the church is called to *do for them*, not anything it might *exact of them*, that he brings formally into notice: they are contemplated throughout as the fitting objects or recipients of a special kind of beneficent treatment from the religious community. It is certain, also, that from the commencement of the church, and pre-eminently in that mother church which in such things gave the tone and impulse to the other churches, widows merely as such were brought prominently into view; and that not only was adequate provision made for the relief of their necessities, but a special class of officers also appointed to see that the provision was properly administered: so far from being required to do anything like deacon work, they were themselves the subjects in whose behalf such work was called into operation. Further, it is undoubted that all the earlier commentators understood the apostle's description of widows merely as the *almswomen* of the church (Chrysostom, Jerome, Theodoret, Œc., and Theophylact): the conditions specified for enrolment were viewed by them merely as the traits of character which qualified those who possessed them for being the accredited pensioners of the church's bounty. And in a matter of this sort, which touches upon the general sense and usage of the church, the concurrent testimony of those ancient expositors is entitled to the greatest weight, and is far more than sufficient to counterbalance some obscure allusions or stray usages appearing in particular localities. Finally, the age at which the enrolment of widows was to be made—not under sixty, a period of life in such a district as Asia Minor relatively much higher than in our cooler and healthier climate — confirms the supposition that, as a rule, no active labour was expected of them. They were already of the aged and infirm class; and if they were expected to serve the interests of the church, it must have been chiefly by the more contemplative and quiet exercises of piety—"by supplications and prayers night and day." These were, no doubt, important services, and are the only ones in the least hinted at by the apostle; but they were such as belonged to the private sphere of the Christian life, and required no ecclesiastical consecration or official standing to authorize and sanction them.[1] In short, from the whole tenor of the apostle's description, viewed in con-

[1] Such, also, was the view taken by Neander: "Since Paul only distinguished them (*i.e.* the widows in question) as persons supported by the church, without mentioning any active service as devolving on them; since he represents them as persons who, as suited their age and condition, were removed from all occupation with earthly concerns, and dedicated their few remaining days to devotion and prayer; and since, on the contrary, the office of deaconess certainly involved much

nection with what is known of the circumstances of the time, there seems no reason for supposing any other class of persons to have been meant under the designation of enrolled widows, than those commonly known by the *name* of widows; yet only such of that class as from their advanced age and approved character were deemed worthy of the church's affectionate care and support. After the lapse of some centuries, notices occur of a particular dress, and a separate place in the church, being assigned to such widows; but Scripture and the earlier church records know nothing of this, nor of any specific work of a diaconal or presbyteral kind, having been by the church generally required of them. Younger widows, we have good grounds for believing, were not unfrequently accepted to the office of deaconess; but there is no proper evidence whatever to show that such widows as those here mentioned by the apostle were invested with any sort of office, or were called to do anything but such pious and free-will service as their own hearts might prompt, and their limited opportunities might enable them to perform.[1]

In regard now to the particular qualifications indicated by the apostle for the widows who were to be put on the list, it is to be borne in mind that, while the persons possessing them were alone to have the full recognition and enjoyment of what was due to the church's almswomen, there is nothing in his instructions to warrant the supposition that widows who in some respects fell short of them might not be admitted to occasional relief, and receive all proper ministrations of kindness. Such, for example, as active employment, we have no ground whatever for finding in this passage deaconesses, or females out of whose number deaconesses were chosen."—*Planting of Christian Church,* B. iii. c. 5.

[1] In this I state merely the general result, and consider it unnecessary to examine the few passages in detail which are relied on by those who hold another view, but which are far too vague and general for their purpose.

were comparatively young—far from having reached the age of sixty—might for a time require very great sympathy and liberal support; but it would have been a misfortune, rather than a benefit for them, if an apostolic injunction had been issued, giving them something like an abiding claim on the church's beneficence, and entitling them henceforth to rank among its objects of charity. That would have only served to paralyze personal exertion, and relax the ties of family relationships. The regular widow list—the list of such as were really desolate, infirm, and helpless—was wisely associated with a comparatively advanced age.—As to the construction, the γεγονυῖα should undoubtedly be connected with what precedes: *who is*, or *has become, not less than sixty years old;* comp. Luke ii. 42. Our translators, after Jerome, Luther, Calvin, etc., joined it with what follows.

Wife of one man. The proper determination of the term *widow*, as here used by the apostle, may be said to carry along with it a corresponding explanation also of this expression—to establish for it a freer, in opposition to the more stringent, sense sometimes put on it. For nearly all the arguments and authorities which are adduced in favour of its being understood of absolute monogamy, proceed on the supposition that the class of persons referred to were not simply widows of advanced age, but of ecclesiastical rank, invested with a measure of sacerdotal dignity, and hence called to a somewhat peculiar sanctity. We have already seen that this notion rests on no solid ground, that the persons in question were merely the desolate and helpless widows whom God's providence had thrown on the bounty of the faithful—the aged almswomen of the church. And of such persons, surely the whole that could justly be required, either by the dictates of reason or by the great principles of Scripture on the subject of marriage, was that they should be chargeable with no indecency in their married life, and never stood related to but one living husband. This much was necessary to their occupying the position of exemplary widows; but one cannot say more, whether the matter is viewed with respect to the law of God or to the known usages of society. The correct sense, therefore, I believe to be that given by Theodoret:[1] "It is hence manifest that he (the apostle) does not reject second marriages, but ordains that they live chastely in matrimony; for, having before established the lawfulness of a second marriage, *he* did not prohibit her that had entered into a second marriage from enjoying her bodily nurture— *he*, namely, who clearly exhibits what is good for all." And Chrysostom, though, from a misapprehension as to the position and duties of those designated widows, he supposed the expression before us intended to exclude second marriages of any kind, yet did so only on the ground of affording leisure for increased spiritual activity:[2] "Why, I ask, does he not permit second marriages to be contracted? Is it because he disapproved of the thing? By no means. For to do that was the part of heretics; but that the widow might be able to devote herself to spiritual things, and be occupied with virtue: for it is not impurity, but want of leisure, which marriage brings along with it."

It is needless to go into any detailed proof on the subject; for what is said here in respect to widows is but another aspect of the same question which has already been discussed at some length in respect to ministers at chap. iii. 2, and much of the proof which was advanced there is

[1] Καὶ ἐντεῦθεν δῆλον, ὡς οὐ τὴν διγαμίαν ἐκβάλλει, ἀλλὰ τὸ σωφρόνως ἐν γάμῳ βιοῦν νομοθετεῖ. οὐ γὰρ ἄνω τὸν δεύτερον γάμον νομοθετήσας σωματικῆς ἀπολαῦσαι θεραπείας ἐκώλυσε τὴν δευτέροις ὁμιλήσασειν γάμοις, ὅς γε τὸ ἀγαθὸν ποιεῖν πρὸς πάντας διαγορεύει σαφῶς.

[2] Διὰ τί γάρ, εἰπέ μοι, δευτέροις οὐχ ὁμιλῆσαι γάμοις προτρέπει; Ἆρα κατέγνω τοῦ πράγματος; Οὐδαμῶς· τοῦτο γὰρ αἱρετικῶν· ἀλλ' ἀπησχολῆσθαι βουλόμενος λοιπὸν αὐτὴν ἐν τοῖς πνευματικοῖς, καὶ πρὸς τὴν ἀρετὴν μεταταξασθαι· οὐ γὰρ ἀκαθαρσίας, ἀλλὰ ἀσχολίας ὁ γάμος.

à fortiori applicable here. A considerable show of proof for the opposite view can no doubt be produced, and has been produced, in particular by Vitringa (*Synag. Vet.* L. iii. P. i. c. 4), and others who have followed in the same line. But the passages chiefly relied on are greatly more numerous than cogent. One large class of them — the one most directly bearing on the point—originated in the heretical asceticism of the second century, and owes its ecclesiastical form and prevalence mainly to the vigorous Montanism of Tertullian. All passages of that class should be put entirely aside. Then the rest, being those which celebrate the superior merit of women who were *univiræ*, and as such were alone deemed fit for performing certain rites in the Cerealia,—passages chiefly relating to earlier Roman feeling and usage,—have respect to an essentially different sphere from that which concerns the constitution and government of the church of Christ. They relate partly to the conscious worth, sometimes proud self-assertion, of Roman matrons, grounding itself on the strength and constancy of attachment to a loved and honoured spouse, and partly to the conviction of special honour and felicity belonging to such as had enjoyed an unbroken conjugal relationship. As more peculiarly favoured by the gods, ceremonies performed by these were naturally supposed to be more acceptably and auspiciously done than by others. But for the time and region in connection with which the apostle here wrote,—for the class of persons in respect to whom he wrote, and the interests he had more immediately in view,—for all this there is no proof that can justly be said to bear upon the point at issue ; none, that is, tending to show that second marriages by women were *per se*, and apart from anything illegal and indecent in the mode of contracting them, deemed so questionable in their relation to female honour and virtue, as to debar the persons who contracted them from a title, in their old age, to the respect, and sympathy, and beneficence of the better portion of society. In the absence of all proof of this description, and on the great principle set forth by the apostle himself here and in other parts of his writings, we hold that the specification, *wife of one man*, should be taken as expressive simply of a chaste and faithful spouse—one true to her marriage vow while the person to whom it was made lived, whether that vow might be taken once merely, or again.

The other qualifications are: *well reported of in respect to good works, if she brought up children, if she entertained strangers, if she washed the feet of saints, if she relieved the distressed, if she followed after every good work.* The things mentioned call for no particular explanation or defence; they are the prominent characteristics of an exemplary Christian matron, partly under the distinctive forms suited to those ancient times, but in spirit applicable to all times. The verbs are all in the indefinite past—implying if at any time a widow has so acted—if her past conduct has been of such a kind! The bringing up of children must refer to the members of her own family, and, of course, could only be intended as a qualification in the cases where such a family existed—not excluding those who might in all other respects have maintained the most blameless deportment, but wanted the opportunity of proving themselves to be good nurses and trainers of children. Viewed generally, the things required of those who in old age and dependent circumstances were to receive the esteem and support of the church, were such as gave evidence of a faithful, kindly, maternal disposition amid the ordinary duties of domestic life.

Ver. 11. *But younger widows decline*—namely, to put on the list of widows entitled to special guardianship and sustenance on the part of the church. The reason follows: *for when they shall become wanton*[1] *against Christ they desire*

[1] The future, καταστρηνιάσουσιν, seems the better reading, being that of ℵ, C, D, K, L.

to marry. The compound verb καταστρηνιάω is found only here, but in Rev. xviii. 9 we have the simple verb στρηνιάω, which occurs also in the later Greek comedy, and in the sense of wantoning, or living deliciously; so that καταστρ. is to *wanton against,* to surrender oneself to a carnal and luxurious course of life, as antagonistic to the claims and calling of Christ. Though the apostle represents this as a general thing to be expected in the case of young widows, if they should be admitted to a place on the regular widow list, it is clear he can only be understood to mean that it is what would not be unlikely to happen; and even a few cases happening of a palpable drawing back into a vain, worldly, pleasure-seeking course of life, after being formally received among the desolate, world-renouncing, heart-stricken widows of the church, could not but bring great reproach and scandal upon the religion of the gospel. If any should actually fall into such a backsliding course, it would be at least a mitigation of the evil that the church had not formally numbered them among its orphaned household. As to the marrying, however, or desiring to marry again, which is given by the apostle as the evidence of a wanton disposition, it must plainly not be isolated, but viewed in connection with the circumstances. They might have re-married, as he presently states, without incurring any blame, yea, with his own approval and advice. But as contemplated by him, the re-marrying was the fruit of a growing insensibility to spiritual things, the result of a light, frivolous, sensual tone of mind, fretting under the yoke of Christ, and seeking to break loose from the restraints imposed by it upon the heart and conduct. So that nothing less than an utter shipwreck of the spiritual life was supposed to be involved in the new and backward direction taken by the parties in question.

Ver. 12. Hence the severe judgment pronounced on their case: *having condemnation, because they made void their first faith*—not broke their vow or promise to the church to remain in perpetual widowhood, and which, if it had been referred to, could at most have been designated their *former*, not their *first* faith; but their simple faith in Christ and consecration to His service when they first assumed the Christian name, and were admitted by baptism into the church. Bengel: *Prima fides*, primi temporis fides, quam initio habebant, priusquam viduis adscribebantur. So also Calvin, who, with reference to the other view, justly remarks, it affords too tame a sense, and asks, why the apostle should in that case have said *first faith ?* He therefore holds that the charge is of a much heavier kind—namely, " that they had fallen away from the faith of their baptism, and from Christianity. For so is it wont to be the case, that they who once overstep the bounds of modesty prostitute themselves to all manner of shamelessness." The greater part of modern commentators follow Tertullian, Chrysostom, and others of the ancients, whose ascetic tendencies naturally led them to see here the breach of a promise of widowhood, coupled with active service to the church. But of such a promise and of such service nothing whatever (as we have seen) is said by the apostle, and indeed it belongs to a much later period. If the placing of the persons in question on the church's list of widows proceeded on a sort of tacit understanding or purpose that they would continue in widowhood, it is the whole that can fairly be supposed. And to represent a simple departure from such an understanding or purpose as of itself inferring a renunciation of their Christian faith, and an incurring of divine condemnation, had been a severity which it seems impossible to reconcile with the genius of the gospel, or with the liberty conceded and sanctioned by the apostle himself. It is not, therefore, we conclude, the simple question of adherence to a state of widowhood, or of departure from it, but such a course of defection from the decorum and purity becoming the gospel of Christ as argued a virtual abandonment of the faith.

Ver. 13. Other proofs are here given of their tendency in that direction, and such as would naturally grow by the comparative ease in which they might be enabled to live in consequence of the pecuniary support ministered to them by the church. *Moreover, they learn also to be idle, going about from house to house.* The connection seems plainly to require that the expression in the first clause, ἀργαὶ μανθάνουσιν, should be taken in the sense here ascribed to it; for it immediately follows, *and not only to be idle, but tattlers also*, etc., clearly implying that idleness had been predicated of them in what went before. The construction is certainly peculiar, but is merely, after all, as well stated by Winer (*Gr.* § 45), " an abbreviated mode of expression, such as we sometimes find elsewhere with an adjective (Plato, *Euthyd.* 276, *b*, οἱ ἀμαθεῖς ἄρα σοφοὶ μανθάνουσιν, and frequently διδάσκειν τινὰ σοφόν), which does not, like the participle, include the notion of time and mood. This exposition," he adds, " which is adopted by Beza, Piscator, and others, and has recently been approved by Huther, is supported by the fact that ἀργαί is taken up again in the following clause as the principal word." He therefore justly discards the interpretation which had been given by some previous expositors, coupling the verb μανθάνουσιν with the participle following, περιερχόμενοι, and rendering, *they learn to go about idle.* But this is not really the sense that would be gained by so construing the passage, as μανθάνειν, when followed by a participle having reference to the subject, signifies, not to learn, but to *perceive, understand*, or *remark* (see also Jelf, *Gr.* § 683). The apostle justly regarded it as a great evil, and the proof of a frivolous, unsanctified, worldly spirit, that young widows should fall into idle, gossiping habits, and unwise in the church to place them in circumstances which would tempt them into such ways. The later expressions in the verse merely point to the different forms which the evil in the case supposed naturally assumes: φλύαροι, *loose talkers*, babbling out whatever might come into their minds; περίεργοι, busybodies, intermeddling with affairs which did not properly concern them; λαλοῦσαι τὰ μὴ δέοντα, *speaking things which they ought not*, which were not befitting, or, as it may be explained, carrying about reports and sayings from one family to another, and so giving rise to serious misunderstandings, jealousies, and strife. The plain remedy for all this, the most effective check against it, would manifestly be to throw those younger widows as much as possible on their own resources, and encourage them to take any fitting opportunity that might present itself of obtaining a settlement in life, and having households of their own to occupy them. And this is precisely what the apostle advises in the next verse.

Ver. 14. *I wish, therefore, that the younger* [widows]—this is certainly what must be supplied, widows alone being the subject of discourse, not generally women—*marry, bear children, manage the house, give no occasion for reproach to the adversary.* The *therefore* indicates the connection with what precedes: Since the case is such, so great a tendency among the younger widows to turn from the chastened, spiritual course which becomes them, and betake to the improprieties just mentioned, I give as my deliberate mind (for such is the force of βούλομαι) that they should marry, etc. In their position as widows, especially if widows alimented by the church, they were exposed to temptations which usually they were unable to resist; let them therefore get, if they can, into circumstances which will withdraw them from the temptations, and afford scope for the exercise of the ordinary domestic virtues. And when it is said, as a further reason for this, that occasion of reproach would be cut off from the adversary, by the adversary must plainly be understood, not any particular individual either in this world or the world of spirits (Chrys., also Huther, *the devil*), but collectively such as stood arrayed against the cause of the gospel, and were ready to catch hold of anything in the life of Christians which might be turned into a weapon of assault. The closely parallel passage of Tit. ii. 8, though differing in the mode of expression, confirms this view : " that he that is of the contrary part may be ashamed, having no evil thing to say of you." Here also the hostile party are personified as one.

Ver. 15. *For already some have turned away after Satan;* taking him, as it were, for their leader and guide, though in what precise way, or to what extent, is not stated. But it can easily be gathered from the preceding representation. Some of those who were the subject of discourse—namely, the younger class of widows whose names were on the list of the church's almswomen—had already given evidence of the wanton, idle, and troublesome behaviour complained of, so that they had become more like Satan's followers than Christ's. Therefore the apostle would have them regarded as beacons, warning the church not to continue the over-indulgent treatment it had begun to exhibit toward such. This argues nothing as to the time of the composition of the epistle; for a very few cases of the kind referred to, and such as might well enough have occurred within a comparatively limited period, would have been quite sufficient to justify the reference, and the advice grounded on it.

Ver. 16. *If any woman that believes hath widows, let support be given to them,*[1] *and let not the church be burdened, that*

---

[1] There are two variations here from the received text. The first and most important is the simple πιστή (instead of πιστός ἢ πιστή), the reading of ℵ, A, C, F, G, P, also the Vulg. as represented by the Cod. Amiat. (si qua fidelis), Cop., Arm., and some of the Fathers. The other reading is found only in D, K, L of the older MSS., and was doubtless introduced as a correction, because it seemed strange that a charge of

it may relieve those who are widows indeed. A return is here made to the principle of *private* beneficence with respect to young or widowed relatives, and *that* for the purpose of extending it somewhat beyond the line indicated in vers. 4 and 8. In these earlier verses the children and widows spoken of were relatives of the nearer kind; they belonged to the believer's household, and had consequently the strongest claim on the means and resources of the house. But now a wider circle is embraced. There might be widows, the apostle suggests, who were not constituent members of a believer's family, such as a sister, or step-daughter, or niece; and in cases of that description, the home resources (if adequate) should, according to the apostle, be charged with the maintenance of the bereaved, so as to allow the benefactions of the church to be applied to the support of those who were widows in the stronger sense, destitute in themselves, and without the sympathy of any near Christian relative to fall back upon. The direction is founded on the great principle everywhere recognised in the gospel, that the grace of salvation comes, not to supplant, but to sanctify and elevate, the relations of nature, and the affections these are fitted to call forth; so that its influence should be manifested in honouring to the full the claims of kindred, and rendering obedience to them more prompt, and generous, and noble. That only a believing woman is mentioned as possibly having widows to whom such private kindness and support should be extended, is merely to be regarded as defining more closely the class of cases referred to—cases in which a widow might be conveniently taken charge of by a Christian female, and

the kind given here should be connected with believing females only, and not also with men. But the whole section treats of female obligations; and the oversight of widows in a household properly belonged to the female head of each. The other change is ἐπαρκείσθω, instead of ἐπαρκείτω, the reading of ℵ, A, F, G.

made part of the household. A very limited class, usually; and the charge is put somewhat generally: Let support be given them, without saying how. She must interest herself in obtaining it.

Ver. 17. *Let the elders who govern* (or preside) *well, be counted worthy of double honour, especially those who labour in word and teaching.* That elders alone are mentioned in connection with the government or presidency of the churches, is again a clear proof that they were the only spiritual overseers known to the apostle. But whether the passage is available to prove that there was in the apostle's days a formal distinction among those who bore the common name of presbyter—as that some were set apart to the work of both teaching and ruling, and others to that simply of ruling—is certainly not expressly said, and has often been disputed, as well by Presbyterian and Independent writers as by Roman Catholics and Episcopalians. Vitringa has discussed the matter at considerable length in his work on the Synagogue (L. ii. c. 3); and though on other grounds favourable to the existence of a body of ruling elders in congregations, and deeming them capable of doing much good service, he yet holds this passage to be incapable of rendering support to such a view, and especially on three grounds:—1. That the term *presbyters* is everywhere used by Paul and by the other sacred writers in reference to the stated, ordinary, and perpetual pastors of the church. 2. That the qualifying epithet also, προεστῶτες, is always applied to the same class of officers, and to these only. 3. That the τιμή required to be given them has respect, if not exclusively, yet mainly, to the support due to them on account of their official ministrations,—a support proper only to those who were known to be engaged in the discharge of clerical functions. These are substantially the grounds on which the same view is maintained still, with the additional consideration of a historical kind frequently introduced, that ecclesiastical antiquity is silent respecting a class of presbyters whose duty was to rule merely, as contradistinguished from both ruling and teaching. Here we have to look at it simply in an exegetical point of view; and in this respect, the closing portion of the note of Ellicott gives, so far, what must be regarded as the fair and natural import of the apostle's language: "The concluding words, ἐν λόγῳ καὶ διδασκαλίᾳ, certainly seem to imply *two* kinds of ruling presbyters—those who preached and taught, and those who did not; and though it has been plausibly urged that the *differentia* lies in κοπιῶντες, and that the apostle does not so much distinguish between the functions as the execution of them (see especially Thorndike, *Prim. Gov.* ix. 7), it yet seems more natural to suppose the existence, in the large community at Ephesus, of a clerical college of governing elders, some of whom might have the χάρισμα of teaching more eminently than others." But it must in fairness be added, that this teaching qualification appears here rather as a separable adjunct than an essential attribute of the presbyteral function,—a gift which, in so far as possessed and faithfully exercised, would materially contribute to the efficiency of the office, and entitle him who so held it to special honour, yet not so as to disqualify those who wanted it from discharging, and even discharging with credit, its primary duties. Seeing it was a spiritual community which was here under consideration, a certain didactic power must be understood to have belonged to every one who could rightly take part in the government of its members; for it belonged to his office that he should at least be able to discern between carnal and spiritual in the characters of men, be capable of testing their knowledge in divine things, and by private fellowship and friendly admonition, if not otherwise, subserve the interests of truth and righteousness among them. So much must be supposed inseparable from the office of presbyter, as held by every qualified person; but the gift of teaching in the more distinctive sense, or, in modern phrase, of preaching the gospel with intelligence to the edification of others, is not represented as indispensable. A man might as a presbyter govern, and even govern well, without it. And, indeed, as Lightfoot remarks (*Com. on Philip.* p. 192), having respect to the actual state of things in most of the early churches, "*government* was probably the first conception of the office,"—hence also in this passage *governing* is the distinctive epithet coupled with presbyters; yet he justly adds, "that the work of *teaching* must have fallen to the presbyters from the very first, and have assumed greater prominence as time went on." This was a species of development which, in the natural course of things, could not but take place, as the visits became rarer of the first heralds of the gospel, as the more special *charismata* of the Spirit also began to be withdrawn, and the churches themselves grew in their membership, and naturally called for greater fulness and variety in public ministrations of word and ordinance. The teaching function would naturally, in such circumstances, come more and more into requisition; and the presbyters who more peculiarly possessed it would also, as a matter of course, rise into greater prominence, and in process of time come to be regarded as alone properly entitled to the name of presbyter. Yet the process was very slow and gradual, as in the Ignatian epistles, with all the extravagance that otherwise characterizes them, the president of the presbyterate (bishop, as he is there termed) appears to have taken upon himself nearly all the more distinctive parts of public worship; and so late even as Cyprian's time, presbyters and presbyter-teachers were still spoken of as sometimes distinct — indicating, apparently, that persons might possess the one function without also possessing the other (Ep. 23, Oxford Ed. 29).

On the whole, therefore, we seem warranted to draw from the passage the following conclusions: That while it furnishes no ground for maintaining that any formal distinctions were made between one member and another of the presbyteral body as to ruling and teaching, the function of government was originally the more prominent element in their collective calling; that the discharge of this function, from its very nature, involved a certain capacity for conveying spiritual instruction, though it might often be only in a private and conversational manner; that, however, the gift of ministering publicly in the exhibition of gospel truth became gradually more important for the interests of religion, and necessarily distinguished, according to the degree in which it was possessed and exercised, one presbyter from another; so that the respect and honour due to all for their office sake, more especially gathered around those who, besides being faithful in governing, also proved successful in instructing and edifying the members of the flock.

As to the mode of expression to be given to this higher estimate of that class of elders, indicated here by *double honour*, διπλῆς τιμῆς, there can be no doubt, from what follows in the next verse, that it includes pecuniary remuneration; but "that τιμή here designates only such remuneration, or precisely a definite salary, is what cannot be made out, either from the expression or from the connection. Τιμή is consideration, honour, here certainly used with a particular respect to remuneration as the special mode of expressing it" (Huther). Consequently the epithet *double* is not to be taken in the strict sense, as if the presbyters in question were to have awarded to them exactly twice as much as the others, or, as some would take it, twice as much as the widows mentioned in ver. 3; for this would imply that the term *honour* must be limited to the definite sense of *pay* or *salary*, which it does not properly bear. Hence, also, the supposed allusion (by Hammond, for example) to the double portion of the first-born, indicating that "the bishop who dischargeth his duty or prefecture well, should be looked upon in all respects as one that hath the primogeniture of maintenance as well as dignity," falls of itself to the ground. *Double* is but a specific mode, common in all languages, of expressing *much* or greater in comparison with something else (hence Theodoret explains by πλείονος); and this emphatic attribution of honour, expressing itself in substantial gifts and marks of respect, was to be given to those who devoted themselves most to the ministry of the word,—in proof, as Milton puts it, that "laborious teaching is the most honourable prelaty that one minister can have above another in the gospel."

Ver. 18. *For the Scripture saith*,—the *for* implying that the passage to be quoted supports the sentiment just expressed,—*Thou shalt not muzzle an ox while treading out*, namely, the corn; or, as it might be expressed, Thou shalt not muzzle an ox when threshing. But the form of expression points to the peculiar mode of threshing in the East, by driving oxen over heaps of corn lying on the barn-floor, and either by their feet, or by means of a hurdle drawn after them, bruising the mass so as to separate the grain from the straw and chaff. It was a clumsy and imperfect style of operation, but the prevalent one in Bible lands and times. The passage respecting it is taken from Deut. xxv. 4, and is one of a series of directions enjoining kind and considerate behaviour. It is the only one that has immediate respect to the lower animals; all the rest bear on the conduct that should be maintained toward one's fellow-creatures, and especially toward those who might be in the unhappy position of bondmen; so that we can scarcely suppose this somewhat exceptional instruction could have been designed for the exclusive benefit of oxen.

We may rather suppose it was intended, by carrying the injunction to cultivate a tender and beneficent disposition so low, to make it all the more sure that such a disposition should be exercised toward brethren of one's own flesh, most especially toward those who were laying themselves out in self-denying labours for the public good. It is therefore a perfectly legitimate application which is made of the passage here, and in 1 Cor. ix. 9, to the labourers in the Christian ministry. Such an application is in entire accordance with its spirit and aim, and can hardly be termed, in the ordinary sense of the word, *typical*. It is merely to carry the kind and considerate treatment which it sought to foster and call forth into a related but higher sphere—to claim for the divinely-commissioned labourers in God's spiritual harvest something akin to what a provision in the law had required of men toward the inferior animals that helped them in the harvest-field of nature. One claim, in a manner, and yet another; for the higher species of labourers here, and the unspeakably nobler service rendered by them, obviously gave an immensely greater strength to the obligation. If *that* was fitting, then how much more this!

The apostle, however, enforces his exhortation by another saying—one relating to the service of rational creatures: *And the labourer is worthy of his hire.* Is this also to be reckoned a scriptural quotation? or is it referred to simply as a maxim of ordinary life? The former opinion has the sanction of several commentators, and latterly it has been advocated by Baur and those of his school as one of their arguments for transferring the authorship of the epistle to a period subsequent to the apostolic age,—a period when New Testament Scripture had come to be formally quoted, as previously was done with the writings of the Old Testament. It is a kind of argument in which the wish is father to the thought. There is no reason for supposing that the apostle meant his reference to Scripture to extend further than the peculiar passage selected from Deuteronomy. What follows is a common proverb, which did not require to be backed by inspired authority, and which in a similar way is employed by our Lord in an address to His disciples (Matt. x. 10; Luke x. 7). It is perfectly possible, and indeed altogether probable, that St. Paul was cognisant of the use which had been made of it by our Lord: for both in his First Epistle to the Corinthians (chap. vii.), and in his address to the elders of Ephesus, he expressly alludes to specific utterances of Christ—in the latter case, indeed, to one that has found no record in any of the Gospels (Acts xx. 35); and it is not to be imagined that the apostle should have remained ignorant to the close of his life of so important a part of our Lord's instructions as the great missionary address in which this passage occurs. But that affords no ground for supposing that he, or any other person in his name, meant the maxim under consideration to be regarded as a formal quotation from it: the object in view was best served by adducing a proverbial saying, which the common sense of mankind—their sense of what is just and right—has made current in respect to those who have laboured for their interest, that the labourer is worthy of his hire. If so in the commonest relations and employments of life, how should it be otherwise in that special field of labour which is occupied by the faithful minister, and which involves much that is peculiarly trying to flesh and blood? But this prudential maxim, it should be added, is introduced, like the legal prescription before it, merely for the sake of the general principle embodied in it; and to argue from it, as some do, that only pecuniary remuneration or salary was all that the apostle had in his eye in the honour due to teaching presbyters, is to press the matter too far, and to make a use of the one saying that cannot properly be made of the other.

Ver. 19. *Against an elder* (that is, manifestly, one in the presbyteral office) *receive not an accusation, except it be* (ἐκτὸς εἰ μὴ, a double negative to strengthen the proviso) *upon two or three witnesses,* — namely, upon their united testimony as the ground of formal proceedings. According to the ancient Jewish law (Deut. xvii. 6, xix. 5), the testimony of two was required to substantiate a charge against any one, whatever might be his position in society; and various reasons have been suggested why only in the case of a presbyter adherence to the common rule should have been pressed. It will certainly not do to say, with Bengel, that the apostle is here speaking only of *receiving* an accusation, not of *accrediting* the charge; for he obviously means receiving it in the sense of making account of it. But the special mission of Timothy must be borne in mind. He had to make inquiries into matters which must often have been of a delicate and somewhat indefinite kind. Occasionally he might be tempted to go upon information which was partial and defective; and he should therefore be the more careful to insist upon sufficient evidence, especially when one in the position of an elder was concerned; otherwise he might entangle the church in worse evils than those he sought to remedy. But this, of course, implied that in all ordinary circumstances the same method should be generally followed; and attention was specially called to the case of presbyters only because a certain deference was due to their position, and the consequences would naturally be of a graver kind should any false step be taken. The sense of ἐπί adopted by Winer (§ 48, 8, *c*), also preferred by Huther, *coram*, in the presence of,—as if the meaning were, that Timothy should only decide on an accusation against an elder when he had two or three others beside him,—is grammatically unnecessary (see Ellicott; also Jelf, *Gr.* § 584), and would give an unnatural turn to the instruction conveyed respecting the cases in question.

Ver. 20. *Those that sin rebuke before all, in order that the rest also may have fear.* The participle being employed to designate the offending parties, τοὺς ἁμαρτάνοντας, implies more than an occasional act of transgression; it denotes persons who are given to sinning, or are known as sinners. Such Timothy is instructed to rebuke openly, before all (for there can be no doubt that the ἐνώπιον πάντων is intended to qualify the rebuking). He was to adopt so severe a method in order to vindicate the cause of righteousness in the community, and to strike fear into others, that they might be deterred from pursuing like devious courses. Hence the case of such is to be distinguished from that of those who may have been overtaken in a fault, and who should, as elsewhere advised, be tenderly dealt with (Gal. vi. 1); and in the original instructions given by our Lord respecting grounds of offence among the members of His community, it was clearly implied that a quiet settlement of matters which involved a certain amount of moral blame may and often should be effected, sometimes without the intervention of any church action, and sometimes again by means of it (Matt. xviii. 15). From the very nature of things, it must always be matter for thoughtful consideration how rebuke should be administered so as best to secure the ends of discipline. Not merely the particular kinds of sin to be dealt with, but the state of society also at the time, must be carefully taken into account, though still there are great landmarks to be stedfastly maintained; and a faithful church must leave no room to doubt that "she cannot bear them that are evil." Some would understand the class of persons described as sinning, and in consequence deserving of rebuke, only of the elders mentioned in the preceding verse. But this is arbitrary, as in the words themselves there is no proper ground for the limitation; and the one verse does not appear to be any way dependent on the other.

Ver. 21. *I solemnly charge thee before God and Christ Jesus,*[1] *and the elect angels, that thou keep these things without prejudging, doing nothing by partiality.* The rendering of διαμαρτύρομαι by *adjure*, as is done by Alford, seems rather too strong; judging from the general use of it by the apostle, a solemn charge or asseveration is what appears to be meant by it (1 Thess. iv. 6 ; 2 Tim. ii. 14, iv. 1). For the purpose of enforcing upon the attention of Timothy, and impressing deeply upon his conscience, the directions which had been given respecting the right ordering of things in the house of God, the apostle now brings his disciple face to face, as it were, with the Redeeming God and Saviour, together with the holy angels in the sanctuary above, and charges him before these glorious witnesses to carry out his instructions, and do all in the sincere, earnest, conscientious manner which became a true servant of Christ. That the angels meant are holy angels, admits of no doubt ; but why they should here—here and nowhere else—be designated *elect*, is not so easily determined. By some (for example Mosheim, Conybeare) it has been understood to denote angels of a more select class—the guardian angels of Timothy and the church of Ephesus, or such angels as were wont to be employed in fulfilling special embassies to men—an altogether fanciful notion. By much the greater number of interpreters take the epithet in the sense of *good* or *holy*, so as to make it comprehensive of all who are not fallen or apostate angels ; and so, apparently, we must hold in substance, though still without losing the more distinctive import of the term *elect*, which implies, indeed, their holiness, but presents them rather as the select objects of God's love (Huther), and perhaps also as His more peculiar instruments of working. As regards the

[1] This is undoubtedly the correct reading, being that of א, A, D, F, Ital., Vulg., Cop., Æth., etc., while the received text, Κυρίου Ἰη. Χ., has quite inferior support.

nearer circle of His intelligent and willing agents, they are His chosen ones; and as such they are here brought into consideration, along with God the Father and Jesus Christ, with the view of stimulating the mind of Timothy to the conscientious discharge of his duty, and carrying him above all the sinister motives and inferior considerations which might tend to create an improper bias in his mind, and dispose him to act from respect of persons. A realizing sense of the glorious beings who were looking down upon him from the world of spirits, would be the most effectual safeguard against such a weak compliance.

Ver. 22. *Lay hands on no one hastily:* with what design? Was it for ordination to ecclesiastical offices? or absolution from scandalous offences? The latter view has found not a few supporters both in former and present times; it is advocated at great length by Hammond, who adduces quotations from the Fathers to show how common the practice was, on receiving offenders back into church communion, to grant them absolution by the imposition of the bishop's hands; so, too, De Wette, Wiesinger, Ellicott. But the evidence is of too late a kind: it altogether fails for the apostolic age, or even the generations immediately subsequent to it. Nor, when the practice had come in, were the better patristic commentators influenced by it in their interpretation of the passage: Chrysostom, Theodoret, Theophylact, all understand the apostle to refer to imposition of hands as connected with ordinations. Thus, Theodoret briefly notes, as if there were no proper room for difference of opinion: "For one ought first to inquire into the life of him on whom hands are to be laid (or who is ordained), and so to invoke on him the grace of the Spirit." Besides, as a man's own writings are our safest guide to a correct understanding of his expressions, we have two other passages in these Pastoral epistles which make mention of the laying on of hands (chap. iv. 14;

2 Tim. i. 7), and they both refer to the matter of ordination. In both, indeed, Timothy himself was the subject, having been by imposition of hands set apart to special service in the gospel, and entitled to look for corresponding endowments of the Spirit to qualify him for it. With these examples before us, it would obviously be quite arbitrary here to suppose the apostle starting off to matters of an entirely different kind, without the slightest intimation that he was now using the expression in another sense than he elsewhere employed it. It is true he had just been speaking of offences, and of the importance of dealing with them in an impartial and faithful manner. But it was in perfect keeping with this, that an exhortation should be given Timothy to beware of making rash appointments to the ministerial office—to take pains beforehand to ascertain the godly life of the persons who should receive the appointment, lest he should be found stamping with his formal approval, and raising to the government of the church, men who were themselves, perhaps, of doubtful character, or amenable to discipline. Hence it is added: *neither participate in other men's sins.* He would virtually have done so, if he was remiss in his appointments to the higher offices in the church, and did not carefully distinguish between the worthy and the unworthy. And further: *keep* THYSELF *pure.* The emphasis is on *thyself*, which is hence placed first in the original. Not only beware, by hasty ordinations or otherwise, of coming into improper alliance with the sins of others, but see that thine own conduct is free from any marked blemishes, and that no one may have occasion to take up against thee the taunt, "Physician, heal thyself." The epithet *pure* (ἁγνός), therefore, should be taken in its general sense of *blameless,* or *holy* (2 Cor. vii. 11; Phil. iv. 8; 1 John iii. 3), not in the specific sense of *chaste,* to which there is nothing in the context to limit it. At the same time, there can be

no doubt that impurity of this description, or even any approach to it, would of all things be the most fatal to Timothy's character and usefulness.

Ver. 23. *No longer drink water*—that is, water exclusively—*but use a little wine for thy stomach's sake, and thy frequent ailments.* The direction here given is in itself plain enough. For some reason not specified, but probably from a desire to testify against prevailing excess by the strictest example of moderation, Timothy had become what is now called a total abstainer: he drunk only water; and the apostle counsels him to relax to some extent in this practice; and instead of restricting himself to water as a beverage, to use a little wine, on the special ground that this might be (medicinally) beneficial to his stomach, and a corrective to his frequent ailments. This has appeared to many too low a ground, considered by itself, for a direction carrying with it apostolic authority, and occurring in the midst of others bearing on pastoral duty. It has consequently been regarded by some, and still is by Ellicott, as having a moral rather than a dietary aim—as a kind of qualification or counterpoise to the charge immediately preceding: Keep thyself pure, but do not therefore deem it necessary to refrain from using a little wine, as thy health may occasionally require, or think of going into ascetic rigour regarding it. Undoubtedly the passage quite naturally admits of being applied against abstinence from wine on ascetic principles, since it shows that the materials of food and drink are to be primarily considered with reference to the sustenance and health of the body, and that there is no merit in abstinence from their moderate use *per se:* in so far as they may be temporarily or habitually disallowed by any one, it should be only on grounds of fitness and expediency, whether derived from the physical or the moral aspect of things. But that is all. To say that the direction was occasioned by the actual appearance of the ascetic tendency in the church, and with the design of checking its progress, is a quite gratuitous assertion, and has the natural cast and impress of the direction against it; although, when that tendency did discover itself, and even led some to object to the use of wine in the Lord's Supper, this passage was most justly appealed to as a proof to the contrary. But when we find the apostle himself assigning a reason for the particular advice he tendered to Timothy, why should any other be sought for? Was it unbefitting one ambassador of Christ to charge another, amid the toils and troubles of his work, to pay some regard to his bodily health, and to take such food and nourishment as was deemed best for the purpose? No one surely will be disposed to allege that—especially since our Lord Himself did not think it beneath Him, in one of His last discourses with His disciples, to give them instructions of a quite cognate nature: He charged them, with a view to their bodily protection and support, to take with them scrip as well as purse, and a sword and garments (Luke xxii. 36); in other words, to neglect no proper precautions for their outward safety and well-being. This instruction to Timothy bears the same general character. He had a great, and in many respects irksome, work to do, with the disadvantage of a delicate and often ailing frame; and if care were not taken to place it under proper dietary treatment, he would inevitably become more or less incapacitated for duty: there might especially ensue that sort of nervous debility and depression, which more almost than anything besides, unhinges the firm resolve of the soul, and disposes it to shrink from the less pleasing parts of pastoral duty. The principle involved, then, in this prudential advice to Timothy, is in its most natural and obvious sense capable of the fullest vindication; it is, indeed, of practical moment for all times; the laborious pastor or evangelist, if he is wise, will never neglect it: for his work's sake, as well as for his personal comfort and advantage, he will endeavour to keep his bodily frame in a sound and healthful condition. And as regards the specific means recommended for this end, the taking of a little wine, the apostle is to be contemplated merely in the light of a friend, exhorting to the use of what was then understood to belong to the proper regimen for such infirmities as Timothy was labouring under. Granting even that wine might not, in the present advanced state of medical science, be found the best specific for his peculiar ailments, that would argue nothing against the propriety of the prescription as coming from the pen of an apostle. He necessarily wrote from the point of view common to him and his contemporaries, having regard to what was *then* believed to be best; and possibly, if we knew more fully the circumstances of the case, it might even still be deemed such: no one, at least, can certainly affirm it to have been otherwise. On every account, therefore, we ought to take the advice tendered by the apostle in its simplest and most obvious import. So considered, it has its value (as already stated in the Introduction) in an apologetic respect, incidentally witnessing to the apostolic authorship of the epistle; its value, also, as an indication of the regard that should be had, even by the most distinguished of God's servants, to the proper regimen and health of the body; and finally, its value as a testimony to the lawfulness of such kinds of food as are adapted to the weal of the body, subject only to considerations of propriety, as contradistinguished from the restrictive prohibitions of a false asceticism.

But if, in dealing with a matter of this kind, we may in one respect take into consideration the change of times, so should we also in another. "How few are there now-a-days," Calvin justly asks, "for whom it might be necessary to interdict water! how many who have to be urged to the restricted use of wine! Moreover, we see here how needful it is for us, even when we desire to act rightly, to seek from the Lord a spirit of prudence, that we may keep the moderation which He would have us to observe! A general rule is laid down, that we should maintain such temperance in meat and drink as may be conducive to our personal health, not for the purpose of prolonging life, but that so long as we continue in life we may be serviceable to God and our neighbours." He then refers to the Carthusians, who carry their asceticism so far, that they would rather die than taste a bit of flesh; and adds: "But if the temperate and abstemious are enjoined not to injure their health by too great reserve, no slight punishment awaits the intemperate, who by surfeiting and drunkenness impair their energy. Such persons are not to be admonished, but rather, as brute animals, to be driven from their pabulum."

Ver. 24. *The sins of some men are manifest*—πρόδηλοι, the πρό having respect to place rather than to time, manifest before or in the sight of men — *going before to judgment; with some, again, they follow after*. The connection of this passage with the preceding cannot be regarded as very close. That it has respect to persons seeking ordination seems to me improbable. It may most fitly be viewed as a supplementary remark that on reflection presented itself to the apostle in respect to the sins of men, which had been the subject of discourse a little previously. Thoughts more directly personal to Timothy, yet growing out of that subject, had meanwhile been introduced by the apostle; and now he reverts to the subject itself, for the purpose of drawing a distinction between one class of sins and another. Some are so notorious, whether from their own nature or from the manner of their committal, that no doubt or uncertainty can prevail respecting them: they are unmistakeable violations of the law of God, and, as it were, herald the doers of them to judgment, crying (like the blood of Abel) for vengeance. By *judgment*, therefore, I would understand chiefly God's, though not excluding man's. It is not said how Timothy should deal with persons guilty of such offences; but the conclusion was obvious. What so manifestly defied the authority and provoked the condemnation of Heaven, must meet with an uncompromising opposition on the part of Christian pastors, and call forth merited rebuke. But besides these, there are sins of a less heinous and more covert kind, which seem rather to follow after than to go before the person who commits them, yet so follow as inevitably some time to let the mournful secret out. But as this may not be immediately, all needful precautions should be taken that the real state of things should be ascertained.

Ver. 25. *In like manner also, the works that are good are manifest, and those that are otherwise cannot be hid.* The τὰ before καλὰ is evidently designed to give prominence to the quality of the actions as good ; and this is best brought out in the English idiom by rendering, not *the good works,* but *the works that are good.* It is a general proposition, and is not to be limited to the *some men* immediately preceding, whose bad deeds done in secret ultimately come to light. Deeds fully deserving the name of good have a kind of self-evidencing character; they speak in a manner for themselves; and those which are of a different description, even though for a time, or under certain aspects, they may appear otherwise, will by and by be discovered in their true character. *They cannot be hid* — that is, when the searching light of God's judgment is let in upon them ; but the saying is strictly applicable only to that, and so confirms the view taken of the *judgment* in the preceding verse. But Christian men, of course, and especially Christian rulers, should, as far as they are called to act in such matters, be at pains to have the truth brought to light.

CHAPTER VI.

Ver. 1. *Whoever are under the yoke as bond-servants, let them reckon their own masters worthy of all honour.* The rendering in the Authorized Version, " as many servants as are under the yoke," gives not an incorrect impression of the meaning to an English reader; but it does so merely from the ambiguity of the term *servants*, which may or may not mean bondmen. But in the Greek δοῦλοι there is no such ambiguity; its proper meaning was *slave* (having its root in δέω, I bind—hence bondman), and, as ordinarily used, the δοῦλοι were those under yoke.[1] The general description properly goes first—*as many as*, or *whosoever*

---

[1] It must be noted, however, that while the meaning here and in many other passages is plain enough, the usage of the New Testament in regard to δοῦλος is of some latitude. The usage, indeed, is derived from the Sept., in which the Hebrew עֶבֶד is sometimes rendered by δοῦλος, even in the case of persons whose service was entirely free (as David's towards Saul, 1 Sam. xix. 4, xxvi. 18, xxix. 3, etc.). It is, moreover, applied there to the relation and service of God's more peculiar instruments of working, very often by David to himself with reference to God, to whom he felt bound to render the fullest obedience (2 Sam. vii. 21; Ps. xix. 11, xxvii. 9, and often elsewhere). This naturally led to a more extended and honourable use of the word by the New Testament writers than is found with classical. It is applied there to true Christians generally (Rom. vi. 16; 1 Pet. ii. 16; Rev. ii. 20, vii. 3, etc.); to apostles, prophets, and ministers of the New Testament church (Matt. xx. 27, xxiv. 45; Luke ii. 29; Acts iv. 29; Gal. i. 10; 2 Tim. ii. 24, etc.); to Moses, the highest authority in the old dispensation (Rev. xv. 3); and even to Christ, the highest in the new (Phil. ii. 7). In all such cases, the rendering *slave*, or *bondman*, would convey an entirely false impression; for while there is implied in the relation a binding or constraining element, it is that of willing, devoted love—not of legal or outward compulsion. In some cases, also, when the relation is simply human, the term δοῦλος denotes plainly the higher class of dependants—stewards or overseers (as in Matt. xviii. 23 sq., xxi. 34, xxv. 14 sq.), not bondmen of any sort.

are under the yoke; and then δοῦλοι specifies the particular kind of yoke—under the yoke as bondmen. The tendency and purport of the exhortation manifestly is, to caution this part of the Christian community to beware of abusing their liberty in the gospel, of imagining that their spiritual calling and privileges entitled them to spurn the outward restraints under which they lay, and disregard the duties of their station. They were rather, on this very account, to behave toward their masters with becoming regard and submission, lest otherwise, as Chrysostom puts it, " if the master should see them carrying themselves loftily because of their faith, he should blaspheme, as if the doctrine were the ground of their insubordination; whereas, if he should see them obedient, he may the more readily believe, and attend to the things that are spoken." Hence the special reason given by the apostle for the dutiful behaviour of the Christian bondmen is, *that the name of God and His doctrine* (or the teaching, namely, of the gospel) *may not be blasphemed.*

Ver. 2. But supposing the masters themselves had embraced the gospel, and master and slave stood on the common footing of brethren in Christ, were those under the yoke still to be held bound to esteem and honour the masters who so held them? Should not the old relations in such a case rather give way? *Practically*, no doubt, they would in a great measure do so. But *formally* it was not the slave's part to demand this, or to act as if, by reason of his church-fellowship with his master, he could claim civil freedom as his right; for this had been to turn the gospel into a political charter, and give rise to the greatest confusion. The change in that direction must be wrought *for* the slave, not asserted *by* him, and could only be brought about by the gradual diffusion of right views respecting men's relation to God, and, growing out of this, their relation one to another. Meanwhile, the most effectual way to secure a partial amelioration, and ultimately a general abolition, of the evil, was by the Christian slaves themselves bearing their burden and doing their part with Christian meekness and generosity, as the apostle here exhorts: *But such as have believing masters, let them not despise them, because they are brethren*—as if the spiritual equality had effaced the civil distinction; *but the rather serve them, because they who receive the benefit are faithful and beloved.* Some (for example, Wetstein) would understand these latter epithets of the slaves, which grammatically might be considered tenable; but the connection is against it, as the object of the apostle manifestly is to present motives which should induce Christian slaves to continue stedfastly in a course of well-doing; and here, in particular, from the position and character of the masters. They were faithful and beloved; and whatever benefit might accrue from the conscientious and diligent labour of the bondmen, these had the satisfaction of knowing it was reaped by persons who were worthy to receive it. The verb ἀντιλαμβάνω, elsewhere used in the sense of laying hold of, with a view to helping or aiding (Luke i. 54; Acts xx. 35), must here mean to lay hold of in the sense of sharing in, or obtaining the participation of the accruing good,—a sense of the word not unknown in other writers. *These things teach and exhort*—those, namely, which had respect to the behaviour of bondmen.[1]

Ver. 3. *If any one teacheth other doctrine, and does not assent to sound words, those* [*namely*] *of our Lord Jesus Christ, and the instruction that is according to godliness.* This description of the false teacher incidentally arose out of the charge in the immediately preceding clause, to teach and exhort after the manner enjoined by the apostle. The word ἑτεροδιδασκαλεῖν has already occurred—chap. i. 3; and both there and here means to teach otherwise, or differ-

[1] For further remarks on the New Testament treatment of slavery, see Appendix C.

ently, that is, as compared with a proper kind of teaching, expressed or understood. This latter sort of teaching has here again, as at chap. i. 10, the epithet *sound* or *wholesome* attached to it, and is explicitly connected with the prophetic agency of Christ—*the sound words of our Lord Jesus Christ;* not necessarily meaning those which were directly spoken by Him, but such as bear upon them the stamp of His authority; along with His own, therefore, those also of His divinely commissioned apostles and evangelists. The teaching which emanated from this source was emphatically of a healthful character, being at once clear in its enunciations and practical in its aim, disposing the soul to grapple with the great interests of its being, and creating in it a distaste for idle speculations and questions that cannot profit. Hence it is said of such Christian teaching, that it is *according to godliness;* that is, in accordance with the nature and interests of godliness. Hence, also, it augured ill for any persons wishing to be regarded as teachers in the church, that they should refuse to come into proper accord with it. Προσέρχεσθαι is the word employed;[1] it means primarily, to come near to, to approach, then to coincide with, to assent to; thus used also by Philo, *de Gigant.*, μηδενὶ προσέρχεσθαι γνώμῃ τῶν εἰρημένων; *Migr. Abr.*, προσελθόντες ἀρετῇ.

Vers. 4, 5. Here follows the result, in a didactic point of view, of the person who so turns aside from the right course of instruction: *he is carried with conceit* (or besotted with pride; see at chap. iii. 6), *knowing nothing* (that is, having no right sense or apprehension of anything), *doting* (νοσῶν, as in a distempered and sickly condition, the opposite of a

---

[1] Tisch., in his eighth edition, follows the single authority of the Sinaitic in adopting here the easier reading προσέχεται, instead of προσέρχεται, which has the support of A, D, F, G, K, L, P, the Goth., Syr., Sah., Cop., Ethiop. versions. The received text seems clearly entitled to the preference.

state adapted to receive the wholesome food of the gospel) *about questions and word-fightings:* things of little or no moment in themselves, but hurtful from the pugnacious spirit which they served to engender and exercise. For thence, as the apostle states, come *envy, strife, blasphemies, evil surmisings, settled feuds:* διαπαρατριβαί, the correct reading,[1] in which the διά, as usual, intensifies the meaning of the compound term, giving it the sense of continued enmities, or conflicts of a more lasting kind (Winer, *Gr.* § 16, *b;* Ellicott). And these settled feuds are further characterized as pertaining to *men corrupted in their mind* (τὸν νοῦν used, as often in New Testament Scripture, of the whole inner man, with respect to moral as well as intellectual qualities), and *destitute of the truth, who suppose that godliness is gain;* not as our translators have put it, "that gain is godliness," which the position of the article before εὐσέβειαν alone renders grammatically untenable, and also against the general feelings of mankind; for no one scarcely would think of identifying gain absolutely with godliness. But there have never been wanting those who suppose godliness to be gain, consider it as a lucrative concern, and profess it only in so far as they find it serviceable to their worldly interests. We have the same sentiment expressed, and with reference to the same class of corrupt teachers, in Tit. i. 11, where they are said to "teach things which they ought not, for the sake of base gain." How the selfish end aimed at by such was actually accomplished, we are not distinctly informed. We may certainly infer it to have been carried on altogether apart from the constituted order and worship of the church—by privately humouring the capricious tastes and unregulated fancies of certain individuals of a semi-religious, speculative cast. Setting themselves forth as men of profound lore, teachers of curious

---

[1] It is that of ℵ, A, D, F, L; the παραδιατριβαί of the received text has no uncial support whatever.

and far-fetched knowledge about sacred things, they drove a trade which found dupes enough to make it by no means unremunerating. It is well known that, both before and subsequent to the gospel era, many of the more depraved and covetous Jews resorted to even baser methods than these, cunningly working upon the fears of the superstitious by plying the arts of magic and soothsaying, in the face of the most express prohibitions and threatenings of the law of Moses. One need not, therefore, be surprised to learn that others with somewhat less, at least, of *open* disregard of the authorities they professed to reverence, yet with the same low desire for worldly gain, should have sought to gratify the religious idlers and speculatists of the time by pretended disclosures of the unseen world, and dogmatical assertions on matters that were at best learned frivolities. They might not inaptly be designated the spiritualists and rappists of early times, and in some cases perhaps stood in a similar relation to the Christian church that persons of that description do now. They were real, though not always the professed, antagonists of its sound doctrine and holy aims.[1]

Ver. 6. *But godliness with contentment is great gain:* the true, in contrast to the fancied or false. It is the mark of a base disposition to cultivate godliness for the sake merely of the temporal gain it may yield; but there is, at the same time, a real and most important temporal gain connected with it (for it is plainly of gain in this sense alone that the apostle here speaks), only it must be godliness of the right stamp: hence godliness with contentment; that is, godliness cultivated for its own sake, not as a stepping-stone to wealth or worldly consideration, and so bringing its own dowry of good along with it, making the soul " satisfied from

---

[1] The addition in the received text, ἀφίστατο ἀπὸ τῶν τοιούτων, from such withdraw thyself, is wanting in the best authorities, ℵ, A, D, F, and most of the versions; only two uncials have it, K, L.

itself." A thought not materially different is expressed by the apostle in Gal. vi. 4: "Let every man prove his own work, and then shall he have rejoicing in himself alone." For to prove one's own work is but a fuller mode of expressing what is meant by true godliness; and the rejoicing that follows—rejoicing in oneself alone—is nothing else than the sweet content and peace of soul which comes from the possession of a conscience purged from dead works, and enabled to relish the communion and service of God.

Ver. 7. A reason is here given for the preceding statement, that the real good for man lies in what he is as a rational and moral being, not in the outward means and possessions he may gather into his lot: *for we brought nothing into the world, because neither are we able to take anything out of it.* Such seems to be the correct reading. The received text has δῆλον before ὅτι with MSS. K, L; but the best authorities, ℵ, A, F, G, want it, and it was in all probability inserted to soften the apparent hardness or difficulty of the connection between the two clauses, and render the import more perspicuous. Taking the passage as it stands in the best supported form, the apostle not merely says that we both enter and leave the world in a state of destitution as to worldly goods, but that the one is ordered with a certain respect to the other: we brought nothing with us of earthly treasure when we were ushered into life here, because neither could we take aught with us when we leave it; thus having a lesson embodied in our very birth, in order that we might keep in view the solemn exemplification it was to find at the hour of death. If we do so, we shall live in the habitual recollection that all we can accumulate of the things of earth during our sojourn in it, is adventitious merely—of the nature of a temporary appendage—and not, therefore, for a moment to be compared with the state of the soul itself in reference to God and righteousness. Here, and here alone, lie the essential elements of our well-being.

Ver. 8. *But* (δὲ, contrasting the avaricious desires of some with what we actually need) *if we have food and raiment, with these we shall be satisfied*, or have sufficient; ἀρκεσθησόμεθα, fut. pass., we shall be sufficed, have all that we really need. Many, after Luther, among others our translators, have taken it in an imperative sense, which the future sometimes undoubtedly bears (Winer *Gr.* § 43. 5). But here it is best to retain the original form, as the apostle is indicating what, on the condition supposed, should be regarded as a fact. The two words employed in the conditional clause—διατροφὰς and σκεπάσματα—occur only here in the New Testament; and though the latter has sometimes been taken in the more general sense of *covering*, so as to include our dwellings as well as our clothes, yet the other is the more natural, as the apostle is speaking simply of what is proper to the individual man—to his proper life and being. In this sense it is taken by the ancient expositors, and is found also in Josephus (*Wars*, ii. 8. 5) and other writers (see in Robinson's *Lex.*). If one, therefore, has these two essentials for the bodily life, more may be dispensed with; nature has the little it can do with; whatever besides is given may be thankfully received and found available to usefulness and comfort—only, not necessary.

Ver. 9. *But they who aim at being rich* (the opposite class of characters to the preceding, having their hearts set upon the superfluities of life, large possessions), such persons get into a perilous, and what usually becomes a downward and ruinous course: first, they *fall into temptation*—that is, are in danger of betaking to means of compassing their end which are not consistent with integrity of character; not only into temptation, but also a *snare*—their haste to be rich involving them in entanglements through which they find it impossible to work their way with a good conscience;

then, as riches increase, the carnal desires and appetites to which these minister grow, they fall into *many foolish and hurtful lusts*, indulge in pleasures and gratifications which are in themselves unreasonable, and in their effects deteriorate the moral well-being of the soul. And these, again, have their downward and deepening tendency—they are *such as* (αἵτινες) *sink men into destruction and perdition.* Truly a *tristis gradatio*, as Bengel remarks; and one that in all ages, and within the pale also of the professing church, has ever-recurring exemplifications. We see it constantly proceeding before our eyes; nor can anything effectually arrest it but that grace of God which brings salvation, and carries the affections of the soul upwards to the things which are not seen and eternal.

Ver. 10. *For a root of all evils is the love of money*—or simply, root of all evils. Putting it in the latter way, the exact counterpart of the original, which also gives prominence to the term *root*, as the apostle undoubtedly meant, we might evade the question whether, if an article were employed, it should be the definite or the indefinite. It is certainly more in accordance with English idiom in such a passage to use an article; and if one is used, then I think, with Middleton, Huther, Conybeare, and Ellicott, against Alford, that the indefinite is the fittest—*a* root of all evils is, etc., or the love of money is *a* root of all evils. No doubt the definite article might also be employed, as Alford contends, for the purpose simply of emphasizing *root*, designating avarice as such a vicious passion, that if it stood alone, all manner of evils might spring out of it. But, on the other hand, the expression so put is ambiguous; for it may also mean that it is the one thing which is so prolific of evil—there is no other of which the same could be predicated: and that is not the case; for it might be said of ambition, and some other passions as well. The question is not, therefore, as Alford seems to consider, whether one might not here, as in other cases, use the definite article in English, where there is none in the Greek, in order to bring out the proper emphasis: one may well enough do so, as in the passage referred to by him (1 Cor. xi. 3), where, as there is but properly one thing of the kind to be thought of, it can occasion no ambiguity. But where the reverse is the case, as in the present instance, it is better to avoid it by employing the indefinite article, even though it should be with a partial sacrifice of the emphasis. The sentiment is, that there is no kind of evil to which the love of money may not lead men, when it once fairly takes hold of them. And the apostle further characterizes the affection by saying, *which some, reaching after, have wandered away from the faith, and pierced themselves through with many pangs.* There is a certain looseness in the structure of the passage, since avarice, or the love of money ($\phi\iota\lambda\alpha\rho\gamma\upsilon\rho\iota\alpha$), being itself an affection of the mind, a lust, one cannot strictly be said to reach or long after it. The passion is obviously identified by the apostle with its object—money as a thing loved and sought after; and some, he says, reaching forth in their desires after this, made a twofold shipwreck: first, of their Christian principles, departing from the faith; and second, of their happiness, piercing themselves through ($\pi\epsilon\rho\iota\epsilon\pi\epsilon\iota\rho\alpha\nu$, transfixed) with many pangs. What precisely these were we are left to infer; but the expression seems to point to inward rather than to outward troubles—to sorrows of heart, the pungent rebukes of conscience, which came upon the individuals referred to when they saw, and had time to reflect on, the shameful course they had pursued.

Ver. 11. *But thou, O man of God, flee these things;* different in character and aims, let your course be also different. The designation *man of God* was in ancient times in frequent use for prophet, because standing in a peculiarly close relation to God, acting as His representative and spokesman to the people; and it is but natural to suppose that, with some reference to that ancient usage, the designation is here applied to Timothy,—reminding him by the very term, that in the special, semi-apostolic agency now entrusted to him, he in effect stood on the relatively elevated position of a prophet, and should take heed to conduct himself accordingly. It might, no doubt, with many commentators, be understood in a more general sense, with reference simply to Timothy's state and calling as a believer. But the whole passage evidently has respect to Timothy's destination as a public witness and servant of the Lord ; and the distinctive epithet, both in itself and in its usage, best accords with that idea. It is again similarly used in 2 Tim. iii. 17 ; and these are the only two passages where it occurs in New Testament Scripture. The things Timothy is exhorted to flee are plainly those mentioned in the immediately preceding context—the love of money, and all the hurtful lusts, and corrupt as well as foolish and unbecoming practices to which it gives rise. But with this negative exhortation the apostle couples a positive : *and follow after righteousness, godliness, faith, love, patience, meekness of spirit* ($\pi\rho a\ddot{v}\pi a\theta\epsilon i a v$, the reading of א, A, F, somewhat stronger than the received $\pi\rho q\acute{o}\tau\eta\tau a$). " As Christian virtues to which Timothy must apply himself, Paul names six, of which each pair stand in a close relation to one another : the two most general ideas go first — righteousness and godliness ; then follow faith and love as the fundamental principles of the Christian life ; and finally, patience and meekness of spirit, which denote the conduct proper to a Christian amid the enmity and opposition of the world to Christ's gospel " (Huther).

Ver. 12. *Maintain the good contest of the faith*—literally, contend the good contest; but this does not quite accord with English usage ; and I deem it better to depart a little from the precise form of the original, than to use an unsuitable combination of words, or convey a wrong impression.

This last is what is done by *fight the fight* of the Authorized Version, and *strive the strife* of Ellicott and Alford. Neither strife nor fight suggests to an English ear the kind of struggle here indicated under a form of expression that bears respect to the ancient games. These games were simply strenuous contests for the mastery in trials of strength and skill; and it is of importance to retain the term *contest*, though we can scarcely couple it with the cognate verb. The contest, however, is characterized as *good*, to distinguish this spiritual contest from the carnal and ambitious wrestlings on the arena. And it is further characterized as that *of the faith* —meaning thereby the specific exercise of faith in the person and work of Christ. The adherents of this faith were like men contending for the mastery against the powers of evil working everywhere in the world around them; they must therefore quit themselves like men, in order to succeed in the conflict. Then the connection is indicated between the contest and the prize: *lay hold of eternal life*, which, as Winer notes (*Gr.* § 43, 2), must mean, Do it in and through the contest; for the laying hold of eternal life is not represented as the result of the contest (though it might have been so), but as itself the substance of the contest: one must grasp the reality, in a measure *now*, in order to maintain the struggle aright, and reach the life in its full and final heritage of blessing.[1]

Having mentioned eternal life, the apostle now drops the figure, and brings the great reality into connection with the Christian calling: *unto which thou wert called, and didst confess the good confession before many witnesses.* The period referred to is undoubtedly that of his formally embracing the faith of Christ's gospel. Timothy was then called to

---

[1] The change of tense, too, is significant, the first imperative in the present, ἀγωνίζου, the second in the aorist, ἐπιλαβοῦ—the former having respect to an action already commenced and to be continued, the latter to an action which is in a manner done at once (see Winer, § 43, 3).

receive the gift of eternal life (Rom. vi. 23; 1 Pet. v. 10); and then also made confession of his belief in the truth in Christ, though the precise moment of his doing so in public before many witnesses, as it is here put, might be either at his baptism or his ordination to the work of the ministry. These are the occasions that naturally present themselves to one's mind in connection with such a statement, and it is needless to think of any other.

Ver. 13. The mention of that confession or witness-bearing which had been made by Timothy seems to have suggested to the apostle's mind another and still higher act of the same kind, which he interweaves in a solemn appeal and charge to Timothy: *I charge thee before God, who preserveth alive*[1] *all things, and Christ Jesus, who before Pontius Pilate witnessed the good confession.* The object of this appeal, and of the specific characters under which God and Christ are here presented, is obviously to strengthen the exhortation which follows, and brace the mind of Timothy to its faithful discharge. God is represented as the preserver of all, and consequently as able to minister protection and support to those who were ready to obey His will, and hazard all for His glory. Then, as the highest example of One who did thus show that He made account of nothing in comparison of the fealty he owed to the claims of truth and righteousness, the apostle points to the fearless and uncompromising testimony given by Christ before Pontius Pilate. (Ἐπὶ admits of being taken in the sense either of *under*, with the Vulgate, Gothic, English versions, De Wette, Ellicott, etc., or *before*, as the Syriac, Chrysostom, Huther, Alford, etc.; but the latter seems the more natural sense, as it is only in connection with the closing scenes of our Lord's

---

[1] The correct text appears to be ζωογονοῦντος, the reading of A, D, F, G, not ζωοποιοῦντος, which is the received text, and is the reading of א, K, L; and the meaning of ζωογ. in the sense of preserving alive is confirmed by the only other passages where it occurs, Luke xvii. 33, Acts vii. 19.

life, and especially with the testimony He then bore to His own person and kingdom, and so shortly after sealed with His blood, that the evangelical record brings Him into contact with Pontius Pilate.) And in regard to the testimony itself, there is, I think, room for the distinction drawn between it and Timothy's in the preceding verse, indicated by Bengel: *testari* confessionem, erat Domini; *confiteri* confessionem, Timothei. The one was of a fundamental or primary character, the other responsive and secondary. Christ bore witness to the truth respecting Himself and His kingdom, as in the closest manner identified with it, and being it; and His confession, as Bengel justly says, " animates all other confessions"—Timothy's among the rest—gave birth to them, indeed. But we may still say, with Huther, that the confession which the disciple of Christ is called to make, and which is declared to have been made by Timothy, is as to its nature nothing else than that which was testified by Christ; and hence it is in each case "*the* good confession"—a specific and formal utterance in respect to the essentials of the Christian faith—differing, it may be, and doubtless often does, in words, but coinciding in the substance of the doctrines confessed. Some commentators appear to broaden the difference between the confessions beyond what the language necessarily implies, or even properly admits of.

Ver. 14. Here follows the thing charged upon Timothy: *that thou keep the commandment spotless and unrebukeable until the appearance of our Lord Jesus Christ.* Various shades of meaning have been put upon *the commandment* ($\tau\grave{\eta}\nu$ $\grave{\epsilon}\nu\tau o\lambda\acute{\eta}\nu$) which Timothy was enjoined to observe or keep. As there is nothing of a special kind mentioned in the preceding context to which it can fitly be referred, it is most naturally understood of the moral obligation generally, the injunction or rule implied in the very nature of the gospel to adhere to the great principles of truth and righteousness, or to give the gospel as to what it teaches and requires a practical and embodied form. This practical imperative of the gospel (if we may so speak) the apostle calls Timothy to keep spotless and unrebukeable, —a somewhat peculiar form of exhortation, certainly, as these epithets are strictly applicable to persons only, though there are not wanting instances of a more extended application in other writers (as in Philo, *de Opif.*, ἡ ἀνεπίληπτος τέχνη; Plato, *Phil.* 43, ἀνεπιληπτότερον τὸ λεγόμενον). Considered by itself, of course, a thing inherently good cannot become subject to any real tarnish or defilement: it must ever remain what its own essential nature makes it; and of nothing involving moral obligation may this more properly be said than in respect to the ethical bearing of the gospel. But contemplated from a popular point of view, a reproach or charge is naturally conceived to be brought on a scheme of doctrine or duty when its acknowledged representatives give an exhibition of it which palpably offends against men's notions of the pure and good; or, in the case of the gospel, is contrary to its real character. And this is plainly what is meant here: it is that Timothy might be careful so to bear himself in the ministry of the gospel, and the intercourse of daily life, as to prevent God's word and service from suffering reproach through his failures; and though the expressions used by the apostle have immediate respect to the commandment itself, not to the observance of Timothy, yet practically it is all one with saying, as Chrysostom puts it, that Timothy should beware of contracting any stain in respect to his doctrine or manner of life. And this *till the appearance* (*the epiphany*) *of our Lord Jesus Christ*—the second advent, which was certainly contemplated by the eye of faith as near, yet not so as to be confidently expected at any definite period, or within the limits of that generation. This is rendered clear by the statements of Paul in one of his earliest epistles

(2 Thess. ii. 1–12), and also in a measure by what follows here.

Vers. 15, 16. These verses begin with a more particular description of the expected appearance of Christ in its relation to God, and then run out into a doxology, celebrating the incomparable greatness and glory of God. This Baur and others would regard as a protest against the semi-polytheism or dualism of the Gnostics—an entirely fanciful and unnatural view. The object seems rather to have been to fortify the mind of Timothy to a consistent and persevering adherence to the Christian faith and life amid the scorn or opposition of worldly powers of the stamp of Pontius Pilate, by placing distinctly before him the sole supremacy, the peerless eminence, and infinite sufficiency of Him who has decreed the future manifestation in glory of Christ, as He had done that of His past humiliation. This affords a reason perfectly cognate to many others introduced by the apostle in this epistle (chap. i. 18, 19, ii. 5–7, iii. 15, 16, v. 21, etc.), and in proper keeping with the connection. *Which* (namely, appearance) *in His own seasons He shall show,* [who is] *the blessed and only Potentate, the King of kings and Lord of lords, who only has immortality, dwelling in light that is unapproachable, whom no man hath seen nor can see: to whom be honour and power everlasting. Amen.* In regard to what is said at the outset about the appearing of Christ, that it is to take place in God's *own seasons,* there is plainly indicated a certain indefiniteness, as in regard to a matter which belongs to the secret things of God, not therefore to be pronounced upon by the superficiality and littleness of human foresight (Bengel: brevitatem temporis non valde coarctuans). The words remind us—perhaps were purposely designed to remind us—of the address given by our Lord before His ascension to the disciples on this very subject: "It is not for you to know the times or the seasons, which the Father hath put in His own power"

(Acts i. 6),—the seasons, namely, which concern the greater movements of Christ's kingdom, and especially, as here, His advent in glory. Nay, our Lord Himself had previously told them, that as regards the precise period when He should come to manifest Himself in the glory of that kingdom, even He did not know it in His humiliation (Mark xiii. 32), doubtless because He *did not wish* to know it; the knowledge would have been unsuited to that transient and provisional state of things. God is here designated *the blessed*, as at chap. i. 11—the antithesis of everything that can be called sorrow or vexation; also the *only Potentate* (μόνος δυνάστης)—alone in the universe possessed of independent right, absolute sovereignty. The epithet *King of kings and Lord of lords* is, with a slight variation in the form, directly applied to Christ in Rev. xvii. 14, xix. 16; for in this, as in all divine prerogatives, "all that the Father hath is His." But it is plainly God the Father that is here the subject of discourse, as some parts of the description are not properly applicable to Christ as the God-man. When it is said of God that He only has immortality, the meaning plainly is, He alone has it of Himself—it is in Him as its fountainhead. John v. 26, which declares the Father to have life in Himself—life in the full and absolute sense—is substantially parallel. Further, He is represented as dwelling in an atmosphere of light—light that from its excessive splendour and intense brilliancy is incapable of being approached or looked upon by the eye of man: compare John i. 18; 1 John i. 5; Ps. civ. 2. The whole of this sublime representation concludes, and is most appropriately wound up, with an ascription of honour and power to God, as alone entitled to receive the homage and adoration of His intelligent creatures.

Ver. 17. The apostle here again reverts to the subject of riches, but now under a different aspect, with reference not to those who made wealth their idol, and were ready to sacrifice principle and character for its attainment, but to such as, having acquired riches, still retain their Christianity, and are willing to use what they possess in accordance with the truth of God and their own best interests. *Charge them that are rich in this world not to be high-minded, nor to set their hopes on the uncertainty of riches, but on God, who ministers to us all things richly for enjoyment.* The instruction to give such a charge obviously implies, that there already were persons in the church at Ephesus to whom the epithet *rich* might not improperly be applied. But that, as every one knows, is a relative term, and in one country or one stage of social progress might include persons whom none almost would think of associating with it in another. It is absurd, therefore, to find an argument against the early existence of the epistle—as is done by Schleiermacher and others—in the mention of rich persons in the church at Ephesus; and, indeed, the disturbance occasioned there many years before the real date of the epistle by Demetrius and his craftsmen, was alone a proof that even then the movement from the old worship in favour of Christianity must have embraced individuals in various grades of society; not a few that were well-to-do in the world, as well as those who were comparatively poor. The persons who might be deemed relatively rich were to be exhorted not to be high-minded, nor to have their hopes set on *the uncertainty of riches*—ἠλπικέναι ἐπὶ πλούτου ἀδηλότητι, a very striking expression. The verb is in the perfect; and being used in connection with a charge to the persons in question, it must mean that they ought not to have done so in the past, nor continue to do so now—not so to hope in such an object as if it were a settled and abiding habit of mind. Then, instead of putting riches as the object of the hope, the apostle rather *indicates the quality* in riches which rendered it peculiarly unsuitable for such a purpose. It is a rhetorical rather than a strictly grammatical construction ; for the term for riches is undoubtedly the principal substantive, and the natural construction would have been to put it in the dative, and couple it with an adjective, expressive of the uncertain element adhering to them — πλούτῳ τῷ ἀδήλῳ. But the mode of expression in the text is not arbitrary ; as Winer remarks (*Gr.* § 34, 3, *a*), " it is chosen for the purpose of giving more prominence to the main idea, which, if expressed by means of an adjective, would be thrown more into the background : hence it belongs to rhetoric, not to grammar." To trust in riches, the apostle would have it understood, is virtually to make uncertainty one's confidence, since both their continuance with us, and our possession of them, may at any moment come to a termination. The contrast to such an insecure foundation is God, the eternal, the all-sufficient, who ministers richly to His people's necessities and just desires, and who, as a source of enjoyment to those who trust in Him, can never fail.

Ver. 18. Here we have in one or two particulars the positive aspect of rich men's duties : *that they do good* (ἀγαθοεργεῖν), *that they be rich in excellent deeds* (ἐν ἔργοις καλοῖς, deeds inherently noble and praiseworthy), *free in distributing, ready to communicate* (or, as Alford puts it, *free-givers, ready-contributors*), not merely imparting of their substance to the relief of the needy and the promotion of good objects, but doing it with a frank generosity and a liberal hand. To act thus is nobly to realize the stewardship of wealth, and, according to the word of our Lord, to make to oneself friends of what, taken merely by itself, is the *mammon of unrighteousness* (Luke xvi. 9).

Ver. 19. The description is here wound up by a word which very strikingly exhibits the connection between such a course of action on earth and its issues in eternity : *treasuring up* (ἀποθησαυρίζοντες, *off* from what would otherwise be lost, and so *up*) *for themselves a good foundation for the future, in order that they may lay hold of what is life indeed.*[1] Two important practical points are here forcibly presented. The first is, the doctrine of a future recompense, the proper employment of one's means in charitable and pious uses, and consequently the doing of good deeds generally, being said to constitute a treasure for the world to come; a treasure which is not an uncertainty, like riches when contemplated by themselves and sought for their own sake, but a *foundation* ($\theta\epsilon\mu\acute{\epsilon}\lambda\iota o\nu$), or well-grounded basis of hope, for the great future. The doctrine could scarcely be more unequivocally put, and is the more remarkable as coming from him who was emphatically the preacher of grace: he saw no incompatibility between a free salvation, the gift of sovereign grace to the sinful, and the placing of those who have become partakers of grace under the law of recompense. And in the teaching of our Lord Himself, the same two doctrines are equally marked characteristics (comp., for example, in Matt. v. 3-10, the first four beatitudes with the second four; or the two parables, Luke xvi. 1-12, Matt. xviii. 23-35). The link of connection between the two is, that the grace which brings salvation as a divine gift, becomes from its very nature to those who receive it their great talent, wherewith they must do service to God, and hereafter be dealt with according as they have themselves done. But is not such a prominent exhibition of the doctrine of reward at variance with the disinterested nature of true excellence? It might be so, if isolated from other parts of the Christian system, but not when taken in its proper connection. "For the

---

[1] Such seems to be the correct reading, $\tau\widetilde{\eta}s$ $\check{o}\nu\tau\omega s$ $\zeta\omega\widetilde{\eta}s$, ℵ, A, D, F, Ital., Vulg., Syr., Cop. versions, and most of the Fathers; while the received text, $\tau\widetilde{\eta}s$ $\alpha\grave{\iota}\omega\nu\acute{\iota}o\upsilon$ $\zeta\omega\widetilde{\eta}s$, is the reading of only two uncials, K, L, with little collateral support. This is also the reading which might naturally suggest itself as an explanation

truth is, that the Christian's love of virtue does not arise from a previous desire of the reward; but his desire of the reward arises from a previous love of virtue. The first and immediate effect of his conversion is to inspire him with the genuine love of virtue and religion; and his desire of the reward is a secondary and subordinate effect, a consequence of the love of virtue previously formed in him. For of the nature of the reward it promises, what does the gospel discover to us more than this, that it shall be great and endless, and adapted to the intellectual endowments and moral qualities of the human soul in a state of high improvement? 'It doth not yet appear what we shall be; but we know that when He shall appear we shall be like Him, for we shall see Him as He is.'"[1] This resemblance is even represented in Scripture as the most essential element both of the Christian state here and of the heavenly state hereafter; and therefore not the actions simply which appear in the life, but the motives also and principles from which those actions proceed, must go together in any just expectation that is formed of future recompense. Beneficent deeds and good deeds generally are valuable most of all on this account, that they are the indications and fruits of a regenerated nature; and such a nature, so proved and exercised, will at last "as by its own elasticity spring to heaven," while that which is in an opposite condition shall not less certainly " descend by its own dead weight to kindred darkness " (A. Butler).[2]

[1] Horsley's 2d Sermon on Phil. iii. 15.
[2] A well-known passage in Newman's discourses puts the matter happily, as regards the *present* relation of goodness to the beneficial consequences that spring from it:—"All virtue and goodness tend to make men powerful in this world; but they who aim at the power have not the virtue. Again: Virtue is its own reward, and brings with it the truest and highest pleasures; but they who cultivate it for the pleasure-sake are selfish, not religious, and will never gain the pleasure, because they can never have the virtue."

The other point here presented is the emphasis laid on *life* in the higher sense — life that really may be called such: rich Christians are exhorted to deal with their earthly means in the manner prescribed, in order that they may *lay hold* of this. Simply as rich men, they were in danger of suffering it to escape from them; certain to fail of it, if they set their hearts on worldly lucre, and the enjoyments to which it ministers. What is meant by such life? It is nothing else than that participation of a divine nature already referred to, which has its beginning here in all spiritual excellence and fruitful working, but will reach its consummation when that which is in part shall be done away, and the perfect shall have come. In this passage, it may be added, St. Paul approaches more nearly to St. John's mode of representation concerning the Life ($\zeta\omega\eta$) than anywhere else—Life, without anything further; Life in the reality being viewed as the one and all of a blessed condition. To exhibit this life as having its fountainhead in the Father, and coming to men as His gift in Christ, is the common teaching of both, and indeed of all the New Testament writers; to St. John only it is peculiar to represent Him, through whom the gift comes, as the Life (John i. 4, xi. 25, xiv. 6, etc.). "In the Father, things are shut up and hidden which manifest themselves in the Son; therefore all things which the Son has belong to the Father: but in the Son the properties of the Father are revealed to men, in order that His name may be celebrated with praise. Life thus lying concealed with the Father in the beginning was manifested to men in the Son; so that when the Father is manifested, the Son is to be seen" (Olshausen, *Opuscula*, p. 193). In regard to men, life in this higher sense is predicated only of such as have, through the action of the Holy Spirit on their souls, been brought to participate of that which is in Christ. The merely natural man ($\psi\nu\chi\iota\kappa o s$) is dead, even while as an inhabitant of the world he lives; "it is the Spirit that quickeneth." And this quickening energy entering into the soul, and linking it through faith in Christ to the proper heritage of life, the body also, by reason of its connection with the soul, must share in the glorious possession; and when both soul and body reach thus their destined perfection, there shall be the full enjoyment of what is here called the life indeed—life in its completeness of purity and blessing.

Vers. 20–22. The conclusion, containing another very earnest charge to fidelity: *O Timothy, keep the deposit* (τὴν παραθήκην, used again in 2 Tim. i. 12, 14, and each time with the same verb). What deposit? Neither here nor in the other two passages in which the word is employed, first with reference to Paul, and then with reference to Timothy, is any further description given of it: the apostle himself commits to Christ's keeping what he calls a deposit; and Timothy had committed to him a deposit to keep, which is simply characterized as *good*. So far, however, the connection here throws some light upon the subject; for the deposit is plainly represented as what, if faithfully kept, would preserve Timothy from the false teachings of the Gnostic school, which were already beginning to make themselves heard: *turning away from the profane babblings and oppositions of knowledge* (the gnosis) *falsely so called, which some professing, erred concerning the faith.* So that remaining stedfast in the one, he should avoid the dangers of the other. And what could possibly avail for such a purpose, but the sound faith or doctrine of the gospel? This is what the apostle himself, in various passages, sets against the false tendency in question, as the only true antidote; for example, at chap. i. 3, 11, 18, iv. 6, vi. 3, etc. So Chrysostom, who identifies the deposit with faith, on the ground that "where faith is not, there is no knowledge; when anything is produced of one's own thoughts, it is not knowledge:" in other words, the errors to be guarded against are the teachings of man; the safeguard against them is what is received by faith from the teaching of God. Tertullian also not only explains it in the same way, but argues against the abuse made of the passage by the Gnostic teachers, to support their assertion that the apostles taught certain things secretly and to a few, which they withheld from others. "What (says he) is this deposit, so secret, that it may be reckoned another sort of doctrine?" And referring to the charge given in chap. i. 18, vi. 13, of this epistle, as probably pointing to the same thing, he proceeds: "From what is written in the preceding and subsequent context, it will be perceived that there is no allusion in the form of expression to any secret doctrine, but rather that he is warned against admitting any other doctrine than that which he had heard from himself (viz. Paul), and that openly—*Before many witnesses*, says he (2 Tim. ii. 2). If by those many witnesses they are unwilling to understand the church, it is of no moment; since nothing could be secret which was set forth in the presence of many witnesses" (*de Præscrip. Hæret.* c. 25). The modern advocates, therefore, of a secret traditional doctrine handed down from Patristic testimony, follow not the Fathers, but the Gnostics, in their use of this passage; and in the interpretation they put on it, they always assume two things which are absolutely incapable of proof,—first, that Timothy's deposit embraced something of importance not in Scripture; and second, that Patristic tradition is an infallible informant as to what that deposit was (see Goode's *Rule of Faith*, ii. p. 78). Even Vincentius Lirinensis, in a long passage regarding the deposit in his *Commonitorium*, expressly designates it, like Tertullian, as no more of private teaching, than of private invention: "Quid est depositum? . . . rem, non ingenii sed doctrinæ, non usurpationis privatæ sed publicæ traditionis;"—nothing else, in short, than the great facts and principles which constituted the burden of apostolic teaching.

The profane babblings and oppositions of the falsely named knowledge have already been referred to, both in the Introduction to the epistles and at chap. i. 6, 19, 20. What is meant is that peculiar kind of religious speculation which originated in the East, but gradually spread westward to Asia Minor, Greece, and Egypt, and which bears the general name of Gnosticism, because of the predominant account it made of *gnosis*, or knowledge. It was this, however, still only in an incipient form, not as ultimately developed into the regularly constructed systems, which appeared one after another in the second and third centuries, and which, though courting alliance with Christianity, were always denounced as essentially antichristian by the Fathers. It was this in spirit and character, even in its earlier and more sporadic existence, in which it assumed a variety of phases and manifestations; so that it cannot be either very particularly characterized or identified with any single locality and individual, but was the native fruit of the spirit of the age, animated and influenced by the circumstances of the time (see Reuss, *Theol. Chretienne*, vol. ii. p. 641). But being in its very nature of a presumptuous and pragmatical tendency, whenever yielded to, it was sure to lead men away from the simple and earnest faith of the gospel.

The grace (namely, of God) *be with you!*[1] or simply, Grace be with you: thee, and those with thee.

(For the subscription, see close of INTRODUCTION.)

[1] The best authorities have ὑμῶν, ℵ, A, F, G, P, which at 2 Tim. iv. 22 is the reading also of the received text.

THE EPISTLE OF PAUL TO TITUS.

THE precise period of St. Paul's visit to Crete for the purpose of preaching the gospel and organizing Christians, as already stated in the INTRODUCTION, is not certainly known. But from the great similarity between certain parts of this epistle and the First Epistle to Timothy, the probability is, that the visit took place some time during the later operations of the apostle in Asia Minor and Greece, and that consequently this epistle to Titus, who had been left behind to complete the work begun by the apostle, must have proceeded from his pen at no great interval from the time when he indited the first to Timothy. The Second Epistle to Timothy belongs to a period considerably later, and presents us with the last record we have of the apostle's thoughts and experiences. In a consecutive exposition, therefore, the Epistle to Titus fitly takes precedence of the Second to Timothy.

CHAPTER I.

Ver. 1. *Paul, a servant of God, also an apostle of Jesus Christ, for the faith of God's elect, and full knowledge of the truth that is according to godliness; 2. in hope of eternal life, which God, that cannot lie, promised before eternal times; 3. but in its own seasons manifested His word in preaching, which was entrusted to me, according to the commandment of our Saviour God; 4. to Titus, [my] true son in respect to the common faith: Grace and peace from God our Father, and Christ Jesus our Saviour.*

St. Paul's mode of designating himself here does not exactly coincide with his form of expression in any other epistle. Elsewhere he calls himself a servant, or bondman of Christ (Rom. i. 1; Gal. i. 10; Phil. i. 1; Col. iv. 12), but here only of God: a noteworthy variation, not on its own account, but as a mark of genuineness; for it is impossible to conceive what motive could have induced any imitator to depart in such a manner from the apostle's usual phraseology. The δέ coupling his calling as an apostle of Christ with his relation to God as a servant, cannot be taken in an adversative sense, for there is really no opposition; but it is used, as not unfrequently, "to subjoin something new, different, and distinct from what precedes, though not strictly opposed to it" (Winer, *Gr.* § 53, 7). The rendering of Ellicott, *and further*, while giving the proper shade of meaning, seems somewhat too formal, broadening more than is natural in a brief introductory description, the difference between God's servant and Christ's apostle. But what is to be understood by this apostolical calling being κατὰ πίστιν ἐκλεκτῶν Θεοῦ? If one were to render, with the A.V., after the Ital., Vulg., and many modern commentators, "*according to* the faith of God's elect," it is difficult to understand why this should have presented itself to the apostle's mind as anyhow the measure or rule of his apostleship. It appears, indeed, so understood, to invert the proper order of things; for there can be no doubt that he received his apostleship with a view to promote or bring into exercise the faith of God's elect, and in connection therewith the knowledge of the truth, and not inversely. The preposition, therefore, must here (with Winer, *Gr.*

§ 49, d. *c*, and many of the best commentators,—Theodoret, ὥστε πιστεῦσαι τῆς ἐκλογῆς ἀξίους,—Huther, Ellicott, Alford, etc.) be taken in the sense of destination *for* or *to*—as, in classical Greek, κατ' ἀτιμίαν λέγω means, I speak for dishonour—with a view thereto (Her. ii. 152; Thuc. v. 7, vi. 31). The apostle indicates the faith of God's elect and the special knowledge of divine truth, on which it is grounded, as that with respect to which he had been made an apostle, and toward which, therefore, all he did in this character must be mainly directed. For the elect's sake, he elsewhere tells us (2 Tim. ii. 10), he endured all things, and for their sake too he held his commission as a divinely authorized teacher of the gospel, that God's purpose concerning them might reach its end. As the elect, or genuine people of God, not only have a knowledge, but a special or peculiar knowledge of the truth, so the word used is ἐπίγνωσιν—knowledge intensified, or in the fuller sense (see at 1 Tim. ii. 4). And it is said to be κατ' εὐσέβειαν—knowledge that has respect to, or tends in the direction of, godliness. So that the sense of the preposition here is much the same as in the preceding clause. True Christian or saving knowledge is thus sharply distinguished from all that is of a merely speculative kind, or is without any moral aim; this throughout bears on the cultivation and exercise of holy principle. And the fact is of importance for the preachers of the gospel now, as well as for the apostle then; their preaching is not what it should be, except and in so far as it aims at the same practical result.

Ver. 2. *In hope of eternal life* — ἐπ' ἐλπίδι, on this as the basis. But to what did it form the basis? Was it St. Paul's office as an apostle, or that which it ministered to— namely, the faith and knowledge of God's elect? Manifestly, this latter is the more natural reference. That faith and knowledge were doubtless great things in themselves, but they stood connected with something that might be called greater still; they rested on a background of promise and hope, which, in a manner, stretched from eternity to eternity, having God's primeval promise for its origin, and a participation in His everlasting life for its end. What an elevated thought! And how peculiarly fitted, both to enhance the spiritual attainments which carried with them the realization of such a hope, and to exalt the ministry which was appointed to bring them, instrumentally, within the reach of men! The expression πρὸ χρόνων αἰωνίων can scarcely be rendered otherwise than *before eternal times*, though being connected with a promise, not with a purpose simply or decree, of God, it must be understood of eternity in the looser sense; that is, of a period indefinitely remote before the ordinary historical epochs of the world. So Calvin, substantially, and in this expressly differing from Augustine and Jerome, who would carry the matter up beyond all temporal epochs, and lose themselves in the thought of ages strictly eternal. "Here, however (says Calvin), because the discourse is of a promise, it does not comprise all ages, so as to lead us beyond the creation of the world; but it teaches that many ages had elapsed from the time that the promise of salvation was given." Or, as he again puts it, that the promise "in the long order of ages is very ancient, because it began presently after the foundation of the world." In short, it might be said to date from beyond the ages, which to man's view seem to stretch into a kind of interminable past. The characteristic of God as in His nature the antithesis of all that is false or deceptive—ἀψευδής—incapable of lying, is designed to inspire confidence in the word of promise: though given so long beforehand, it is fresh and living still, having its root in the unchangeable, ever-faithful Jehovah.

Ver. 3. The structure of the sentence here has a somewhat irregular appearance; but it is better to leave it so, and give a natural interpretation of the words as they stand, than for the sake of a formal correctness to put a strain upon the meaning. It would have seemed to us, perhaps, the most orderly and consecutive way of speaking to say, "the eternal life which God promised before eternal times, but in its own seasons manifested through the word;" and it is much in this way that Beza (quam promiserat Deus ante tempora seculorum, manifestam autem fecit præstitutis temporibus suis, [videlicet] sermonem illum suum) and others have explained the passage; while some again, including Calvin, by *the word* understand Christ Himself: from primeval time God had promised eternal life, but since the gospel era He manifested His Word. Such explanations are manifestly of too artificial a cast. But taking the expression *His word* in its ordinary sense, and as the object of the *manifesting* which distinguishes the gospel from all preceding times, we are to regard the apostle as here introducing an independent sentence—contrasting the manifestation now, in its own seasons (see at 1 Tim. ii. 6), with the period of promise preceding, but not precisely of the eternal life, which was the subject of the promise—for it still is in great part future—and, therefore, instead of saying *which*, or *which life He manifested*, he says, *manifested His word*, in which everything pertaining to the nature of the life, and the means of attaining it, is brought clearly to light. (See, for other instances, Winer, § 63, 1.) By the addition *in preaching* coupled with the word, the preaching with which Paul was entrusted, it is plainly intimated that the word meant is the gospel,—*the word* emphatically, as declaring God's mind, not by dark intimations merely, or distant promises, but in great facts and blessed assurances as to the present and eternal good of His people. In regard to the expression, *according to the commandment of our Saviour God*, see at 1 Tim. i. 1, where it also occurs with only a slight variation in the order of the last words.

Ver. 4. In the address itself to Titus there is nothing

calling for much remark. He is called, like Timothy, a *true child*, and that according, or rather *in respect, to the common faith*. He may have been, and very probably was, a convert of the apostle's; but that is nowhere distinctly stated, nor does the language here necessarily imply it (see at Tim. i. 2). The designation *child* is indicative partly of endearment, and partly of comparative youth, in relation to the apostle. The received text has *grace, mercy, peace*, as at 1 Tim. i. 2, 2 Tim. ii. 2, with A, K, L, Philox., Theodoret; but the reading *grace and peace*, the same that is found in all the other epistles of St. Paul, except the two to Timothy, has the support of ℵ, C, D, F, Ital., Vulg., Syr., Pesh., Copt., Chrysos., etc. The latter must therefore be regarded as the preferable reading, and is now generally followed. The other was probably adopted to assimilate the text to the other two Pastoral epistles.

Ver. 5. *For this cause I left thee behind in Crete, that thou shouldst further set in order the things which are wanting*—general indication of the work which had been assigned to Titus in Crete, which the apostle, for want of time to do it himself, left him behind (ἀπέλιπον)[1] to carry forward. In the verb ἐπιδιορθώσῃς, the ἐπί " does not serve the purpose of strengthening = omni cura corrigere, but expresses the idea of addition : still further bring into order " (Huther). Matters had been so far put in a right condition by Paul himself; what further remained to be done was left to the charge of Titus. The kind of rectification meant can only be learned from what follows ; but the first, and apparently the most prominent point, concerned the official organization of the churches : *and mightest appoint elders in every city, as I directed thee.* This was virtually to say that each church or Christian community was to have its governing body of elders ; for in the very infancy of the Christian cause in

---

[1] The best supported reading being that at first hand of ℵ, A, C, D, F, I, —the received has κατέλιπον.

Crete, it is not to be imagined that each town could have more than one such community. Even that, in most cases, must have been comparatively small. Not only was the appointment of elders to each several congregation to be made, but it was to be done in accordance with the instructions which had been given by the apostle—the main part of which are doubtless embodied in the description, which immediately follows, of the qualifications to be sought in the persons who were to receive the appointment.

Ver. 6. *If any one is blameless*—that is, such an one only as is blameless—*husband of one wife, having faithful children, not accused of profligacy* (lit. not in accusation of it, in a position that such accusation could be brought), *or unruly*. The qualifications have already been considered at 1 Tim. iii. 2 sq.

Vers. 7, 8. *For a pastor must be blameless*—δεῖ εἶναι, ought to be so, should not be a pastor unless he is blameless—*as God's steward:* showing at once the original identity of elder and *episcopos*, by the substitution here of the one name for the other, and the weighty reason why he should be of irreproachable character, since by the very nature of his office he has to manage the things of God (Luke xii. 42 ; 1 Tim. iii. 15). The statement of Pearson, quoted here with approbation by Ellicott, that "Episcopal government was *under* the apostles, *from* the apostles, *in* the apostles," is peculiarly out of place in connection with this passage, which speaks only of a constitution by presbyters settled over each church, and these presbyters, each and all, bearing the name of *bishop*—pastor, or overseer of the flock. But see at 1 Tim. iii. 1, 10; also the Essay of Lightfoot, appended to his commentary on Philippians, on *The Christian Ministry*.

Not self-willed, not soon angry (irascible, ὀργίλον), *not a brawler, not a striker, not greedy of gain;* ver. 8, *but hospitable, a lover of good, discreet, righteous, holy, temperate.* Again, very much the same qualifications as were associated with the pastoral office in the First Epistle to Timothy. They indicate one possessed of that prudence and self-control, that uprightness of character, that kind, generous, disinterested, gracious disposition, which were fitted to command the respect, and secure the confidence and affection of a Christian community,—one altogether such as might serve for a pattern to the flock over whom he was appointed to preside, and guide their affairs with discretion.

Ver. 9. Then follows at the close what more especially pertained to the teaching function of his office: *holding fast the faithful word according to the teaching, in order that he may be able with the sound doctrine both to exhort and to convince* (or reprove) *the gainsayers.* There can be no reasonable doubt as to *the faithful word* which the true Christian pastor is to hold fast: the expression is often used in these epistles (1 Tim. i. 15, iii. 1, iv. 9; 2 Tim. ii. 11, iii. 8), and always means the word which is entitled to our confidence, the word which is in itself the proper ground of trust and hope—God's word. The only question is, in what sense or respect is it said to be *according to the teaching?* Does this mean, what the person has been taught, or what he himself teaches? Of itself the expression might be taken either way, and has been so taken by commentators, though both the more natural, and the more generally received view, is that which understands it of the teaching imparted by the apostles, and which constituted by way of eminence the teaching—the church's normal instruction and rule in spiritual things. The Authorized Version gives unambiguous expression to this, by rendering "the faithful word as he hath been taught," putting, however, the other view on the margin ("in his teaching"). It was natural that the apostle, when he was going to refer to a sort of teaching that was unsound and perilous, should not only point attention to that which was of another character, and might fitly serve as a corrective, but should also give some hint of its nature—should indicate the source whence it came, and the authority on which it rested. This is what he does, briefly yet not uncertainly, in the expression: "the faithful word according to the teaching;" that, namely, which is recognised as true and authoritative in the apostolic church. Hence, as standing on this solid foundation, and having such choice materials to handle, he should be able by his own sound doctrine both to exhort and to convince the gainsayers. But as the pastor is supposed here to accomplish the end in question by his own sound doctrine or teaching, this confirms the view taken of the preceding statement—that the teaching there spoken of was what he had previously received, and by which he was qualified for giving forth a teaching that should be at once sound and effective. This teaching is presented under a twofold aspect—one having respect to those within, and the other to those without the Christian community. It was the first part of the duty of the overseers of such a community to *exhort*, that is, to instruct and edify its own members; and only secondarily, and as occasion required, to resist and expose the false teaching of those who assailed the Christian faith, if so be they might be able to convince them of their errors. So that the qualification here associated with the true Christian pastor corresponds to the *aptness to teach* mentioned in 1 Tim. iii. 2; only here it is more specifically described, and its importance indicated with reference as well to the hostile as to the friendly elements, amid which the church in Crete was placed. Having there very pragmatical and troublesome disputants to deal with, much necessarily depended on the men who stood at the helm of affairs being possessed both of enlightened views and strong convictions; as they might otherwise, even with the best motives and intentions, misrepresent and embarrass the cause of the gospel. But both duties had to be discharged; therefore, "he is the true bishop who holds the right faith, and who properly uses his knowledge to edify the people, and check the wantonness of the adversaries" (Calvin).

Vers. 10, 11. The apostle now, taking occasion from the last clause in the preceding verse, proceeds to discourse of the peculiar character of the adversaries whom the infant church in Crete had to contend against: *For there are many unruly vain talkers and deceivers, especially they of the circumcision.* It would appear, from various incidental notices, that many Jews had settled in Crete; but it is sad to learn that the most noted for troublesome wranglings and practices of deceit were of that class. Perhaps it is not meant that they were absolutely the worst in Crete, but the worst only of those with whom the Christian church came into contact; for, the most depraved portions of the people would as yet be but little touched by the apostolic movements around them. I should, however, hesitate to say that "those of the circumcision" were (as many expositors hold) not simply Jews, but rather Jewish Christians. They must have been, one would suppose, more or less favourably disposed toward the Christian cause; but as yet scarcely won over to its side. It is by no means probable, considering what Jewish converts had everywhere to encounter, that at so early a period after the introduction of Christianity into the island of Crete there should have been great numbers of the more reprobate class of Jews, who were ready to brave the risk, and, for any considerations likely to be appreciated by them, should have actually pressed into the Christian fold. Some better evidence would be required for this than the present passage affords. For the characters here described are introduced simply as a specific portion of the opponents or gainsayers mentioned in ver. 9, and the most insidious and pestilent section of them. The more probable supposition regarding them is, that they did, indeed, somehow place themselves alongside the Christian communities,—feigned, perhaps, a measure of sympathy and goodwill toward them, but mainly for the purpose of insinuating their objections to the truth of the gospel, ventilating their own frivolous and fanciful conceits, and prosecuting with advantage their selfish aims. Their whole spirit and conduct, as depicted by the apostle, ran counter to a genuine, or even credible, profession of Christianity: instead of children of peace, they were sowers of strife and discord; sedulous pliers of the arts of seduction, not lovers of truth and righteousness; and so intent on worldly pelf, that *for the sake of base gain they subverted whole houses, teaching things which they ought not.* As it was by word of mouth that they sought to compass their ungodly ends—by teaching things which they ought not—the subverting ascribed to them must be taken in a spiritual sense: they perverted the views, overthrew the faith—and that of whole houses or families (comp. 2 Tim. ii. 18). The precise form of representation differs from what we find in 1 Tim. i. 4 sq.; but the relation in which the respective parties stood to the law on the one side, and to the gospel on the other, appears to have been much the same; and so, in both places alike, the apostle charges his evangelists to see that an uncompromising opposition be given to them: *there*, they were to be testified against and shunned; *here*, where the evil apparently was more rampant, *their mouths must be stopt*—they must be reduced to silence.

Ver. 12. The apostle now passes on to the Cretans generally. They had in a measure been referred to already; for while persons of the Jewish race had been more particularly noticed, it was only as forming the most troublesome and dangerous class of adversaries to the cause of Christ in Crete. But the Cretans at large were noted for characteristics akin to those charged upon the Jews; and he brings in proof an unimpeachable witness : *One of them has said—their own prophet—The Cretans are always liars, evil beasts, idle bellies* (Κρῆτες ἀεὶ ψεῦσται, κακὰ θηρία, γαστέρες ἀργαί). This passage, which is a regular hexameter line, has been ascribed by some to Callimachus, a Cyrenæan, but improperly; the better informed of the Fathers (Jerome, Chrysostom, Epiphanius) associate the words with Epimenides, who was a native of Phæstus or Cnossus, in Crete, and who had the name and repute of a prophet (Diog. Laertius; Cicero, *de Div.* i. 18; Plato also calls him θεῖος ἀνήρ, *Legg.* i. 642). He lived about 600 years before Christ. It was a dreadful testimony for him to bear against his countrymen, when he charged them with being addicted to falsehood, ferocity (κακὰ θηρία, wild, fierce like beasts), and gluttony (γαστέρες ἀργαί, lit. *idle bellies*, but used of persons given to luxurious living, and through that growing into a corpulent habit of body). The first characteristic was so notorious, that it was the subject of frequent remark; the very expression here used of it is also found in a hymn to Zeus by Callimachus; and Hesychius in his Lex. explains Κρητίζειν by the synonymous words, ψεύδεσθαι and ἀπατᾶν : *to play the Cretan,* was just to lie and deceive. (See in Wetstein an immense array of quotations on all the expressions, and on the first with special reference to the Cretans.) The description, of course, is to be understood as applying only in the general to the Cretan population, while admitting, doubtless, of many individual exceptions. But being so general, as to have become a kind of byword and reproach to the island, it was to be expected that the noxious qualities would not be long in making their appearance in the Christian church; on the side especially of these qualities danger was to be looked for to the cause of a pure and healthful Christianity.

Ver. 13. Hence in this verse the apostle calls for sharp reproofs against the prevailing evils : *This testimony is true;*

wherefore reprove them sharply, that they may be sound in the faith. It were wrong to infer from such words, though it is sometimes done, that the members of the church generally in Crete had already given way to the common vices, or had not abandoned them when they assumed the Christian profession; just as in regard to the early church at Corinth, the outbreak of licentious tendencies in one or two individuals by no means argued a general corruption. But happening where licentious practices so fearfully abounded, even a very partial appearance of the evil was sufficient to awaken apprehensions, and called for instant repression. It would naturally be the same in Crete in regard to the corrupt tendencies which had obtained such wide and continued prevalence there; and the purport of the exhortation given to Titus on the subject, was simply that he should maintain a firm protest against practices of such a nature, and in so far as they appeared among the members of the Christian church, subject the doers of them to admonition and rebuke. And when the apostle presents it as the object of such dealing, that the offending parties become sound or healthy in the faith, he as much as says, that faith, when in a state of health, fulness, and vigour, cannot ally itself to such corrupt practices as were prevalent in Crete: such practices betoken either the total absence of faith, or faith in a very feeble and sickly condition.

Ver. 14. Further, and with the view especially of securing real soundness of faith, the apostle would have them exhorted not to give heed to *Jewish fables and commandments of men, who turn away from the truth.* The same exhortation substantially was given at 1 Tim. i. 4 and iv. 3. The lying and deceptive tendency which had obtained such prevalence in Crete seems to have begotten a fondness for those fables, and have led also to the introduction or pressing of merely human commandments, as if they were divine. These probably related very much to distinctions in food and punctilios of outward observance, and from their nature necessarily indisposed both teachers and taught toward the truth of God. In such a case deceivers and deceived could only present different shades of what was essentially the same radical error.

Ver. 15. *To the pure all things are pure:* a great counter principle set over against that on which those Jewish semi-Gnostic sciolists were trading to the perversion of their own and other people's consciences. Judaism in part, and Gnostic asceticism still more, associated moral good and evil with certain outward distinctions: " Touch not or take not this, and you are holy; touch or take it, and you are defiled." No, the apostle virtually replies, these are but superficial distinctions; and even when they were to some extent of God, it was only as temporary and provisional arrangements—supplying for a season the lack of clearer light. All things which lie outside a man,—the things of whatever kind which he can use as articles of food, or turn into instruments of service,—these are in themselves indifferent; there is no power of intelligent and voluntary choice in them, and therefore no element of sanctity or corruption: this can only be where moral qualities reside, in the region of thought, desire, will; let there be but purity there, and then those external things assume a corresponding character, because they receive an impress and a direction from the spirit of him who uses them. It is but a fresh enunciation of the truth long before uttered by our Lord, and laid by Him as an axe to the root of the mistaken ceremonialism of the Pharisees. He told them that washed or unwashed hands, clean or unclean in food, had of themselves nothing to do with religious or moral purity: that for this everything depended on the state of the heart, from which proceed, as to good or evil, the issues of life (Matt. xv. 11–20; Mark vii. 14–16). It is obvious, from the mere statement of this principle, that in the *all things* spoken of as pure to the pure, errors of doctrine and corrupt practices cannot be included, for these come from an impure source : they are what they are in spirit and character, as the soul is which gave them birth ; they are not of God, but of the evil one. It is also obvious that the converse of the statement must hold equally good with the statement itself; as, indeed, the apostle expressly affirms: *but to them that are defiled and unbelieving is nothing pure.* Surely a solemn thought for persons of this class, who are not wholly steeled against conviction! They have within a fountain of pollution, which spreads itself over and infects everything about them. Their food and drink, their possessions, their employments, their comforts, their actions—all are in the reckoning of God tainted with impurity, because they are putting away from them that which alone has for the soul regenerating and cleansing efficacy. The apostle, however, carries it even further ; he brings out the evil more distinctly on its positive side: *but both their mind and conscience are defiled.* In saying this, he no doubt indicates the reason why nothing external is pure to them : but he does not give it formally as a reason ; he rather advances it as an additional disclosure of their defilement, showing how it embraces both the intellectual and moral parts of their nature, and lays alike the powers of thought and the workings of conscience under bias to evil.

Ver. 16. The description is wound up by a fearful announcement of their morally shipwrecked and hopeless condition: *they confess that they know God, but in works deny [Him], being abominable and disobedient, and unto every good work reprobate.* The description, it must be borne in mind, relates to those who have come within the sphere of religious truth, who have had their minds instructed in its principles and obligations, and have withal not formally renounced the profession of godliness which they naturally involve; but who have all along, from sinister motives, withstood the truth in their hearts, have talked big and done little; nay, have become adepts in evading the plainest calls of duty, and following courses at variance with the great principles of morality and religion. Of persons who have pursued such a career it may justly be said, that the very foundations of their moral being are out of course; and according to God's ordinary methods of dealing, there is no hope of recovering them to truth and righteousness. By calling them *reprobate* in regard to every good work—ἀδόκιμοι—the apostle means that they are of no worth or account in that respect: when the question is about a good work, such persons may be rejected as having no proper affinity to it.

CHAPTER II.

Ver. 1. In contrast to the false teachers mentioned in the preceding verses, and the pernicious results of their teaching, the apostle now urges, and with reference to all ranks and classes in the church, the sound practical teaching of the gospel. *But speak thou the things which become the sound instruction of the gospel:* sound, or wholesome, because it does not run out upon fables and frivolous prescriptions of human invention, but bears throughout with practical energy upon the duties of everyday life. Christianity is primarily, indeed, a doctrine, but only that it may be in the true sense a life; and the two can never be kept apart from each other in the public teaching of the church without imminent peril to both.

Ver. 2. In accordance with the rule, that after verbs of *saying, thinking,* and such like, the infinitive sometimes expresses, not what, according to the speaker's assertion, *is,* but *what ought to be* (since those verbs involve the notion of advising, requiring, or commanding, Winer, *Gr.* § 44, 3, *b*), we have now in a series of accusations with the infinitive the substance of the general order to speak the things becoming sound doctrine. The more advanced believers are taken first: *that the aged men* (πρεσβύτας, not πρεσβυτέρους, which might have been understood only of persons in office: the word is found again at Philem. 9, and Luke i. 18) *be sober* (νηφαλίους, 1 Tim. iii. 2), *grave, discreet* (1 Tim. iii. 2, 8), *sound (healthy) in their faith, their love, their patience.* It seems quite necessary to take these three latter terms in the subjective sense: love and patience must certainly be so taken, and this seems to fix down the meaning in like manner of the first. The article, therefore, prefixed to each of the terms, points to the individuals supposed to be addressed: *the* faith, etc.,—namely, of those individuals = *their* faith, etc. The exhortation is, that they should not only possess those Christian graces, but have them in a healthy condition, so that the exercise of them might be free, natural, regular, and consistent—such every way as might be expected from persons living under a felt apprehension of the great realities of salvation. The various things mentioned in the exhortation are peculiarly appropriate for persons in advanced life; they are the qualities in which it behoves them in an eminent degree to adorn the Christian faith.

Ver. 3. *In like manner the aged women, that they demean themselves as becomes holiness* (lit. that in demeanour they be holy, beseeming, ἐν καταστήματι ἱεροπρεπεῖς). The expression καταστ. is of comprehensive import, and has respect to everything in appearance and bearing which is indicative of the state of feeling within; and the design of the exhortation is, as Jerome explains, that "their very walk and motion, their countenance, speech, silence, may present a certain dignity of holy propriety." We get the exact idea when, assuming them to be possessed of a devout and reverent frame of mind, their entire manner and deportment are in suitable keeping therewith, the appropriate aspect and clothing of a mind rightly attempered toward things sacred and divine. The passage 1 Tim. ii. 10 is nearly parallel, only that the exhortation there has a more specific reference to becoming fitness and modesty of dress. *Not slanderers*—μὴ διαβόλους—given to do the work of him who is emphatically the accuser of the brethren. Old women, who usually have little to do, and with the garrulity, are not unfrequently visited with the querulousness, of advanced age, have special need to be warned against this tendency; it is a fine exhibition of Christian love and contentment when they can rise above it, even though there may be many things in their circumstances which are fitted to nourish it. *Not enslaved to much wine*—μὴ οἴνῳ πολλῷ δεδουλωμένοις—a very moderate demand in this respect certainly, but probably indicating by that very moderation, that a slavish addictedness to the evil was not uncommon among the female population of Crete, and that even a rational freedom from such slavery would be no small or unimportant testimony to the power of the gospel. Both of these exhortations are in substance pressed, though in different terms, at 1 Tim. iii. 8, 11, the first on females, the second on deacons. *Teachers of what is good*, not, of course, in public, but by private converse, and personal example in their proper sphere.

Vers. 4, 5. The apostle goes on to specify what more especially should be taught by the elderly female members of the church to the younger sisterhood, not intending thereby to supersede instructions of the same sort by the pastors of the church (comp. 1 Tim. v. 2), but coming in aid of them, and giving them a point and application which could scarcely be done in public. *That they school* [1]

---

[1] The reading σωφρονίζουσι, present indicative (after ἵνα), instead of the regular and grammatical σωφρονίζωσι, is plainly the best supported, being

the young women to be lovers of their husbands, lovers of their children; ver. 5, *discreet, chaste, workers at home, good, submitting themselves to their own husbands, that the word of God may not be blasphemed.* The verb σωφρονίζειν, which rules all that follows, does not precisely correspond to the Authorized Version's *teach to be sober*, or the Vulgate's *prudentiam doceant*, otherwise there would plainly have been no propriety in the term σώφρονας being afterwards included among the special characteristics. The word, though originally signifying to *make discreet or prudent*, came often to be used in the more general sense of schooling, or admonishing, with a view to the possession of certain things; and the reason, probably, why the apostle here used it, instead of some word expressive simply of teaching or instructing, was, that on account of the youth of the parties in question, he contemplated the necessity of a kind of authoritative disciplinary treatment from the older to the younger Christian females. The teaching recommended was to be of the more severe and urgent kind. (Hence the distinction made by means of this and another verb in Dio Cassius, p. lv. 560: δεῖ τοὺς μὲν λόγοις νουθετεῖν, τοὺς δὲ ἀπειλαῖς σωφρονίζειν.) In the epithets themselves, which mark the different characteristics that were to be the objects of the schooling, there is no proper difficulty; they are all such as especially became young women who were disposed to bring their Christianity to bear on the regulation of their conduct in daily life, and through this reflect honour on their Saviour. In regard to one of them, there

found in ℵ, A, F, G, H, P; while for the other there are C, D, E, K, L. Two other almost undoubted instances of the same usage with ἵνα in St. Paul's writings occur in Gal. iv. 7, 1 Cor. iv. 6; also in John xvii. 3. Various modes of explanation have been offered; but perhaps the most probable is, that it is the adoption in a few cases of a faulty construction, which is known to have become somewhat common in later Greek (Winer, *Gr.* xli. *b.* 1).

is a difference of reading: instead of οἰκουρούς, keepers at home, a number of the best MSS. (א, A, C, D, E, F, G) have οἰκουργούς, which means, *workers at home*, active housewives—undoubtedly a good sense; and the reading is preferred by Lachmann, Tisch., and Alford. Having such support, I hesitate to reject it, though the ancient versions, Ital., Vulg., Syriac, also Chrys., follow the other reading; while Theophyl. and Œcum. join the term οἰκουρούς to the ἀγαθάς, so as to make *good housekeepers, economical housewives*. This conjunction of epithets, apparently independent, is not to be justified; and the latter expression (ἀγαθάς) must be regarded as indicative of goodness generally, not with reference simply to household management = kindly, benignant. The last characteristic, *submitting themselves to their own husbands*, naturally winds up the description as by a sort of climax; for a heady and high-minded behaviour here would inevitably spoil the effect of all other qualities; it were utterly inconsistent with a proper conjugal bearing; and so with it as the immediate antecedent, is coupled the great end (negatively expressed) to be aimed at: *that the word of God may not be blasphemed*. In a measure, however, this must be carried back over the whole description; for in any one respect a behaviour contrary to that recommended would more or less have the effect of bringing reproach on God's word.

Ver. 6. *The younger men, in like manner, exhort to be sober-minded*—σωφρονεῖν, to accustom themselves to that becoming, prudent self-restraint, which is not inaptly expressed by being sober-minded—see at 1 Tim. ii. 9—a habit of mind which, when really formed, saves the young from many a vicious indulgence and foolish extravagance.

Ver. 7. Not only teach and exhort so, but—having respect to Titus, as himself comparatively a young man—*showing thyself* (the σεαυτόν used with the middle voice, though it might have been dispensed with, for the sake of greater distinctness and emphasis; see Winer, *Gr.* § 38, 6, who points to a similar instance, with the same verb, in Xen. *Cyr.* viii. 1, 39, παράδειγμα τοιόνδε ἑαυτὸν παρείχετο) *in all things a pattern of good works*—(τύπον used here only with the genitive of the thing)—*in your teaching* [showing] *incorruption, gravity.*[1] The latter of these two expressions must plainly be referred to the manner, not to the matter, of the teaching; and this renders it natural that we should also regard the other in the same light—should understand it subjectively of the teacher, not of what was taught by him. This is confirmed also by the circumstance, that the verse which follows has respect to the substance or matter of the teaching. By requiring Titus to show a spirit of incorruption, as well as gravity, in his teaching, the apostle appears to have meant, that in his very mode of communicating divine truth, he should give unmistakeable evidence of a mind freed from all corrupt tendencies and prurient imaginations—a mind in full accord with the sublime realities and holy aims of the gospel of Christ.

Ver. 8. And now comes the character of the instruction itself: *sound discourse that cannot be condemned, in order that he who is of the contrary part may be ashamed, having no evil thing to say of us.*[2] The same peculiar aspect is here given to true evangelical teaching, which is of such frequent occurrence in these Pastoral epistles; it was to be *sound* (ὑγιῆ), or healthy, as opposed to everything fitted to nourish a sickly and distempered pietism. Being such, it could not, of course, be condemned by any competent judge; and, what was more, those who had the will would find they

[1] The correct text here evidently is ἀφθορίαν, σεμνότητα. L and certain cursives insert ἀφθαρσίαν after the two; and instead of ἀφθορίαν, ἀδιαφθορίαν is the reading of L and some others.
[2] ἡμῶν is the reading of ℵ, C, D, E, F, G, K, L, Ital., Vulg., Syr., by much the best supported.

lacked any proper ground to speak reproachfully against the doctrine taught, and for shame sake might be reduced to silence. Although the party contemplated as ready to assume a hostile position is spoken of in the singular, "he who is of the contrary part," yet this is plainly but an individualizing mode of representing a class, and both the connection and the form of expression employed forbid us to suppose any other than human adversaries, heathen or Jewish, to have been in view. *May have nothing bad* or *foul to say*—μηδέν, having reference to the subjective condition of the adversary: however desirous, he could get hold of no ground of blame.

Ver. 9. The slave portion of the Christian community naturally presents itself for separate counsel: *Bondmen* [exhort, supplied from ver. 7] *to be in subjection to their own masters, in all things to be well-pleasing* (viz. to their masters; so that, written in full, it would be εὐαρέστους εἶναι δεσπόταις;—the rendering of the Authorized Version, "to please them well in all things," gives the correct sense); *not gainsaying* (or contradicting; Vulg. contradicentes; the "answering again" of the Authorized Version is too weak); *not purloining* (νοσφιζομένους, setting apart for oneself, self-appropriating; comp. Acts v. 2, 3), *but showing all good fidelity* (πᾶσαν πίστιν ἀγαθήν, good faith of every sort, a thoroughly trustworthy spirit); *in order that in all things they may adorn the doctrine of our Saviour God*. Here, again, as at ver. 5, also at ver. 8, the high spiritual aim of the gospel, in what it teaches of doctrine and exacts of obedience, comes prominently out. The glory of God's name and character among men is involved in it. And it is noticeable that the strongest expression given to this, in connection with the different classes of believers, is precisely here where the lowest in social position are concerned: previously it was that God's word might not be blasphemed, or that nothing morally bad might be found in those who appeared as His peculiar representatives; but now it is that the conduct of the poor bondmen who avowed themselves believers might *adorn* the doctrine which is of God. " God thinks it meet" (to use the words of Calvin) " to receive an ornament from bondmen, whose condition was so mean and wretched that they were scarcely reckoned among men. For servants are not meant as such are now in use, but slaves, who were bought with money, and were possessed as oxen or horses. But if *their* life (he justly adds) is an ornament of the Christian name, all the more should they who are in honour see to it that they do not mar it by their base behaviour."

Vers. 11-14. Taking occasion from what he had just said of the connection between the conduct of Christians and the doctrine they professed to have received, and the connection of both with the glory of God, the apostle proceeds in these verses to ground the whole of his exhortations respecting the behaviour of Christians in the essentially moral nature and design of the grace of God as now manifested in the gospel : *For the grace of God, having salvation for all men, was manifested, disciplining us*, etc. Two grammatical points call for remark here. One is whether the *all men* (πᾶσιν ἀνθ.) should be connected with the verb (ἐπεφάνη) or with the adjective (σωτήριος). Our translators expressed the former construction in the text ("hath appeared unto all men"), but placed the other on the margin ("bringeth salvation to all men"). The earlier English versions followed the other mode (Tyndale, Cov., Cran., Genev.); and that is the construction which is now generally approved by scholars, and which certainly, from the position of the words, is the most natural. The import of the verb, also, is complete without the "all men," since manifestation, or shining forth, involves of itself the idea of an unrestricted exhibition. The other point has respect to the exact relation and bearing of the adjectival clause, σωτήριος πᾶσιν ἀνθρ., which might be taken as a distinct predicate: "the grace of God was manifested as bringing salvation." But this, as Ellicott remarks, "would subjoin a secondary reference that would mar the simplicity of the context, παιδεύουσα clearly involving the principal thought." The clause, therefore, must be held to be merely explanatory, defining more exactly the nature of the subject before speaking of its practical operation and results among men; it is the grace of God in its saving design and properties toward men—"that grace of God (as Bishop Beveridge puts it) whereby alone it is possible for mankind to be saved," which also, it may be added, presents and offers salvation to all, and in that sense brings it. The article is not used in connection with πᾶσιν, so that "the notion of *all* is merely general, neither signifying expressly the whole class, nor all the parts of a class" (Jelf, *Gr.* § 454, 1). In a word, the salvation-bringing grace of God is without respect of persons; it is unfolded to men indiscriminately, or to sinners of every name, simply as such. The apostle says of this grace, it was *manifested* (ἐπεφάνη)—not simply "appeared," but shone forth, came openly to view; referring doubtless to what had taken place in Christ, yet not merely, as some would understand it, to the Epiphany, or the incarnation of Deity in His person, but to everything connected with His appearance and work among men. It was this in its totality which brought, as it were, to the light of noon-day that grace which had previously remained comparatively hid in the bosom of God: *now*, emphatically, the darkness was past, the clear light shone (John ii. 8; comp. also John i. 18, Matt. xi. 27).

Ver. 12. In this verse we have the main point presented to us of the apostle's testimony respecting God's grace—the particular aspect under which he here presses it on our regard; and this, it must be remembered, takes quite naturally its hue from the preceding context, in which the

Christian life, in its habitual resistance to sin and diligent practising of all moral excellencies, was the great theme. Hence, the saving grace of God comes into consideration as the pædagogic or moulding power, by means of which our naturally wayward and corrupt souls are formed to that higher scheme of life: *disciplining us to the end that, denying ungodliness and worldly lusts, we might live soberly, justly, and godlily in this present world.* We have no word that exactly corresponds to the παιδεύουσα of the apostle. With classical writers it bore the sense simply of instructing or educating; in which sense, as elsewhere noted (1 Tim. i. 20), the word occurs, once at least, in the New Testament (Acts vii. 22). But a deeper meaning came to be infused into the verb and the cognate noun (παιδεία) by the more profound and earnest spirit of the gospel; for, as Trench well remarks, the sacred writers "felt and understood that all effectual instruction for the sinful children of men includes and implies chastening, or, as we are accustomed to say, out of a sense of the same truth, correction." The expression here, therefore, bears respect to the native tendency of the human heart, as requiring to be chastened and subdued, that it may be delivered from its inherent superfluity of naughtiness, and formed to the pure, upright, and benignant character which becomes the gospel of Christ. And this corrective influence, or internal discipline, is what the grace of God in Christ Jesus comes to effect; but does so, of course, according to its proper nature, less by imposing any conscious restraint, than by infusing and nourishing the desires which breathe after conformity to the will of God. Herein lies the difference between the law and the gospel; yet their common end, the moral aim of the disciplining in question, is expressed first in the negative, then in the positive form: in the former respect it shows itself in a denial of ungodliness and worldly (κοσμικὰς, only occurring once again in New Testament Scripture, Heb. ix. 1) lusts; that is, in a disrelishing and avoiding of those things which tend to dishonour God, and pamper desires and appetites which are of a merely terrene nature. It is impossible, of course, in such things to draw on every side a sharp boundary line between what is allowable and forbidden, for the one will often seem, in actual life, to approach very near to the other; while still, in every real child of grace, and the more always that grace is living and active in his experience, there will never fail to be such a shrinking from the corruptions, and such a reserve even in regard to the common pleasures of the world, as to render his course easily distinguishable from that of those whose "portion is in this life." We have the same thought as to the renunciation of worldly lusts expressed, and somewhat more strongly, in 1 John ii. 15-17.

A positive, however, must go along with this negative; for an active following after the good is the necessary counterpart and complement to a renunciation of the evil; and this the apostle describes as a life marked by three prominent characteristics: that we might live soberly, justly, and godlily, in this present world. We may not say, perhaps, that in these words the apostle intended to mark a threefold distinction of moral duty; but commentators have not unnaturally observed, that they do in fact admit of special application to oneself, one's neighbour, and God. *Soberly* expresses the self-command and restraint which the Christian should always exercise over his thoughts and actions; *justly*, the integrity that should regulate all his dealings towards his fellow-men; while *godlily* or *piously* indicates the state of mind and conduct he should maintain in his relation toward God. And all these are given as distinctive features of the life he should lead, he should be ever living (for the aorist ζήσωμεν sums it up into one ideal whole), in this present world, notwithstanding that there is so much in it to tempt to a contrary course. Through grace the believer must triumph over all; as the apostle says of himself elsewhere, "I can do all things through Christ strengthening me" (Phil. iv. 13).

Ver. 13. *Looking for the blessed hope and manifestation of the glory of the great God and our Saviour Jesus Christ.* This statement, expressing the attitude of believers with reference to the future, can scarcely be regarded as included in the disciplinary action of the grace of God as now revealed in Christ; it comes in rather as an appendage or fitting sequel to the other, and for the purpose of showing how the past manifestation of the grace of God in Christ, when it works its proper effect upon the heart of the believer, naturally leads on to the expectation of another manifestation—a manifestation in glory. Such an expectation will doubtless help the disciplinary process, by bringing to bear on the higher principles and desires of the soul the potent influence of an elevating hope; but it does not itself possess a disciplinary character. When believers are said to look for the hope, it is clear that hope is, if not altogether, yet mainly, viewed in an objective light—identified with the object hoped for; yet, being said to be looked for, there is here also an exercise of hope in the same direction. There is the same apparent anomaly in what St. Paul says of the Jews respecting the resurrection at Acts xxiv. 5: "Having hope toward God, which [hope] they also themselves look for" (προσδέχονται, the same word as here), "that there shall be a resurrection:" a hope possessed, and at the same time looked forward to as still in the future (see also Gal. v. 5, Col. i. 5). The apostle seems to have been in the habit of contemplating the hope of coming glory so much in connection with its actual realization, that it sometimes presented itself to his mind as a kind of substantive thing, standing outside the believer, although still the believer's existing position was conceived of by him as one of hope; and at other times he represents him as being peculiarly influenced by the power of hope (see Rom. viii. 24, Col. i. 27, Tit. i. 2). The hope, considered with respect to its realization, is here called *blessed*, because of the happy results with which it shall be associated in the experience of all to whom it properly belongs. But the hope itself is more closely defined by what follows—*the manifestation of the glory:* so, certainly, should ἐπιφάνειαν τῆς δόξης be rendered, not by hendyadis, as in the Authorized Version, "glorious appearing," for the manifestation of the glory as a thing to come stands here in a kind of antithesis to the manifestation of the grace which has already taken place. But the chief difficulty in connection with this latter portion of ver. 13 lies in determining whether the manifestation of glory spoken of is to be connected both with God and with Christ, or simply with Christ as at once God and Saviour. If the latter view were adopted, then the proper way to avoid all ambiguity would be to render, with Ellicott and many others, "the manifestation of the glory of our great God and Saviour Jesus Christ;" while, if with the Vulgate, Syr., and all the English translations, except the Genevan, we render, "of the glory of the great God and of our Saviour Jesus Christ," we naturally think of God and Christ as distinguished from each other. A decision has been sought in favour of the former view, by Middleton and many others, on the grammatical principle, that the article τοῦ, standing simply before μεγ. Θεοῦ, and omitted before σωτῆρος, covers the two expressions as attributives of one and the same person. On the ground of this principle, Middleton says: "It is impossible to understand Θεοῦ and σωτῆρος otherwise than of one person." Had two been meant, the article must have been repeated before σωτῆρος. Ellicott, however, frankly admits that "it is *very* doubtful whether the interpretation of the passage can be fully settled on this principle." And Winer, while he allows that "σωτῆρος ἡμῶν may be regarded as a second predicate, jointly depending on the article τοῦ," still holds to the other interpretation, and considers "the article to have been omitted before σωτῆρος, because this word is defined by the genitive ἡμῶν, and because the apposition precedes the proper name: *of the great God and of our Saviour Jesus Christ*" (*Gr.* § xix. 5). Alford is of the same opinion, and thinks that σωτήρ was one of those words which gradually dropt the article and became a *quasi* proper name—referring in proof to 1 Tim. ii. 1, iv. 10—the article here also being the less needed on account of the pronoun ἡμῶν. Both writers, however, as also Huther, De Wette, and several others, confess themselves to be chiefly influenced by a regard to St. Paul's usual style of representation, especially in the Pastoral epistles, in which the relation of God to salvation is not identified with, but distinguished from Christ's: 1 Tim. i. 1, ii. 3–5; Tit. iii. 4–6; also Jude 24. There is, undoubtedly, something in this consideration; and it can scarcely be maintained that there is any quite parallel passage in St. Paul's writings, if he should here be held to have designated Jesus Christ at once "the great God and our Saviour."

On the other hand, there are especially two considerations which must be allowed to have considerable weight in the opposite direction. One is, that the notion expressed by ἐπιφάνεια is in New Testament Scripture specially applied to the Son, not to the Father (2 Tim. i. 10; 2 Thess. ii. 8; 1 Tim. vi. 14; 2 Tim. iv. 1, 8); the nearest approach to it in connection with the Father is at Matt. xvi. 27, where it is said that Christ shall appear in the glory of His Father, though still the appearing or manifestation itself is Christ's. The other consideration is, that nearly all the Fathers—Greek, as well as Latin—who refer to this passage, understood it simply of Christ. Thus Chrysostom, after quoting the words, says: "Where are they who speak of the Son as less than the Father? Of the great God, he says, and Saviour. When he couples great with God, he does not say great in respect to what, but great absolutely, since there is nothing great after Him." So Jerome: "Where is the serpent Arius? Where the snake Eunomius? Jesus Christ, the Saviour, is called the great God. Not as the first-begotten of every creature, not as the Word or Wisdom of God, is He so called, but as Jesus Christ—names which belong to Him as having assumed humanity." Quotations to the same effect have been produced from Clemens Alex., Hippolytus, Basil, Gregory Nys., Epiphanius, Aug. (see Waterland, *Works*, ii. p. 135). This striking unanimity as to such being indisputably the meaning of the passage, must be held conclusive to this extent, that the application of the epithets "great God" and "our Saviour" to Jesus Christ, appeared to persons conversant with the Greek as a living tongue, not only a competent, but by much the most natural interpretation. So that no one who takes this view can be charged with doing violence to the passage, considered by itself. The only question that seems open is, whether the other view, which distinguishes between God and Christ, is not in somewhat better accord with the usual language of the apostle. In a doctrinal point of view, it is of little moment which interpretation is adopted; for, while I see no reason for saying, with Alford, that this latter interpretation "even more strikingly asserts Christ's equality in glory with the Father," than that which directly ascribes to Him the designation of the great God, it is inconceivable that the name of Christ as Saviour should be associated equally with the Father in that manifestation of glory which is the culminating hope of the church, unless He had been essentially divine—unless, indeed, the peculiar glory of the Father had been that also of the Son. I am disposed, with Calvin, rather to press this aspect of the matter, as being, on the whole, the more sure and satisfactory. Feeling some doubt whether the epithets should be applied solely to Christ, or disjunctively to the Father and the Son, and having referred to the mode in which the orthodox Fathers sought to confute the Arians from the passage, Calvin characteristically adds: "More briefly and certainly may the Arians be refuted thus, since Paul, when speaking of the revelation of the glory of the great God, presently conjoined Christ, so that we might know that that revelation of glory was to be made in *His* person; as if he said, when Christ shall have appeared, then shall be disclosed to us the magnitude of the divine glory."

Ver. 14. In this verse we have an expansion of the term *Saviour* applied to Christ, so presented as to bring out a fresh exhibition of the grand moral aim contemplated in the grace of the gospel: *Who gave Himself for us*—Himself, ἑαυτόν, as contradistinguished from any inferior gift, and that *for us*, ὑπὲρ ἡμῶν, not exactly in our room or stead (which ἀντὶ ἡμῶν would have expressed), but in our behalf. It was altogether in our interest that the great self-sacrificing deed was done; and in what respect is immediately stated: *in order that He might redeem*—λυτρώσηται, by the paying of a ransom free—*us from all iniquity, and purify to Himself a peculiar people, zealous of good works.* It is what may be called the redemptive, not the atoning or propitiatory aspect of Christ's work, which is here brought into view, though the two are very closely interconnected, and the one now under consideration presupposes and is founded upon the other; for it is only by virtue of the reconciliation with God, effected through the propitiatory death of Christ, that there is attained by the sinner such a participation in the life of Christ, and such renewing and strengthening aid from the Spirit of grace, as may enable him to break the bonds of his spiritual captivity, and rise into the pure and glorious liberty of God's children. Having through His obedience unto death paid the costly ransom through which this happy change is accomplished, Christ is therefore said to have redeemed from iniquity those who share in His salvation, and purified them to Himself as a peculiar people—λαὸν περιούσιον, a people over and above, occupying a position separate and peculiar, like one's *peculium* or special treasure. The expression, as used here, is taken from Ex. xix. 5, Deut. vii. 6, xiv. 2, where the Sept. gives it as the equivalent of the Heb. *segullah* (סְגֻלָּה), *treasure*, or peculiar possession. In meaning, it substantially coincides with the λαὸν εἰς περιποίησιν of 1 Pet. ii. 9, a people for doing about, preparing, and fashioning for one's special use, hence peculiar (οἰκεῖον, Theodoret). Jerome, with substantial correctness, and on the ground of those Old Testament passages having explained the phrase, adds: "Rightly, therefore, Christ Jesus, our Great God and Saviour, redeemed us by His blood, in order that He might make a Christian people peculiar to Himself, who should then indeed be peculiar, if they proved to be zealous of good works." So that while the direct subject of the passage is sanctification, this is here, as in New Testament Scripture generally, made to spring out of that which is primarily the ground of our justification and peace with God.

Ver. 15. *These things speak, and exhort, and reprove with all authority.* A short retrospective utterance, for the purpose of impressing upon the mind of Titus the importance of the things which had just been declared respecting the salvation of God in Christ, and of his bringing them to bear in every possible way upon the understandings and hearts of the people. They were, therefore, first to be spoken, or taught in plain and intelligible language; then they were to be made the subject of exhortation, that is, pressed as matters of obligation upon the conscience; and finally, when these failed to secure the requisite attention and compliance, reproof was to be added—and this with all authority, μετὰ πάσης ἐπιταγῆς—with every sort of imperative earnestness, as of one speaking under authority, having a right to enjoin as well as to teach and exhort. The word ἐπιταγή is used only by Paul, and always in much the same sense— an authoritative order or command (Rom. xvi. 26 ; 1 Cor. vii. 6 ; 1 Tim. i. 1 ; Tit. i. 3). *Let no man despise thee;* that is, maintain your place as a delegated ambassador and servant of Christ, and act in such a manner that others shall see your determination to secure what in this respect is due to your office. Admonitions of this kind, given more than once to Timothy (comp. 1 Tim. iv. 11, 12, v. 21, vi. 13, 14, 2 Tim. iv. 1, 2), seem to imply that his weak point lay here, and that he required to be stimulated to the display of firmness and resolution in standing to the rights and duties of his office.

CHAPTER III.

Ver. 1. Passing from the more direct and spiritual obligations of the gospel, the apostle proceeds now to indicate the proper bearing of Christians toward the constituted authorities. It is not improbable, though it cannot be held certain, that he may have been led to give such prominence to this, from a known tendency on the part of the Cretans to insubordination and turmoil. Before their subjugation to Rome, which was accomplished by Metellus, B.C. 67, they had the reputation of being somewhat quarrelsome and seditious (Polybius, vi. 46: στάσεσι καὶ φόνοις καὶ πολέμοις ἐμφυλίοις ἀναστρεφομένους) ; the different tribes and free cities displaying a good deal of jealousy in regard to their respective rights, and a readiness to take up arms in vindication of them. The Jews also, who are known to have existed in considerable numbers throughout Crete, were everywhere beginning to show signs of insubordination towards the Roman yoke about the closing period of St. Paul's labours, and the storm was already gathering among them, which, in a few years more, was to burst forth with terrible fury. In such circumstances, it can readily be supposed that there might have been special, as well as general, reasons for the apostle here pressing the duties of civil obedience: *Put them in mind to submit themselves to magistrates, to authorities,*[1] *to obey rulers, to be ready to every good work.* There is a striking redundancy in the terms indicative of the kind of obedience required, as if to exclude all possibility of evasion: the civic rulers are designated ἀρχαὶ and ἐξουσίαι, as in Luke xii. 11, intended, doubtless, to include all classes of governing powers, but without meaning, apparently, to denote by the one a lower, and by the other a higher grade. And, besides being required to submit themselves to these, the people were also to be enjoined πειθαρχεῖν, a term which of itself comprehends the entire circle of obedience: it may be taken either generally, *to be obedient*, or more specifically, *to obey rulers;* in the former it occurs at Acts v. 29, 32; but here, considering the connection, the *kind* of obedience as to persons in authority may perhaps be indicated. That the *being ready to every good work* should follow on such precepts respecting civil subjection, was probably suggested by the thought of the magistrate's office having for its professed object the repression of evil, and the encouragement of well-doing (Rom. xiii. 3); so that the possession of a mind ready for every good work would in ordinary circumstances render civic obedience comparatively easy, would make the yoke in a manner unfelt. Of course, the requirement had then, as it has still,

---

[1] The καὶ of the received text between ἀρχαῖς and ἐξουσίαις is wanting in ℵ, A, C, D, F, G, and should therefore be omitted.

its limitations: the duties of rulers and ruled are reciprocal; and absolute unrestricted authority on the one side is no more to be contemplated than unqualified submission on the other, for neither is in accordance with the essential principles of truth and rectitude. Obedience to external authority can be due only in so far as that authority has a right to command; when it oversteps this, and issues injunctions which reach beyond its proper line of things, the higher principles of obligation come in: "We must obey God rather than men;" "Be not partaker in other men's sins."

Ver. 2. A quiet, inoffensive demeanour in the more private relations of life is now inculcated: *to revile no man, to be not contentious, forbearing, showing all meekness unto all men.* The first verb, βλασφημεῖν, imports more than to speak evil in the ordinary sense; it is to act the part of a reviler or slanderer; and when used of conduct from one man toward another, always betokens the exercise of a very bitter and malignant spirit. Titus was to charge the Christians of Crete to give no exhibition toward any one of such a spirit, nor to show a quarrelsome disposition, but, on the contrary, to cultivate a mild, placable, and gentle temper.

Ver. 3. As a reason for the manifestation of this mild and benignant spirit toward others, even degraded and ignorant heathen, the apostle refers to their own similar state in the past, and the marvellously kind and compassionate treatment they had, notwithstanding, experienced from their heavenly Father: *For we also* (we, namely, who are now Christians) *were once foolish* (or void of understanding; see Gal. iii. 1, Eph. iv. 18), *disobedient, going astray, serving diverse lusts and pleasures, living in malice and envy, hateful, and hating one another.* It is a dark picture of the natural state of men, and must be understood in the general, as more or less applicable to all who are left to the workings of corrupt nature, especially when that nature has developed itself amid the manifold temptations and pernicious examples of heathenism, but not without a measure of exemplification also even in such as, like St. Paul himself, have been brought up amid the decencies of a religious profession, so long as the heart has remained a stranger to the renewing grace of God. If, therefore, we may justly enough say that Paul was not thinking of himself *primarily* here,—was thinking rather of those in whom, up to the period of their conversion to the faith of Christ, the propensities and dispositions of nature had taken their free course,—there is no reason, on the other hand, for supposing that the apostle could have dreamt of excepting himself, as if he had not been conscious of possessing the same elements of character in his natural state. Elsewhere he has expressly affirmed as much of men universally, including himself (Rom. i. 18 sq., ii., iii. 9–20, vii., etc.); and it can scarcely be characterized otherwise than as absurd in Schrader to speak of the writer here forgetting the representation given of the apostle at 2 Tim. i. 3 as a man who from his forefathers had served God with a pure conscience. For in our passage, in so far as he contemplates himself, it is as lying in the corruption and following the tendencies of nature; while in the other he thinks only of what he was from the time that the sense of religion had been awakened in him, and he entered intelligently into the faith and spirit of his believing ancestry. The particular expressions are all simple enough. It may be doubted whether πλανώμενοι should be taken in the neuter or the passive sense—*going astray*, or *led astray, deceived*. It occurs in both senses in New Testament Scripture: comp. Matt. xxii. 29, Mark xii. 27, Gal. vi. 7, with John vii. 47, 1 Cor. vi. 9, 2 Tim. iii. 13; but here, where the whole tenor of the passage has respect to evil in its more active manifestations, the neuter sense seems to be the more suitable. So the Vulg. *errantes;* also the Syriac, Ellicott, Huther, and others. The term here used for pleasures—

pleasures, namely, of a grovelling or sinful kind—ἡδοναῖς, is not elsewhere found in St. Paul's writings, but occurs in other books, Luke viii. 14; Jas. iv. 1, 3; 2 Pet. ii. 13; and the idea of doing service or being in bondage to such things is employed more than once by our apostle, Rom. vi. 6, 16, xvi. 18. It cannot therefore with any justice be called an un-Pauline form of expression. Living, spending life (διάγοντες, *sc.* βιόν), in malice and envy, expresses only what is implied of men in their natural state at Eph. iv. 31, Col. iii. 8. The term στυγητοί is found only here, but is of the same import as μισητοί (Hesych.): it indicates the possession of qualities which are fitted to awaken the dislike of others—selfishness in some one or other of its aspects; and in proportion as this existed there could not fail to be exhibitions of the remaining quality, *hating one another.* Comp. Gal. v. 15. In regard to all the qualities, the degrees of strength and forms of manifestation might be infinitely diversified; but of this the apostle says nothing.

Ver. 4. *But when the kindness and the love toward man of our Saviour God was manifested:* it might almost be put *kindness and philanthropy,* for our *philanthropy* is but the English form of the original, and bears much the same sense. The Vulg. has *humanitas.* In New Testament Scripture it occurs again only in Acts xxviii. 2, where it is employed to characterize the humane and kindly behaviour of the people of Malta. In reply to De Wette's remark on the word, that "it is an unusual mode of expressing the idea of χάρις," Huther properly states that "the reason why Paul here uses this word is given in ver. 2, where he exhorts believers to show meekness (πραΰτης) toward all men; χρηστότης corresponds [nearly at least] to meekness, and with reference to the 'all men' φιλανθρωπία is added by the apostle. The goodness and man-ward love of God, in which our salvation is grounded, should impel us to the exercise of meekness and gentleness toward all men." In

John iii. 16, the pregnant expression, "God so loved the world," corresponds to the φιλανθρωπία here; and in this passage as well as in the other, the love to man which is celebrated as appearing in the procedure of God is strictly associated with redemption; it is the love of our Saviour God (see at chap. ii. 11, 1 Tim. i. 1). That it must here also be understood of God the Father, seems plain from the mention afterwards of Christ as the instrumental agent— "through Jesus Christ."

Ver. 5. Here the apostle carefully guards the divine benignity and loving-kindness with respect to the freeness of its actings: *not of works—works in righteousness—which we did,*[1] *but according to His mercy He saved us.* The act of God, though expressed only at the close, covers the whole of the passage: He saved us, not on one ground, but on another. *Not of works*—that is, out of them (ἐξ) as the formal or meritorious cause. And then the works are more exactly defined as τῶν ἐν δικαιοσύνῃ—those, namely, done in righteousness as the state or sphere in which we moved, or, with Winer (*Gr.* § 48. 3, *e*), in the spirit of a righteous person; and to make the meaning plain in English, we require either to repeat *works*, or to insert some such word as *done* or *wrought*. Bengel rightly states that "the negative belongs to the whole announcement: We had not been in righteousness; we had not done works in righteousness; we did not possess works through which we could be saved." The works of righteousness, in respect to which salvation is denied, are contemplated as past with reference to God's

---

[1] There is a diversity of reading here: the received text has ὧν ἐποιή-σαμεν—the ὧν by attraction for ἅ, as very commonly in the New Testament—with E, K, L, and many later MSS.; but the reading of ℵ, A¹, C¹, D¹, F, is ἃ ἐποιήσ., which is adopted by Tisch., Lachm., Huther, Alford, who regard the other as a correction of the scribes in accordance with the law of attraction. It may have been so; but apart from that, this is the reading of our best MSS., and on that ground should be adhered to.

saving act: they were non-existent when that act came into effect, consequently had no influence in calling it forth; it proceeded entirely irrespective of them. And then, in contrast to this negation as to things on our part—works that *we* had not done—there is introduced the real ground of action—God's own mercy. The connection is expressed by κατὰ, which in such a case denotes the occasion or reason, and is much the same as "in consequence of," "by reason of" (see Winer, *Gr.* § 49. d. *b*, and similar examples in Acts iii. 17, 1 Pet. i. 3, Phil. ii. 3). So that the wellspring of salvation is here represented as lying in the kind and loving propensions of God toward men, and these coming forth in the character of provisions and overtures of mercy in behalf of the undeserving, the sinful (comp. Luke i. 72, 78; Rom. ix. 23; Eph. ii. 4). As the apostle, however, is speaking of the actual experience of salvation, the mercy of God is contemplated mainly in connection with the application of the provisions of grace to individual souls. For, as well noted by Wiesinger, "it is only the part which God performs in our salvation that is held up to view; and so it did not admit of that being mentioned which is required on the part of man, as the subjective instrument or condition of his entrance on salvation. Hence it is not said, διὰ τῆς πίστεως (as in other passages); for the apostle's aim here is not to describe the new state of the man, but to point to the act and saving agency of God in regard to the individual, by which the new state is brought about, and which shows, more than anything else, that this new state does not rest on man's merit or his own doing."

Then follows an indication of the means through which the divine mercy realizes itself in experience: *through the laver of regeneration, and* [*through*] *renewing of the Holy Ghost.* Such appears to be the proper rendering of the text. The word λουτρόν, which in New Testament Scripture occurs only here and in Eph. v. 26, has been very variously understood. *Washing* is the sense adopted by Wycliffe and the Authorized Version; but Tyndale, Cranmer, and the Geneva have *fountain;* the Rheims, after the Vulgate (*lavacrum*), has *laver*. This last is the only ascertained sense of the word: taken literally, it signifies not the act of washing, but the vessel or bath in which the act was performed. And the only question is, how the expression, when coupled here with *regeneration*, is to be explained. Some have taken it in an altogether figurative sense, as emblematically representing the spiritual change; some, again, of the Holy Spirit, or of the word—the one as the efficient, the other as the instrumental, cause of regeneration. But these cannot be termed quite natural explanations; and neither here nor at Eph. v. 26 do they seem to have once occurred to the ancient interpreters. They all apply the expression to the baptismal ordinance: thus Theodoret, by the complex phrase λουτρὸν παλιγγενεσίας, understands τὸ σωτήριον βάπτισμα, *saving baptism;* Greg. Naz., "We call baptism λουτρόν, as being an ablution"— ὡς ἔκπλυσιν (see further in Suicer, *Thes.*, under the words λουτρόν and παλιγ.). "I do not doubt (says Calvin) but that he at least alludes to baptism; nay, I readily admit that the passage is to be explained of baptism, not because salvation is included in the outward symbol of water, but because baptism seals to us the salvation procured by Christ. . . . But the apostles are wont to deduce an argument from the sacraments to prove the reality sealed therein; since that beginning ought to convince pious minds that God does not mock us with empty figures, but by His own power inwardly accomplishes what He exhibits by an external sign. That man will rightly hold the proper use and virtue of the sacraments, who shall thus connect the sign and the thing signified, so as neither to make the sign empty or inefficacious, nor yet, with the view of extolling it, detract from the Holy Spirit what is His own." When interpreted thus, the passage yields no countenance to a ritualistic and superstitious use of the ordinance, such as became common with the Fathers, when they regarded the very waters of baptism as being, when rightly administered, impregnated with the power of the Spirit—*trans-elemented*, as it was called—so as by a kind of sacred magic to produce the spiritual result.[1] It is simply as an ordinance of God—an ordinance that has specially connected with it the promise of God's Holy Spirit—that the apostle here speaks of it; implying that, if entered into with the same sincerity on man's part that it is appointed on God's, the promise will assuredly be made good; while to the hypocritical and unbelieving it may not less certainly prove, in common with other divine ordinances, altogether fruitless. If, therefore, we say that the natural import of St. Paul's words here obliges us to hold that he speaks of baptism, it is of baptism, we must remember (to use the words of Ellicott), "on the supposition that it was no mere observance, but that it was a sacrament, in which all that was inward properly and completely accompanied all that was outward. He thus could say, in the fullest

---

[1] It was a source of inextricable confusion in the Patristic theology, and the occasion of much practical error and superstition, that the Fathers identified, in the unqualified manner they did, the ordinance of baptism with regeneration. Mr. Mozley's endeavour to justify them in so doing (in his *Primitive Doctrine of Baptismal Regeneration*), though containing much valuable matter, cannot be regarded as satisfactory; for their usual style of representation was clearly fitted to mislead, and in Augustine particularly was inconsistent with his doctrine of grace. But occasionally they could distinguish well enough. Augustine, for example, speaks of the possibility of the *laver* of regeneration being unaccompanied with the *grace* of regeneration (*Enar.* in Ps. lxxvii.), and of conversion of heart being sometimes where there is not baptism, and of baptism being where conversion of heart is not (*De Bap.* iv. 25). So Jerome speaks of persons who do not receive baptism with a full faith, and says of them that "they have received the water, but have not received the Spirit" (*Com.* in Ezek. xvi. 4, 5).

sense of the words, that it was a *laver of regeneration*, as he had also said (Gal. iii. 27) that as many as were baptized into Christ had put on Christ—entered into vital union with Him." The most exact parallel, however, is 1 Pet. iii. 21, where, with reference to the salvation wrought for Noah through the deluge and the ark, the apostle says that "baptism now also saves *us;*" but then baptism of what sort? Not that (he presently adds) which is simply outward, and which could avail only to the purifying of the flesh, but that which carries with it "the answer (or interrogation) of a good conscience toward God through the resurrection of Jesus Christ." It was baptism of such a kind as involved an earnest and conscientious dealing with God in respect to salvation, and an appropriation of the new life brought in for believers by the death and resurrection of Christ.

In our passage, what is said of baptism is further guarded and defined by what follows respecting the work of the Spirit: *through the laver of regeneration, and renewing of the Holy Ghost* (καὶ ἀνακαινώσεως Πν. ἁγίου). So far as grammatical construction is concerned, ἀνακαινώσεως might be made dependent either on λουτροῦ or on διὰ: it might be rendered either "through the laver of regeneration and of the Holy Ghost's renewing," or "through the laver of regeneration, and through renewing of the Holy Ghost." With the view of securing the latter rendering, several MSS. insert a second διὰ (D, E, F, G); Jerome also expresses it, *per renovationem*, though the Vulgate has *renovationis:* hence connecting renovation as well as regeneration with laver. By renovation, however, as used in New Testament Scripture, is meant a progressive change to the better—a growing advancement in the divine life, of which the Holy Spirit, indeed, is the efficient agent, but in which also there is a concurrent action of the regenerated soul. The grace that works in it is not converting, but co-operating and strengthening grace. And while baptism is the seal of the new birth, and gives assurance of the Spirit for all redemption blessings, it is never formally represented as the seal of spiritual progress, nor could it with propriety be so. For it has respect to our introduction into a new state, but not to any future and successive advances thereafter to be made in it. The ordinance of the Supper, in a sacramental point of view, stands related to this, not baptism. There are therefore two things marked here—first baptism (as the laver of regeneration), and then the renewing of the Holy Ghost, which is but another name for progressive sanctification. And as the apostle, in predicating salvation, or an experimental acquaintance with the saving mercy of God in Christ, speaks only of such as have partaken alike of baptism and of the Spirit's renewal—partaken not of one of these merely, but of both—it is a departure from the precedent of apostolic teaching to use language indicative of a saved condition, where one only of the two can be said to have come into play. If people *will* speak of baptismal regeneration, let them take care, as Alford has justly cautioned, to bear in mind what baptism in such a case should be understood to mean: "not the mere ecclesiastical act—not the mere fact of reception by that act among God's professing people; but that, completed by the divine act, manifested by the operation of the Holy Ghost in the heart and through the life." Precisely similar language, it may be added, is often used regarding the word which is here applied to baptism: it, too, is coupled with regeneration, or a saving change (John i. 12, 13; 1 Cor. i. 18, 21; Rom. x. 9; Jas. i. 18; 1 Pet. i. 23; 1 John v. 1); but then it is always on the understanding, expressed or implied, that the word has been received into the heart, and produced through divine grace its proper effect.

Ver. 6. Having named the Holy Spirit as the efficient

author of the renovation accomplished in believers, the apostle goes on to indicate, in further proof of the loving-kindness and mercy of God in the matter of our salvation, the copiousness of the gift; it is bestowed, not with a grudging, but with a free and benignant hand: *which He poured out* (οὗ ἐξέχεεν, the οὗ by attraction with the preceding Πνεύματος ἁγίου, not in any way dependent on λουτροῦ) *on us richly through Jesus Christ our Saviour.* The form of expression is derived from the language of Old Testament prophecy (Joel ii. 28; Zech. xii. 10), adopted by the apostles at the commencement of the New Testament church (Acts ii. 17, 33, x. 45)—language proceeding on the similitude of the Spirit's grace to quickening and refreshing streams of water. As such He is represented, not simply as given, but as poured out,—nay, poured out richly, in order to convey some idea of the plenteous beneficence of the gift. This rich bestowal is peculiar to New Testament times; and here, as elsewhere, it is expressly connected with the mediation of Christ, who as Saviour has opened the way for it, and Himself sends forth the Spirit as the fruit of His work on earth, and the token of its acceptance with the Father (John xiv. 16, 26, xvi. 7; Luke xxiv. 49; Gal. iv. 6; Eph. iv. 7-11). So that the whole Trinity appears here as concurring in the blessed work of our salvation: we are saved by God the Father, through the ministration of His life-giving ordinances, rendered such by the presence and agency of the Holy Spirit; and this, again, proceeds on the ground of what was done for us by Christ as our Saviour, and what He still does in mediating between us and the Father respecting the bestowal of the Spirit. Such a style of representation could never have been used unless Father, Son, and Spirit had been co-ordinate agents in the work of salvation. And as regards the more specific topic in this verse—the rich outpouring of the Spirit—there can be no doubt that, as the apostle is speaking more immediately of the salvation of individuals, it must be primarily understood with reference to this, though still of this only as a part of that general effusion of the Spirit's grace which commenced on the day of Pentecost. The individual, in such a case, cannot be viewed apart from the general; and it is needless here to distinguish minutely between the two.

Ver. 7. In this verse we have the important practical design of the salvation-work described in the three preceding verses : *in order that, being justified by His grace, we might become heirs according to the hope of eternal life.* The expression *by His grace* (τῇ χάριτι ἐκείνου) must be connected with God the Father, since it is He always who is represented as conferring the grace which justifies the ungodly. Concurrently, however, with the Father's procedure in respect to justification, there is an indispensable action of the Holy Spirit, uniting the sinner to Christ, and so establishing a vital bond between the guilty and the righteous. For, however gratuitous the act of justification is as bestowed on its objects, not only without any good deeds on their part, but in spite of many bad deeds, there is nothing arbitrary in it. It proceeds upon such a connection between the soul and Christ as secures for it a participation in His infinite worth and sufficiency, so that God is just even when He justifies the ungodly (Rom. iii. 26). When it is said, further, that this justification is effected that we might become κληρονόμοι κατ' ἐλπίδα ζωῆς αἰωνίου, the explanation may run, either heirs in respect to hope of eternal life—heirs of that life, yet meanwhile having it only in hope ; or heirs in conformity with the hope of eternal life—of all that such a hope entitles to. Grammatically, the one explanation is as admissible as the other. But I think, with Alford, against Huther and Ellicott, that considering the expression used by the apostle at the commencement of this epistle, ἐπ' ἐλπίδι ζωῆς αἰωνίου, it is more natural here to couple *hope* directly with *eternal life,* and regard the heirship spoken of as comprehending all that is conformable to, or is embraced in, the hope of eternal life. But the difference between the two modes of exposition is of a philological rather than a doctrinal kind: in substance the meaning is much the same either way; and to the popular apprehension, it will matter extremely little whether we say of the justified that he is heir of eternal life, as to hope, or that he is heir of whatever the hope of eternal life warrants him to look for. Niceties of this description in the interpretation of Scripture, if they may be noticed, should certainly not be dwelt upon.

A few practical advices to Titus now close the hortatory part of the epistle, followed up by some personal notices and salutations.

Ver. 8. *Faithful is this saying* (that, namely, contained in the immediately preceding verses respecting God's method of procedure in respect to salvation; for the form of expression, see at 1 Tim. i. 15); *and concerning these things I would have thee strenuously affirm* (διαβεβαιοῦσθαι, make asseveration; see at 1 Tim. i. 7), *to the end that they who have believed God be careful to practise good works*—προΐστασθαι, set forward, practise such works. The governing verb φροντίζειν, which is sometimes, though rarely, as here, followed by an infinitive, nowhere again occurs in Scripture; but it denotes the application of earnest and continued thought, a careful striving of soul in this direction, that the belief in the doctrines of the gospel should be substantiated by a steady performance of its commanded duties. *These things* —namely, the things involved in this practical teaching and concern—*are good and profitable to men:* in themselves good (καλὰ), and in their tendency and results profitable (ὠφέλιμα) to others.

Ver. 9. In contrast to such sound teaching, he again warns against that frivolous and disputative sort of teaching which he had previously characterized (i. 10–14): *but foolish questionings, and genealogies, and strifes, and conten-*

tions about the law, avoid—περιίστασο, keep out of the way of, turn from them. And on this account, *for they are unprofitable and vain*—utterly wanting in the practical element which so remarkably characterizes the true doctrine of the gospel.

Ver. 10. *A heretical man, after one and a second admonition, shun.* The word αἱρετικὸς only in part corresponds to our term *heretical;* perhaps *schismatical* or *factious* would more nearly approach to it. It denoted one who set himself to make a αἵρεσις or party, separate from the community of the faithful. In the history of the Acts the designation is applied to the sectional divisions among the Jews—the *sects* (as the word is rendered) of the Pharisees and the Sadducees (chap. v. 17, xv. 5). On one occasion Paul applies it to himself, and his former co-religionists, in a good sense; he spoke of it as a thing creditable to them that they formed "the strictest sect of their religion" (chap. xxvi. 5). This, however, might be called an exceptional use; for, shortly before, Paul himself confesses that, in a way which his countrymen called *heresy* (αἵρεσιν), he worshipped God, and was stigmatized by his accusers as a ringleader of the Nazarene heresy or sect (chap. xxiv. 5, 14). Also in St. Paul's own writings the expression is similarly used—Gal. v. 20, 1 Cor. xi. 19; the latter of which passages especially throws light on the import of the word in the apostolic church. In the preceding verse he had mentioned with grief that he heard there were schisms or divisions among them; and then he adds, "for there must be also αἱρέσεις among you, that they who are approved may be made manifest among you." It is clear that the persons who taught the αἱρέσεις were just those who caused the schismatical divisions—formed some kind of separate interest by unduly elevating a human mode of teaching, or teaching what was in itself at variance with the principles of the gospel. I conclude, therefore, with Campbell (*Preliminary Disserta-*

tions on the Gospels, ix. 4), that the heretical man of our text "must mean one who is the founder of a sect, or at least has the disposition to create sects in the community, and may properly be called a *factious* man. The admonition here given to Titus is the same, though differently expressed, with what Paul had given to the Romans when he said, 'Mark them which cause divisions, and avoid them'" (chap. xvi. 7).[1] A person of this conceited, opinionative stamp Titus is counselled not summarily to cast off, but to deal with him as an offender against the peace and good order of the church—to give him one and even a second admonition; and then, if these failed to reclaim him from his waywardness, to shun him as an evil-doer. The apostle does not carry the matter further; he does not advise formal excommunication, the course he had himself adopted in the case of others (1 Tim. i. 20); but the kind of shunning or avoiding enjoined was a *virtual* excommunication, as it plainly involved a resolution not to recognise him as a Christian brother so long as he pursued his divisive and factious course. And the reason given in the next verse for the action recommended confirms this view.

Ver. 11. *Knowing that such an one is perverted, and sinneth, being self-condemned.* The language throughout is very strong: first he is *perverted*—the rendering of Tyndale, Cranmer, and Gen., and upon the whole better than the Authorized Version, *subverted:* the compound verb ἐκτρέπω signifying to turn out of,—namely, the proper way or course; and when used, as here, in the passive of one who, notwithstanding even a second admonition, persists in following his self-willed line of action, "denotes a complete inward corruption and perverseness of character" (Ellicott).

---

[1] The dissertation on this point is in general good, but carries to an extreme the idea of false doctrine having nothing to do with *heresy* in the gospel age. False or erroneous teaching must certainly have been an element.

Then, he *sinneth*—ἁμαρτάνει, lives in sin, or errs knowingly and deliberately, because he cleaves to his own way, after having been expostulated with about its erroneousness by an authorized messenger of God. And so, finally, he is said to be *self-condemned:* not as if he formally pronounced judgment against himself, or was conscious of acting a part which he consciously knew to be wrong, but because his conduct was such as of itself to betray a desert of condemnation. The meaning is much the same as that expressed of similar characters at 1 Tim. iv. 2—both alike spoken of persons whose inward sense or conscience has got into a state which is palpably at variance with the mind of God, as made known through His authorized representatives.

Ver. 12. *When I shall send Artemas to thee, or Tychicus, make haste to come to me at Nicopolis.* Artemas is nowhere else mentioned; but Tychicus is described at Col. iv. 7 as "a beloved brother, and a faithful minister and fellow-servant in the Lord;" and very nearly the same expressions are employed respecting him at Eph. vi. 21. He was an Asiatic (Acts xx. 4), but we want materials for a closer determination. The Nicopolis at which St. Paul intended to pass the winter is uncertain. Three towns of that name are well known to have existed at the time, within the sphere of the apostle's labours: one in Cilicia, another in Thrace, and a third in Epirus. Each of these has been fixed on by different commentators as the one probably meant in the passage before us; but it is impossible to adduce anything of a decisive nature in favour of either. If the epistle was written from Macedonia or some part of Greece, then it would likely be Nicopolis in Epirus, which was by much the more important of the two in that quarter; but if from some place in Asia Minor, then Nicopolis in Cilicia should rather be understood. But whichever it might be, when the apostle states his intention to spend the winter *there* (ἐκεῖ), it is clear he was not at Nicopolis when he wrote the epistle.

Ver. 13. *Zealously forward on their journey Zenas the lawyer, and Apollos, that nothing may be wanting to them.* The σπουδαίως πρόπεμψον evidently means that Titus should hasten the departure of the brethren mentioned, and do it, as the context shows, by furnishing them with things needful for their journey. This is the only passage in which the name of Zenas occurs; nor is it certain whether the designation *lawyer* is to be taken in the Jewish sense (one who had been skilled in Hebrew law, and from former times still retained the name), or with reference to the study and practice of law in a civil sense. The majority of commentators prefer the former view. But the mention of Apollos here along with Zenas, as one whom Paul wished to have beside him, so near the close of his earthly labours, is a clear proof of the good understanding which subsisted between these two eminent servants of God, and how little ground there is for the serious differences in respect to their doctrinal teaching which have sometimes been alleged by modern rationalists. As Apollos commenced preaching when still but imperfectly taught in the gospel, and then received fuller instruction from some of Paul's most intimate friends (Acts xviii. 26), the probability is, that whatever divergence might appear was confined to the earlier part of his labours: and even of that we know next to nothing.

Ver. 14. The task of supplying Zenas and Apollos with things requisite for their journey, seems to have suggested to the apostle the thought that the brethren generally in Crete should be admonished to lend their help and co-operation in matters of that description. *But* (though I ask you to take this in hand, it is not you alone I mean, but) *let ours also* (the brethren generally) *learn to practise good deeds for necessary uses*,—namely, for such strictly proper and important ends as supplying the wants of Christ's servants when going on their Master's work; and this, *in order that they may not be unfruitful*—may not spend life unsuitably to their profession.

Ver. 15. The conclusion is brief and simple: *All that are with me* (that is, probably, such as were labouring with him in the ministry of the gospel) *salute thee; salute those that love us in the faith; the grace* (namely, of God) *be with you all.* No other epistle of the apostle's ends quite similarly. The mode of salutation may be said to be Pauline in spirit; but in form it differs too much from those found in the other epistles, to have been at all likely to occur to any one but the apostle himself. But including, as it did, all who loved the apostle in the faith, it implies that the epistle was to be made known to the churches in Crete.

THE

SECOND EPISTLE TO TIMOTHY.

———◆———

THIS is admitted, by all who hold the authenticity of the Pastoral epistles, to be the last writing we have from the pen of the apostle. He had himself evidently despaired, at the time he wrote, of getting deliverance from the hand of his persecutors, or even of having his martyrdom long delayed. An early termination of his course by an unjust and violent death appeared now to be inevitable ; and the brief epistle in which he gave expression to his last utterances of faith and hope, is altogether worthy of the occasion. The probable date has been already discussed in the INTRODUCTION. A measure of uncertainty must always hang around it ; but a variety of convergent circumstances seems to point to the year A.D. 68 as the most likely period.

CHAPTER I.

Ver. 1. *Paul, an apostle of Christ Jesus by the will of God, according to the promise of life which is in Christ Jesus.* The descriptive designation which Paul here employs respecting himself is so far peculiar, that it does not precisely accord with any other found at the commencement of his epistles, while still there is nothing in it which is not also found in some of them. That he was an apostle by, or through, God's will, is very frequently expressed—1 Cor. i. 1; 2 Cor. i. 1; Eph. i. 1; Col. i. 1: in the First to Timothy it was by God's *appointment*, which occurs only there. In connecting his apostleship here, and so frequently, with God's will, he sought to place it above, not merely any choice or desert of his own, but also every kind of elective agency that was simply human, and to bring it into immediate connection with the mind and purposes of the Supreme. To show this more distinctly, he adds: *according to the promise of life which is in Christ Jesus*. This promise of life, or, as it is expressed in Tit. i. 2, "hope of eternal life, which God, that cannot lie, promised before eternal times," is presented as the primary ground out of which the specific acts and arrangements of God proceeded in reference to the work of salvation in the world, and among others, Paul's own calling to the apostleship, which formed an important link of connection between the promise and its actual realization among men. The life meant, of course, is life in the higher sense, comprehensive of all the blessing and glory, both in this world and the next, which flow from an interest in the redemption of Christ. It is therefore not life simply, but that life which is in Christ Jesus (see at 1 Tim. vi. 19). Timothy is thus again reminded, at the outset, that the character in which Paul now wrote to him, and consequently the counsels and admonitions which in that character he might express, bore on them a divine impress: they stood in near proximity to the eternal purpose and will of the Father.

Ver. 2. *To Timothy,* [*my*] *beloved child.* I cannot but regard it as a very frivolous question, to ask here, with some commentators, why the apostle should have addressed Timothy as his *beloved* (ἀγαπητῷ), and not, as in the first epistle, his *true* (γνησίῳ) child? and whether his doing so did not bespeak a somewhat diminished confidence now in respect to Timothy? (Mack, Alford.) Why should an apostle, any more than another person, be expected, if he has once employed a particular epithet on an endeared friend, to confine himself ever afterwards to the same? For anything we know, it might be the very reason why Paul did not use *true* here, that he was conscious of having used it in the former epistle; for love itself, when fervent, instinctively shrinks from formal repetitions. And did not Timothy now need to be greeted with an *endearing* rather than a *confidential* epithet, separated as he was unwillingly, and at such a crisis, from his spiritual father? The tears shed by the youthful disciple at that separation, which were still fresh in the remembrance of the apostle's heart (ver. 4), would alone prompt the latter to select a term that would be expressive of tenderness and affection. If there *are* certain things in the epistle (as Alford alleges) which seem to indicate a "somewhat saddened reminding, rather than one of rising hope and confidence," toward Timothy, the designation of *beloved child*, so appropriate in the circumstances, is assuredly not one of them; and the attempt to turn it to such account belongs to fancy, not to exposition. *Grace, mercy, peace from God the Father, and Christ Jesus our Lord.* The same form of salutation as at 1 Tim. i. 2, which see, with reference especially to the inclusion of *mercy*, a peculiarity of these two epistles.

Vers. 3–5. *I give thanks to God, whom I serve from my forefathers in a pure conscience.* The form of expression at the commencement, χάριν ἔχω, occurs only once again in St. Paul's acknowledged epistles—1 Tim. i. 12; elsewhere it is εὐχαριστῶ (see there). In mentioning God as entitled, on a certain account, to receive and actually receiving thanks from him, the apostle couples a statement as to his own present and past relation to Him: the God he now served was also the God of his forefathers, and the service was done in a pure conscience toward Him, as theirs also had been. By *forefathers* (προγόνων) may be understood either the nearer or more remote ancestry, but most naturally the former; as also at 1 Tim. v. 4, where the same word is used of grand-parents, the parentage just a step further off than the immediately preceding — *Scottice*, forbears. The apostle's service or worship (λατρεύω) formally, indeed, differed from that of his forefathers, inasmuch as it was all offered in the name of the Lord Jesus Christ; but then, holding this Jesus to be the Messiah promised to the fathers, and ever looked for by them, there was both the same God, and essentially the same worship, with him and with them. The one faith which he and they alike professed was only more developed now, and the worship adapted to the fresh stage that had been reached; and he would have Timothy to bear this perpetually in mind, not only because he also stood in the same relation to a pious Jewish ancestry (presently to be noticed, vers. 5, 6), but also because the apostle's approaching condemnation and death as the abettor of a new religion was sure to expose Timothy to opposition and danger on the same ground. It was meet, therefore, that he should know well here the foundations of his faith, and hold firmly by them. Substantially, the same assertions respecting his worship, and the manner in which he discharged it, were made by St. Paul in Acts xxiii. 1, xxiv. 14–16. And that what he says here is no way inconsistent with the admissions he makes respecting his native depravity, see at Tit. iii. 4.

But for what precisely does the apostle give thanks to God? That it is mainly for what he believed to be in Timothy,—the unfeigned faith which he had, in some sense, as a heritage from his ancestors, but which he personally and stedfastly continued to hold,—there can be no reasonable doubt. But this is not formally introduced till ver. 5, and there is an involved construction of two or three clauses going before, commencing with the particle ὡς, which presents some difficulty, and has been variously explicated by commentators. Some, as Chrysostom, Luther, Authorized Version, take ὡς in the sense of *that* (which it never properly means), and so make the apostle's remembrance of Timothy in his prayers the direct object of his thanksgivings,—this being only supplemented afterwards by a reference to Timothy's sincere faith. That, however, appears unnatural; and so also are the renderings of ὡς by *when, as often as* (Calvin, Conybeare, "whenever I remember thee"), *because, quod, quoniam* (Common Vulg., Chrys., Leo), or even by *as*, which is adopted by Winer, De Wette, Huther, Ellicott. For though, by this latter method, as indeed also by the others, we get the substantial import of the passage, yet not in the precise form in which it seems to have been presented by the apostle: he would be made to tell Timothy, that since he did constantly in fact remember him in his prayers, he could, while he did so, bring into consideration his unfeigned faith. It seems best, most in accordance with the order and connection of the several clauses, to take ὡς in the ordinary sense of *how, quam* (which is the rendering also of the Vulg. in the *Codex Amiat.: quam sine intermissione habeam tui memoriam*), and thereby bring the prayerful remembrance of Timothy into a somewhat closer relation to the thanksgivings than if it were merely parenthetical. Thus: *I give thanks to God . . . how unceasing remembrance I have of thee in my prayers night and day, longing to see thee, mindful of thy tears, that I may be filled with joy, recollecting the unfeigned faith* [*that is*] *in thee, which dwelt first*, etc. Reading the passage thus, in what seems the most natural and simple manner, the apostle must be regarded as including the perpetual mention of Timothy in prayer as a ground of thanksgiving; but then it is not so properly the mention or remembrance itself, as the way in which he found himself able to do it, that he is thankful for: it was that he had, and still continued to have, such an image upon his mind of Timothy's affection to himself and his faith in God, that he could unceasingly bring him into remembrance before God for an interest in the divine favour and blessing, being assured that in so doing he might look for acceptance with Heaven. There is nothing strange in such a line of thought; but it obviously proceeds upon the conviction of Timothy's spiritual state and character being such as to awaken only grateful feelings and recollections; and it does seem strange that any one should think of discovering, in so friendly and glowing a representation, indications of spiritual declension on the part of the much-loved evangelist. This is what Alford does, but on the slenderest possible grounds.

The epithet of *unceasing*, which the apostle couples with his mention of Timothy in his prayers, must, as its prominent position indicates (ὡς ἀδιάλειπτον ἔχω τὴν μνείαν), be emphasized: it was an *unceasing* reminiscence in ever recurring acts of devotion, because the tender and agreeable impressions on his mind respecting Timothy pressed him continually into the foreground of his thoughts and desires, when drawing near to God. Something of this the apostle ascribes to the working of natural affection—*longing to see thee*, ἐπιποθῶν, "participle dependent on ἔχω μνείαν, expressing the feeling that existed previously to, or contemporaneous with, that action, and connected with the final cause, ἵνα πληρωθῶ" (Ellicott) — the full experience of joy. The apostle's longing, he goes on to state, was much increased by the remembrance of Timothy's tears—the tears, doubtless, which he shed at parting with his beloved father in Christ, and shed afresh, we can well suppose, as the perils deepened around the apostle's condition. He could not, therefore, but wish to have this dear companion again at his side, in order that their common sadness might be turned into joy; nor can we doubt that the ordering of events, so as to accomplish this natural desire, was one of the things which he sought from God, when making such frequent mention of the object of his affectionate regard. But such considerations and desires, however proper in themselves, and suitable for expression in prayer to God, would have failed in their end, nor would they have found any record here, unless they had been associated with another—from the first the more essential element in the apostle's estimate of Timothy's condition as a subject of thanksgiving and prayer—namely, the recognition he could make of his unfeigned faith. The expression is a little peculiar, ὑπόμνησιν λαβών, literally, taking reminiscence, or simply *recollecting;* as λήθην λαβών, in 2 Pet. i. 9, is unquestionably *forgetting,* and ἀρχὴν λαβ. λαλεῖσθαι, *took beginning = began to be spoken.* This recollecting of Timothy's faith is not to be connected with the apostle's longing to see him, but is to be referred back to his thanksgivings and constant remembrance of Timothy in prayer; such recollection gave him confidence in naming Timothy to God, and filled him with gratitude. And in designating the faith *unfeigned,* he clearly ascribes to it the most essential attribute of goodness; it was a genuine principle, the opposite of a hypocritical or wavering profession. That the possession of this faith was also an abiding characteristic of Timothy—a thing of the present as well as of the past—is plainly implied in the unceasing mention made of him by the apostle to God as a man of faith.

The faith in question is further characterized as that *which also* (ἥτις, *quæ et,* Vulg., that sort of faith which) *dwelt first in thy grandmother Lois;* meaning, not first absolutely in this ancestral line, but first in that portion of it with which the apostle and Timothy had personal acquaintance —the first so far as they could take cognizance of it;—

and thy mother Eunice; and not only so, *but I am persuaded* (πέπεισμαι, have been and still am persuaded) *that in thee also* (viz. ἐνοικεῖ, *dwells*). That there is a want of entire confidence expressed here, as Alford, after some earlier commentators, thinks, has no proper foundation. Paul simply expresses his persuasion that Timothy had the same unfeigned faith which belonged to his godly parentage on the female side; and we have no more reason to imagine that this connection with the past implies suspicion in regard to Timothy's stedfastness, than the apostle's declaration a little before respecting himself, that he served God from, or after the example and spirit of, his forefathers, bespoke some failing in his own piety.

Ver. 6. *For which cause*—namely, because I have full confidence that such is your spiritual condition (Theophylact, διότι οἶδα σε ἀνυπόκριτον ἔχοντα πίστιν; Theod., ταῦτα περὶ σοῦ πεπεισμένος παρακαλῶ). Cocceius justly compares 1 John ii. 21, "I have not written unto you because ye know not the truth, but because ye know it," and adds: "Each apostle guards against the supposition that his writing or excitation should seem to insinuate either ignorance or unbelief of the truth; and, on the contrary, shows that the knowledge and faith of the truth dwelling in them was the cause of writing them and stirring them up. Such incitement would certainly have been in vain with persons ignorant of the truth, or not exercising faith in it." In accordance with this is the mild form of the exhortation that follows: *I remind thee* (ἀναμιμνῄσκω, admonish is too strong) *to stir up* (ἀναζωπυρεῖν, lit. *to kindle up*, the subject being viewed under the image of a fire) *the gift of God which is in thee through the laying on of my hands.* That the verb here used (ἀναζωπ.) does not necessarily imply any previous decay or slumbering—that it means to kindle *up*, as well as *re*-kindle, the force of ἀνα being *up*, or *upwards* (Ellicott)—is put beyond doubt by the examples given in

Wetstein. (The synonyms given by Hesych. are ἀνεγεῖραι, ἀναζῆν ποιεῖν; by Suidas, ἀνανεῶσαι, ἀνεγεῖραι.) Very similar is the language of St. Peter when he speaks of stirring up the disciples by way of remembrance, or putting them in mind (διεγείρειν ὑμᾶς ἐν ὑπομνήσει, 2 Pet. i. 13). The circumstances of the time, especially as connected with the apostle's fresh imprisonment, and now all too probable destination to capital punishment, rendered such an exhortation every way fitting. On such a mind as Timothy's, disposed to lean rather than to lead—accustomed to take a subordinate, not a principal part—those circumstances could not but have a depressing effect. The danger for him, the apostle would readily foresee, was that he would lose heart in the conflict, and perhaps withdraw into some more retired and humble position than his calling and acquirements qualified him to occupy. He is therefore urged to brace himself for the occasion, and stir into vigorous action the gift he had received for the service of God. The gift itself (χάρισμα) is undoubtedly the special endowment or gift of grace qualifying him for the evangelistic work to which he was appointed. It was referred to in the former epistle (1 Tim. iv. 14), and is there connected instrumentally with the laying on of the hands of the presbytery, as here with the laying on of St. Paul's own hands. There is no contrariety between the two statements, as both parties no doubt took part in the ordination service (see at the former passage); but here it was natural and proper that the apostle should have reminded Timothy of his own act of imposition, as now more than ever Timothy was likely to be called to stand, to a certain extent, in the apostle's room, and enter into his labours. It was of great importance, therefore, that he should now feel his increased responsibility, and apply himself to the cultivation of the grace which had been conferred upon him, undeterred by any discouragements or dangers which might stand in the way.

Ver. 7. *For God gave us not the spirit of cowardice, but of power, and love, and correction.* By *spirit* here may be understood either God's Spirit working in a certain manner in us, or our own spirit as wrought upon and formed by God; practically, it comes much to the same thing, since either way the gift is of God, obtained by direct fellowship with His Spirit. But spoken of as a thing that, hypothetically at least, might take a wrong as well as a right direction, it most naturally presents itself to our view in the subjective, concrete aspect—as the inwrought spiritual disposition or temperament which, by the Spirit of God conferred on us as ministers of the word, we were at once called and empowered to exercise. Now, as such it was not, the apostle says, *the spirit of cowardice* (δειλίας, more than φόβου, *fear*, which is capable of a good as well as a bad sense) —such as would dispose us to shrink from the discharge of duty when it becomes irksome, or to compromise our principles when it is perilous to hold them. Not this is the spirit with which we were endowed by God (as at Rom. viii. 15 it was denied to be the spirit δουλείας, of bondage), *but of power*, manfully to bear up against trials and difficulties, to hold our ground when others are ready to yield and give way; *and love*, which seeks not its own, but the good of others and the glory of God, even at the expense of what is personally dear and amiable to it; *and correction.* In regard to this last expression, σωφρονισμός, it is impossible, perhaps, to get an English word that exactly corresponds with the original. Our translators have rendered it *sound mind*, substantially following Beza, *sanitatis animi;* the Vulg. and Erasmus have *sobrietatis*, not much different, but giving the import of σωφροσύνη rather than σωφρονισμός: for the latter, as Suicer remarks, *Thes.* ii. p. 1224, " expresses the authority which admonishes and restrains those who walk in a disorderly manner, and is opposed to cowardice;" so that this spirit shows itself in a capacity to check what, either by corrupt motions from within, or by threats and allurements from without, would lead us into foolish and perverse ways : it is the power of authoritative control and wise restraint, which if we but have in sufficient measure, we shall not weakly bend to adverse circumstances, but make these bend to us. This coincides, in part at least, with one of Chrysostom's explanations ; and Theodoret gives the sense of the whole thus : " God has given us the grace of His most Holy Spirit, not that we should dread the perils that beset godliness, but that, being replenished with divine power, we might both ardently love Him and repress the disorder of the affections that agitate us ;" as also, it should have been added, might reprove the false compliances and disorderly behaviour prevalent around us. Hence the word, in later times, came to be applied to ecclesiastical censures ; see in Suicer.

Ver. 8. *Be not thou therefore ashamed of the testimony of our Lord, nor of me His prisoner.* Having received from God such a spirit, show it now by repressing all emotions of shame, and boldly avowing your adherence to the faith of Christ, and your connection with me as His apostle. The exhortation does not imply that any indication had yet been given by Timothy of an improper sense of shame ; rather the reverse, indeed,—it is a fatherly admonition, *lest he should* give way to the feeling ($\mu\grave{\eta}\ \dot{\epsilon}\pi\alpha\iota\sigma\chi\upsilon\nu\theta\hat{\eta}s$, coupled here, as elsewhere, with the accusative, ver. 16, Rom. i. 16). But amid the painful experiences of the apostle at the time of his writing,—seeing how one after another of his old friends had been dropping away from him, and now only one faithful companion remained to stand by him (chap. iv. 10, 11),—we cannot wonder that he should have manifested solicitude about his beloved Timothy, and called him to exhibit another spirit. The testimony of Christ, or, as it is put somewhat unusually, of our Lord (see, however, 1 Tim. i. 14, Heb. vii. 14), is certainly not Christ's personal *martyrion*, His martyr death, or the witnessing that had to be borne respecting it, but all that the faithful servant and minister of Christ was bound to testify concerning His person and work, His life and death. The genitive, therefore, is the genitive of the object (μαρ. τοῦ Κυρίου) : the primary aim of apostolic and evangelistic work was to bear witness about Him (Acts i. 8, ii. 32). And with this primary testimony St. Paul couples himself as the Lord's prisoner,—a prisoner, that is, for the Lord's sake, and in a sense also (though this only by implication) by the Lord's appointment. It was the duty of Timothy to be no more ashamed of the apostle in such a crisis than of the gospel itself: for Christ was, in a manner, suffering in His servant; and to turn the back on the one (considering the closeness of Timothy's relation to him), would have been virtually to turn it on the other.

From what Timothy should not do, the apostle proceeds to say what he should : *But suffer hardship with me for the gospel, according to the power of God.* The preposition (σὺν) in the verb—συγκακοπάθησον—seems to be most naturally referred to the apostle; as the question which now presented itself for solution was, whether Timothy would join himself with the apostle in suffering for the gospel, or to avoid the suffering would stand aloof. Not, therefore, as in the A.V., "be partaker of the afflictions of the gospel" (which also somewhat harshly represents the gospel as susceptible of suffering), but be partaker of affliction, or suffer hardship with me, for the gospel—εὐαγγελίῳ—the Dat. of interest, for its sake, or on its behalf. We have a similar mode of expression in Phil. i. 27, "Striving together for the faith of the gospel" (συναθλοῦντες τῇ πίστει τοῦ εὐαγ.). When the apostle exhorts Timothy to share with him in this readiness to suffer for the gospel *according to the power of God*, he points to the great things done by God in the matter of salvation as a ground and motive for something corresponding being done by us: Consider what power He has displayed in meeting with and overcoming the evils of our condition, and in that power show that you have become a partaker. Chrys.: "Because it was a hard saying, *Suffer hardship*, he again comforts him, saying, *not according to our works;* that is, Do not think to bear these things by thine own power, but by the power of God; for it is thine to choose and be ready to undertake, but it is God's to relieve and to give rest. Then also he brings forth proofs of His [God's] power: Consider how thou wert saved; how thou wert called. As he says elsewhere, *According to His mighty power that works in us.* Thus there is greater power required to persuade the world than to make the heavens. How wert thou called?" he asks: "*By a holy calling.* That is, He made those holy who were sinners and enemies; and these things are not of us—they are the gift of God."

Ver. 9. The apostle now proceeds to give a brief but graphic description of this manifested power of God in the matter of salvation: *Who saved us, and called us with an holy calling, not according to our works, but according to His own purpose, and the grace which was given us* [grace that which was given = the grace which was given] *in Christ Jesus before eternal times.* The passage as a whole, including what follows in ver. 10, has a close resemblance to Tit. iii. 4–6, only with the introduction here of certain phases of the work of God, which bear directly on the mighty power and energy displayed in its execution. The purpose of the apostle in so distinctly referring to God's more peculiar work naturally led to this; since it was designed to brace and fortify the mind of Timothy to that life of vigorous action and hardy endurance which was in accordance with the gospel scheme, and would be a fitting reflection of it. In saying that *God saved us and called us*, it is plainly God the Father that he more specifically refers to, as with Him, in Scripture, salvation as a whole, and in particular the calling of believers, is commonly associated. The calling, in this aspect of it, is all one with being brought into a state of salvation. And the work itself, with this individual application of it, is ascribed, as to its origin, simply and exclusively to the sovereign goodness and electing love of God, projecting themselves into the future before it could properly be said there was either a past or a future : the fountainhead of all was *His own* (ἰδίαν) *purpose and grace*, and that not waiting to be evoked by the events and circumstances of human life, but *given in Christ Jesus before eternal times*. How carefully is the doctrine of God's saving grace here guarded from dependence on anything external or creaturely ! It is traced up to the infinite depths of the Father's loving-kindness, not merely as regards the general idea and principal lineaments of the plan, but also in respect to the glorious gift it secures for the individual believer. The grace was *given* us by Him—given before eternal times; for, as even De Wette puts it, " what God determines in eternity, is as good as done in time." And given in Christ, who, as sponsor for His own in the everlasting covenant, could then also receive for them what the Father in His good pleasure gave : so that, as regards those who shall ultimately share in the blessings of the covenant, all from the first is well ordered and sure. Much the same thought as to the primal and thoroughly independent character of God's purpose of grace is presented in Tit. i. 2, only connected with a promise instead of a purpose.

Ver. 10. *But*—passing from the secret purpose of grace in eternity to its unfolding in time—*manifested now by the appearing of our Saviour Jesus Christ, who abolished death, indeed, but brought life and immortality* (or incorruption) *to light*. Christ's appearing must certainly be understood in the larger sense—not of the incarnation simply, but of the incarnate Son in His entire mission and work on earth. By means of that He gave full manifestation of the Father's eternal purpose of grace; and did so, the apostle tells us, by a twofold act—a sort of double agency, on the one side destructive, on the other salutary and glorifying. The two necessarily stand in contrast, yet not without a close and inward connection; for the one is but the reverse side of the other. Hence the particles μέν—δέ, indicative at once of connection and contrast (which should not be overlooked in the rendering): *who abolished death, indeed, but brought life and immortality to light.* In the one respect He acted as a destroyer, but only that He might place as in the light of day the destiny of His people to an everlasting heritage of life and blessing: salvation in its highest issues necessarily carrying along with it a work of destruction.[1] In so speaking of the manifestation of God's grace, and identifying the whole with the appearing of Christ among men, there is a close resemblance, in point of form, to the representation previously given of the eternal purpose of grace. This was contemplated by the apostle, not only as taking shape in the divine counsels before the world began, but as finding there an ideal realization in the (predestined) gift of salvation-blessings in Christ. So now, here, with respect to the *manifestation* of the grace, he sees its accomplishment in the personal triumph and glorification of the Redeemer, as potentially carrying along with it and imaging the common experience and destiny of His people. For in *His* triumph over death *theirs* also was involved; and in that immortal life to which He rose, they have their life hid (1 Cor. xv. 20–22; Col. iii. 3). Or, as St. Peter puts it, "they are begotten again to a living hope by the resurrection of Jesus Christ from the dead, to an inheritance incorruptible, undefiled, and that fadeth not away" (1 Pet. i. 3, 4).

Viewing the passage thus as an exhibition in the personal Saviour of what is distributively, in due time, to be realized in the experience of all genuine believers, we are saved

[1] See, on this principle, *Typology of Scripture*, B. ii. c. 16, s. 2.

from the necessity of inquiring in what precise sense death is here to be understood—whether as a personal adversary, or as a state in respect alike to body and soul, or as a power pervading and overshadowing the world (Ellicott). There seems no need for going into such an inquiry, and breaking up what is here presented as a unity into a variety of parts. Death as triumphed over and abolished in Christ comprehends all that can justly be included in the name; primarily, no doubt, the extinction of animal life, but that only as the natural issue and result of the mortal elements or powers of evil, which are at work in the temporal condition of mankind. In Christ's resurrection from the dead, and entrance on the power of an endless life, a complete and final end is made of them all; as shall be done also in the case of the redeemed, when the purpose of God respecting them is finished. But what appeared like one great act in Him, who knew no sin, and had the Eternal Spirit dwelling in Him above measure, can in them be only gradually developed. And while the work is proceeding in their experience—proceeding amid many trials, and with the sure prospect of a temporary sojourn in the grave, they should strive to keep the eye of faith fixed on the glorious pattern of the risen Redeemer, as that to which they are destined to be conformed. For thus they will feel, that it is not for them to quail before the difficulties and trials of time, but in the face of all such to remain stedfast to their calling in Christ, and endure hopefully to the end.

The verb φωτίζειν, though sometimes used intransitively, is here and elsewhere (1 Cor. iv. 5; John i. 9; Rev. xxi. 23) taken actively. It means, not for the first time to disclose, but to bring into the clearest light what had hitherto lain in comparative obscurity. The thing so shone upon, objectively illuminated, is *Life*—life, as elsewhere spoken of in these Pastoral epistles (here, ver. 1; 1 Tim. iv. 8; Tit. i. 2), in the higher sense—such as it exists, pure and blessed, in the presence and kingdom of God. It is here conjoined with, and explained by, ἀφθαρσίαν, immortality or incorruption—indicating, not anything properly distinct from the life, but the imperishable and incorruptible nature of this life (as is done also in 1 Pet. i. 4). Finally, while the manifestation of God's grace, as destroying death and exhibiting life and immortality, took place in Christ, it is also associated with the gospel—is spoken of as in a manner done through this, because by the gospel the certain knowledge of it is communicated to men; and instrumentally, everything depends on the sincere belief and faithful proclamation of this gospel by the ministers of Christ.

Ver. 11. The reference to the gospel, introduced so casually at the close of the preceding verse, is taken by the apostle as a link to introduce what follows respecting his office, and what it called him to suffer, as well as to do, for the sake of Christ: *for which I was appointed a herald and apostle, and teacher of the Gentiles.* The same description exactly that was given of his office in the first epistle, chap. ii. 7. What follows, however, is different, having respect to the sufferings associated with the calling, as formerly it stood connected with his authority to prescribe and rule in church affairs.

Ver. 12. *For which cause also I suffer these things:* the things, namely, alluded to in ver. 8—his persecutions, imprisonment, and sufferings. *But I am not ashamed; for I know whom I have trusted, and am persuaded that He is able to keep my deposit against that day.* The chief question here is, What is to be understood by *my deposit*—τὴν παραθήκην μου? Is it what the apostle had committed to God, or what God had committed to him? Having just expressed his trust, and his assurance that this, whatever it might be, God was able to guard or keep (φυλάξαι), one most naturally thinks of it as something which he had committed to God. And this is the view expressed in the

Authorized Version—"that which I have committed to Him;" that also which many able expositors, in former and present times, have adopted, with only minor shades of difference as to the thing committed (his *soul*—Grotius, Bengel; *soul, body, and spirit*—Conybeare, Alford; his *salvation*—Calvin, Huther; his *final reward, crown of righteousness*—Theophylact, Beza, Calov, Wolf). But the view undoubtedly lies open to two somewhat serious objections. First, the personal pronoun connected with the word—*my* deposit—seems rather to connect its possession with Paul than with God; it was his as contradistinguished from another's, and his in connection with the cause for which he was suffering. Then, the word as used presently after, ver. 14, and in 1 Tim. vi. 20 (the only other passages where it occurs), expresses what is committed by God to a person, and for which he is answerable to God. And there is force, it must be allowed, in the question of De Wette: "How could a writer use the same word so shortly afterwards [or before], in a different sense, without giving some indication of the difference?" Considering, also, that the matter has respect to a peculiar Greek mode of expression, there is some weight to be attached to the circumstance that this is the sense which all the Greek expositors seemed to regard as the natural and patent one, though they differed as to what precisely should be understood by it. According to Theodoret, the deposit was "the spirit of grace which God had given to the apostle." What was the deposit? asks Chrysostom; and answers it by saying, "Faith, preaching." But he hesitates, and gives, as another possible answer, *the faithful:* and these, either as committed by God to the apostle, or by the apostle to God. Theophylact, as usual, adopts all Chrysostom's, and adds another also from himself,—namely, the future recompense: for "whosoever has done anything that is good lays it up with God, that he may in due season be crowned for it."

There is obviously a good deal of guess work in several of these explanations; in themselves fanciful, they are also little suited to the connection. On the whole, however, the weight of probability, in a linguistic point of view, seems plainly to favour the opinion which regards the deposit as something entrusted to the apostle. Then, looking at the connection, the same impression forces itself upon us. For it will be observed that the apostle is here accounting for the fact, that though now in the extremity of peril and suffering for his apostolic calling and his missionary labours, he was not ashamed. Had he yielded to the sense of shame, what would have happened? He would have renounced his connection with the gospel of Christ as a thing unworthy of him—too weak to stand in the hour of trial. But when he thought of Him who had sent him on such a warfare, and had put him in trust with so precious a treasure, he felt there was no room for shame, and scorned the temporizing policy which shame would dictate. The all-powerful Guardian and Protector in whom he confided, and who had borne him through so many troubles in the past, would assuredly uphold him still, and enable him to preserve his calling, with all its sacred prerogatives and gifts, unimpaired to the end. So that in the great day of account, nothing properly belonging to it should be found wanting—nothing forfeited or lost.[1]

This I take to be the most natural explanation of the passage, and the train of thought which it embodies. The attempt of Alford to vindicate the other view has too artificial an appearance, and overlooks, as it seems to me, the more important points, on which the determination of the

---

[1] It might be added, in proof of the naturalness of the interpretation which identifies the deposit with the apostolic calling of Paul, that he often elsewhere speaks of *being put in trust with the gospel*; 1 Tim. i. 11; Tit. i. 3; Gal. ii. 7, etc.

question must turn. The *day* referred to in so emphatic a manner, is undoubtedly the day of the Lord's appearing for judgment. But εἰς ἐκείνην τὴν ἡμέραν is not *until, up to* that day, but *for*, or, as in the Authorized Version, *against* it, in view of its proceedings.

Ver. 13. *Have* (or possess) *the pattern of sound words, which thou heardest of me in faith and love which are in Christ Jesus.* The term ὑποτύπωσις occurs only here and in 1 Tim. i. 16; nor does it mean more than pattern or exemplar, only this in the more active or vital sense: "a living expression of things (as Calvin puts it), as if they were visibly presented to the eye." The verb with which it is connected, ἔχε, has been taken by many commentators, also in the Authorized Version, as substantially equivalent to κάτεχε, *hold fast.* But this is untenable. The examples appealed to do not bear out the interpretation: in several of them the meaning may fairly enough be expressed by *hold*, but this only in the sense of having as a possession; so, for instance, at 1 Tim. i. 19, we can indifferently render " *having* " or " *holding* faith and a good conscience," and at chap. iii. 9, " having " or " *holding* the mystery of the faith in a pure conscience." The verb in each case denotes nothing more than an actual personal possessing. Abiding, then, by this only allowable sense, what is to be understood by the exhortation to Timothy, that he should possess the fresh pattern of sound words, which he had heard from the apostle? Many would take it, with Calvin and Beza, of " that form and method of teaching " which he had learned from Paul; and others, somewhat more definitely, of an outline or written sketch, which the apostle had furnished him withal (Herder, Schrader, De Wette). Alford objects to this as in one respect too specific (reading ὑποτύπωσιν as if it were τὴν ὑποτύπ.), and in another too general—away from any immediate connection with the present discourse. He would therefore render, " Have (take) an example of (the) healthy words which thou heardest of me;" and he would regard it as pointing to the declaration just uttered by the apostle in the immediately preceding verse: *q.d.*, Take these as a specimen or example of the sound words which thou hast so often heard from me. But this also is an explanation which has an artificial aspect, and requires too much to be supplied. Had the apostle meant precisely what it ascribes to him, we should have expected him to employ language that pointed more explicitly to the preceding declaration; nor is ἔχε, with such a rendering, exactly in its place, as is clear from the virtual displacing of *have* in the translation by the bracketed *take*. There is certainly no need for excluding the declaration in question from the sound or healthy words spoken of by the apostle; and it is quite probable that the exhortation of this verse was suggested by the healthful utterance of faith and practice therein contained. But the *general* form of the exhortation, and the reference at the close of it to things formerly heard by Timothy from the lips of the apostle, forbid our giving it so limited an application.

Perhaps the main scope and spirit of the exhortation could not be more happily expressed than has been done in the following comment of Chrysostom's: "What is it that he says? I have, as it were, after the manner of painters, impressed an image of virtue on thee, and of all the things which are pleasing to God, as a certain rule and archetype and declaration which I have let down into thy soul. These things, therefore, possess; and if thou shouldst have to give counsel respecting faith, or love, or self-control, take thence your exemplars: you shall have no need to seek a pattern from others, having all these provided to your hand." The apostle thus expresses the wish that Timothy should retain, for his own safety against error and backsliding, the many things he had heard from the apostle as the kind of living type and embodiment of whatever was healthful in the life of faith—should remember it, and keep it beside him, like a faithful monitor and guide. Not, however, that he should do this in a mechanical and formal manner—out of regard merely to the authority from which he had derived it—but in the spirit of a true disciple, as one dwelling *in faith and love that are in Christ Jesus:* in these, that is, as the spiritual element, or frame of mind, in which the pattern of things exhibited to him should be remembered and applied. He must with a kindred spirit appropriate them, and endeavour to carry out the high moral ends for which they were given.

Ver. 14. Very naturally and fitly coming after this exhortation, rightly understood, is the charge in this verse: *the goodly deposit keep through the Holy Spirit that dwelleth in us.* The goodly deposit, or good thing entrusted to him, is just the scheme of divine doctrine and obligation, which he had received in trust as a believer and an evangelist, and the living type of which had formed itself in his heart from the apostolic words he had so often listened to. He is called to keep or guard this ($\phi\acute{u}\lambda a\xi ov$); yet not as in his own strength and wisdom, but through the indwelling of the Holy Spirit. So that there is no inconsistence between what is thus charged on Timothy respecting *his* deposit, and what the apostle represented himself as doing in regard to his own—trusting in the faithfulness and power of God to keep it. In both cases alike the effective guardianship was of God—the assurance of a safe and triumphant issue stood in their personal relation to Him; but God's keeping, in their case as in all others, had man's for its necessary counterpart—through this alone could it be justly expected to realize itself.

Ver. 15. A few sad notices are now introduced of persons who had failed to do toward the suffering cause of Christ in the apostle what he had been earnestly pressing upon Timothy. *Thou knowest that all who are in Asia turned away from me.* Who these might be we cannot tell, except as regards the two individuals specially mentioned, *of whom is Phygellus and Hermogenes;* nor of these do we know anything more than the names, for no other notice exists regarding them. But the "all in Asia" can only refer to some definite number in that region—the Roman province which bore the name of Asia—with whom the apostle had, in his hour of trial, some sort of recognised connection. As Timothy knew, at least, the general circumstances referred to, the apostle naturally left a good deal to be supplied. He does not even say where the conduct he felt so painfully was exhibited; but the natural supposition is, it was at Rome, and in connection with the accusation brought against him, or the trial and imprisonment to which it led. In this emergency those Asiatics (with one noble exception presently mentioned) *turned away from him,* ἀπεστραφήσαν—not "*are* turned away," as if they had gone into settled alienation and apostasy—for it refers to a specific act of unkindness toward the apostle; yet not, perhaps, so marked as that implied in the translation of Alford—they *repudiated* him; for the verb does not strictly import more than to stand aloof: when they should have showed friendship, they ignored him. Even this was bad enough, and betrayed a culpable lack of sympathy with one who had done so much for them, and a kind of halfheartedness to the cause of which he was the peculiar representative.

Vers. 16, 17. There was, however, a noble exception to this faint-hearted procedure: *The Lord give mercy to the house of Onesiphorus, because he ofttimes refreshed me, and was not ashamed of my chain*—that, namely, which bound him as a felon to the soldier who guarded him. It implies that others were ashamed, and, shrinking from the ignominious treatment which his unflinching zeal had brought on him, turned away. The more gratifying must have been the conduct of Onesiphorus, whose Christian principle and fellow-feeling carried him above the discouragements and perils of the time, and, regardless of consequences, enabled him to do the part of a genuine comforter. He *ofttimes* did it, says the apostle—even after the chain had turned to imprisonment in the capital; for it is added, *when he had arrived in Rome* (γενόμενος ἐν Ῥώμῃ, not merely was there, but had come to the city, or arrived in it), *he sought me out with greater diligence, and found me.* The expression is striking, as showing that what led others to turn away from the apostle was the very thing which prompted the friendly search and beneficent ministrations of Onesiphorus. "The comparative [in σπουδαιότερον] does not imply any contrast between Onesiphorus and others, nor with the diligence that might have been expected, but refers to the increased diligence with which Onesiphorus sought out the apostle when he knew that he was *in captivity*. He would have sought him out σπουδαίως in any case; now he sought for him σπουδαιότερον" (Ellicott).

Ver. 18. *May the Lord grant to him that he may find mercy from the Lord in that day.* The repetition of LORD is peculiar—the Lord grant that he may find from the Lord! —but is certainly not to be explained, with some, both in earlier and later times, as having respect in the first case to the Father, and in the second to the Son as the Judge. If such a distinction had been intended to be made, we may be sure it would have been more broadly marked. We may explain it (with Huther, Alford), by regarding the first expression, "May the Lord grant" (δῴη ὁ Κύριος), as so common a formula in such brief requests to Heaven, that the repetition in the second part was not noticed. But Calvin's seems preferable: "It might be that the vehemence of affection moved Paul to an unnecessary repetition, as is wont to happen." And he properly adds: "This prayer teaches us how much greater a reward shall await those who, without the hope of any earthly recompense, have done offices of kindness to the saints, than if they had received a present reward from the hand of men." It is noticeable, also, as he still further remarks, that mercy is the thing prayed for, doubtless because the apostle had respect to the Lord's own exposition of the law of recompense: "Blessed are the merciful, for they shall obtain mercy;" and again, "Blessed . . . because I was sick and in prison, and ye visited me." The circumstance that St. Paul asks simply a future blessing for Onesiphorus—mercy of the Lord in that day, the day when all things shall come into judgment—coupled with the other circumstance, that when speaking of the present he twice over names merely *the household* of Onesiphorus (ver. 16, iv. 19), has given rise to the inference that Onesiphorus must have already ceased to live. The inference may certainly be regarded as probable, though we can scarcely deem it altogether conclusive. For, possibly, such special mention was made of the household, because Timothy was at the time in their neighbourhood, and the father of the household may have been known to be still absent from them. But the matter is of little moment. More important is the circumstance which the apostle adds respecting this good man, to show that what he did at Rome was no isolated thing, but a following out of the course he was wont to pursue at home: *And how many things he ministered at Ephesus, thou knowest very well* —βέλτιον—literally, better—namely, than I can tell you, or than needs to be told. In these Ephesian ministrations the apostle doubtless shared; but as they are mentioned quite generally, they may justly be regarded as embracing the Christian community there, and its common interests. The A.V. has "ministered *unto me*," and in the later copies of the Vulgate *mihi* is inserted, but the earlier and better copies want it; and there is nothing corresponding to it in the Greek.

CHAPTER II.

Ver. 1. *Thou therefore, my child, be strengthened in the grace that is in Christ Jesus.* This is the practical result which the preceding statements were intended to produce in the mind of Timothy. The *therefore,* which indicates the connection, points back mainly to the apostle himself, and subordinately to his sympathizing friend Onesiphorus, who had shown themselves to be possessed of a moral power that was adequate to the greatest trials and emergencies of life. And this power the apostle had also been careful to represent as derived solely from the grace of a redeeming God. Therefore, when calling upon his child Timothy to follow in the same path of suffering and obedience, his primary exhortation is as to the source of strength: *Be strengthened*—ἐνδυναμοῦ—not simply "be strong," for the verb in the passive signifies to become strong, to get strength (comp. Rom. iv. 20, Eph. vi. 10); and this *in the grace that is in Christ Jesus*—that is, in the supply of the Spirit of life, which is ever ready to be given to those who are savingly united to Him. The being in Christ by a child-like faith is the sphere in which the gift of grace is to be found. But the injunction to be strengthened therein, implies that, in order to be realized, it must be actively laid hold of by the believer. The grace that is provided to sustain him and carry him forward in the life of faith, is cooperating grace; and at every step it requires his willing respondency and implicit obedience. This is what was seen so nobly exemplified in the case of Abraham (Rom. iv. 18-22), and is explicitly enjoined upon all believers (Phil. ii. 12, 13). So that the "more grace" which is said to be given to believers (Jas. iv. 6), is always given in proportion as they feel their need of more, and are prepared to receive and use it.

Ver. 2. A direction is now given how best to secure the transmission of the testimony he was called to bear for Christ, and its faithful maintenance in the church: *and the things which thou hast heard from me with many witnesses, these commit to faithful men, such as shall be able to teach others also.* The things that had been heard are undoubtedly the same as those referred to in chap. i. 13, and are no more in the one case than in the other to be confined to what was uttered on some particular occasion. It is the whole scheme of doctrine and duty as taught by the apostle, and which Timothy had enjoyed numberless opportunities of listening to, that is here meant; not simply, as many commentators suppose, what was delivered of it at Timothy's ordination. This were an unwarranted abridgment, and is no way countenanced, but the reverse, by the mention of many witnesses in connection with the things delivered—διὰ πολλῶν μαρτύρων, literally, *through* these; but as at 2 Cor. ii. 4, where the apostle speaks of writing *through* many tears, meaning with tears accompanying and giving a specific impress to his work, so here the "through many witnesses" must signify *with* them, their presence forming a clear indication of the character of the things spoken and heard. These were no private communications, no secret doctrine delivered in a corner, as if adapted only to the wants of a select few, or intended to minister merely to personal gratification. They were the great things which concern the salvation of men and the glory of God; therefore things which all ears should hear, and which it was important to have committed in every particular church to faithful men (πιστοῖς ἀνθρώποις, men worthy of such a trust), in order that these might testify aright concerning them, and in turn find others who should receive and deliver the testimony to the generation following. This is the true apostolic succession; the kernel lies here, in the maintenance from age to age of the same grand fundamental principles of faith and practice. External organizations are but the shell which may more or less fitly serve to guard and perpetuate the treasure ; and it is by the possession of this, the kernel, or gospel treasure, that the worth of the other is to be tried, not that other which is to determine or modify it. Both the *doctrina arcani* (the secret traditionary doctrine) of the Catholics, and the so-called impressed character and inherent virtue of a ministerial sacerdotalism in the Christian church, are here virtually struck at the root.

Ver. 3. *Suffer hardship with me* (συγκακοπάθησον, the reading of ℵ, A, C, D, F at first hand, is undoubtedly the correct text, not σὺ οὖν κακοπάθησον of the received text), or "take thy share in suffering" (Conybeare), intimating that the disciple in this must not expect to be above his master: if he would do his work faithfully, he must lay his account to experiences of trouble. *As a good soldier of Jesus Christ.* This is the first of a series of illustrative examples showing the necessity, for those who in any department would do effective service, of being in habitual readiness to endure hardship. Every believer, and pre-eminently the believer who is also a minister of the gospel, is a soldier of Jesus Christ, enlisted under Him as the Captain of salvation, to contend against the powers of evil ; therefore hardship of some sort is inevitable (2 Cor. x. 3 ; Eph. vi. 11 sq.).

Ver. 4. *No one serving as a soldier* (Scholfield, *Hints*) *entangles himself* (taking the verb ἐμπλέκεται as in the middle) *in the businesses of life*—that is, in the ordinary affairs and occupations of a worldly calling, such as of the forum or the market-place—*in order that he may please him who has called him to be a soldier*—literally, who enrolled him as a soldier, for such is the exact import of the verb στρατολογεῖν, *milites conscribere;* but, with a very natural extension of the meaning, also to call or choose one so to serve. The fact stated is notorious : no officer engaged in earnest warfare would hire soldiers who did not engage to separate themselves for the special service, so as to be ready at any moment to do his commands. A similar disentanglement is needful to the Christian warrior from everything that might keep him at a distance from his Divine Master, or impede him in the service he is called to render. But only thus far; not that he must absolutely withdraw from all employments of a secular kind. The great mass of believers must serve Christ *in* these; and even for the Christian pastor, his specific relation to them must depend, to some extent, on circumstances. Ordinarily he *should* be free from any business of a worldly kind; but like Paul himself, with his tent-making, some work of that description may even form a part of his soldier-service to Christ.

Ver. 5. *But* (δέ, introducing a fresh illustration—Winer, *Gr.* § 53, 7, *b;* not only so, but there is this further case) *if any one also strive in the games*—another good rendering of Scholfield's, and decidedly preferable to that of the Authorized Version, "if a man strive for the masteries," which is too general, and scarcely suggests to the mere English reader the specific kind of striving referred to. It is impossible, except by such a circumlocution, to give the force of the Greek ἀθλῇ. The Vulgate also had to take the same course—*certat in agone. He is not crowned unless he have striven lawfully*—adhering with whatever self-sacrifice to the prescribed rules. This alone entitles him, even if his striving have been such as to place him in the foremost rank, to obtain the crown of victory. The inference is plain: if so in the lower sphere, and with respect to a perishable distinction, how much more in regard to the great struggle between righteousness and sin, light and darkness in ourselves and in the world, which carries with it issues of eternal moment!

Ver. 6. *The toiling* (κοπιῶντα, hard-working) *husbandman must first partake of the fruits,* or, must be first in partaking of them; his very character as a man of hard labour gives him in this respect a precedence and superiority over others: he *first* partakes, partakes even while he works, somewhat like the ox who might eat while in the act of treading the corn (1 Tim. v. 18). So, the apostle means to say, it is in the Lord's husbandry. There is here also a compensation; for they who grudge not the hardship, the present sacrifice involved in doing God's work, have a blessing which others know not—they reap, in a measure, while they labour, having an immediate satisfaction in the fruits which they have been enabled to gather. Such appears to be the precise import of the apostle's statement; and it is one quite suited to the connection, though we would rather, perhaps, have expected him to put it somewhat differently, so as to express the idea that the husbandman must first labour if he is to partake of the fruits, or labour before he can do so. This is, indeed, what many commentators have actually extracted from his words, with so exact a scholar as Winer to countenance the exposition as grammatically tenable (*Gr.* § 61, 5, *f*). But it is without support from any properly parallel passages, and manifestly does violence to the natural order and meaning of the words. The object of the apostle in using the illustration was not, seemingly, to mark the distinction between the active and the idle husbandman: he assumes that Timothy would not be exactly idle, that he would be a worker in the Lord's vineyard; but he would have him to be a worker in the stricter sense, like the husbandman who labours hard, who *toils* at his employment, and so reaps the first and fullest recompense. This is so clearly the preferable sense of the passage, that it is needless to recount other interpretations, and equally needless to go into the various applications which have been made of it by the Fathers and others in later times. Some of these are fanciful enough. We must keep hold of the great principle which the statement is brought to establish—*that the most willing and hard labourer is the most speedily and richly blessed.* This holds good in the spiritual as in the natural sphere; and only those things which can be called real exemplifications of such a principle are fair applications of the apostle's similitude.

Ver. 7. *Understand what I say*—so the verb (νόει) properly means, Lat. *intellige*—not simply consider, or observe; and it was said with reference to the figurative language employed in the immediately preceding verses. "For since it was a parabolical mode of speech, it was necessary that he (Timothy) should be stirred up to search into the meaning of the hidden sense" (Theodoret). And he couples with the exhortation an expression of confidence that the requisite assistance would be given from above: *for the Lord will give thee discernment in all things.* The correct reading seems to be δώσει, not δῴη, having the support of ℵ, A, C, D, F, with the Latin and Cop. versions; and the thing which the apostle expresses his confidence would be given to Timothy is σύνεσιν ἐν πᾶσιν, a *complete understanding in all things*—such an exact and comprehensive knowing as "grasps the connection, with its grounds and consequences" (Beck)—or a clear and intelligent discernment. Combining thus personal application with the assurance of divine grace, the apostle virtually said to Timothy, "Seek, and ye shall find."

Ver. 8. *Remember Jesus Christ as having been raised from the dead, of the seed of David, according to my gospel.* This I take to be the exact rendering of the original—not "remember that Jesus Christ has been raised"—with the Vulg. (*Jesum Christum resurrexisse*), Authorized Version, and, among others, Alford, who tries to distinguish between the use of an accusative after μνημόνευε, and a genitive, as if in the former case it was a *fact* that was to be borne in mind, rather than an object or a person. Any one who will compare the following examples, in the two first of which the object of the verb is in the genitive, and the other two in the accusative (Luke xvii. 32; John xvi. 21; Matt. xvi. 9; 1 Thess. ii. 9), may see that the alleged distinction is entirely fanciful. When in the first of those passages our Lord called His disciples to remember Lot's wife, He surely meant Lot's wife as embodying a memorable fact, not less than when in the third of them He called His disciples to remember the five loaves of the five thousand; and so with the others. The verb seems to have been indifferently coupled with a genitive or an accusative of the object—in classical writers more frequently with the accusative, in the New Testament more frequently with the genitive; but with whichever case, the import is much the same—namely, to remember or bear in mind the person or object expressed in the noun that follows. So here it is, Remember Jesus Christ, but Jesus Christ in a specific aspect, as "having been raised from the dead," while still "of the seed of David." Why should an injunction have been laid on Timothy to keep so specially in remembrance the fact of a risen Saviour, and a Saviour sprung from the seed of David? We are left to conjecture; but it was partly, no doubt—perhaps we should say primarily—by way of encouragement: for, having his eye ever fixed on one so sprung and so glorified, he had in a manner before him the fulfilment of all promise, and the pledge of all just hope and expectation. Why should he therefore faint under his duty of service, or quail before the assaults of the persecutor? He knew that his Redeemer, the destined Head of God's chosen heritage, lived after having triumphed over sin and death, and was set down at the right hand of the Majesty on High. But in the same great facts, grasped by a childlike and reliant faith, he should have a secure position against the more subtle dangers which had begun to arise from that Gnostic spirit which, in its disparagement of flesh, at once ignored the natural descent of Christ, and made void the truth of His literal resurrection. And this also may have been in the view of the apostle, though there seems no reason for supposing, with some, that it was the only consideration to which he had respect in introducing the subject; nor, looking to the connection, even the more prominent one. The more immediate point is, how to endure hardship, to brave persecution, for the truth of Christ; and, surely, holding fast by Christ's royal lineage, which was essential to His being the Messiah promised to the fathers, and by His resurrection from the dead, which was equally essential to His right to reign over the house of God, could not but form the best preparation, as it was indeed the indispensable condition, of stedfastness.

Ver. 9. The truths respecting Christ, which Timothy in the preceding verse was exhorted to bear in mind, were spoken of in connection with St. Paul's gospel—the gospel which had been committed to him (1 Tim. i. 11); he now adds, *in which* (that is, the gospel, as his appointed sphere of action) *I suffer hardship up to bonds as a malefactor.* Corresponding phrases are, Phil. ii. 8, μέχρι θανάτου, up to death; Heb. xii. 4, μέχρις αἵματος, up to blood; so in the Vulg., *usque ad vincula.* But (though as to my personal condition I am in chains) *the word of God is not bound:* this still ran, and was glorified. It did so partly, indeed, through the apostle himself testifying of it, even in his bonds, before rulers and kings, so that his gospel as well as his bonds came to be known in Cæsar's household (Phil. i. 13, iv. 22), and in his letters sounding it forth far and wide; but partly also through the instrumentality of others who gave themselves to the same blessed work, and some of whom, he intimates, waxed bold through his bonds to speak more abundantly the word of God (Phil. i. 14). Thus, when an arrest is laid on one, freedom and boldness are given to others to spread abroad the good seed of the kingdom.

Ver. 10. *For this reason I endure all things for the sake of the elect, in order that they also may obtain the salvation that is in Christ Jesus with eternal glory.* The connection between this and the preceding cannot be taken so close, as with Bengel, "Because through my chains the gospel runs, therefore I endure." He, no doubt, has in view the diffusion of the word, because it was in connection with that his sufferings had come upon him; but in the present passage that circumstance rather lies in the background, recognised and felt, yet not distinctly exhibited; for he has a more special point which he wishes to bring into notice in relation to the preaching or diffusion of the word, viz. the salvation of God's elect. This was the aim of his preaching, yet not of his preaching merely, but also of his sufferings; for these, too, had an important bearing on the contemplated issue. We must therefore connect the διὰ τοῦτο at the commencement with what follows, as is usual in similar constructions, where these words stand related to a succeeding ἵνα, as at 1 Tim. i. 16, "For this reason I obtained mercy, that in me first," etc. (διὰ τοῦτο ἠλεήθην, ἵνα ἐν ἐμοὶ πρώτῳ), and so again at Philem. 15. The explanation of Chrysostom is quite to the point: "For what cause do I suffer these things? For the benefit of others, that they may obtain eternal life. What, then, do you promise? He did not say simply, for the sake of some persons, but for the sake of the elect. If God chose them, we ought to suffer all things for them, in order that they also may obtain salvation. When he says, *that they also*, he means to say, *as also we;* for God chose us also; and as for us God suffered, so also we for them." Under the name of *the elect* the apostle may certainly be regarded as having primarily in view those who belonged to that number in his own day; for them he was called more immediately to think and act, yet by no means exclusively. His apostolic work, as well in suffering as in preaching and writing, he knew well was for all countries and for all time; and the elect of this present age are in many ways reaping the benefit of his self-denying and devoted labours. Nor is it unimportant to mark how he heightens the good he sought for them—not their salvation merely, but the salvation that is in Christ Jesus, and that *with eternal glory:* so that if their salvation has to be made good through trial and suffering, its connection with Christ, and with the mass of glory laid up with Him in eternity, justifies, and unspeakably more than justifies, the sacrifice. So in 1 Pet. v. 10 the present suffering condition of believers generally is, in like manner, connected with their call to God's eternal glory.

Vers. 11–13. *Faithful is the saying, For if we died with Him, we shall also live with Him.* Does the saying point to what precedes, or to what follows? Commentators are divided on the question; and as nothing very decisive can be urged for the determination either way, they are still likely to be so. Certainly, as Ellicott contends, and Huther also admits (though he adopts the forward reference), the *for* (γὰρ) which follows the proverbial saying seems to point backwards, and to introduce a confirmatory statement of what had been uttered immediately before; and this is the view taken by all the ancient Greek commentators. But there is no need for pressing the matter closely either way, as it is substantially the same line of thought that is indicated in both the preceding and the following context—only in the former more individually, in the latter more generally. Whether viewed with respect to Paul himself and his fellow-labourers in the gospel, or with respect to those who in any place or time would lead the Christian life, one must be prepared to look for the same kind of mixed experience—temporal evil followed by a glorious compensation; hardship and suffering as the condition of ultimate victory; death even as the pathway to life, never-ending and full of glory. The truth of the gospel in this respect is a faithful saying: it holds good every way; the apostle himself was in the course of realizing it in his own experience, with the full consent and approval of his own mind. So he had said just before; and now he makes a quite general and comprehensive application of it: *For if we died with Him* (namely, when by a living faith we embraced Christ as our Saviour, entering into the fellowship of His sufferings ánd death), *we shall also live with Him*, sharing at last in His resurrection-power and blessedness of life, as spiritually we do in a measure now. *If we endure* (ὑπομένομεν, patiently undergo trial and hardship,—namely, *with Him*, or in His cause and service), *we shall also reign with Him:* as our Lord Himself repeatedly testified (Matt. xvi. 24–27, xix. 28, 29; Luke xxii. 28–30), and as is stated also in other passages (Rom. v. 17, vi. 8, viii. 10, 11, 17; Col. iii. 3, 4; Rev. iii. 21). *If we shall deny (Him)*,—put contingently, as a thing that might possibly happen in the future,—*He also will deny us;* a virtual repetition of our Lord's solemn words: "Whosoever shall deny me before men, him will I also deny before my Father who is in heaven" (Matt. x. 33). Finally, *if we are unbelieving*,—ἀπιστοῦμεν, not merely prove unfaithful in times of trial, shrink from confessing what we inwardly feel to be the truth concerning Him, but, rejecting or quitting our hold of the truth, pass over entirely into the region of unbelief,—if we should thus estrange ourselves from the common ground of faith, still *He abides faithful*—remaining perpetually true to His declarations and promises, whether we accredit them or not. And the reason follows: *For*[1] *He cannot deny Himself.* This implies that the word given as the ground of our faith in Scripture is the expression of His own essential nature; it reveals what, as possessed of that nature, He is in His relation to us, what

---

[1] The received text omits γὰρ, but it is found in the best copies, ℵ, A, C, D, F, L, and is admitted by all the best critics.

He purposes toward us, or has done in the execution of His purposes. To disown this, therefore, were to deny Himself; and *that* it is impossible He should ever do, seeing He is the unchangeable Jehovah (Mal. iii. 6); and so, His word, like Himself, "liveth and abideth for ever."[1]

Ver. 14. There follow now a series of exhortations to Timothy, founded upon the important statements contained in the preceding verses, and bearing directly on the manner in which he should ply the work of the ministry, and withstand the errors which were already beginning to prevail in the church. *Put them in mind of these things* (ὑπομίμνησκε, sup. αὐτοὺς, which in a similar exhortation at Tit. iii. 1 is expressed). The things meant were, no doubt, those mentioned immediately before. Timothy was first rightly to apprehend and grasp them for himself, and then act as a faithful monitor in enforcing them upon others. *Solemnly charging them* (διαμαρτυρόμενος, the διὰ intensifying the meaning of the verb, and the verb, though primarily signifying to bear witness or testify, evidently meaning, in such a connection as this, to deliver a protest or charge, 1 Tim. v. 21) *before God not to wrangle about words*,—a practice already mentioned in 1 Tim. vi. 4, and warned against as characteristic of a class of persons who were unsound at the very core, and of itself fitted to produce much mischief. So here it is declared to be *profitable for nothing* (χρήσιμον having for its object λογομαχεῖν, the art or practice of mere word-fighting); no one is in a moral respect the better for it. And worse than that, it is *upon the subversion of them that hear:* an elliptical clause, but plainly meaning that the practice tends to this melancholy result. And the reason is obvious; it serves to beget and nourish a captious, sophistical state of

---

[1] As regards the question whether the passage vers. 11-13, from its somewhat measured and rhythmical structure, was not part of some Christian hymn, I would be inclined to give the same judgment as in regard to 1 Tim. iii. 16—which see.

mind, the reverse of that babe-like spirit which receives the sincere milk of the word, and rests with a firm trust in the testimony it brings. If the parties in question were deficient in this before, they were sure to depart further from it by listening to such teaching: it would lead them entirely off from the foundations.[1]

Ver. 15. *Give diligence to present thyself to God approved:* δόκιμον, one who can stand, or has actually stood, the test appointed by God, and come forth stamped with His approval. The object of the exhortation was to lead Timothy, in contrast to the frivolous disputes mentioned before, to realize himself as a servant of God, and to guide his course through the trying and perilous circumstances around him, so as to be able to appear before the Divine Majesty as one that had proved faithful to the trust reposed in him. *A workman not ashamed:* ἀνεπαίσχυντον, in New Testament Scripture found only here, and in classical Greek signifying *shameless, impudent*, but used by Josephus in the sense of *not being ashamed of,* or *having no occasion to blush for* (*Ant.* xviii. 7. 1, μηδὲ δευτερεύειν ἀνεπαίσχυντον ἡγοῦ: "nor think that one should not be ashamed to be inferior to" . . . ; so also in Agapetus, quoted by Wetstein). The sentiment is the same as that expressed by Paul respecting himself in Phil. i. 20, ἐν οὐδενὶ αἰσχυνθήσομαι, In nothing shall I be ashamed—meaning that his behaviour would be such as to

[1] There is some variation both in the reading and the pointing of this text. Instead of μὴ λογομαχεῖν, MSS. A, C have μὴ λογομάχει— the imperative : Do not wrangle about words ; and this forming a clause by itself, necessitates another distribution of the preceding words : Put them in mind of these things, solemnly charging them before God. But this is an unnatural sort of arrangement, and differs from the apostle's usual practice ; for elsewhere διαμαρτύρομαι *precedes* the exhortation to which it belongs : 1 Tim. v. 21 ; 2 Tim. iv. 1. And though the reading above noticed must have early crept in, appearing as it does in the Latin versions, yet λογομαχεῖν is the text of ℵ, D, F, K, L, and is exhibited in the Syr., Coptic, and Gothic versions.

afford no occasion for such a feeling. And as the more special ground of this confidence, we have the still further characteristic—*rightly handling the word of truth*. Here again there is a word of singular occurrence in the New Testament—ὀρθοτομεῖν, primarily signifying to *cut straight*, with reference, as is supposed by some, to the cutting and distributing of bread (Calvin, Vitringa); by others, to the right division of the victims in sacrifice (Beza, Mel.); by others, to the drawing of straight furrows in ploughing (Theodoret); but by the majority to the cutting of a line of road, in which sense it occurs figuratively in Prov. xi. 5, Sept. The question is, how the word may most naturally be understood when applied, as it is here, to the treatment of God's word? To *divide rightly*, in one point of view, might give an appropriate meaning, but scarcely one quite suited to the connection; for as the subject under discussion is the true as opposed to the false, the serious and earnest as opposed to the frivolous and unprofitable, dealing with spiritual things by a minister of the gospel, one does not so naturally think of the *mode of distributing* or administering the word of truth among the hearers (a matter of tact and wisdom rather than of fidelity), as of a fair and conscientious or straightforward handling of the word itself. This, as opposed to all kinds of tortuous interpretations, or by-plays of ingenuity for sinister purposes, is pre-eminently what becomes the teacher who would stand approved in the judgment of God: like a sincere and honest workman, he must go right on in his use of the word, maintaining it in its integrity, and applying it to the great spiritual ends for which it has been given. This appears at once the simplest and the most suitable explanation of the phrase; it is that which substantially was expressed by the Vulgate, *recte tractantem*, and is acquiesced in by Huther, Alford, and others.[1]

[1] Deyling has the merit of establishing the correct view in a very full

Ver. 16. Here, again, the apostle returns to the things to be avoided—the corrupt practices of false teachers : *But profane babblings shun*—περιΐστασο, *stand aloof from*, as one naturally does in respect to any object of dislike or terror. It was used at Tit. iii. 9, much in the same way, with reference to unprofitable questions about the law, genealogies, and such like contentions. See also at 1 Tim vi. 20, where profane babblings are mentioned as things which Timothy should turn away from. Here it is added, by way of strengthening the exhortation, *for they will advance to more of ungodliness;* which the succeeding context shows must be understood of the persons who teach the profane babblings, not of the babblings themselves. The sense also requires this; for it is only the teachers of such things, of whom a forward movement in the wrong direction could justly be predicated. But readily enough of them : for exhibiting, as they did, a relish for modes of thought and discourse which could be characterized as at once empty and profane, their downward progress might be reckoned on as certain; the rather so, as now the great moral earnestness which appeared in the true teachers of the gospel would reflect unfavourably upon them, and almost inevitably drive them into extravagances of a more startling and pernicious kind.

Ver. 17. *And their word will eat as a gangrene.* A gangrene is described by Galen as "an eating sore," or a tumour in the state between inflammation and entire mor-

dissertation on the verse; *Obs. Sac.* vol. iv. p. 2, c. 3. After examining the other views, and stating that here, as in many other compound words, we cannot adhere to the etymological sense of *cutting*, he adds : Nam quemadmodum καινοτομεῖν non est res novas secare, sed *res novas moliri*, ita similiter ὀρθοτομεῖν est recte tractare, et ὀρθοτομία, tractatio recte, prout decet, instituta, traducta significatione a specie ad genus. Idem confirmat versio Syriaca pervetus, quæ ὀρθοτ. τὸν λόγον transtulit *recte prædicare sermonem veritatis*, hoc est, recte tractare et exponere Scripturam sacram, etc.

tification, and tending to the latter. Though not strictly synonymous with our word *cancer*, it might not improperly be represented in popular language as a sort of cancerous affection, and, like this, spreading or finding pasture (νομὴν ἕξει) on the contiguous parts of the body. It was therefore a fitting image of the evil tendency in such false teaching to diffuse itself among the people, because ministering in one respect or another to the weaknesses and follies of human nature. As the moral disease in the teachers themselves would get worse, so their word would eat outwards, catching hold of others, and bringing them under its noxious influence. It is a general statement, but to what extent applicable then, or to any particular error arising in later times, must always depend, partly on the kind of error which seeks propagation, and partly in the more or less congenial elements amid which it has to work.

Ver. 18. The apostle now points to specific examples of what he meant: *of whom is Hymenæus and Philetus, men who* (οἵτινες) *concerning the truth swerved* (or went astray, see at 1 Tim. i. 6), *saying that the resurrection has already taken place, and overthrow the faith of some.* One of the names mentioned here, Hymenæus, occurred in the First Epistle to Timothy, chap. i. 20; and, as was stated there, the name in both cases had respect, in all probability, to the same person. In the former passage he was represented as a man who had sunk into a bad moral condition—had thrust from him faith and a good conscience, and so concerning faith had made shipwreck. It is not materially different to say here of him, that he had gone astray respecting the truth, and did so to such an extent as to overthrow the faith of some. This, of course, implies that his own faith had previously suffered shipwreck—that he had virtually abandoned the ground of faith, and discarded the truth of God as taught by His authorized ambassadors. In this apostasy Philetus is coupled with him, of whom nothing is known except what is stated in this brief notice.

The specific error charged upon the persons in question, that they held the resurrection to have already taken place, is no proof of Marcionite teaching, as Baur and his school assert. There was no need of Marcion to account for the broaching of such opinions. The First Epistle to the Corinthians (chap. xv.) shows plainly enough how ready the Grecian mind was to stumble at the doctrine of a literal resurrection; and no wonder, since the doctrine was so entirely alien to the whole spirit and tendency of the Greek philosophy. Tertullian expressly affirms, that however much the philosophic sects might differ on other points, they were at one in denying that doctrine of the gospel (*De Præscr. Hær.* § 7); and hence, when St. Paul, in his discourse before the Athenian Areopagus, came to refer to the resurrection of the dead as a fact in history, already exemplified in Christ, the patience of his audience could stand it no longer; the assembly broke up amid jeers and laughter, as if some incredible absurdity had been uttered in their hearing. This, therefore, was precisely the point in respect to which it might be expected that heathen converts to the gospel would be apt to stagger; and such as were of a more speculative tendency, while admitting it in words, would deny it in reality. Within a few years of the first planting of the church at Corinth certain parties did so there, as several years later others appear to have done at Ephesus. In both places, very probably, the explanations fallen upon were of the kind mentioned by Tertullian: some identifying the resurrection with the soul's spiritual renewal by the doctrine of the gospel, causing it "to burst forth from the sepulchre of the old man;" while others understood it of the soul's departure from the body, "the world in their view being only the habitation of the dead" (*De Resurr.* § 19). The Hymenæus and Philetus here noticed must have taken somewhat of the former view, holding, as they did, the resurrection to be already past. It was altogether a spiritual thing in their account, a quickening merely of the soul's activities to newness of life; and thus, by their excess in spiritualizing, they loosened the very foundations of the Christian system; for the position they assumed involved by necessary inference the denial of Christ's resurrection, and the saving efficacy of His death (1 Cor. xv. 12-19).

Ver. 19. *Nevertheless* (μέντοι, here only in Paul's writings, but frequently in John's, *certe quidem*, expressive of opposition to the preceding, and preparing for an announcement of a contrary nature) *the firm foundation of God stands, having this seal,* "*The Lord knoweth them that are His.*" There can be no doubt that this is the proper mode of rendering—not, as in the Authorized Version, "The foundation of God standeth sure," which is grammatically untenable. The apostle's assertion is, that, notwithstanding the existence of such cases as he had just mentioned of defection from the truth and the consequent loss of salvation, there is a firm or strong foundation of God which remains stedfast. What, then, is the foundation? To this a great variety of answers have been given: with some it is the doctrine of the resurrection, denied by the heretics of the preceding verse; with others, the word of promise, or the plighted faith of God; with others, Christ or the Christian religion; with others, including Calvin, Calov, Wolf, and various besides, the election of God. It is quite possible to explain the apostle's assertion in connection with each of these views, and to say only what is in perfect accordance with the truth of things, and has also a certain bearing on the matter immediately in hand. Yet, unless it be the last, they fail in presenting such a contrast to the evil, which the thought here suggested was intended to meet with an adequate corrective, as exactly suits the requirements of the case. The evil was an actual falling away in some from the belief of the truth, and their consequent loss, with all who came under their influence, to the church of Christ. Now, to meet this, and reassure the hearts of believers under it, something more was plainly needed than to point attention to the certainty of the fact itself of a coming resurrection, or of the word generally and promises of God, or of Christ as the manifested Saviour, and the religion introduced by Him. For all these might have been conceded to be as they are represented in Scripture, and yet the defection in question gone on unchecked, nay, possibly spreading and growing till everything was involved in ruin. There was needed to set over against it an objective good, which should practically circumscribe the evil, set bounds to its operation, by securing that there should be a succession of living witnesses to the truth, whom no temptation could mislead, nor false teaching beguile, into a betrayal of its interests. Such a security might be said to be furnished by the election of God, yet in this only as actually realized in a company of faithful men, who abide in the truth, and resist the errors that tend to undermine it. It is also only such a living embodiment of the election of God, not the abstract idea or doctrine itself, which could fitly be designated a foundation; for this necessarily has respect to an objective reality, a structure of some sort (material or spiritual), whereof it forms a part. So that, not precisely the divine act of election, but "the faithful elect," as put even by the Catholic Estius, or, "which is the same thing, the church in the elect"—those chosen in Christ before the foundation of the world, and who are prepared and kept by omnipotent grace for the glory to which from the first they were destined—in a word, the members of the true or invisible as contrasted with the simply outward or professing church: these are what we may here most naturally understand by the foundation of God. They constitute His *firm* foundation, which stands amid both the assaults of adversaries and the defection of unstable souls, because held fast by His own eternal purpose and efficacious grace.

This, accordingly, is the view now generally adopted by commentators—for example, by De Wette, Huther, Wiesinger, Ellicott, Alford; and it is the only one that fitly accords with what follows about the sealing, which has immediate respect to Christ's true people, not to Christ Himself. Of course they are what they are only from their relation to Him; so that by this view He is not excluded from the foundation, but, as it were, subsumed; and they who would find Christ more directly in the passage are still obliged, when they come to the sealing, to couple His people with Him, and even to have special regard to them.

The notion of sealing with reference to a foundation is peculiar to this passage. For a literal foundation it were somewhat out of place, but not so when understood spiritually of those appointed to a particular calling or destination. It is in this way that the action of sealing is commonly employed in New Testament Scripture; it represents persons as somehow certified of God, or having a special pledge of security granted them (John vi. 27; 2 Cor. i. 22; Eph. i. 13, iv. 30). Such, at least, is the prominent, if not in every case the exclusive, idea conveyed by the expression. It is plainly in that sense used here; the persons spoken of as sealed are those who derive from their peculiar relation to the divine foreknowledge what ensures their permanent stability and progress in the divine life. Genuine believers are God's firm foundation, because they have their place and calling under this certification: "*The Lord knoweth them that are His;*" that is, knoweth them as such; and knowledge being necessarily for Him the ground of correspondent action, He regulates His procedure toward them accordingly. The passage itself, thus identified with the seal of God, is taken, with the substitution merely of Κύριος for Θεός, from the Sept. of Num. xvi. 5, ἔγνω ὁ Θεὸς τοὺς ὄντας αὐτοῦ—literally, *God knew them that are His* (all the verbs in the passage being in the past): He knew from the first who stood in that peculiar relation, and (it is implied) would take steps for making this manifest to all, as the Hebrew, indeed, quite distinctly states: He will show, or give to be known. It was spoken of those whom He had chosen to the priesthood, as contradistinguished from Korah and his company, who were seeking to thrust themselves into the office. When quoted, however, as a general statement, nothing depends upon the particular tense; and we may as well render *knoweth* as *knew* who are His. For the knowledge of God is not affected by the evolutions of time: what He knows now, He knew with equal certainty in the past; and it is not the time *when* the knowledge was possessed by Him, but *the manner how* it bears on the state and destiny of those who are the objects of it, that is the point of special moment.

The apostle adds another sentence, which cannot, like the former one, be regarded as a quotation, though in substance it occurs in other parts of Scripture: *And let every one that names the name of the Lord*[1] *depart from iniquity.* To name the name of the Lord is to do more than call upon Him, or profess some knowledge of His mind and will; it is to assume that name as the one by which we would be called, or to identify ourselves with the cause and interests it represents. The expression points back to Old Testament usage, where we find not only "naming the name of," but having "the name named upon," sometimes "called," or "put upon" one—that is, the name of Jehovah upon the people of His covenant. To have it so named or put upon them, implied the existence or expressed the acknowledgment of such a relationship (Gen. xlviii. 16; Num. vi. 27; Isa. xxvi. 13, xliii. 7; Amos ix. 12, etc.). And for

[1] There can be no doubt that Κυρίου is here the correct reading, being that of ℵ, A, C, D, F, K, L.

any one to name the name of the Lord, in the sense meant by the apostle, is, in other words, to give himself out for a true believer in Christ, and formally to take up his position among those who look to Him for salvation. Let every one who does this, says the apostle, depart from iniquity, or unrighteousness, because everything of this description is at variance with the position assumed; it would be a practical lie upon it. This call, therefore, to depart from iniquity, expressed in the second apophthegm, we can readily see, forms a fitting sequel and counterpart to that contained in the first: the naming of the Lord's name, and, in consequence, departing from iniquity, is, on man's part, the reflex and practical outcome, as well as evidence, of the blessed distinction of being known by God as emphatically His. But it seems rather fanciful to consider the second word, couched in the form of an exhortation, as equally with the first included in the designation of *seal*, and forming, so to speak, the inscription on its reverse side. For seals had not, like coins, a reverse side, from which another impression different from the primary one could be made. Nor could an exhortation to a particular course of life, like a divine, perpetually influential act, have properly attributed to it anything of sealing virtue. The relation of the two sayings to each other may rather be regarded as corresponding to a similar pair in Eph. iv. 30, " Grieve not the Holy Spirit of God, whereby ye are sealed unto the day of redemption "—where the sealing is made to stand simply in the indwelling grace and action of God's Spirit; and the call not to grieve Him is an exhortation to the line of duty which such a near and blessed relation to the Spirit involves as a natural sequence or imperative obligation. There is no need, or even propriety, in pressing the connection further here. It is God who seals the firm foundation, or secures a living and abiding membership in His church, by choosing and recognising those who belong to it as His;

and the proof that this seal really exists in any particular case, because the sure, unvarying result in which it expresses itself, is the departure of him who has it from iniquity—his treading in the paths of righteousness. This bespeaks his living connection with the Holy One, while the want of it would as clearly indicate his alienation from Him.

Ver. 20. Here the apostle passes to another and apparently somewhat contradictory aspect of the church—from the church viewed as God's firm foundation, all solid and compact, to the church as a house composed of various and, to a certain extent, heterogeneous materials. The distinction is simply that of the real and the professing, or the invisible and the visible church. *But* (δέ, the adversative, indicating something diverse from the preceding) *in a great house there are not only vessels of gold and of silver, but also of wood and of earth, and some to honour, others to dishonour.* That by the great house is to be understood the church as an outstanding, visible institution, is the nearly unanimous opinion of commentators, although Chrysostom insists on its being taken to mean the world, as the apostle (he says) wished everything in the church to be considered of gold and silver. But the question is as to the facts of the case, not what the apostle might wish to be such; and the whole tenor of his discourse here has respect to what in some way or another stands related to God as His household, in a religious point of view, in which respect there can be no doubt that there is a mixed condition of things— a false as well as a true. Considered in this light, there are certain obvious resemblances between it and the utensils of a large dwelling-house, accompanied, no doubt, as usual in such comparisons, with underlying differences, which require to be kept in the background. But, so far as here put, the similitude is apt and natural: the vessels of gold and silver in such a house, being in themselves of costly material, and reserved for honourable uses, differ widely, though pertaining to the same establishment, from those of wood and earthenware, which are of little intrinsic worth, and fit only for meaner services. And such relatively to each other are the two great parties in God's professing church: the one God's true elect, His jewels, as He elsewhere calls them, or peculiar treasure, preserved by His faithful guardianship, and destined to His eternal glory; the other, those who have but an outward standing in the household, and if capable, perhaps, of performing some inferior offices, yet never attaining either here or hereafter to the honour of God's saints, because destitute of the spiritual life which constitutes the essential property of such. This is the highest that can be said of the latter class; for if in certain things they may do a little service to the interests of the church, in others of a more vital nature they cannot; but, as a rule, do much *dis*-service. In the great conflict which is proceeding between good and evil, God does not receive from them the honour to which He is entitled, and they in turn must be treated by Him with dishonour, awaking at last to "shame and everlasting contempt." They are of Israel, yet not Israel; called, but not chosen.

Ver. 21. There follows, therefore, a virtual exhortation to separate oneself from this class, and make sure of reaching the state and destination of the other. Without explaining what corresponded to the two kinds of vessels, taking for granted that this was understood, the apostle says, *If any one, then, shall have purged himself from these*—that is, as Bengel well explains, shall by purifying himself have gone out of their number, those, namely, represented by the vessels associated with dishonour—*he shall be a vessel for honour, sanctified, serviceable to the Master, prepared for every good work.* Looking at the matter simply from a human point of view, and as connected with each man's personal responsibilities, the apostle merely points to the result to be aimed at and attained, leaving it to be ascertained from the great principles of the gospel how the end in question was to be accomplished. He contents himself with putting before men a plain practical issue : moving no question about election, or about adoption into the family of God ; but simply teaching, as Calvin well puts it, " that all who would consecrate themselves to the Lord must purge themselves from the filthiness of the ungodly—the same, indeed, that God everywhere teaches. For we hear nothing else in this passage than what we find in many other parts of Paul's epistles, and particularly in his second to the Corinthians : Be ye clean who bear the vessels of the Lord. It is hence clear beyond contradiction that we are called to holiness. But the calling and duty of Christians is one thing, and it is another whence the faculty or power of effecting it. That the faithful are required to purify themselves, we deny not ; but that this is a matter which belongs to the Lord, He declares Himself, when through the prophet Ezekiel He promises to send forth the Holy Spirit, that we may be cleansed (chap. xxxvi. 25). Wherefore we should rather beseech the Lord to purge us, than vainly make trial in such a matter of our own strength without His aid." In a word, the thing itself must be done by *us :* every individual should lay it upon his conscience as a condition he is morally bound to have made good ; but when he comes in earnest to attempt it, he finds he can only succeed by throwing himself on the redeeming mercy and sanctifying grace of God.

Ver. 22. *But flee youthful lusts*—Vulg. *juvenilia desideria* —primarily, no doubt, sensual indulgence, yet not this alone, levity of spirit also, love of pleasure, vainglory, and things of a similar kind (Theodoret). Such an advice was still suitable to Timothy, who, though now in ripe manhood, was yet not beyond the period when the mind is liable to aberration or excess, from the undue impulse of the lower affections (see INTROD. sec. iii.). And the advice is introduced by the adversative particle (δὲ), in order more distinctly to mark the importance of the thing here required, if the well-qualified condition for doing good service, noticed immediately before, was to be attained: but remember this at least is indispensable—you must keep clear from the gratification of youthful lusts. *But* (instead of yielding to those lusts) *follow after righteousness, faith, love, peace with them that call upon the Lord out of a pure heart;* in short, maintain a character such as becomes the gospel of Christ, adorned with the graces and virtues which it especially inculcates. The lesson here comes out again, so often already and in so many ways presented in these Pastoral epistles, that a sound moral condition is above all things essential to fitness for effective ministerial service in the divine kingdom. Other things may more or less be helpful, but this is indispensable. The peace spoken of is undoubtedly to be understood of peace in the closer sense—a state of inner harmony and agreeable fellowship; because it is such as is to be maintained with them that call upon the Lord out of a pure heart. This connection obviously reflects upon the nature of the peace intended.

Ver. 23. *But foolish and ignorant questions avoid, knowing that they do gender strifes.* The same advice substantially was given to Titus (chap. iii. 9); and the tendency of discussions about questions of the kind here indicated to give rise to fruitless contention, is distinctly stated at 1 Tim. vi. 4. The only point which calls for explanation is the precise meaning of the second epithet applied to the questions—ἀπαιδεύτους. Our translators have rendered it *unlearned*, which may be said to express the etymological sense, like the Vulgate's *sine disciplina*, or Alford's *undisciplined*. But to proscribe unlearned or undisciplined questions, with an implied sanction of such as could fitly be called learned or disciplined, is certainly not what the apostle meant, in the ordinary sense of such expressions. The Greek word nowhere else occurs in the New Testament; but in the Septuagint it is employed in a considerable variety of significations (if we may judge from the Hebrew terms it is taken to represent) — not only untaught or undisciplined (Prov. v. 23), but worthless (1 Sam. i. 16), senseless or foolish (Prov. viii. 5, xv. 13, 15), etc. (See Schleusner, *Lex.*, on the word.) *Ignorant* is probably as good a secondary meaning, and as suitable to the connection here, as any that can be employed,—understanding thereby something closely allied to the other epithet, *foolish*, with which it is conjoined—*senseless, stupid;* such questions as might be raised by persons who had undergone no proper instruction or training in the things of God. Questions of that description the thoughtful and earnest minister of God's word will do well to eschew: he should feel like one that has no heart or time for them; and a little observation will soon convince him that they are, when entertained, as the apostle intimates, a fruitful source of strife.

Vers. 24-26. *But the servant of the Lord*, it is added, *must not strive, but be gentle toward all:* not a person of contentious and combative disposition, but of mild and conciliatory bearing. Every one who is a true believer in Christ, and in any sphere of life is called to do service to Him, ought to be such; for it is what Christ Himself, the great pattern of believers, pre-eminently was; but the connection makes it plain that *servant of the Lord* is here taken in the more emphatic sense — of those who, like Timothy, were set apart to special service—evangelists and ministers of the word. In such a case it is more in accordance with our idiom to say *the* than *a* servant of the Lord, though the δοῦλον of the original is without the article; but the prominent position of the word, at the very commencement of the sentence, and its being coupled also with a defining genitive (Κυρίου), serve substantially the same purpose as our definite article. Besides being gentle in his bearing, the Lord's servant must be *apt to teach* (1 Tim. iii. 2, which see), *patient of wrong* (ἀνεξίκακον, enduring evil), *in meekness correcting those who oppose themselves*—meaning thereby persons within the professing church, but who, taking up some false notions, or misled by perverted counsels, set themselves to withstand the pure teaching and goodly order of Christ's kingdom. Such persons need to be firmly met, and brought under a corrective, wholesome administration (παιδεύοντα, see at 1 Tim. i. 20, Tit. ii. 12), yet conducted with a meek and forbearing spirit. And the reason follows: *if peradventure*, or *sometime perchance, God may give them repentance unto the full knowledge of the truth.* The form of expression is peculiar, indicative of hope, yet mingled with much doubt and hesitancy: μήποτε δῴη αὐτοῖς ὁ Θεός, literally, *lest at any time God may give them.* But what is meant is, plainly, not something to be dreaded, but something to be desired and hoped for, only of so uncertain or improbable a kind, that there was only a faint prospect of seeing it realized. "Μή is here used somewhat irregularly, in its dubitative sense; ποτέ, with which it is united, is not otiose, but brings its own signification of indefinite time; and while marking clearly the complete contingency of the change, still leaves the faint hope that at some time or other such a change may, by God's grace, be wrought within" (Ellicott). See also Winer, *Gr.* § 56, 2, *b*, note by Mr. Moulton, who suggests as a translation, *whether haply;* and Scherlitz, *Grundzüge der Neutest. Gräcität*, p. 365, perhaps fully better, *whether God may not still give.* It is an elliptical sentence, and cannot, as it actually stands, be very definitely construed; while yet there is plainly enough expressed a hesitating, yet not altogether groundless hope, that the desired good might be ultimately reached. The *if peradventure*, therefore, of the Authorized Version gives the sense nearly as well as any rendering that could be adopted.

In regard to the good itself to be sought in behalf of the opposers in question, a twofold description is given: first, that through a μετάνοιαν, a benignant change of heart wrought by the grace of God, they might come to the *full knowledge* (ἐπίγνωσιν) *of the truth*—might not know it in part merely, or in so superficial a manner as to leave the spirit and temper of the inner man still unsubdued by its hallowed influence. Only the full knowledge, apprehended and embraced by a properly receptive heart, would be sufficient to win them over to the obedience of Christ. The other aspect presented of the good in question is contained in the next verse, 26: *and that they may return to soberness out of the snare of the devil.* Such is the only ascertained sense of the verb ἀνανήψωσιν, found only here in the New Testament writings. The parties in question are contemplated as having sunk into a kind of drunken or benumbed state, through the artful devices of the great adversary, and capable only of being recovered to sobriety of thought and soundness of moral perceptions by being dealt with in a kindly and temperate, yet faithful exercise of authority. In that case, with God's blessing on the means employed, the delusive spell might possibly break, and a position of freedom and safety be gained by them. The sentence is here, again, elliptical; and the full import plainly is, that they may return to soberness, [and so escape] out of the snare of the devil. The bewildered or stupefied state into which they had fallen was as if they had been caught in a snare of the wicked one; and so the dispelling of the one brought an escape from the other.

The remaining clause is attended with some difficulty, and has been variously interpreted: ἐζωγρημένοι ὑπ' αὐτοῦ εἰς τὸ ἐκείνου θέλημα, *being*, or *having been, taken captive by him, for*, or *according to the will of him.* Such is the plain rendering of the words, which in themselves are simple enough. But in the original there are two pronouns, which are at least most naturally referred to different subjects, as indeed they do refer, in a passage quite near (chap. iii. 9), where the one (αὐτός) has respect to a nearer, the other (ἐκεῖνος) to a more remote party. Cases have been produced in which both pronouns, when occurring in a single sentence, have respect to the same subject (Kühner, § 629, 3). But they are somewhat exceptional, and, as stated by Alford, it took place only when it was sought by such a use of ἐκεῖνος to emphasize the subject. The meaning, therefore, can hardly be that given by the Vulgate, *a quo captivi tenentur ad ipsius voluntatem;* reproduced in our English version, "who are taken captive by him at his will," adopted still by De Wette and Huther; for, so rendered, the devil would be the subject of both pronouns, with no more emphasis in connection with the one than the other: αὐτοῦ would have served equally well in both places. The objection applies also to the view of the Greek expositors, who ascribe the taking captive not to the devil, but to God, and as the product of His will, which is liable to the further objection that it represents men, who had just returned to the free use of their intellectual and moral powers, as now taken captive, though in a better sense than before—borne away by another power than their own. Nor is the matter much mended by Bengel, Wetstein, and others, who would refer the αὐτοῦ, who takes captive, not to God Himself, but to the servant of God, through whose instrumentality the blessed captivity is effected, and God's will in this respect made good. This gets rid, indeed, of the objection as to the two pronouns being made to refer to one subject; but there still remains the apparent unnaturalness and impropriety of representing persons, just restored to sense and liberty, going into captivity—carried captive, on this supposition, by a human agent, who, immediately before, was taught to regard his working upon them to any good purpose as only a bare possibility. A transition of this sort wants verisimilitude. It seems necessary, therefore, to a satisfactory explanation, that we understand by the power who takes captive the devil, and, as a matter of course, that the captivity so effected be associated with the preceding period of spiritual intoxication, when the parties lay locked, as it were, in a stupefying delusion. The tense also confirms this view—the perfect, not the aorist—pointing, therefore, not to a single act, but to a continued state: *having been taken captive by him.* Then the concluding clause, εἰς τὸ ἐκείνου θέλημα, *unto* (in pursuance of, or for the carrying out of) *the will of Him*—namely, of God: this may grammatically be connected, either with their captivity to the power of evil, which in that case comes to be regarded as under His appointment and control; or, as appears more natural, with their recovery from that state—the restoration to sobriety of mind, which is all one with escaping from the snare and captivity of the devil, being the fulfilment, in their experience, of His gracious will. The whole passage, then, might be read, pointed, and slightly paraphrased thus: *In meekness correcting those who oppose themselves, if peradventure God may give them repentance* [to come] *unto the full knowledge of the truth; and that they may return to soberness,* [and so escape] *out of the snare of the devil (by whom they had been taken captive), according to the will of Him* (God), who for this end seconds the efforts of His servant, by giving the spirit of repentance and true enlightenment.

CHAPTER III.

Ver. 1. *This know,*[1] *however, that in the last days grievous times shall set in.* The introduction of the mournful topic

[1] It is scarcely worth while to advert to the plural reading of A, F,

discussed in this section of the epistle is made with a *but*, or a *however*, because forming a sort of contrast to the hopeful issue indicated at the close of the preceding chapter respecting the opponents there referred to. Timothy, and those following him in the administration of the affairs of the church, are warned against entertaining too sanguine expectations—admonished to bear in mind that, however they may succeed with particular persons in repressing incipient disorders, and winning men back to sobriety of mind, there was to be a great development of evil in the approaching future, not only of the outlying world, but also of the Christian church. This gloomy prospect is associated with *the last days* (ἐν ἐσχάταις ἡμέραις—without the article, because the expression itself is sufficiently individualizing as to the time meant; Winer, *Gr.* § 19). But while in one sense this term is specific enough, in another it is attended with a considerable amount of vagueness. In prophecy it was often used for the far distant future, especially as connected with Messianic times (see the Sept., for example, at Num. xxiv. 14; Isa. ii. 2, ix. 1; Jer. xxiii. 20; Dan. ii. 28, x. 14, etc.). And about the gospel age, it would appear that the expression, with some slight variations—such as John's ἐσχάτη ὥρα (1 John ii. 18)—had become appropriated generally to the period or dispensation of Messiah. So, in Heb. i. 1 and 1 Pet. i. 23, this whole period is distinguished from the times of the fathers and the prophets which preceded, by being designated "the last days," or "the last of the days;" and we learn from other sources that the Jews of later times familiarly used the same mode of speech (Schöttgen, *Hor. Heb.*, on this passage). It does not appear that in this respect they were wont to distinguish between the "latter" days and the "last" days (see at 1 Tim. iv. 1). And it is somewhat doubtful how far the apostles attempted

γινώσκετε, strangely preferred by Lachmann and Huther; for γίνωσκε has the support of ℵ, C, D, K, L, Vulg., Syr., and Coptic versions.

to go beyond their countrymen in any more discriminating use of such expressions. They were discouraged by our Lord from expecting to get definite revelations of the times and the seasons pertaining to the future of His kingdom (Acts i. 6); and while they throw out, from time to time, prophetic intimations of events, both of an adverse and a prosperous kind, which should mark its progress, they leave us much in the dark as to either the absolute or the relative times of their occurrence. In particular, the deplorable manifestation of corruption and godlessness which here, for example,—and at 2 Pet. iii. 3, also in 1 John ii. 18, and 2 Thess. ii. 1-12,—is coupled with the last days, appears from the descriptions to deepen as those days proceed, and to reach, one is apt to think, a culmination not far from their close in the second advent; while yet the evil is represented as either actually begun in the apostolic age, or just on the eve of beginning to develope itself. The grievous times or seasons ($\chi\alpha\lambda\epsilon\pi\text{οί}$, grievous in a moral respect; difficult, hence perilous) which the apostle in this passage associates with the last days, are at the same time said to be pressing on—$\dot{\epsilon}\nu\sigma\tau\acute{\eta}\sigma\text{ονται}$, *aderunt* (Bengel), they will immediately be present, are even now close at hand—so that all should be on the outlook for them. Indeed, consisting as they do in spiritual defections from the life of the gospel, and consequent moral depravations, they are never wholly wanting in any age of the church, though at certain periods and in particular localities they become more rife and rampant than in others. "I think," says Theodoret, "that it was our time which is here predicted. For our life is full of these evils; and while we bear about us an aspect of piety, it is the image of wickedness which we produce by our works." So, many have in substance said, of their particular time, both before and since; so, doubtless, they will say in the future; and what is written of the evil in the epistolary or apocalyptic portions of New Testament Scripture, is but an expansion of the prophetic glimpses given by our Lord in some of His parables (such as the Wheat and Tares, the Wise and Foolish Virgins), and in His discourse on the last times, which speaks of false teachers and prophets, delusions, iniquity abounding, and the love of many waxing cold (Matt. xxiv.). It was not that Christianity was in any measure to produce the corruptions and disorders that were in prospect, but simply that they should exist in spite of the divine grace and reformatory agencies it was bringing into play, and to some extent also should take advantage of its hallowed name under which to cloak, or more effectually prosecute, the work of evil.

Ver. 2. *For men* (οἱ ἄνθρωποι, men, not universally indeed, yet, as the article seems to indicate, in large numbers) *shall be selfish* (φίλαυτοι, self-lovers, each seeking his own, comparatively regardless of another's good), *covetous, boastful, haughty* (ὑπερήφανοι, carrying themselves with a lofty and supercilious air), *slanderers* (βλάσφημοι, offensively speaking evil of others, vilifying them), *disobedient to parents, unthankful, unholy.* Ver. 3. *Without natural affection* (ἄστοργοι, wanting the instinctive sense of endearment which links together parents and children, στοργή), *implacable* (ἄσπονδοι, not truce-breakers, as in the Authorized Version, but such as would not enter into a truce; *sine pace,* as the Vulgate, or as Luther, *unversöhnlich,* not to be appeased—see Lexicons), *false accusers, incontinent* (ἀκρατεῖς, without moral power or self-control, unbridled), *fierce, haters of good* (ἀφιλάγαθοι, the opposite of the φιλάγαθον commended and required in Tit. i. 8). Ver. 4. *Betrayers, headlong* (προπετεῖς, ready to precipitate matters by hasty speech or action), *carried with conceit* (see at 1 Tim. iii. 6), *lovers of pleasure rather than lovers of God* (φιλήδονοι—φιλόθεοι, both ἅπαξ λεγόμ., but quite natural compounds, and found in Philo; see Wetstein). Ver. 5. *Having a form* (μόρφωσιν, an outward show or appearance) *of godliness, but denying the power thereof*—that is, by their immoral lives and wicked deeds belying their profession—practically disowning that godliness was an actual power in their experience.

It is a dreadful picture, and from the very darkness of the characteristics it delineates, plainly requires to be understood with some limitations. If such characteristics were to become general in any particular age or country, society could not long continue to exist; it would fall to pieces by the weight of its own corruptions. We must therefore suppose the apostle to mean, that in the coming future there would be ever and anon persons appearing with those vicious qualities more or less characterizing their behaviour—not that all of them should meet in the same individuals, and still less that any entire community should be pervaded by them. But in proportion as the spirit of selfishness should at any time prevail, the others might be expected in a corresponding ratio to follow. That spirit fitly stands at the head of this black catalogue of moral evils, being in a manner the root-quality out of which the rest will, as circumstances admit, inevitably spring, and being that also, which more almost than any other bespeaks the disregard of Christian verities, and the absence of their influence on the heart. And if, from being simply a negation, there should come to any extent to prevail an antagonism to the fundamental truths and love-inspiring influences of the gospel, one can easily understand how the barriers which restrain the selfish spirit, and oblige it to maintain a certain moderation and formal decency, would one after another give way, and a fierce, unscrupulous, reckless opposition to whatever is pure, lovely, and of good report, rise to the ascendant. In such a case the reigning spirit of the time would necessarily be, if not *avowed*, at least *virtual* atheism; and the atheist, as has been justly said, "holds all mankind in contempt, and would be ready with a jest to blot out life from the world. Let but the day come, when it shall be fearlessly and commonly professed that death is annihilation, and that therefore the pleasures of appetite, graced by intelligence, are the best portion of man, and this horrible opinion shall quickly become parent to a giant cruelty, loftier in stature, and more malign, than any the earth has hitherto beheld. Even the most sanguinary superstitions have had some profession of sanctity and of mercy to maintain; a reserve, a saving hypocrisy, a balance of sentiments, which has set bounds to their demands of blood. But atheism is a simple element: it has no restraining motive, and must act, like itself, with a dreadful ingenuousness."[1] The nearest approach to this on a large scale which the world has seen since the diffusion of Christianity, was the state of France at the close of the last and the beginning of the present century. But the disturbing elements which brought on that terrible state of things, there can be no doubt, are again actively at work in many parts of Christendom; and it can scarcely be said to be beyond the bounds of probability that "the last days" of the present dispensation are destined to witness, in certain quarters, a realization of the prophetic picture before us more appalling than has yet been exhibited in the history of the past.

And from these turn away. Such an exhortation clearly implies that the state of moral pravity described was not regarded by the apostle as belonging entirely to the future; that persons were even then to be found in whom its features partially at least appeared; and consequently, that what was said at the outset of "the last days" as inclusive generally of Christian times, holds also here.

Vers. 6, 7. The apostle now not only presupposes the existence of parties to whom his description in a measure

[1] Isaac Taylor's *Saturday Evening*, chap. xiii.

applied, but also points to a specific line of operations carried on by them. *For of these are they who creep into houses, and take captive silly women, laden with sins, led away by diverse lusts.* A sly and cunning mode of procedure is indicated, as of persons in a low moral condition, watching their opportunities, and ready to take advantage of the infirmities and troubles of others to compass their own selfish ends. They *creep into houses:* ἐνδύνοντες, not necessarily more than entering into, but here, as also sometimes in classical writers, with the collateral idea of doing so by secret, stealthy movements; so that, as Chrysostom states, "something dishonourable is implied—deceit, cozening." Their object in this is said to get thoroughly under their power (αἰχμαλωτίζοντες, a word said to be of Macedonian origin, meaning literally, to take captive—Luke xxi. 24; figuratively, to get dominion over, or bring under one's control—Rom. vii. 23; 2 Cor. x. 5) γυναικάρια (a diminutive, ἅπαξ λεγόμ., expressive of contempt), *little,* or *silly women.* And these are further described as *laden* (σεσωρευμένα, heaped up, hence laden) *with sins, led away,* or borne along (ἀγόμενα), by various kinds of lusts: in ver. 7 further characterized as *ever learning, and never able to come to the full knowledge* (ἐπίγνωσιν, knowledge in the true and proper sense) *of the truth.*

It is not quite easy to get a perfectly satisfactory view of the sort of women here referred to, or why the designing and corrupt characters spoken of should have especially sought to win their confidence. It may naturally be supposed that they were possessed of wealth, though of small worth as to personal qualities, and that it was this the intriguers were mainly intent on acquiring. Such, probably, was the case, but it can only be matter of inference: the fact is not directly stated. Reference has been made to the well-known circumstance that the Gnostic leaders sought to lay hold of females, used them as instruments for the propagation of their false doctrines, and not unfrequently carried on with them, under high-sounding pretensions, the most licentious practices. Irenæus (*Hær.* i. 13), Epiphanius (*Hær.* xxvi. 12), and others, have given special notices of these; and Baur finds, in the supposed allusion here to those wily and corrupt proceedings of the second century heresiarchs, a proof of the sub-apostolic origin of this epistle (*Pastoralbr.* p. 36). But the character of the women as described here is not such as we are given to understand were chiefly sought after by the Gnostic leaders: these were, as might be expected from the Gnostic pretensions, and as Irenæus expressly tells us, "the well-bred, elegantly attired, and very wealthy;" and it was rather (if we except the fables of a later age about Simon and Nicolaus) the fascinating and corrupting influence which the Gnostic teachers contrived to exert over women hitherto reputed honourable and good, that the accounts in question complain of, than their intercourse with women of loose character, carried away by sinful lusts. But it is of such the apostle speaks—women, not sinners merely, but *laden with sins* (which we have no right to interpret, with De Wette, whom Alford follows, burdened in their consciences with a sense of sins, labouring under convictions of guilt; for such were not the indications of *silliness* in the early church, nor was it customary then any more than now to represent people as laden with sins in any other than an objective sense). And, finally, it is not said by the apostle that the persons who acted this treacherous and ensnaring part to the women in question were teachers: they were adversaries and opponents of the gospel, because agents of deceit and corruption, while it was all intent on the interests of truth and purity; but nothing more is known of them, and the allusion that follows to the Egyptian magicians, and a little after to others of a like description now (ver. 12), rather leads us to suppose that they were of the class generally called sorcerers or magicians—the class to which Simon the Samaritan, Elymas, and the sons of Sceva belonged (Acts viii., xiii., xix.)—men of bloated consciences and reprobate minds, who, for merely selfish ends, played upon the weakness and credulity of mankind, and pre-eminently upon certain portions of the female section of them. We have undoubted evidence of persons of that description abounding in apostolic times about Ephesus and its neighbourhood; and from what is known of them, nothing seems more likely than that they should have presented themselves to the apostle as the prototypes of the most worthless and depraved characters of the latter days.

Taking this view of the deceivers, we can scarcely hesitate where to find the deceived. They were, as the words of the apostle naturally import, the loose, the frivolous, worldly-minded ladies, who lived for the most part in fulness and pleasure, but, as frequently happens with such persons, were visited at times with recoils of feeling, guilty compunctions, fears of a judgment to come; and yet, when casting about for relief, and desirous of learning what might be for their good, continued still too light-hearted and unstable to embrace a life that aims at conformity to the example of Christ; hence they were peculiarly in danger of being caught by the arts of those who pretended, by some heaven-taught secret, to charm away from their disciples the powers of evil. It is precisely among such that impostors of that stamp have ever found their readiest dupes and their richest harvest.

Ver. 8. *Now in the same manner* (ὃν τρόπον δὲ) *that Jannes and Jambres withstood Moses, so do these also withstand the truth.* The reference to these ancient magicians shows, as already stated, the class of corrupt opponents more immediately in the eye of the apostle. It appears that a very old tradition among the Jews had handed down the two names here mentioned as those of the leading magicians who endeavoured to rival the miracles of Moses, and foil him in his mission. The names appear in the Chaldee paraphrast, at Ex. i. 15, very nearly the same as here —Janis and Jimbres; and again as Janis and Jambres at Ex. vii. 11. Other modes of spelling the names in the Rabbinical writings (such as Jonos and Jombros, Janos and Jambrinos), with various, evidently fabulous, accounts respecting them, are given by Schöttgen on this passage; also by Wetstein. It is needless to go into these tales, which apparently belong to different periods, and are not always consistent with each other. But there is no reason to doubt the correctness of the tradition as to the names and the persons they represented, there being no conceivable temptation in such a case to depart from the truth, and a very great probability that the truth so far should have found some place in Jewish memorials of the past. As regards the substance of the historical allusion, nothing depends on the specific names; for the action ascribed here to Jannes and Jambres is the same that in the narrative of Exodus is associated with the magicians generally; nor can it be doubted that a body so peculiar in the powers they professed to exercise, and so influential in their position, would have their recognised heads and leaders, by whatever names they might be called. In proud reliance on their thaumaturgical skill, and doubtless supposing that Moses and Aaron were only members of a similar craft with their own, they withstood the claim to a divine commission and a strictly supernatural power which was put forth by those men of God, entered with them into a competitive trial, and so completely failed in the attempt that they were obliged to own themselves vanquished. Such, too, the apostle affirms, would be the issue of the trial which was then proceeding between the ministers of the gospel and the adversaries—not false teachers, properly so called, but deceitful workers, the professors of secret lore and magical art. The conflict now, as of old, was essentially one between God's truth on the one side, and the devil's lie on the other; between the one grand remedy of Heaven for the ills of humanity, and the wretched devices of self-seeking, fraudulent men,—*men, it is added by the apostle, corrupted in their mind, reprobate* (or worthless) *concerning the faith.* Such was generally the condition of the class of persons who assumed the delusive pretensions referred to, and plied the infamous traffic connected with them. From the very nature of things, their consciences must have been entirely sophisticated, and a moral state induced strongly repellent to the faith of the gospel.

Ver. 9. *But* (such is the conclusion of the matter) *they shall not make progress* (οὐ προκόψουσιν ἐπὶ πλεῖον, lit. shall not advance to more, or rise to a stronger position); *for their folly shall become manifest to all, as* THEIRS *also came to be.* The triumph of truth over error, of reality over presumption, should now, as of old, become apparent. An opposition has been thought to exist between this passage and chap. ii. 16, where it is said of the teachers of profane and vain babblings, that they would advance to more of ungodliness. But the cases are really very different, for the persons spoken of here were not of the same class as the others; and having become already thoroughly corrupt and reprobate, an advance in this direction was impossible. The advance, however, which is denied respecting them has reference not to their personal state, but to the godless cause they were seeking to promote: in this they should not make progress; the course of events would expose their folly, and leave them, like the old wonder-workers of Egypt, exposed to obloquy and shame.

Ver. 10. *Thou, however, hast closely followed*[1] *my instruc-*

[1] The received text has παρηκολουθηκάς, the perfect, with D, E, K, L, the great majority of cursives, Chrys., Theod., Damas.; but ℵ, A, C

tion, my manner of life, my purpose, my faith, my long-suffering, my love, my patience, etc. In contrast to the selfish and crafty proceedings of the parties just referred to, the apostle now reminds Timothy of the very different line of conduct he had been made familiar with in the apostle's own case—what proofs it had afforded of sincere devotion to the truth, self-denial, and all the higher graces of a pure and earnest life. *Thou hast closely followed my course*, says Paul, in all this, hast gone along with me therein as a sympathizing and approving disciple (see at 1 Tim. iv. 6). The aorist, or indefinite past, is thought by some preferable to the perfect here: not that the reading, as stated in the note, is the better supported, but that it affords a fitter sense, conveying, as it would do, a kind of latent admonition to Timothy to take heed that it was as well with him now in this respect as it was in the past; or, as Alford more strongly puts it, the aorist bears something of reproach with it, virtually implying that Timothy was not the man now he had formerly been. In an earlier part of this epistle the same meaning was extracted from certain things said by the apostle, but without any just grounds, as we endeavoured to show; see at chap. i. 3–7. If the aorist *were* ascertained to be the correct reading, it would still convey no such reproach; it would only indicate that for some reason the apostle thought fit to refer specially to the earlier trials he had undergone, and the spirit he had manifested under them, rather than to those of a later period. Some explanation has been given of it by Paley and others, when tracing the coincidences between this epistle and the narrative in the related chapters of the Acts (chaps. xiii., xiv., xvi.); the old scenes of persecution and trial which took place at and around Timothy's earthly home naturally pre-

read παρηκολούθησας; also F, G, the simple verb ἠκολούθησας. Tischendorf now adopts the second, as do also Alford, Ellicott, Huther, chiefly on internal grounds, which are referred to in the text.

senting themselves afresh here, and this in the very order in which they occurred: ver. 11. *My persecutions, my sufferings, such as befell me in Antioch, in Iconium, in Lystra; such persecutions as I endured: and out of them all the Lord delivered me.* "We have thus the strongest reasons for believing that Timothy was a witness of St. Paul's injurious treatment; and this, too, at a time of life when the mind receives its deepest impressions from the spectacle of innocent suffering and undaunted courage. And it is far from impossible that the generous and warm-hearted youth was standing in the group of disciples who surrounded the apparently lifeless body of the apostle at the outside of the walls of Lystra" (Howson). We can thus sufficiently account for the peculiar stress laid by the apostle here on matters connected with his first and second mission tour in Asia Minor, and for the reference being couched in the indefinite past, if so be that the aorist is the correct reading. But the other, the perfect, appears to me fully as natural (though the aorist has been retained in the text), because the reference of the apostle is not by any means exclusively to his remote experiences at Antioch, Iconium, and Lystra, but rather to the spirit, temper, and behaviour exhibited by him during the whole of Timothy's acquaintance with him, but especially so in connection with what may be called the formative period of Timothy's Christian life and ministerial agency. Commonly as an eye-witness, always in intimate fellowship and sympathy of spirit, Timothy had made common cause with him in all; and could thus judge at how high a moral elevation he stood above the low and worthless impostors against whom he was warning—yea, had himself shared in it.

The article prefixed to the several items in the apostle's delineation of his course—τῇ διδασκαλίᾳ, τῇ ἀγωγῇ, etc.— individualizes them much in the same manner as our possessive pronoun, and may be said to carry forward the μου, which stands at the beginning: the teaching of me, the conduct, namely, of me = my conduct, and so on.

Ver. 12. *Yea, and all* (καὶ πάντες δὲ, or, and all too) *who are minded to live piously in Christ Jesus, shall be persecuted.* The apostle had spoken of his own persecutions, how he himself bore them, and how God delivered him out of them; but he now generalizes, in a manner, his own experience: others may look for a measure of the same. None, indeed, are excepted; *all who are minded* (οἱ θέλοντες, having their will set) *to live piously in Christ Jesus*—in Him, or in union with Him, as the one true source of living godliness—*shall be persecuted.* He does not say how or to what extent; but merely states the fact, that persecution in some form or another shall be their portion. And even this general announcement obviously presupposes as its ground, the existence in the world around of a spirit of alienation and hostility with respect to vital godliness. But that might not be always and everywhere the same; it could not but vary as Christianity itself rose to power, or the reverse; and so, as regards quantity and force, a certain conditional element necessarily enters into the statement, which may be put thus: In so far as the world retains its native character, those who are bent on leading in it lives of piety shall have to meet persecution. If through the diffusion of the gospel the old has to a considerable extent passed away, and a better order of things taken its place, then the persecution may narrow itself to taunts, reproaches, spiteful or contemptuous treatment, when at the behest of holy principle a stand is made against worldly compliances or fashionable vices. In these, however, the persecuting spirit breathes, only less coarsely and vehemently than when fire and sword are its weapons (Gal. iv. 29). So that the apostolic utterance still has its application to the Christian life; and they who would prosecute this life must be ready to brave such persecution. But they should never court it; they are as much bound to avoid provoking it by indiscretions, as to bear it meekly when excited by their virtues.

Ver. 13. *But evil men and deceivers shall grow worse and worse, deceiving, and being deceived.* We have here, by way of contrast to the life and experience of such as live piously in Christ, a return to the wretched characters formerly discoursed of—the modern representatives of the Egyptian magicians. For the language employed is strictly applicable only to such: *evil men and* γόητες — we have no precise synonym for it; *deceivers* is too general, though we must take it for want of a better; but the word is expressive of a specific class of deceivers—the class of magicians, sorcerers, thaumaturgists, or wonder-workers, as they were variously called, who by dexterous sleight of hand, mysterious incantations, and consummate hypocrisy, wrought upon the hopes and fears of the credulous. In naming these, the apostle is plainly not to be understood as introducing a new class, for they bear the very lineaments of those already described and denounced; but their course of life and its fruits are now placed over against those of the true followers of Christ. How different! Living in an element of deceit, they come to be themselves deceived; their sin becomes their snare and their punishment: so that, in so far as they are capable of progress, the progress is from bad to worse; and if their manner of life is such as to save them from persecution at the hand of others, it brings recompenses of evil far more to be dreaded, and these prepared by their own hands. The assertion of Huther, that the term γόητες in this passage is only in a kind of secondary or figurative sense applied to the parties in question, that it merely represents them as exercising a sort of magical power over their weak, especially female, followers, is without foundation. The unqualified use of such a term cannot justly be understood otherwise than as identifying them with the wily and unscrupulous professors of the magical art.

Ver. 14. *But do thou* (σὺ δὲ emphatic, in contrast to the deceivers in the preceding verse) *continue in the things which thou didst learn* (lit., in what things thou didst learn), *and wert assured of*—ἐπιστώθης—not, were committed to thee, as the Latin and Gothic versions, which would have required ἐπιστεύθης. Hesychius, ἐπιστώθη : ἐπείσθη, ἐπληροφορήθη, *persuasus est, certum et exploratum habuit.* (See much more to the same effect in Suicer, *in voce.*) The things had not only been learned by Timothy, but learned in such a way as to give them a firm place in his belief. *Knowing of whom thou didst learn them*—namely, of persons who were entitled to the fullest confidence, utterly incapable of practising the deceit, by which others are misled to their ruin. The reference must primarily be to his mother Lois, and his grandmother Eunice.

Ver. 15. *And that from a very child* (ἀπὸ βρέφους, from an infant, the youngest period of childhood) *thou knowest the holy Scriptures, which are able to make thee wise unto salvation.* This is only a further specification and enhancement of the preceding statement, bringing out more distinctly the kind of learning Timothy had received, and from what period it dated. The expression τὰ ἱερὰ γράμματα for the divine word is peculiar, so far as the New Testament is concerned; but it occurs in Philo and Josephus (see in Wetstein), and always in the definite sense, *the* sacred writings, or the Holy Scriptures, namely, of the Old Testament. Here also, of course, it is Old Testament Scripture that is meant. And the things contained in them are represented as still possessed of saving virtue—possessing it even for such a believer as Timothy: *which are able* (δυνάμενα, the present, not the past, as the οἶδας, *knowest*, virtually is) *to make thee wise unto salvation*—σοφίσαι εἰς σωτηρίαν (the verb used in this sense also, Septuagint, Ps. xix. 7, cv. 22); yet not now as apart from the revelation of Christ in the gospel, but *through the faith which is in Christ Jesus* (or, through faith—that, namely, which is in Christ Jesus). When ability to such an extent is ascribed to the Old Testament Scriptures, *instrumental* agency is all that can be meant— available means in regard to salvation when intelligently and faithfully used ; which they can be *now* only as handmaids to the faith in Christ—the end to which they all more or less pointed ; not when employed as a barrier to keep men at a distance from Christ, as if they were in themselves God's perfected revelation. It was necessary that the apostle should thus guard himself in respect to Old Testament Scripture, considering the abuse to which the unbelieving Jews were ever applying it. But having so guarded himself, he proceeds in the next two verses to give a fuller deliverance of his sentiments respecting the value and importance of sacred Scripture.

Ver. 16. *Every scripture* [*is*] *given by inspiration of God, and* [*is*] *profitable for teaching,* etc. ; or, *Every scripture, given by inspiration of God,* [*is*] *also profitable for teaching,* etc. It is now admitted by all competent scholars that either of these translations is grammatically admissible ; no valid objection can be urged against either from the construction. Take the one or the other, and it will be found quite easy to support it by parallel examples ; so that it is from the subject, and the connection in which it stands, that our grounds of preference must be drawn. Indeed, it matters little for the interpretation which we adopt, if the subject itself be rightly determined. What precisely is meant by πᾶσα γραφή? *Every scripture*, as it must be rendered, since there is no article after πᾶσα. Can this, as some would have it, be taken in the sense of scripture, or written production of any sort ? If it could, then the nearest adjective (θεόπνευστος) should have to be regarded as an attributive of the subject, distinguishing between one kind of writing and another :—Every writing God-inspired—not writings of all sorts, but whatever writing has this origin and character—

is also profitable, etc. The expression, however, cannot be so taken. The usage is against it. There are as many as fifty passages in the New Testament in which γραφή occurs; and in every one of them, whether it has the article or not, —whether, also, it is in the singular or the plural (the singular, besides here, in John xix. 37, 2 Pet. i. 20),—the word has but one meaning: it signifies uniformly *sacred* Scripture, which virtually determines the meaning here. But the context conclusively fixes it; for there the subject of discourse is not writings generally, but specially the sacred writings—those which Timothy had as a child been instructed in. These alone were in the eye of the apostle at the time; and so the πᾶσα γραφή, which follows, cannot fairly have any other sense attached to it than that of every part of the previously mentioned whole. He spoke *first* collectively of the Holy Scriptures; *now* he speaks individually of the component writings. So Chrysostom: "*All*, of what sort? That of which, says he, I said all holy; of which he was just declaring that from a mere child thou hast known the Holy Scriptures."

Holding this, then, to be the subject in hand—Holy Scripture in one and all of its parts—it is plainly of no moment, as regards the substantive import of the passage, whether we say, Every scripture given by inspiration of God is also profitable; or, Every scripture is given by inspiration of God, and is profitable. For in the former the theopneustic or divinely-inspired character is made to extend to every part of the sacred volume as well as in the other. In both, indeed, there is a virtual predication of the divine element; only, according to the first, the quality is assumed under a specific attribute or title, stamped, as it were, on the formal character of the writings; while, according to the second, it is directly affirmed of them. That is really the whole amount of the difference when you limit the reference in γραφή to sacred Scripture alone, and make the attribute of divine inspiration associated with it co-extensive with each and all of the component parts of Scripture. For in that case the expression, Every scripture given by inspiration of God, is equivalent to, Every scripture being given by inspiration of God; which, as already said, is a predicate in the form of an assumption. Such, precisely, is the way Origen explains, who is commonly represented as denying the predicative force of the θεόπνευστος here. He says: "Let it be to us according to our faith, whereby we have trusted, that *every scripture, being God-inspired* (θεόπνευστος οὖσα), *is profitable.* For one alternative you must admit regarding those scriptures—either that they were not God-inspired, since they are not profitable; or that, since they are profitable, they are God-inspired" (*Op.* vol. ii. p. 443, ed. De Larue). Clearly, therefore, Origen attached a predicative force to the θεόπνευστος; not less (only with a slight difference in the mode of exhibition) than Chrysostom, when, after explaining the "every scripture" here to be inclusive of all the sacred writings, he adds: "The whole of this, therefore, is divinely inspired; doubt not, then," says he—namely, as to the truly divine character of Scripture—"in every part it is of God."

Since nothing, then, as to the import of the passage depends on the mode of construing it, the only question touching the construction is, which of the two modes seems the more natural. Was it more likely that St. Paul would seek to confirm the soul of Timothy in his early-imbibed regard to Scripture, and appreciation of its value, by directly asserting the divinely-inspired character of each of its parts, and then indicating what, as possessing such a character, were the important uses which it was calculated to serve? or that, on the assumption of its divinely-inspired character, he should simply point attention to those various uses? I cannot but think (after all that Huther, Ellicott, Alford, and others have advanced on the other side) that the former was the more natural. The inspired character of particular portions of Old Testament Scripture, it is alleged, was not then called in question by those who acknowledged an inspired element in any. But are we sufficiently acquainted with all the phases of opinion then afloat, to be sure that such was the case? No one *can* be sure; and besides, Timothy was coming into contact with modes of thought which set light by the very heart and substance of the Old Testament revelations. Even apart from such things, might not Timothy himself—not the less, one might almost say all the more, that he had been familiar with the Scriptures from his very childhood—be the better for having his mind thus arrested on the higher element in their composition? Would it not serve to bind him the more closely to them, and render him disposed to apply them to the uses for which they were designed? Surely, if it was not unnecessary or out of place to press on him such simple exhortations as to remember that Jesus Christ, of the seed of David, was raised from the dead, and that St. Paul was a minister of His truth and an apostle to the Gentiles, it could not be superfluous to impress upon him a sense of the divine character of Old Testament Scripture. And then, as to the objection that on this view "the καὶ, being copulative, would seem to associate two predications,—one relating to the essential character of Scripture, the other to its practical applicabilities, which appear scarcely homogeneous" (Ellicott),—the simple reply is, that according to the structure of the passage, the καὶ is to be taken as καὶ *consecutivum*, presenting what follows as a consequence growing out of what precedes (Winer, *Gr.* liii. 3):—Every scripture is given by inspiration of God, and hence is profitable; because it is that, then, as a matter of course, it is also this. The ancient versions, it may be added, omitted the καὶ. Thus the Vulgate: *Omnis scriptura divinitus inspirata utilis est;* so also the Syriac; and both Origen and his Latin translator, in the passage formerly referred to. But this probably arose from a desire merely to evade what was felt to have a measure of difficulty in it—they thought it enough to give the substance.

In regard to the subject itself of the inspiration of Scripture, the field is too wide and varied for discussion here. I simply refer to my article on the subject in the *Imp. Bible Dictionary*, and the works noticed there. The quality expressed by θεόπνευστος is primarily and strictly applicable only to men, employed as the instruments of the Spirit in making known His will to the world, writing as they were guided, or speaking as they were moved by the Holy Ghost (2 Pet. i. 21). But it is in accordance with common usage to apply the same epithet to the words or writings that came from them under such an influence: the product of divine inspiration, they might justly enough be said to be themselves inspired.

The things mentioned in connection with the profitableness of Old Testament Scripture call for no special illustration: *it is profitable for instruction* (διδασκαλίαν, or teaching in the things of God), *for conviction* (or reproof, ἐλεγμόν), *for correction, for discipline* (παιδείαν, see at chap. ii. 25, Tit. ii. 12) *in righteousness;* that is, for such a moral training as will lead those who submit to it to live in righteousness. All this, be it observed, is affirmed of the Old Testament Scriptures, even after the fuller light of the gospel had come. They have such uses still to fulfil to the church of Christ.

Ver. 17. Then follows the practical aim and result of this profitableness, when turned to proper account: *in order that the man of God may be perfect* (ἄρτιος, *aptus in officio*, Bengel; every way complete), *thoroughly furnished for every good work*. This explains more fully what is meant by ἄρτιος—denoting one who, by the study of the Scripture, and the intimate acquaintance thereby obtained with the mind and Spirit of God, is well equipped for every good work to which he may be called. The minister of God's word should be this in a pre-eminent sense; what should be found generally in such as can be called *men of God*, should be found more especially in him. And we can scarcely doubt the apostle had persons of that class peculiarly in view: in an emphatic sense, they are men of God; but the expression is not to be limited to such—it must be extended in a measure to all true believers in Christ (see at 1 Tim. vi. 11).

CHAPTER IV.

Ver. 1. *I solemnly charge thee before God, and Christ Jesus, who is going to judge living and dead, and by His appearing and His kingdom.* (On the διαμαρτύρομαι, see at 1 Tim. v. 21. Here, as there, the correct reading is undoubtedly, "before God and Christ Jesus"—the received text inserting on very slender authority (only K, L, Syr.), τοῦ Κυρίου before Χριστοῦ. It also inserts, on equally poor authority, οὖν ἐγώ after διαμαρτ.; but the best MSS. omit them, ℵ, A, C, D, F, L, also the Latin and Syriac versions.) This is, so to speak, the apostle's last charge to Timothy—the last in this epistle, and not improbably the last absolutely; and he therefore puts it in the most solemn form, not only delivering it as in the presence of God and of Jesus Christ, but also the appearing of Christ (τὴν ἐπιφάνειαν, the usual accusative after verbs of religiously charging or adjuring,—Deut. iv. 26; Mark v. 7; Acts xix. 13; 1 Thess. v. 27,—and requiring *by* to be prefixed in our idiom; as also the Lat. Vulg., *per adventum ejus*) and His kingdom. These are obviously added for the purpose of bringing before Timothy the great realities of the future world, which should infinitely outweigh all the present: Christ's appearing, when everything in the past shall be brought into judgment, and His kingdom, when His faithful servants shall reign with Him in glory. Our translators have been quite misled here by the κατὰ, which in the received text stands before τὴν ἐπιφάνειαν, but which is omitted by ℵ, A, C, D, F, also by the Vulg. (according to the better copies) and Copt. versions, and is rejected by all the leading critical authorities.

Ver. 2. Here follow, in a series of imperative sentences, the several things which Timothy was taken bound to do; the imperatives all in the aorist, as noted by Ellicott, indicating rapidity of action, or the vivid nature of the address (Winer, *Gr.* § 43, 3, *a*). *Preach the word*—the word of God generally, no doubt, but that word more especially as connected with the realities, obligations, and hopes of the gospel. *Be instant* (ἐπίστηθι, lit. stand by, or near; and when used here in a moral sense, with reference, no doubt, mainly to what goes before,—the preaching of the word, implying an ever wakeful, ready attitude: be at it) *in season, out of season*—that is, at all times; for what may seem to the careless or lukewarm unseasonable occasions for making mention of the truth, will often by the zealous and faithful pastor be found opportunities of usefulness. It means, says Chyrsostom, "Have no definite time; let it be always time for thee: not in peace alone, or in quietness, or when sitting in the church. And if you should be in perils, if in prison, if compassed about with chains, if even going forth to death, at that very time convince, withhold not the word of rebuke. For then even rebuking is in season, when the work meets with success." Truly and beautifully said, only somewhat too exclusively with reference to the circumstances of the pastor; for, as Calvin remarks, the reference should also be made to the people. "To the pastor, indeed, lest he should give himself to the function of teaching only at his own times, and when it suits his own convenience; but let him apply himself, sparing no labour and trouble. As regards the people, there is this importunate diligence, when they are entreated though in a state of slumber, when the hand is laid upon them while they are hurrying elsewhere, when they are chid as to the vain occupations of the world." Then, as required by the various conditions of those addressed, a corresponding variety in the mode of address is enjoined: *reprove, exhort, rebuke, in all long-suffering and teaching*—διδαχῇ, which occurs only here and in Tit. i. 9, of the Pastoral epistles, while διδασκαλία is of pretty frequent occurrence: the former having respect mainly to the work or mode of teaching; the latter to the thing taught—the instruction. This concluding part of the charge clearly implies that in his ministerial vocation Timothy should have to lay his account with much in the condition of those he had to deal with that would try his patience, and call for earnest pleading and remonstrance. Instead of listening with attentive ears and willing hearts to the gospel message, ready to hail what it taught, and comply with its requirements of duty, the corrupt tendencies of nature, the sluggishness of the flesh, the love of ease and the world, would present to his efforts too often a resisting medium, which would call for something else than soft and honeyed words—what might rather be likened to a sharp and two-edged sword. All faithful ministers must lay their account to a measure of the same, and must consequently know how to reprove and admonish as well as to win, to exhort as well as encourage. But it is of unspeakable importance for the success of their mission, that, when those severer methods have to be resorted to, all should be done in a gentle and patient spirit, or, as it is here, in every kind of long-suffering and teaching, continuing at the work in a forbearing, steady, peaceful manner, if haply the truth may thus find its way into the heart, and bring the stubborn will into captivity to the obedience of Christ. The more any one can carry on his ministerial work in such a spirit, the more is the conviction likely to take hold of his hearers that he really seeks their good, and that it will be well for them to listen to his counsels; whereas, if he should but mock their follies, fiercely denounce their sins, or flare up in passion at their opposition to the calls addressed to them, it is next to certain that no progress will be made—a prejudice rather will be created against the work of the ministry. He must act, as Chrysostom says again well, "not as one provoked, not as inflamed with hatred, not as insulting or as having found an enemy: let all such things be absent. But what? As one who loves and condoles, as sorrowing even more than the other, and grieved at the things which concern him."

Ver. 3. The earnestness and fidelity thus recommended, with all possible gentleness and patient industry in the application, is now enforced by a reference to the foreseen tendencies of the future: *For there shall be a time when they will not endure the healthy instruction* (or doctrine—namely, of the gospel), *but after their own lusts will heap up to themselves teachers, having itching ears*—ears, that is, which were always pricking with an uneasy desire for what would gratify the taste of a carnal, self-willed heart. The evil is drawn in very striking colours, especially considering that it is of persons still professedly within the pale of the Christian church that the apostle speaks. But the delineation is otherwise indefinite; he merely says there will be a time or season when such things shall happen, and urges the prosecution of ministerial work after the style and character he has described, as the only means of postponing its arrival. In the spirit of prophecy he knew it would come; it was but one of the phases of corruption and backsliding which were to characterize the last days. And we who now live in this advanced period of them, have no difficulty in pointing to facts which amply corroborate the apostle's forebodings; not only in these later times of discord and disunion in Protestant Christendom, but even greatly more in those ancient and so-called halcyon times, when the visible church was still in a manner one. For no one who has read with any degree of impartiality the history of those times, and with discernment to understand the lessons it teaches, can be ignorant that the falling away from sound apostolic doctrine, and sliding into the asceticism, the legalism, the endless mummeries and superstitions, which became consolidated into mediæval and Romish Christianity, grew up precisely in the manner here indicated. Men came over into the church from the ranks of heathen superstition and Gentile philosophy, bringing along with them many false notions and degrading practices which should have been left behind; and the teachers of the church, unwisely accommodating themselves to these, preached so as to gratify the itching ears they should have reproved, and kept back the pure word which would have checked the influx of evil. Accordingly, the more the church grew as an outward institution,—growing in that respect, indeed, far too rapidly,—the fewer always became the number who would endure sound doctrine, till they were found only in holes and corners, or, when occasionally occupying more conspicuous places, it was at the hazard of their lives. There is enough of this itching after false doctrine in the scattered communities of Protestantism to humble and sadden any Christian heart; the signs of the times give no doubtful indication of even more yet to come; but it is in the bosom of the great apostasy that the most marked and mournful exemplification of the apostle's prediction is to be met with.

Ver. 4. And so is it also in regard to the further statement concerning the errorists in question made in this verse: *and they will turn away their ears* (lit. their hearing) *from the truth, but be turned aside to fables.* We can scarcely believe, with Ellicott, that this indicates as the result " a complete turning away from every doctrine of Christian truth;" for if such were the result, there would necessarily be an abandonment of the Christian profession—a going over to the ranks of unbelief. But it is rather a depravation within the professing church that the apostle appears to be speaking of, than a formal forsaking of its communion —such a depravation as would disincline the minds of men to sound doctrine; consequently such a turning away from the truth as would cause this to lose its proper character, and by mixing it up with error and fable, would prevent it from effecting its proper aim upon the heart and conduct. Even the Gnostic sects, who shortly became so prominent in this line of things, did not go further than has just been stated—they still retained many Christian elements in their systems; but these did not save their doctrine from being justly denounced as a corruption of the truth, and held as a whole to be essentially antichristian. In a modified sense, the same may be said of the false worship and discipline which now bears the name of Popery: it undoubtedly has many Christian elements in it; but these are so intermingled with error, that the system as a whole is a grievous departure from the truth of Christ. And how large a part fable played in accomplishing that departure,— tales of lying wonders concerning reputed saints and their adversaries in this world and the next,—no one acquainted with the history of the subject, and even with the present state of Catholic belief, can need to be told. The modern tendency in Protestant countries, even when turning away the ear from the truth, can scarcely be said to take this particular direction; the substitute is not fables, but rather science falsely so called—science, not in its ascertained results, but in its speculative processes and rash deductions.

Ver. 5. *But watch thou in all things; endure hardship;*

do the work of an evangelist; fully perform thy ministry. It is as much as to say: Whatever others may do, and whether men will hear, or whether they will forbear, *this* is what *thou* must do. First, *watch*, νῆφε, or be sober, *in all things.* The being sober is the primary meaning of the word—sober in the literal sense; but when used metaphorically, as it is here, it denotes more than we commonly understand by being sober—a vigilant, wakeful, considerate frame of mind, which takes good heed to what is proceeding around, and with calm and steady aim pursues its course. It is an exhortation to maintain the clear perception and even balance of the mind, so as not to be entrapped by false appearances, or by undue excitement turned aside from the onward path of truth and duty. *Suffer hardship*, or tribulation, in respect to which the apostle had already referred to himself as an example (chap. ii. 9). In such times Timothy would plainly be required to show that he had somewhat of the same resolute and hardy spirit. *Do the work of an evangelist*— much the same as a preacher or missionary of the gospel, a carrier of its good tidings, without, as in the case of a pastor, being fixed to any definite locality. In the apostolic age, persons recognised as evangelists seem to have occupied a position between apostles and pastors (Eph. iv. 11), and to have stood in a certain relation to the former with regard to the diffusion of the gospel and the planting of churches. In some respects, therefore, "they were nearest to the apostles, and had an office cognate to these; in respect to dignity alone they were inferior. For at the command of the apostles [sometimes, indeed, without this; Acts viii. 5, 40] they went forth to various churches in order to preach the gospel, and to perfect the work which had been begun by the apostles" (Suicer). Or it might be in the inverse order, the apostles came to perfect what the evangelists had begun; for the relations so far do not seem to have been exactly determined. *Fully perform thy ministry,* πληροφόρησαν — not, as in the Authorized Version, after Beza, "make full proof of;" but as the Vulg. *ministerium tuum imple*—fill it up, perform it fully, or make it, as far as you can, a complete and effective service.

Ver. 6. The course of active, faithful, devoted labour in the work of the ministry thus enjoined upon Timothy is now enforced by a reference to the apostle's own case, his approaching departure from the field, coupled with a brief retrospect of the manner in which he had fulfilled his calling, and the prospect that lay before him of the coming recompense. Commentators have traced the connection variously—some laying stress on one point, some on another. I agree with Alford, that there appears no propriety in confining it to any one; and it may well be put, as he does it, so as to include several weighty considerations: "I am no longer here to withstand those things: be thou a worthy successor of me, no longer depending on, but carrying out for thyself, my directions; follow my steps, inherit their result, and the honour of their end."

For I (ἐγὼ γάρ—emphatic with respect to the thou, σὺ, in the preceding verse) *am already being offered*—ἤδη σπένδομαι, already poured out as a drink-offering. He contemplates himself in the light of a sacrifice, yielding up his life for the cause of the gospel—a sacrifice which might be said to have already begun in the sufferings of a preliminary kind he was called to endure; and the drink-offering, or libation, was thought of as the special kind of sacrifice under which he presented the surrender, because of the resemblance it would be seen to carry to the shedding of his blood. This is so much the most natural explanation of the reference, that it is not worth while noticing any other. The same thought, and expressed in the same language, was employed at an earlier period by the apostle, in Phil. ii. 17. But in the following clause he gives it without a figure: *and the time of my departure is at hand*—

departure, namely, from life; without reference, as some would have it, to leaving the sacrificial feast with a libation, or, as others, to withdrawal from the battle-field. Such allusions are too far-fetched, and instead of adding to the beautiful simplicity and force of the language, tend rather to spoil it. From what he had already seen in the treatment of his case, and the obvious temper of those he had to deal with, he was convinced that the final stage was approaching.

Ver. 7. *I have fought the good fight*—or more exactly, as at 1 Tim. vi. 12, though one is unwilling to alter such familiar words, *I have maintained the good contest*—τὸν καλὸν ἀγῶνα ἠγώνισμαι—referring to the contest for the mastery in the public games; and the perfect tense having here its full significance, for the contest was now in a manner over: he could look back on it as a thing of the past. And why does he speak of having maintained the good contest? "It is (says Chrysostom beautifully) as if a father should console his little son seated beside him, and unable to bear the bereavement, saying: My son, weep not; we lived honourably, and having come to old age we left you; our life has been blameless, we depart with glory; you can also acquire honour from the things that have been done by us." And why emphatically the *good* contest? Let Chrysostom again answer: "Nothing better than this contest; this crown takes no end. It is not a thing of wild olives; it has not a man for presiding arbiter, nor has it men for spectators [of the contest]; the theatre is replenished with angels. *There* they labour for many days, and are fatigued, and in a single hour they receive the crown, and the pleasure presently is gone. But *here* it is not so; for they are always in brightness, in glory and honour." *I have finished the course*—the race being the contest which here, as elsewhere (Phil. iii. 12; 1 Cor. ix. 24; Heb. xii. 1), presented itself to the apostle's mind as the fittest of the Grecian games to symbolize the Christian struggle; so that to finish the course, only expresses in a more specific form the thought contained in the preceding clause. *I have kept the faith*—that, namely, which had been entrusted to him as a sacred deposit—faith objectively, as the great treasure of gospel verities. As to meaning, it is much the same thing over again: the apostle, as Bengel notes, having expressed the matter twice by metaphor, now gives utterance to it in direct speech. Through all trial, and mockery, and persecution, and suffering, he had held fast by the saving truths which he received by special revelation from above, and which as a chosen vessel he was sent forth to declare to a perishing world (Gal. i. 12; Acts ix. 15). In doing this he maintained the good contest, and finished the course.

Ver. 8. *Henceforth* (λοιπὸν, *quod reliquum est*, Beza) *there is laid up* (or aside, ἀπόκειται, reserved) *for me the crown of righteousness;* not *a* crown merely, but *the* crown—that which is associated with righteousness, either as its proper object or its destined possession. A return is made to the figure of the contest; and as the victor in each particular species of game—wrestling, running, etc.—got the crown appropriated to it, so the apostle designates his reward as the crown of righteousness: therefore the righteous crown, or the crown which by divine appointment belongs to it, which is (prospectively) its own. In plain words, it is that kind and measure of bliss which the wrestler in righteousness alone is either entitled or prepared to enjoy — the destiny, as it is put in Rev. iii. 21, to share in Christ's throne, as having previously shared in His triumph over sin. It is reserved, therefore, till this triumph is completed; and then, *in that day*, the terminating point of the believer's struggles and exertions, it *shall be awarded by the Lord as the judge*—the righteous judge or arbiter of the contest. Considered in the light of a recompense, the future inheritance of bliss and glory is fitly connected with the Lord's righteousness or justice—as it is also elsewhere (2 Cor. v. 10; Rom. iii. 6; Eph. vi. 8, etc.)—because the bestowal of it shall be in accordance with the just and holy principles on which the divine government is conducted toward men. Yet grace is not hereby superseded or made of no account. On the contrary, it is regarded as the basis on which the whole administration of reward proceeds in the kingdom of Christ. It is an economical arrangement, made by God in Christ for carrying out the purposes of His salvation; but as the salvation itself, so the bestowal of reward connected with it, is all of grace—to be thankfully received, but never to be claimed as a debt. For without the Spirit of grace working both to will and to do in them that believe, there could be neither righteousness nor reward; and so, while those who, as partakers of grace, have faithfully done their part here, shall all, like the apostle, in the great day receive their crowns from the Lord, they shall again lay them at His feet, in lowly and grateful acknowledgment of the source whence they have been derived, ascribing to Him, as alone worthy, the honour and the glory (Rev. iv. 10, v. 9, 10).[1]

The apostle gracefully concludes by noticing this participation of others with him in the anticipated good: the crown which the Lord the righteous judge shall award, he says, *not only to me, indeed, but to all those that love His appearing* — ἠγαπηκόσιν τὴν ἐπιφάνειαν αὐτοῦ, the second appearing, doubtless, as the connection requires; and the action of the loving being put in the perfect, betokens it as a thing commenced in the past, but continuing on till the proper completion is reached: who have fixed their love on His appearing, and so still love (Winer, *Gr.* § xl. 4, *b*). A remarkable characteristic! How rarely is it possessed by believers as it ought to be! If they might justly be represented as loving Christ, yet how seldom should we think of

[1] Comp. Delitzsch on Heb. vi. 10.

describing them as loving precisely *His appearing*—when He shall come to wind up the affairs of His administration, and distribute to every one as his case may be! To love Him in this particular aspect bespeaks not only faith, but such a full assurance of faith and hope in Him as casts out fear, and carries with it the confidence that, when He appears, we shall also appear with Him in glory. Why should the followers of Christ fail of this peaceful and loving anticipation, when even Old Testament believers hailed the prospect of the Lord's appearing to judgment with songs of joy and hope? (Ps. xcvi. 11, 13, xcviii. 9.)

Ver. 9. From here to the end of the chapter a few notices are given by the apostle of his own condition and prospects, also of some of his companions in the gospel, with the free expression of his feelings and desires in respect to them. *Do thy endeavour to come to me quickly.* An earnest desire had already been expressed for Timothy's coming (chap. i. 4), and now there is the command to hasten it forward: σπούδασον, do it promptly and diligently, lose no time about it. The apostle seemed to have no doubt whatever in his mind as to Timothy's willingness to come: he could thoroughly count on his affectionate fidelity, even while others were falling away from him; which surely implies that nothing had yet occurred to shake the apostle's confidence in the hearty and stedfast devotedness of his disciple.

Ver. 10. The reason follows why he would have Timothy to make such haste to come to him: he now peculiarly needed his sympathy and support. *For Demas forsook me, having loved this present world*—ἀγαπήσας, the participle as expressive of the cause = because he loved, or, through his love of, the present world. There can be no doubt, therefore, that this withdrawal of Demas was the result of carnal influences, and was regarded by the apostle in the circumstances as a dereliction of duty—a kind of desertion of his post. It must have been all the more painful to Paul, as

Demas had formerly stood near to him, and had once and again been mentioned with honour among his fellow-workers (Col. iv. 14 ; Philem. 24). Yet we should perhaps press what is said here too far, if we inferred from it that Demas had made total shipwreck of the faith in Christ. His unworthy conduct at this time may have been the temporary result of the violent measures which in the last mad days of Nero had begun to be taken against Christians at Rome. Demas was meanwhile alarmed at these, and under servile fear withdrew to a safer region : *he is gone* (says the apostle) *to Thessalonica.* But with what view we are not informed. It may have been, as Chrysostom states, his home ; or it may have been to do some ministerial work, where it could be done with less risk; or, finally, to look after some worldly interest. The stress laid by the apostle on his love to the present world, renders the last supposition fully the most probable. And in that painful uncertainty as to his real state and future career, the notices we have respecting him leave us ; and to make positive affirmations, either on the favourable or on the unfavourable side, is unwarrantable.

Crescens [is gone] to Gaul,[1] *Titus to Dalmatia* — the latter a part of the province of Illyricum, on the eastern side of the Adriatic coast. Why these brethren left is not stated. They are not included in the blame associated with the name of Demas, yet we cannot say with Theodoret

[1] This is the reading of א, C, εἰς Γαλλίαν, also 23, 31, 72, 73, 80, several Latin codices, and has the distinct testimony of Euseb. *Hist*. iii. 4, Epiph. *H*. 51. Tisch. adopts it in his eighth edition. Even if Galatia were retained in the text, as it undoubtedly is in the larger number of authorities, we should probably have to understand by it Gaul, as Theodoret expressly states : εἰς Γαλατίαν· τὰς Γαλλίας οὕτως ἐκάλεσε— adding that the ancients were wont so to call it. So, for example, Plutarch, *Cæs*. c. 20; Polybius, iii. 77, 87. Coupled with Thessalonica on the one side, and Dalmatia on the other, it is more likely that Gaul was meant by the word (whichever form was used) than the province in Asia Minor.

that they were absolutely free from blame, and that they were sent into those regions to preach the gospel. The probability is, that they did go with this design; but the language of the apostle implies that they went of their own accord, not that they were sent by him. Of Crescens no mention is made elsewhere, nor have we any reliable traditions of him.

Ver. 11. *Luke alone is with me*—the beloved physician, as he is called in Col. iv. 14; there also, and in Philem. 24, coupled with Demas in salutations—but now different in the relations they now occupy! All the names mentioned in the passage of Philemon referred to again recur here, except that of Aristarchus. De Wette asks what has become of it? and Alford justly replies, that while we have no means of answering the question, "a forger, such as De Wette supposes the writer of this epistle to be, would have taken good care to account for him."

Mark take up (ἀναλαβὼν, here, the literal sense the best, implying that he was to be picked up on the way), *and bring with thee; for he is serviceable to me for the ministry.* There can be no reasonable doubt that the Mark here is John Mark, the evangelist, who caused the unfortunate split between Paul and Barnabas (Acts xv. 36-41), but who at a later period became reconciled to the apostle, and was in close fellowship with him (Col. iv. 10). By being *serviceable for the ministry*—εἰς διακονίαν—cannot be understood otherwise, when spoken in this absolute manner, than of the ministry of the gospel. There is a similar omission of the article at 1 Tim. i. 12, where, beyond doubt, it is that kind of ministration which is meant. Mark, probably, had been more at Rome than most of the other evangelists known to Paul, and was hence better acquainted both with the language (whence not a few Latin words have crept into his Gospel) and the manners of the place. If so, the apostle might see his peculiar adaptation for evangelistic work there, and naturally wish to have him again employed in it.

Ver. 12. *But Tychicus I sent to Ephesus*—not *and* I did so, for in the δὲ there is plainly a certain adversative meaning, though it may be regarded as of the slighter kind. If connected with what immediately precedes, it may have respect to a thought not unlikely to arise in the mind of Timothy when asked to bring Mark with him : Haven't you Tychicus ? But I had occasion to despatch him to Ephesus —for what specific purpose is not said. There must have been some urgent business to attend to when he was sent at such a time ; and it seems to imply that Timothy himself was not now there. He appears to have been also sent, during Paul's first imprisonment, with special greetings and friendly communications to Ephesus and Colosse (Eph. vi. 21 ; Col. iv. 7).

Ver. 13. *The cloak which I left at Troas with Carpus, bring when thou comest, and the books, especially the parchments.* It would seem from this that Timothy was still somewhere in Asia Minor ; if he had indeed left Ephesus, he could not have been very far from it, as Troas lay on his way. The kind of cloak mentioned—φέλονην, Latin, *penulam*—was a long thick cloak, understood to be without sleeves, enwrapping the whole body. The derivation is not quite certain (see in Ellicott). As to the reason for wishing such a cloak, there is no need for looking further than the mention of approaching winter in ver. 21. If his destination to suffer martyrdom should anyhow be postponed till that season, he would need the garment to protect him from the cold. The *books*, as contradistinguished from the *parchments*, were probably written on papyrus, and less valuable than those written on the more costly and enduring material. Hence a request that the latter especially be brought. But what respectively might be their nature and contents cannot be known, further than that, being urgently sought at such a moment, they must have related to things of highest interest—if not Scripture itself, writings more or less bearing on its revelations of truth and duty. When the articles had been left by Paul at Troas we know not; but, as noticed in the Introduction, it could scarcely be on the occasion noticed in Acts xx. 6, which belonged to a period about six years earlier. From the passing nature of the reference, and the things themselves which were left, the probability is, that the leaving of them behind was comparatively recent.

Ver. 14. *Alexander the coppersmith* (or, simply *smith;* for latterly χαλκεύς came to signify a worker in metals of any sort, and particularly in iron, as being the most frequently used) *did me much evil*—ἐνεδείξατο, exhibited it, but which is all one with doing it. *Where* he did it, however, is not said; nor *how*, though the language seems to betoken outward, active malignity. He may have been the same Alexander who is mentioned along with Hymenæus in 1 Tim. i. 20; but it is just as probable that he was not; and possibly the more precise designation here of the person by his trade may have been meant to distinguish him from the other. *The Lord will requite him according to his works*—ἀποδώσει seems clearly the correct reading (being that of א, A, C, D, F, also the Vulg., Cop., Syriac versions, Chrysostom, Theodoret; while the ἀποδῴη of the received text has the support only of K, L, at first hand, and of many cursives). The future, as compared with the optative, may be called popularly the milder sense; and Theodoret seems to lay some stress on so explaining: "It is a prediction, not an imprecation; and it was given forth for the purpose of consoling the blessed Timothy, and teaching him not to be disconcerted by the assaults of the adversaries." In a theological respect, however, there is no material difference; and if the optative *were* the correct reading, no one need stumble at it. For, surely, what it is perceived God is going to do, a believer, an apostle, nay, even the purest of angelic natures, may fitly desire to see accomplished. "Thy will be done" is the prayer of all saints, alike in heaven and on earth; only, when the thing to be done is the execution of deserved judgment upon the wicked, the difficulty is to breathe the prayer without any intermixture of wrathful feeling—with nothing but a pure and simple regard to the glory of God and the interests of righteousness. This may, however, be done even on earth by the ripened Christian, such as the apostle, who might now be said almost to stand midway between earth and heaven. From what he had seen in the behaviour and suffered at the hands of Alexander, he had come to understand that it was meet this man should, in some marked way, receive the due recompense of his misdeeds: the cause of the gospel required it—why should not God do it, and righteous men desire it to be done? It might be the best thing even for the man himself—possibly the one chance for him of being brought to a better mind; as many adversaries and persecutors of the truth have been led to see, only when humbled to the dust by chastisement and rebuke, how vain it is to contend with the Almighty.

Ver. 15. *Of whom be thou also on thy guard, for he exceedingly withstood our words.* That is, he made himself extremely obnoxious as an opponent of the gospel testified and pleaded for by St. Paul; had shown a bitter and determined spirit of resistance, so that Timothy could have no hope of winning him over, and should only beware of falling into his hands.

Ver. 16. The apostle now comes to speak of his own case in its judicial aspects: *In my first defence, no one stood forward with me, but all forsook me.* What is meant here by his first defence can only be understood of his first appearance before a tribunal at Rome to answer to the charge recently brought against him; not, as some, of what happened under his first imprisonment. We have spoken of the probable nature of this charge in the Introduction. It was, in all likelihood, an indictment against him as the setter forth of a new religion, which was forbidden by the laws of the Empire, though there may possibly have been some other accusations mixed up with it; so that, even as regards the matter of the indictment, it might have admitted of falling into two separate parts. Or, if the proper charge was only one, the trial may have been distributed into two distinct stages—the one called, according to the Republican practice, the *actio*, the other the *ampliatio*. It is disputed whether this practice still continued in judicial proceedings under the Empire (see Conybeare and Howson, vol. ii. p. 488); and our knowledge of the circumstances is too scanty to enable us to speak definitely on such minor points. Evidently, from what the apostle himself says, there was somehow a twofold cause to be adjudicated upon, calling for a double pleading or vindication on his part. He had already passed the first, yet with a saddening impression of the forlornness, humanly speaking, of his position. He had to stand all alone, without a patron, without an advocate, without even the sympathy and support of trusty and confidential friends, so disreputable and perilous, on grounds of law, seemed to be the cause with which he was identified. The conduct of friends, deserting him in the hour of need, he naturally felt most. Yet he pities rather than condemns them, and he prays for their forgiveness: *May it not be laid to their charge!* He would have it to be reckoned as a proof of weakness, not of false-heartedness.

Ver. 17. Though alone in one sense, however, the apostle was far from being alone in another: he had better and nobler defences than human advocates or intercessors could provide: *But the Lord stood by me, and strengthened me*— ἐνδυνάμωσέν με, replenished me with might; that is, inspired him with a holy boldness and energy for the occasion. And this, *in order that through me the preaching [of the gospel] might be fully accomplished:* πληροφορηθῇ, not "fully made known," as in the Authorized Version, which the word never signifies, but, as at ver. 5, fully accomplished or performed—not left, so to speak, as an imperfect, half-executed work : *and that all the Gentiles might hear.* This seems strong language to use of a single address of St. Paul, delivered before a judicial tribunal in Rome. It could only have been used by him on the supposition that there was a very great, in some sense a representative, Roman audience present to listen. And the cause, we can easily conceive, did excite a considerable interest there, and bring into court a vast assemblage, partly no doubt composed of Christians and Jews, but still more of the Gentile population of Rome, who usually crowded the Forum. In that case, it was most probably in one of the large Basilicas connected with the Forum, which were capable of accommodating a vast concourse of spectators, that the cause was heard. And Paul, seizing the noble opportunity it presented, and specially assisted by divine grace for the occasion, made his defence by unfolding the great theme of that gospel which had been committed to him; proclaimed the wonderful facts of Christ's life, and death, and resurrection, and of the solemn and momentous bearing which these were destined to have on the present well-being and eternal destiny of mankind. Such a vindication of the blessed gospel, and of his own connection with it, in such a place, and to such an audience, he might not unnaturally regard as the culmination of his work as an ambassador of Christ to the Gentiles.

As regards the immediate design of this great effort, it had the desired result, as is here added : *And he*—that is, the Lord—*delivered me out of the mouth of the lion.* There can be no doubt it means that he was rescued from the immediate danger that threatened him—got his acquittal on the first count, or in respect to the first stage of the charge brought against him. But when one goes to inquire what precisely is to be understood by being delivered out of the lion's mouth, a great variety of answers present themselves: Nero, say some (most of the Fathers); the lions in the amphitheatre, others; others, again, his Jewish accuser (so Wieseler), or the jaws of death (*ex præsenti incendio, vel ex faucibus mortis*—Calvin, Ellicott); perhaps the farthest-fetched of any of them, and in sense the feeblest, is Alford's, from or "in spite of desertion and discouragement." It seems to me that the most natural way is to take the words as an appropriation of figurative language frequently occurring in the Psalms—in those Psalms which describe the experience of the writers in their darkest seasons of danger and distress. Lion or lions was the sort of personification under which at such times they often expressed the fierce and remorseless adversaries or crushing calamities that were ready to devour them; and to be delivered from the lion's mouth was, in plain terms, to be set in a position of safety (Ps. xxii. 21, xxxv. 17, lvii. 4, etc.). So here: deliverance from the lion's mouth was simply escape from the complication of adversaries and intriguers that were gnashing, as it were, their teeth at him: for the moment he was free. Nothing, I believe, will ever be gained by pressing the language closer; on the contrary, by doing so we rather impair its force, and get, besides, into a region of uncertainties.

Ver. 18. From the past the apostle turns to the future, giving expression in this respect also to his filial confidence: *The Lord will deliver me from every evil work, and preserve me safe to His heavenly kingdom.* The *and* (καὶ) with which in the received text this utterance of faith and hope is introduced, is more than doubtful. It is wanting in א, A, C, D, Vulg., Copt., Arm. versions. The καὶ appears only in F, K, L, and is represented in the Syriac versions. While in this reference to the future the apostle uses the same verb as in regard to his late deliverance, he changes the preposition: it was there ἐρύσατο ἐκ; here it is ῥύσεται ἀπὸ, pointing, as Ellicott notes, "more generally to the *removal from* all the evil efforts that were directed against the apostle, and the evil influences around him—not merely all that threatened him personally, but all that in his person thwarted the gospel." Clearly, what he means by deliverance in this connection is a safe issue, as regards all that is really great and important, out of the endless machinations and troubles with which he had to contend here as the servant of Christ in the gospel. He should be so delivered, that none of them would be allowed to bear down his intrepidity, or make him flinch from the path of obedience, so that he should reach in safety the kingdom of everlasting bliss and glory. The expression βασιλείαν τὴν ἐπουράνιον, with respect to Christ's kingdom, is found only here in St. Paul's epistles, and has consequently been deemed *un*-Pauline by the opponents of the genuineness of this epistle. But it is a frivolous objection, as in other places he associates Christ's existence in glory with a present reigning or kingdom (1 Cor. xv. 25; Eph. i. 20; Col. iii. 1).

The passage fitly ends with a doxology: *to whom be glory for the ages of ages*—that is, for ever and ever (1 Tim. i. 17) —*Amen*. The context obliges us to connect this ascription of divine glory with Christ; for it was He, doubtless, of whom the apostle spake as standing by him, strengthening and delivering him.

Ver. 19. *Salute Prisca and Aquila* — with whom the apostle maintained a long, very endearing, and intimate fellowship (Acts xviii. 1; Rom. xvi. 3, 4, etc.)—*and the household of Onesiphorus.* See at chap. i. 16.

Ver. 20. *Erastus abode at Corinth, but Trophimus I left*

behind at Miletus sick. It was shown in the Introduction that these notices could not refer to anything recorded in the history of the Acts, and that they must be understood of later, and indeed quite recent events. On his last visit to Asia Minor and Jerusalem, as related in the Acts, Trophimus, so far from having been left at Miletus sick, went with Paul to Jerusalem, and his appearance there with the apostle gave occasion to the disturbance and accusation that were raised by the Jews (Acts xx. 4, xxi. 29).

Ver. 21. *Do thy endeavour to come before winter*—that is, while still the sea was open for navigation, according to the usages of the time; at the approach of winter, vessels were for the most part laid up till the return of spring (Acts xxvii. 9, 10). *Ex die tertio Iduum Novembris, usque in diem sextum Iduum Martiarum, Maria clauduntur,* is a passage quoted by Mr. Smith, from Vegetius, in his *Voyage and Shipwreck of St. Paul,* p. 45. He has others to the same effect. So that, if Timothy did not reach Rome before winter, his visit would in all probability have to be postponed till the following year; and by that time the apostle should very possibly have finished his course. *Eubulus saluteth thee, and Pudens, and Linus, and Claudia, and all the brethren.* The names mentioned here occur nowhere else in New Testament Scripture. Tradition in one form connects with this Linus the first presidency of the church of Rome after the apostles, while another tradition assigns that honour to Clemens. The Pudens and Claudia here associated have been supposed to be the same mentioned as man and wife in an Epigram of Martial, iv. 13, comp. with xi. 34; and much learned labour has been employed of late to make out the identity. An outline of the discussion may be found in Alford's Prolog. to this epistle—Appendix; also in Conybeare and Howson, vol. ii. pp. 500-2. But the story is woven together by so many slender threads, and has to be eked out by such a variety of hypothetical, sometimes not very probable conjectures, that I confess, with Ellicott, the identification appears to me "very doubtful."

Ver. 22. *The Lord be with thy spirit.* (This is the shortest and probably the correct reading, that of ℵ, F, G ; some authorities add Jesus after Lord, and others Jesus Christ.) *Grace be with you.*

APPENDIX.

APPENDIX A.—Page 119.

THE PECULIAR TESTIMONY FOR GOSPEL TIMES—1 TIM. II. 6.

TO designate the truth that Christ gave Himself a ransom for all, *the* testimony for its own (*i.e.* gospel) seasons or times, is so peculiar, and at the same time so important a statement, that some further illustration of it than could fitly be introduced into the text may not be out of place. Indeed, as matters now stand, it calls for vindication as well as for more lengthened exposition. The peculiarity and importance of the statement consist in the singular prominence given, not to the simple fact of the death of Christ, but to that death in the character of a ransom or redemption-price for sinful men—elevating this to the central place in God's scheme as disclosed for gospel times. The death of Christ on the cross as a historical fact is recorded with great fulness by all the evangelists, and is unquestionably the most prominent subject in their respective narratives. But has it there the same *doctrinal significance* as is assigned to it by the apostle? This is now frequently called in question, and by some the teaching of St. Paul on the subject is expressly affirmed to be out of accord with that of Christ Himself, as reported by His more immediate witnesses. Of the class referred to, Professor Jowett may be taken as one of the most eminent representatives. He says:[1]—" It is hard to imagine that there can be any truer expression of the gospel than the words of Christ Himself, or that any truth omitted by Him is essen-

[1] *Commentary on St. Paul's Epistles*, ii. p. 555.

tial to the gospel. 'The disciple is not above his master, nor the servant greater than his lord.' The philosophy of Plato was not better understood by his followers than by himself; nor can we allow that the gospel is to be interpreted by the Epistles, or that the Sermon on the Mount is only half Christian, and needs the fuller inspiration or revelation of St. Paul, or the author of the Epistle to the Hebrews. . . . How strange would it have seemed to the apostle St. Paul, who thought himself unworthy to be called an apostle, because he persecuted the church of God, to find that his own words were preferred in after ages to those of Christ Himself!" To regard the teaching of the Epistles as an essential part of Christian doctrine, it is again said, " is to rank the authority of the words of Christ below that of apostles and evangelists."

Now, representations of this sort proceed on the idea that Christ and His apostles stood related to each other just as Plato did to his followers; that they were alike simply teachers of certain moral or religious truths; and that, of course, the master-mind must have taught in a clearer and nobler strain than any who might sit at His feet. But this is not the view of the relation given by the Master Himself — not, at least, in its bearing upon the question at issue. Jesus Christ had not simply a doctrine to teach, but a work to do; and a work of which His doctrine in the fuller sense was to be but the proper exposition and the varied application. Hence the promise of the Holy Spirit so largely dwelt upon by Christ before His departure, as requisite to bring His disciples to a full knowledge and appreciation of the truth concerning Him. The revelation He had given of Himself, therefore, in the Gospels could not by possibility be the whole. The *germ* of all, indeed, was there, but not its development into a comprehensive scheme of truth and duty. There are sayings and discourses of Christ which are profound and large enough to embrace everything: as when He said, " God so loved the world, that He gave His only-begotten Son, that whosoever believeth in Him should not perish, but have everlasting life" (John iii. 16); or, " Come unto me, all ye that labour and are heavy laden, and I will give you rest" (Matt. xi. 28); or, " The kingdom of heaven is like a certain man that made a great supper, and bade many" (Luke xiv. 16); and so on. But how much was still required to explicate the meaning of such statements, and show precisely what they involved respecting the work of Christ, and its adaptation to the wants and circumstances of mankind? Then, there were utterances of Christ which were thrown out as occasion offered—like seed-corn scattered here and there—but in which so little regard was had to systematic form or rounded completeness of representation, that, if taken apart, and without regard to acts and operations yet in prospect, which would shed a reconciling light upon them, might have seemed scarcely compatible with each other. For example, we find forgiveness of sin at one time coupled simply with the exercise of a penitent disposition, as in the case of the woman who was a sinner, or in the parable of the prodigal son (Luke vii. 15); on other occasions with the manifestation of a forgiving spirit toward one's fellow-sinners (Matt. vi. 12, 14; Luke vi. 37); while, again, in a different class of statements everything in that respect is made to depend upon the atoning death of Christ—as when He said that He came to give His life a ransom for many (Matt. ix. 28), or that He *must* die, that repentance and remission of sins might be preached in His name (Matt. xvi. 21; Luke xxiv. 44–47), plainly pointing to His suffering obedience as the ground on which all hope of blessing was to rest.

Indeed, this one great fact of the death of Christ—its necessity, its priceless worth, and the essential relation it was to hold to the entire mission of Christ—obviously rendered His own teaching, during the period of His personal ministry, in a great degree fragmentary and incomplete. It was with His death (coupled, of course, with the resurrection that was to follow) that He connected the finishing of His work; it was in that He was to perfect Himself as the Messiah; and till the destined consummation actually took place, the doctrinal significance of it could not possibly be more than very partially revealed. It was *then* only that the mystery which had hung around God's scheme of grace began to clear away, and that it became possible to present anything like a full and harmonious exhibition of the truths and principles embodied in it. All instructions delivered beforehand, though uttered by One who spake as man had never spoken, were in a doctrinal respect necessarily imperfect; they could not possess the perfect clearness of gospel light, because the consummating act still lay in the future, which was to constitute for all time the main ground of God's gracious procedure toward men, and of their confidence and love toward Him. It hence is *the mediatorial death of Christ*, not the moment of His incarnation, or of His entrance on His public ministry, which forms the proper boundary line between the Old and the New. It is with the shedding of His blood for the remission of sins —as He distinctly announced at the institution of the supper —that the new covenant was ratified, and its provisions of grace and blessing were made for ever sure to a believing people. And so the doctrine taught up to that time could not be final; in other words, the utterances and facts of gospel history could not be seen in their proper force and meaning till the events had taken place to which they all more or less pointed. The Gospels, indeed, reveal much; but they themselves close with the expressed need and promise of further revelations, in order to set in its true light, and carry out to its moral results, the perfected work of the Redeemer.[1]

What, then, do we find as to those further revelations, or that more explicit and developed knowledge, when we turn to the other books of the New Testament? Do we find our Lord still acting with a view to impart it? We do. His agency in this respect did not cease with His death, nor even with His ascension to the heavenly places. A

---

[1] Archbishop Whately long ago urged very cogently the considerations just stated: "How could our Lord, during His abode on earth, preach fully that scheme of salvation, of which the keystone had not been laid —even His meritorious sacrifice as an atonement for sin—His resurrection from the dead, and ascension into glory, when these events had not taken place? He did, indeed, darkly hint at these events in His discourses to His disciples by way of prophecy; but we are told that 'the saying was hid from them, and they comprehended it not, till after that Christ was risen from the dead.' Of course, therefore, there was no reason and no room for Him to enter into a full discussion of the doctrines dependent on those events. He left them to be enlightened in due time as to the true nature of His kingdom by the gift which He kept in store for them [the Holy Spirit]. . . . Our Lord's discourses, therefore, while on earth, though they teach the truth, did not teach,

period of instruction, we are expressly informed, intervened between His resurrection from the dead and His ascension to glory, during which He often met with the disciples, and expounded to them the things concerning the kingdom. Of these explanations we are merely told that they turned much upon the necessity of His sufferings and death, in order to the fulfilment of what had been written of Him in the law and the prophets; and the results of the teaching we naturally look for in the discourses and epistles which, under the power and guidance of the Spirit, were addressed by the apostles to those who received their testimony. It had now become, in a sense, the dispensation of the Spirit, but it was not the less the dispensation of Christ, the glorified Redeemer. And it is instructive to mark how beautifully the one is linked with the other in the narrative of the Acts, where the Spirit is represented as working all, yet working as the representative of Christ—carrying forward *His* agency, giving effect to *His* will. Hence, in the march of events we never lose sight of Christ, any more than of the Spirit: everything is done as under the direction of His hand, and the witness of His risen power and glory. It is the same when St. Paul comes upon the scene; it is Christ who, by the Spirit, arrests him in his career of persecuting violence, and calls him to the work of an apostle, furnishing him with the authority and gifts requisite for its discharge. Hence the apostle disclaimed his doing anything as of himself: the commission he bore was not of man, or by the will of men, but by Jesus Christ, or by the commandment of God our Saviour and Lord Jesus Christ: the gospel he preached was received, not of man, but by revelation from

nor could they have been meant to teach, the *whole* truth, as afterwards revealed to His disciples. What chance, then, can they have of attaining true Christian knowledge who shut their eyes to such obvious conclusions as these? who, under that idle plea, the misapplication of the maxim that 'the disciple is not above his master,' confine their attention entirely to the discourses of Christ recorded in the four Gospels, as containing all necessary truth; and if anything in the other parts of the sacred writings is forced upon their attention, studiously explain it away, so that it do not go a step beyond what is clearly revealed in the evangelists? As if a man should, in the culture of a fruit-tree, carefully destroy as a spurious excrescence every part of the fruit which was not fully developed in the blossom that preceded it."—*Essays on St. Paul*, sec. 2 of Essay ii.

Jesus Christ, so that the things he spake and wrote were to be acknowledged as the commandments of the Lord (1 Cor. xiv. 37); and he and his fellow-labourers were but instruments to bear the treasure of the gospel, that others might believe as the Lord gave to every man. In short, the later history of the New Testament was but the varied manifestation of the continued life and agency of the Lord Jesus Christ. Through the instrumentality of His delegated servants, He was, though personally unseen, giving articulate form to His gospel, and applying it to the salvation of souls and the planting of His church in the world. The voice of Paul or the voice of Peter speaking to the churches, was in effect the voice of Jesus. Hence He had Himself said from the outset, "He that heareth you, heareth me; and he that despiseth you, despiseth me" (Luke x. 16).

Was the voice the same now, then, as when it came directly from Christ? The same, we reply, in substance, but with a difference of a circumstantial kind suited to the more advanced stage of things which had now been reached. It was no longer the objective Saviour merely, but this through the Spirit made manifest in the hearts of men: in other words, the facts concerning Christ's person and work known and apprehended as *doctrine;* divine truth entering into human thought and human experience. On this account, also, it might be expected the word would be more effective, since everything would appear now at once in its proper harmony and proportions, and in its thorough adaptation to human wants and circumstances, enlightening the understanding, satisfying the heart and conscience, taking possession of the thoughts and feelings of the inner man.

Now this is precisely what we find in the representations given in the Acts and Epistles. Christ is throughout the great subject, or matter of the testimony delivered, and the instruction imparted. The apostles, we read in the Acts, "ceased not to teach and to preach Jesus Christ;" of one it is said "that he preached Christ unto them;" of another, "that he preached Christ in the synagogues," or, "he preached Jesus unto them, and the resurrection." The Apostle Paul sums up his preaching, in one place, as "Christ and Him crucified, the power of God unto salvation;" in another, as "repentance toward God, and faith toward our Lord Jesus Christ;" or, in the one immediately before us, as " the Mediator between God and man, who gave Himself a ransom for all, the testimony for its own seasons "—Heaven's special testimony for the times of the gospel. In other passages we find the kingdom of God put along with the person of Christ as the subject of apostolic testimony. So St. Peter, for instance, on the day of Pentecost, when he gave the people to know assuredly that the " Jesus whom they had crucified was made both Lord and Christ "—that is, both King and Messiah, or King Messiah; and St. Paul, in the last notice we have of him in the history of the Acts, is said to have received those who came to him, " preaching the kingdom of God, and teaching those things which concern the Lord Jesus Christ."

This mode of representation, it will be observed, carries us back to the kind of preaching or proclamation of which we read in the Gospels: it connects the one with the other, but with an obvious advance as to the mode of doing it. "The kingdom of God is at hand." *That* was the common style of preaching as reported in the Gospels, first of John Baptist, then of Jesus, finally of the twelve; and many a parable was taught by our Lord, having for their common object the kingdom of God, in its nature, its principles of administration, and final issues. But now, since Christ had finished the work which was required for laying the foundation of the kingdom in its New Testament form, the doctrine of the kingdom came to be all associated with Himself; the truth had come to its proper realization in Him; and to preach the things which concerned His person, His work, and the glory that followed, was at the same time to testify of the kingdom. All who really received Christ as the ground of their peace and hope, entered into the kingdom; they were " translated out of darkness into the kingdom of God's dear Son;" and what they thenceforth looked for was His appearance in the kingdom, when they also expected to appear with Him in glory. It was thus that the Spirit, through the preaching of the apostles, glorified Christ, in a way they could not possibly do during His sojourn upon earth. And, as a matter of course, the things testified respecting Him now were no longer simply facts, but facts as the basis of doctrine—facts with an interpretation put upon them which gave them a spiritual significance and power in relation to men's spiritual life and well-being. "The Christ preached by the apostles was one who [had not only lived and wrought righteousness on earth, but also] had died and risen again, and whom the heavens had received till the time of the restitution of all things. In these three facts the manifestation of the Son of God had culminated, and in *them* the true character of His mission had appeared. The old carnal thoughts of it had been left in the grave, and could never rise from it again. It was 'the Prince of Life' who had risen from the dead; it was 'the King of Glory' who had passed into the heavens. And no less did these facts declare the *spiritual consequences* of His manifestation, since they carried with them the implication of those three corresponding gifts—the forgiveness of sins, the resurrection of the body, and the life everlasting."[1]

It thus appears how naturally, and by reason of the inevitable progress of events, the things concerning Christ assumed a more doctrinal form; or rather, how the facts which made up the earthly career of Christ necessarily became, on being completed, *doctrines*, and as such were preached in the name of Christ by apostles, and by the Holy Spirit were sealed upon the understandings and hearts of men. The question now was, not whether men simply believed in Jesus as the Messiah, but with what meaning or to what results did they accept of His Messiahship? Could they say, with St. Peter, "Neither is there salvation in any other; for there is none other name given under heaven among men whereby we must be saved"? Or, with St. Paul, "By Him all that believe are justified from all things, from which they could not be justified by the law of Moses"? To say this was to affirm the doctrine that Christ by His death had done, in respect to the desert of sin, what the old sacrificial system of the law could do only in a symbolical manner—that His death is the one great sacrifice that atones, because in it He bore our sins in His own body on the tree; and, consequently, that legal rites of propitiation must be done away, and no dependence rested on anything for salvation but the perfect work of Christ the crucified. This was the gospel of Peter and Paul; and

[1] Bernard, *Progress of Doctrine in the New Testament*, p. 130.

when Paul accused the Galatians of accepting, through false teachers, another gospel, he did not mean to say that they denied the facts of Christ's holy life and humiliating death, but that they understood these differently, failed to give them their proper moral significance—in other words, did not accredit and appreciate them in their true *doctrinal import*. So, also, when parties in the church of Corinth and elsewhere sought to couple with the faith of Christ a disbelief of the doctrine of the resurrection, or a licence to sin, they were denounced as really subverters of the faith, enemies of the cross of Christ, because practically robbing it of that moral worth and significance which in the scheme of God are inseparably connected with it.

Such is the gospel of Christ in its completed form—completed under the direction of Christ Himself, by the Spirit He gave and the instrumentality He appointed. It is simply the facts of His mediatory work in their spiritual bearing and personal application. Contemplated merely as facts or historical events, they stand outside of us, and may leave us *morally* much as we were. But when apprehended as doctrine, or appropriated by faith as the elements of saving knowledge, they enter into our consciousness; they touch the springs of thought and feeling in our bosom; they form the ground of new aspirations, the motives of a new and higher life. Without the facts, indeed, the doctrine might swim in the air; but without being seen in their doctrinal import, the facts would not be spirit and life to the soul.

We thus perceive the absurdity of attempting to separate Christianity from doctrine. Only as containing elements of doctrine does it become to us matter of truth and duty. Have I faith in Christ as the Son of God and Saviour of the world? Then I hold the doctrine of the incarnation, and realize its importance. Have I faith in the death of Christ, as the ground of my reconciliation with God? Then I hold the doctrine of the cross, or of a crucified Redeemer, as the one thing needful to my peace and hope. Have I faith in Christ as the conqueror of death, the resurrection and the life? Then I embrace Him as the source of a new and undying life, beginning here and perfected in eternity. Have I faith in Christ as ready to come again and appear on the throne of judgment? Then I hold the doctrine of the second advent, and recognise its bearing on my personal condition and destiny. Thus Christianity as a doctrine, is the root of Christianity as a life; reject it in the one respect, and you cut the sinews of its vitality and strength in the other.

But there is no difficulty in understanding how many should be disposed to make such a separation—disposed, that is, to accredit more or less of the recorded facts in Christ's life, but make little or no account of them in their doctrinal aspects. So long as they are considered apart from these aspects, everything about them presents a kind of loose, sporadic appearance; and men may fix, some upon this, others upon that point in the life-history of Jesus as what, in their view, chiefly serves to make it valuable and important. There is, too, so much in that history, brief and chequered as it was, which appears attractive and winning even to the natural man—so much of grace and condescension, of disinterestedness in doing good, of compassion toward the miserable and unworthy, of readiness to brave the fiercest opposition, and to sacrifice life itself in the cause of truth and righteousness, that all the better feelings and sympathies of the heart can without difficulty be awakened, and turned toward the Son of man as exhibited in the Gospels with profound affection and regard; nay, can find there, as they can find nowhere else, what is fitted to interest and instruct them, in the varied circumstances and relations of life. But it is another thing when all that there was in the life, death, and resurrection of Jesus, is brought out in the subsequent parts of the New Testament, and, under the form of doctrinal belief, presented to every Christian bosom as the ground and nourishment of a life devoted to God, and fraught with the fruits of righteousness. Under this aspect of matters the natural heart rebels, and seeks in a thousand ways to escape the unwelcome conclusion. It does so, often, by putting another than the natural interpretation on the facts of gospel history; or, if not, by allowing other things to intercept their due influence on the affections of the soul and the actions of the life. To enter aright into this part of gospel teaching—to accept and relish Christianity as exhibited by the apostles, and by them formed into a system of truth and duty—has for its essential prerequisite a mind that has become profoundly conscious of the guilt and danger of sin, and longs for an interest in the restored favour and blessing of God as the one great good. Whenever men reach this state of spiritual conviction and desire, they will be ready to hail the entire manifestation of the truth in Scripture, and will find but the fitting sequel of Christ's own teaching, and the true explanation of His work in the world, in the discourses and writings of His apostles.

It is incumbent on all who would do the part of faithful representatives of Christ, and true exponents of His mind and will to men, to draw their materials from what He has thus made known to us as the whole of His counsel in regard to salvation. It is of special moment that they should do so in an age like the present, when many persons of note, biassed by the aims and spirit of literary or scientific culture, are disposed to take the gospel only in part, and refuse to go the full length of a cordial appreciation and belief of the truth. They will speak, perhaps, in the most approving terms of the simply human aspects of our Lord's character, and of the moral qualities exhibited by Him in His career on earth; they will also frankly concede the impulse derived from the power of Christianity in raising the tone of thought and feeling among the nations that have received it, and ameliorating in many respects the condition of society. But in all this they restrict themselves to humanitarian ground, and appear to make account of nothing as actually true, or at least appreciable by them, except the incomparable excellence of Christ's character, and the pure morality of the gospel. But had that been all, great and valuable as it is, should the results which even such writers acknowledge to have followed in the train of Christianity have been produced by it? What wonders have been achieved, what moral reformations accomplished, by such a Christianity in the hands of its formal abettors, the modern Unitarians? Has not the history of the past taught us to associate with them the stagnant marshes of Christianity, rather than its vivifying streams and fruitful fields? "The force which Christianity has applied to the world, and by which it has produced that change in the world which it has, is the doctrine of grace. There has been a new power actually working in the system, and that power has worked by other means besides doctrine; but still it is the law of God's dealings with us to apply His power to us by means of our faith and belief in that power—that is, by doctrine. Faith in his own position, the belief at the bottom of every Christian's heart that he stands in a different relation to God from a heathen, and has a supernatural source of strength, —this it is which has made him *act*, has been the rousing and elevating motive to the Christian body, and raised its moral practice."[1]

Yes, for a Christianity of regenerating power and divine blessing, we must have the saving doctrines, as well as the historical facts and moral teaching, of the gospel wrought into men's convictions and experience. The light shall otherwise want power to reach the conscience, and call forth the nobler acts of self-denying love and patient continuance in well-doing, which are the marks of a living Christianity. Only when there is a faith which embraces all the essential elements of truth and hope in Christ, and is itself sustained in the heart by the Spirit of God, is there a principle of life powerful enough to resist the desires of the flesh, and overcome the evil that is in the world. With such faith, however, the followers of Christ have no need to be afraid. They will prevail in the future as they have done in the past. "Their antagonists themselves will be their helpers;" for these will but serve to drive them the more closely to Christ, and cause them to drink more deeply from the well-spring of His salvation.

APPENDIX B.—PAGE 139.

ON THE MEANING OF THE EXPRESSION "HUSBAND OF ONE WIFE," IN 1 TIM. III. 2, 12, TIT. I. 6.

THE explanation given of this expression, under the first of the passages referred to, restricts the qualification indicated by it to an existing relationship, irrespective of the question

[1] *Mozley on Miracles*, p. 182.

whether a previous relationship may or may not have existed, which had been dissolved by death. It simply required that when one was called to office in the Christian church, there should be but one living woman to whom he stood related as husband. And as the expression of itself does not import more, there are various considerations which appear to shut us up to this meaning as the only one that is properly tenable.

1. First of all, let the place be noted which the qualification holds in the apostle's delineation of fitness for office in the Christian church. In both the epistles (1 Timothy and Titus) it stands second in the list of qualifications for the pastorate,—in each also occurring immediately after the epithet blameless or irreproachable, — as if, among the characteristics of a life free from any palpable stain, the first thing that might be expected to start into notice was, whether the individual stood related in marriage to one person only, or to more than one. Now, supposing this latter alternative had respect merely to the contracting of a second marriage after the death of a first wife, is the qualification one that, in the circumstances, we could imagine to have been so prominently exhibited, and so stringently imposed? Or is it what we have reason to think would have been borne up by the moral sense of the community? Quite the reverse in both respects. The legislation and the practice of Old Testament times were notoriously of a different kind. They went to an extreme, indeed, in the opposite direction; and even our Lord, when correcting that extreme, gave no indication of His purpose to introduce a restriction of the nature in question, or to make monogamy, in this sense, a condition either of office or of sanctity. St. Paul himself had explicitly declared, in his earlier writings, that death dissolved the marriage tie, so as to leave the survivor free to enter into another union, if such might be deemed advisable or expedient (Rom. vii. 1–3; 1 Cor. vii. 8, 9). And in the laws and usages of the Greeks and Romans no hindrance was ever known to be put upon men in respect to their use of this freedom; no stigma attached to their doing so, unless it might be in connection with the time and mode of their going about it. Such being the case, is it in the least degree probable, or does it seem

to accord with the wisdom we are wont to associate with the apostle (apart altogether from his inspiration), that he should now, for the first time, and in so brief and peremptory a manner, without even a note of explanation, have pronounced more than a single marriage-union absolutely incompatible with the ministerial function?—nay, should have set it in the very front of admitted disqualifications?—and should even have extended the rule to deacons, whose employment was rather about, than in, spiritual things, serving tables, not ministering in word and doctrine? Unquestionably, if such were the import of the apostle's instruction, a new thing was now introduced into the discipline of God's house, and introduced in a very extraordinary way. A principle of sanctity was enunciated which was without warrant in any prior legislation or recognised usage; a principle, moreover, which, in contrariety to the whole spirit of the apostle's writings, must have given to caste distinctions and ascetic notions of excellence a legitimate footing in the church of Christ. In point of fact, when the sense we contend against began to be put upon his words, it did work powerfully both in the ritualistic and the ascetic direction. And if that sense could be established as the natural and proper one, a difficulty of a very formidable kind would be raised against the Pauline authorship of the Pastoral epistles.

2. A second ground of confirmation to the view we advocate is the general concurrence in its favour on the part of the earlier interpreters; and this in spite of a prevalent feeling and usage tending to produce a bias in the contrary direction. Thus Chrysostom: "He (St. Paul) speaks thus, not imposing a law, as if it were not allowed one to become [an *episcopos*] without this condition [viz. unless he had one wife], but to restrain undue licence (τὴν ἀμετρίαν κωλύων); since among the Jews it was lawful to enter into double marriages, and have two wives at the same time."[1] So, too, Theodoret: "Concerning that saying,

---

[1] His comment on Tit. i. 6, though less explicit, is to the same effect when rightly interpreted. It speaks merely of a double marriage relationship as incompatible with the pastoral office: "chastising the wanton, and not permitting them with a second (or twofold) marriage to assume the governing power,"—οὐκ ἀφεὶς μετὰ δευτέρου γάμου τὴν ἀρχὴν

the husband of one wife, I think certain men have said well. For of old both Greeks and Jews were wont to be married to two, three, and more wives at once. And even now, although the Imperial laws forbid men to marry two wives at one time, they have commerce with concubines and harlots. They have said, therefore, that the holy apostle declared that he who dwells in a becoming manner with a single wife is worthy of being ordained to the episcopate. For, they say, he (that is, Paul) does not reject a second marriage, who has often commanded it to be used." Then, on the other side: "If he have put away his former wife, and married another, he is worthy of blame and deserving of reprehension; but if force of death has deprived him of his former wife, and nature has prompted him to become united to another, the second marriage is to be attributed, not to choice, but to casualty. Having respect to these and such like things, I accept the interpretation of those who so view the passage." Theophylact is briefer, but to the same effect: "*If he be a husband of one wife;* this he said because of the Jews, for to them polygamy was permitted." Even Jerome, with all his ascetic rigour, speaks favourably of this interpretation (in his notes on the passage in Titus); states that, according to the view of many and worthy divines, it was intended merely to condemn polygamy, and not to exclude from the ministry men who have been twice married. Now, considering the general prevalence of ascetic feeling at the time, and the virtue commonly attached to celibacy as a qualification for the proper discharge of priestly functions, the interpretation thus either expressly put upon the expression under consideration by those fathers, or held at least to be allowable, cannot but seem entitled to the greatest weight. It presents a series of testimonies to what may be fairly called the natural sense of the expression, and to what appeared the just and reasonable nature of the qualification demanded by the apostle, in spite of a strong current of feeling, and a very prevalent usage, tending to incline them in the opposite direction.

ἐγχειρίζεσθαι,—not *after* the marriage in question, but *with* it—standing in the twofold relationship at the same time—guilty of a moral wrong, though practised under the forms of law. See Suicer, under Διγαμία, vol. i. p. 897.

3. The commencement and growth of the other view—the view which understands the expression to exclude from the offices of pastor and deacon in the church any one who might have re-married after having lost a wife by death—furnishes an additional argument in favour of our interpretation. For the history of church opinion and practice on the subject puts it beyond a doubt, that the more natural view was abandoned only when a false asceticism began to flow in upon the church, and an ideal of piety unwarranted in Scripture, and at variance with the flesh and blood relations which God has established for men in this life. It is not till near the end of the second century that the ascetic spirit makes its appearance as a disturbing element in this particular line; and when it does so, the perverting influence discovers itself in respect to the members generally of the Christian church, not specifically to those who were called to discharge any spiritual function. It may be questioned whether the *Plea* of Athenagoras or *The Shepherd* of Hermas had, in point of time, precedence of the other. Probably they were nearly contemporaneous; and they are the earliest extant of the Patristic writings which can be referred to on the present subject. Athenagoras is often erroneously adduced as a witness for the other view; for when the passage in his *Plea* is correctly explained, it has respect to bigamy in the proper sense. "A person (he says) should either remain as he was born, or be content with one marriage; for the second marriage (ὁ δεύτερος γάμος) is only a specious adultery. 'For whosoever puts away his wife (says He), and marries another, commits adultery,'—neither permitting a man to put her away whose virginity he has made to cease, nor to marry another (οὐδὲ ἐπιγαμεῖν). For he who deprives himself of his first wife, even though she be dead, is a veiled adulterer, resisting the hand of God" (c. 33). The thought is somewhat loosely expressed, but the reason assigned for the judgment given clearly shows that the second marriage contemplated by the writer is one contracted under the forms of law, after an improper divorce had been effected against a first wife. In such a case a second marriage was justly held to be from the first vitiated—essentially adulterous; and this for all Christians alike, without respect to official distinctions. The passage in *The*

Shepherd is more to the point : " If a wife or husband die, and the widower or widow marry, does he or she commit sin ? There is no sin in marrying again, said he ; but if they remain unmarried, they gain greater honour and glory from the Lord ; yet if they marry, they do not commit sin" (Com. iv. c. 3). This also has respect to the Christian life generally, and makes but a slight advance upon the teaching of Scripture ; for there both our Lord and St. Paul speak of the resolution to abstain from marriage as, in certain circumstances, and with a view to more entire devotedness to the service of God, an indication of spiritual excellence beyond what would be exhibited by a different course. Only here the married state is apparently contemplated more apart, as in itself, especially when entered into a second time, incompatible with the higher degrees of honour in the divine kingdom. It was still but an incipient indication of the leaven which had begun to work. A stage further on, and we meet with greatly more marked symptoms of its operation.

This stage had its commencement with the rise of that pretentious Gnosticism which, especially from about the middle of the second century, in the hands of the Encratites (Tatian and Marcion), sought to elevate the tone of Christianity, and raise the ideal of Christian perfection higher than was done by the acknowledged teachers of Christianity. According to this school, true perfection consisted in working one's self free from the ordinary relations and enjoyments of life : marriage, which formed the common basis of these, was esteemed a kind of service of the devil, utterly at variance with the higher aims of the spiritual life ; the " elect " spirits must have nothing to do with it, and must also abstain from the use of flesh and wine, and give themselves to fastings and other kinds of bodily mortification. The real tendency of this Gnostic spiritualism did not quite immediately discover itself ; it pressed at various points as a reforming influence into the church ; and in some of its more characteristic features it ere long burst forth with great power among the excitable and enthusiastic Christians of Phrygia in the guise of Montanism. Montanus and his followers did not profess, indeed, to stand in any proper affinity to Christians of the Gnostic type ; but they so far coincided with them as to aim at introducing a new and higher style of Christianity, and one that partook largely of Gnostic elements. Having received (as they imagined) the fuller afflatus of the Spirit promised by Christ, they had attained to the position of right truly spiritual Christians; were the pneumatics (πνευματικοί), while others, if Christians at all, were but psychical or carnal (ψυχικοί); and, in proof of their nobler elevation, they renounced not only the pleasures and luxuries, but also most of the comforts of life—fasted oft, and rigidly; courted indignities, self-denials, persecutions; disparaged marriage, and stigmatized second marriages as fornication. Though the movement was opposed by all the leading authorities in the church, and the claim to supernatural guidance was on every hand rejected, yet many were impressed by the apparent elevation and moral strength of the party; and the opinion grew, that the more select class of Christians should cultivate the ascetic virtues, and should either remain in cœlibacy, or at most be but once married. The tendency of Christian thought and practice in this direction received a great impulse from Tertullian, who not only imbibed the distinctive principles of Montanism, but threw himself into the advocacy of them with zeal and energy. On the subject of marriage he occupied what he called middle ground—between those (the Encratites) who repudiated marriage altogether, as a thing inherently evil, and the Psychical party, who maintained the lawfulness of the married state, even when entered into anew after the death of a previous wife. He contended for the absolute singleness of the marriage union, pressing all sorts of considerations into his argument; such as that the first Adam had but one spouse (Eve), the second also but one (the church); that death does not entirely destroy the union of married parties, since the soul still lives, in which the more vital seat of the union resides; that at the resurrection, though there shall be no more marrying, but an angelic state of being, yet those who have been married on earth shall recognise each other as such, etc. (*De Monog.*, and *Ad Uxorem*, L. i.). By considerations like these, Tertullian reaches the conclusion that in no case is more than a single marriage allowable for a Christian, while the state of cœlibacy is to be preferred as one of higher sanctity.

He admits that in 1 Cor. vii. 39 the apostle grants liberty of re-marrying to those who had been deprived of a spouse by death, if only they married in the Lord; but he thinks this had respect to such merely as had been first married in heathenism, so that their union was no marriage in the Christian sense. He also admits that the principle laid down at the beginning of Rom vii. as to death severing the marriage tie, and leaving the survivor free to marry again without being guilty of adultery, is at variance with the view maintained and advocated by him; but finds his escape in the new revelation of Montanism, that as Christ had taken away the liberty which Moses allowed to the Israelites because of the hardness of their hearts, so the Paraclete now takes away what Christ and Paul allowed on account of the infirmity of the flesh, in order that the original ideal of marriage might be restored. So that he concludes second marriages are contrary to the will of Christ—not lawful—next thing to adultery (*juxta adulterium; De Monog.* c. xi.–xv.).

In the course of this strange piece of argumentation, the passages 1 Tim. iii. 2, Tit. i. 6, are naturally brought into consideration, and the expression *husband of one wife* is held, without question, to denote a person only once married: those who married a second time are termed *digami*, bigamists—the first time that such an explanation, followed by such an application of the term, occurs in any Christian writing.[1] Tertullian's argument from the passages is this: The apostle requires of those who hold clerical functions in the church, that they be no more than once married; but this cannot be confined to them, no more than any of the other moral qualifications mentioned in the same connection: if the rest are common to them with believers generally, why should not this also? Or if the clergy alone have to do with this, then they, too, alone must be subject to the discipline of the rest. And is it not the doctrine of Scripture, that all genuine believers are of priestly rank, having one and the same spiritual standing, the same high and holy calling, with official distinctions only for orderly administrations? Here, undoubtedly, Ter-

[1] The word is found in Justin's *Apology*, c. i. 15, but in the usual sense of separating from one wife and marrying another.

tullian got hold of a right principle, though he utterly misapplied it; for it is against the fundamental principles of the gospel (as already indicated) to have class distinctions as to moral attainments—to set up one type of purity or holiness for the pastor, and another for the flock. And it betrayed a departure from the simple faith and true spirit of Christianity when the authorities in the church began, as they did about or shortly after Tertullian's time, to hold that it was allowable for common believers, but not for Christian ministers, to enter a second time into a marriage relationship. This was really to change the constitution of Christ's spiritual kingdom.

The influence of Tertullian's writings on this subject, as on many others, operated far and wide throughout the church, though he failed to carry the formal sanction of his views. In various quarters, second marriages, even among the laity, came to be viewed with disfavour, and were occasionally subjected to a measure of disciplinary treatment. Thus, in one of the canons of the provincial synod of Neo-Cæsarea (A.D. 314), priests are forbidden to countenance the festivities of second marriages by their presence, "since the *bigamus* needed penitence." (Thus early did the ecclesiastical use of the word *bigamus* become distinguished from the civil, in which it always denotes one married to two spouses still living.) The Council of Nicæa sought to interpose a check on this foolish restriction, and required (in its 8th canon) that the *cathari*, or purists, on being received into the church, should formally consent to communicate with such as had been married a second time. Yet a provincial council at Laodicea, held about a quarter of a century later (A.D. 352), ordained, in its very first canon, that persons legally marrying a second time should be received into communion only after fasting and prayer, and *juxta indulgentiam*. The general sense of the church, however, successfully withstood the ascetic tendency in this form of its manifestation; but only that it might be made to concentrate itself upon the select class of the priesthood, in respect to whom the feeling continued to grow that the normal condition was one of entire separation from married life, and that disqualification for clerical ministrations was consequent on a second marriage, especially if the second had been entered into after baptism. A rule to this effect is laid down in the so-called Apostolical Canons, which, though bearing a false title, undoubtedly expressed the general mind of the church about the close of the fourth century. They ordained, among other grounds of exception, that no one who had become involved in second marriages after baptism, or who had married a widow (this being also on one side a second marriage), could be admitted to any grade of priestly standing (Can. 17, 18). In like manner Ambrose, while distinctly asserting that the apostolic precepts do not condemn second marriages (*De Vid.* c. 2, § 10), yet maintains that they were rightly held to be inconsistent with priestly functions (according to the prescription in 1 Tim. iii. 2), and for this among other reasons, that there should not be one rule for the clergy and the people; that the former, as they stood on a higher spiritual eminence, should be held bound to a more perfect mode of life (*Ep. ad Vercell. Ecclesiam*, § 62–64. To the same effect also Innocent of Rome, *De Cr.* 13; and Epiphanius, *Hær.* 48).

Yet, with all this countenance from some of the more prominent authorities of the church, and the steady growth of public sentiment in the same direction, the practice in many places but slowly conformed to what the ascetic spirit, in this alliance with caste distinctions and ritualistic services, demanded as right and proper. Theodoret (whose comment on St. Paul's expression was formerly given) mentions, in a letter to Domnus of Antioch (Ep. 110), that he had ordained one Irenæus, though he had entered into marriage a second time; and that in doing so he had but "followed the footsteps of those who had gone before him." He refers also to various examples of the same kind. And the frequency of the practice, coupled with the impropriety, or rather the palpable indecency, of the church's commonly recognised procedure in excluding from sacred ministrations those who had lawfully entered into wedlock a second time, while persons guilty of concubinage and the grossest immoralities were freely admitted, is denounced by Jerome, in his own peculiar style, when commenting on a case of the former description in his letter to Oceanus. "I wonder," says Jerome to his correspondent, "that you should think of dragging forth one bishop as having transgressed the apostolic rule, since the whole world is full of these ordinations: I don't mean of presbyters, or those of inferior grade, but I come to bishops, of whom I could unroll such a list as would exceed in number the members of the synod of Ariminum." He then refers to a disputation he had with an eloquent man at Rome on the subject, whose syllogistic reasoning he met by a counter reasoning of the same kind; and then he adds: " It is a new thing I hear, that what was not sin shall be reckoned for sin. All sorts of prostitutions, and the filth of public abominations, impiety towards God, acts of parricide, of incest, etc., are purged away in the font of Christ. Shall the stains of a wife still inhere, and brothels be preferred to the marriage-bed? I do not cast up to *you* troops of harlots, lots of catamites, shedding of blood, and swinish indulgences at every feast; and you bring up to *me* from the sepulchre a wife long since dead, whom I received lest I should do what you have done! Let the Gentiles hear it; let the catechumens, who are candidates for the faith, lest they marry wives before baptism, lest they enter into honourable matrimony, but may have wives and children in common—nay, may shun the term *wife* in every form, lest, after they have believed in Christ, it shall prove to their detriment that they had wives, and not concubines or harlots."

Such were the factitious distinctions and the mischievous results which grew out of this unscriptural mode of teaching which the church received mainly at the hands of Tertullian, after he had assumed the heretical position of a Montanist. The view ultimately became associated nearly as much with false notions of the ministry and of the sacraments, as with unwarranted restrictions regarding marriage. And as the development in that direction could not be deemed otherwise than natural, if the principle had been sound on which it proceeded,—that a species of sanctity incompatible with second marriages was required of pastors and deacons which is not required of believers generally,—the development itself may fairly be regarded as a proof of the unsoundness of the principle. Doctrinally, it was wrong; but in a practical respect also, the view could not fail to be accompanied with serious embarrassment or trouble of a domestic kind. Pastors bereaved by death of their wives, and without any female relative to supply the blank, would often find it impossible to have their children properly cared for, and their households ruled well (according to apostolic precept), except by entering anew into married life. And to interdict this would necessarily have forced on them the painful alternative of either perilling the moral well-being of their family, or, to avoid that, renouncing their position as ministers of God's word.

4. There remains still another line of reflection to strengthen the interpretation given—this, namely, that in addition to the objections which have been urged against understanding the expression of absolute monogamy, the other view affords a perfectly good and appropriate meaning. Recent interpreters have sometimes denied this, and laid considerable stress on the opposite allegation. Thus Alford: "The apostle would hardly have specified that as a requisite for the episcopate or presbyterate which we know to have been fulfilled by all Christians whatever; no instance being adduced of polygamy being practised in the Christian church, and no exhortation to abstain from it." If this were anything like a fair and full representation of the matter, it would be hard to account for so many of the early interpreters (conversant, as they were, with the circumstances of the time) taking the other view of the passage, and thinking that, as matters then stood alike among the Jews and Gentiles, ample grounds existed for insisting on monogamy in the ordinary sense — monogamy in contradistinction simply to polygamy and divorce — as a qualification for office in the church. A certain proportion of its membership consisted of converts from Judaism; and though divorce, perhaps, on insufficient grounds, and subsequent marriage, or the undisguised practice of polygamy, might not be very common in the gospel age among the Jews, yet there is not wanting evidence to show that usages of that description did exist, and continued for ages after the Christian era. Justin Martyr charges it as matter of just reproach against the teachers of the Jewish people, that even till now they permitted each man to have four or five wives (*Trypho*, c. 134). And in the year A.D. 393 a law was passed by Theodosius, enjoining that "none of the Jews should retain their own custom in marriage, nor enter into diverse marriage

relationships at one time" (*nec in diversa sub uno tempore conjugia conveniat*),—a law which is not likely to have been enacted without adequate reasons for it, and still less to have been re-enacted, as it was by Justinian a century and a half later. It will readily be understood, that if persons, who in their unchristian state had become entangled in such double or treble marriage relationships, might be admitted, on their conversion, to the communion of the church, they should still not be entrusted with the spiritual administration of its affairs: there was a flaw in their condition which unfitted them for being unexceptionable guides and overseers of the flock. It is notorious, also, that among the Greeks and Romans, although polygamy was not formally sanctioned, yet it virtually prevailed—prevailed under the connivance or sanction of law; and that the most deplorable and wide-spread laxity in this respect existed, both previous to the apostolic age and for long after it. In the later stages of the Republic, with the influx of wealth and luxury, a fearful degeneracy of manners made way among the higher classes of society; many shunned the restraints of marriage, and with those who entered into the bond it was often little more than a temporary contract. Divorce was so common, that "public opinion ceased to frown on it; it could be initiated by husband or wife with almost equal freedom: there was a ready consent of both parties to the separation, in the prospect of marrying again; and this facility was open to all classes who could contract marriage."[1] It was even open to them to do it without any legal process; for, as another authority on the subject tells us, "among the Romans divorce did not require the sentence of a judge; no judicial proceedings were necessary. It was considered a private act, though some distinct notice or declaration of intention was usual."[2]

This great social evil, instead of abating, grew with the introduction of the Empire, and received a powerful stimulus from the scandalous excesses of persons in high places. The two first Cæsars set here an example which was only too closely followed by many of their successors and underlings. Female manners became so loose, that no woman

[1] Dr. Thos. D. Woolsey *On Divorce and Divorce Legislation*, p. 41.
[2] Lord Mackenzie *On Roman Law*, part i. c. 6.

(Seneca could say) "was now ashamed of divorce; and illustrious and noble ladies counted their years, not by the number of consuls, but by the number of their husbands." Hence also the bitter sarcasm of Juvenal:

> Sic fiunt octo mariti
> Quinque per autumnos.—vi. 229.

The influence of such a state of things at headquarters must have told disastrously throughout the empire. The States of Greece are known to have been lax enough even before such an influence began to work upon them; there was little of a high moral tone in the relations of domestic life. Along with marriage, the practice of concubinage was everywhere tolerated, and actions of divorce were effected by common consent, and on the weakest grounds. Even in Sparta, which was probably the least licentious State of Greece, what a light is thrown on the prevailing sentiments and habits of the people by such a fact as this: "To bring together the finest couples was regarded by the citizens as desirable, and by the lawgiver as a duty. There were even some married women who were recognised mistresses of two houses, and mothers of two distinct families,—a sort of bigamy strictly forbidden to the men, and never permitted except in the remarkable case of King Anaxandrides, when the royal Herakleidan line of Eurystheus was in danger of becoming extinct."[1] But without going further into detail, there can be no doubt that corruption in this particular line held its course generally throughout the Roman Empire for centuries after the Christian era, only partially checked by the introduction of the Christian element; so partially, indeed, that "divorce *ex communi consensu* kept its ground all the way down to Justinian" (Woolsey, p. 101). The legislative attempt of Constantine to grant liberty of divorce only on the proof of such heinous crimes as poisoning and adultery, failed from the impossibility of carrying it into effect. It had to be first relaxed, and by Honorius was almost abrogated. "A Christian writer, at the beginning of the fifth century, complains that men changed their wives as quickly as their clothes, and that marriage chambers were set up as easily as booths in a market. At a later period still, when Justinian attempted to prohibit all divorces

[1] Grote's *History*, vol. ii. p. 520.

except those on account of chastity, he was obliged to relax the law on account of the fearful crimes, the plots and poisonings, and other evils, which it introduced into domestic life."[1]

Taking, then, all the known circumstances of the time into account, we see only too ample reason for such a qualification as that specified by the apostle for pastors and deacons—if by that qualification is understood simply fidelity to the marriage vow, or relationship to no more than one living woman as a spouse. The question was not (as put by Alford) whether, after being received into the Christian church, a looser practice might be held compatible with Christian obligations,—a wife and a concubine, or two wives at a time,—but whether those who had in these respects followed the too common practice of the world, should, on becoming Christians, be admitted to office in the church. Had they been so, the church might have seemed to take too light a view of the prevailing immorality; embarrassing complications also might have arisen for the parties themselves in the discharge of duty; so that the part of Christian wisdom with the church evidently was to stand entirely clear, in her administrative capacity, from having any participation in the abounding corruption. It is the very course which missionaries of the gospel are obliged in heathen lands to pursue still. They can often receive parties into church fellowship, because apparently sincere in the profession of the faith, whom yet, on account of essentially adulterous connections contracted in their heathenish state, they have felt it necessary to exclude from positions of honour, especially from functions of government in the church.[2]

It has been thought by some Protestant writers (by Vitringa, for example, *Synag. Vet.* P. i. c. 4; also by Ellicott, Alford, and some others), that the corrupt state of

[1] Milman's *History of Christianity*, vol. iii. p. 290.
[2] The comment of Conybeare and Howson on the passage under consideration, though brief, is in perfect accordance with the view we have given. "The true interpretation seems to be as follows : In the corrupt facility of divorce allowed both by Greek and Roman law, it was very common for man and wife to separate, and marry other parties during the life of one another. Thus, a man might have three or four living wives. An example of the operation of a similar code is un-

matters prevailing at the time may have induced the apostle to lay down the rule of absolute monogamy for rulers in the church—to provide a more efficient check against the evil —but that, as the same motive no longer operates now, the rule is fitly regarded as having had only a temporary significance, and as no longer in force. This, however, is a quite arbitrary supposition. The qualification, as given by the apostle, is coupled with no temporal limitation. It stands, in that respect, on the same footing as the other prescriptions—alike valid, apparently, for all times. Besides, the extremely lax state of morals then prevalent, while it undoubtedly called the church, especially in its official representatives, to be examples of a truly chaste and becoming behaviour, could never have justified the application of tests which went beyond the requirements of God's law and the dictates of sound reason ; for this would have been to make one evil the occasion of opening the door to another. It would have been an attempt, as the ascetic discipline in every form is, to improve upon God's institutions by setting up a higher ideal of purity than is proper to them, and which always ends in bringing on worse evils than those it seeks to correct. In the form now under consideration, it would have given apostolic sanction to false views of marriage, and, against the whole spirit of the gospel, would have formally authorized gradations of sanctity in the membership of the church—a lower that might have sufficed for common believers ; and another and higher, as not only proper, but indispensable, for those who should be called to bear rule in the congregation. A distinction certainly not of apostolic origin, and the fruitful parent, when originated, of grievous errors and perversions !

Special stress is laid, in this connection, by the writers in question on the corresponding qualification prescribed for widows, who were to be admitted to the kindly oversight

happily to be found in our own colony of Mauritius. *There* the French revolutionary law of divorce has been suffered by the English Government to remain unrepealed ; and it is not uncommon to meet in society three or four women who have all been the wives of the same man, and three or four men who have all been the husbands of the same woman. We believe it is this kind of *successive* polygamy, rather than *simultaneous* polygamy, which is here spoken of as disqualifying for the presbyterate."

and benefactions of the church : these were, among other moral characteristics, to be known as having each been *the wife of one man*, chap. v. 9. How, it is asked, could this be understood otherwise than as descriptive of a woman who had been only once married ? And if such is the kind of oneness indicated in this case, how can it justly be regarded as different in the other ? The facts already stated, however, show that the necessity supposed for so understanding the expression in the woman's case by no means existed ; and the very circumstance of a qualification of this sort being necessary to entitle a poor widow to become merely the recipient of the church's charity, may surely be regarded as no mean evidence that the qualification in both cases could have involved nothing of an ascetic nature—could have required only what is due to the claims of decency, and is in accordance with the essential nature and design of marriage. But this is shown more fully in the annotations on chap. v. 9.

APPENDIX C.—PAGE 232.

THE TREATMENT OF SLAVERY IN NEW TESTAMENT SCRIPTURE (I TIM. VI. 2 ; TIT. II. 10).

THIS subject, in its relation to the spirit and teaching of Christianity, naturally falls into three closely-related parts : first, the direct instructions it gave to those standing to each other in the relation of slave and slave-owner ; second, the principles it unfolded tending indirectly, yet most materially, to bear on the relation ; and third, the practical measures which, under the influence of one or the other of these, came to be adopted with a view to the improvement of the existing order of things.

1. As regards the first of these points, it is to be borne in mind that the original heralds of Christianity had to do with slavery as not only an existing, but a time-honoured and widely-ramified institution, with a recognised place in the laws and usages of the empire, and of such gigantic propor-

tions that in the gospel age a slave for every freeman has been thought a moderate computation for the provinces of the empire at large.[1] In particular districts the proportion was much greater, though in others probably somewhat less. It was such, indeed, that in the more populous parts of the empire nearly all menial employments must have been discharged by servile hands, as well as much besides that belonged to the category of skilled labour. Now, with this vast system of legalized property in human flesh, the evangelists and apostles of our Lord came into contact chiefly as it bore on the class, not of owners, but of owned —of bondmen, not of those who held them in bondage; for the gospel drew at first the great body of its adherents from the lower grades of society, and those who ranked immediately above them. Of the first generation of believers in Christ, an extremely small proportion, it may be confidently assumed, would be owners of slaves; but not a few, in all probability, of the slaves themselves, whose depressed and suffering condition would naturally dispose them to hail a religion which looked so benignly on the afflicted, and held out such elevating prospects to all who sincerely embraced it. We thus quite readily account for the circumstance that the prescriptions in New Testament Scripture bearing on the relation in question are most numerous and pointed with respect to the slaves; and that sometimes, when charges are given as to the behaviour becoming *them*, none are delivered on the correlative duties of masters. It was not that the one class required the word of counsel or admonition more than the other; but because there were as yet scarcely any of the higher class who professed subjection to Christ, while there were many of the lower.

Having, therefore, mainly to do with those who occupied the lower place in this relationship, the authorized ambassadors of Christ naturally regarded them as peculiar objects both of pity and concern. They found them in an abject and humiliating condition, which they had no power, however they might have wished it, to alter or amend,—a condition which, in all its essential features, was fixed and regulated by the legislation of the empire. While the gospel of Christ could not break the chains which out-

[1] This is Gibbon's estimate.

wardly lay upon them, it could, and did also, in a moral and spiritual respect, mightily relieve and benefit their state; and, in return, it justly called them to prize the better things which it brought within their reach, and to show their profiting therein by discharging in another manner than before the duty of service exacted of them—to eye, in all they did, the divine rather than the human authority under which they stood: that so they might honour and commend to others the Master whom now it was their delight and glory to serve. They were thus, by their very calling as Christians, elevated within their own sphere to the high rank of witnesses of Christ, and instruments in His hand for diffusing abroad that saving light and truth, by which alone the greater disorders of society could be rectified, and the troubles of the more afflicted portions of mankind effectually removed. By taking the line of conduct prescribed, also, they would pursue the course which was almost sure to react beneficially on their social position. They necessarily became patterns of active virtue; and such were the encouragements given under the system of Roman slavery for obtaining freedom as the reward of good conduct, that Christian slaves, who in their daily procedure exhibited the spirit of the gospel, might be said to be on the high road toward manumission.

So much did the apostles set by conformity in this respect to the mind of Christ, and so confidently did they reckon upon other desirable ends being thus in due time attained, that they scarcely ever touched on the civil aspect of the question—on the acquirement of liberty. Incidentally the subject comes up in the Epistle to Philemon, with respect to Onesimus, his runaway slave; and yet it is so considerately and delicately handled by the apostle, that, while he shows distinctly enough his appreciation of a brotherly as contrasted with a servile relation, he would not have the former in any case acquired by fraud—would not even have it wrung from the legal owner by a reluctant concession; yet, if frankly conferred, would esteem it a most worthy expression of enlightened and sanctified feeling. In another place—a passage in the First Epistle to the Corinthians—the subject is also briefly treated in connection with a more general question, namely, how the reception of the gospel should be regarded as affecting people's family and social relationships? Were they still to continue in these after they had become Christians? Or were they to find in their Christianity a reason for abandoning them? The apostle's direction is: Abide as you are, and where you are, if you can do so consistently with Christian principle; and in so far as anything in your existing relations may be trying and irksome, instead of hastily ridding yourselves of it by a self-chosen method of escape, seek rather by your meek, patient, noble Christian bearing, to rise above the disadvantages of your outward position, and in the interests of godliness triumph over them. This is the general principle of action enunciated; and when applied to those who, on becoming Christians, found themselves oppressed by the yoke of slavery, it meant that they were not to use any power or opportunity they might have to break the yoke violently asunder; that they were rather to regard this as a part of the burden which, meanwhile, they had to bear for the sake of Christ; and that, while it was not good to be in slavery to man, it was possible even in this to be Christ's freeman: and *to be such* was so noble and blessed a thing, that their civil disabilities might be borne, while they lasted, with comparative indifference. This seems plainly the gist and bearing of the apostle's treatment of the subject, however we interpret the particular expressions.[1] It did not, when fairly considered, betoken any insensibility in the apostle's mind to the evils of slavery, taken by themselves. It is impossible, indeed, that he and the other heralds of the cross should have thought lightly of them, seeing they were in themselves so numerous and flagrant, and so contrary to the spirit of philanthropy which breathed in the gospel of Christ, and which was also exemplified so finely in the conduct of its divinely-commissioned teachers. But these men of God knew that the promptings of nature were likely to furnish a sufficient stimulus in that direction, and were not forgetful also of the effect which the new wine of the kingdom might have in the same direction—fermenting, as it would naturally do, in the minds of Christian slaves, with thoughts and aspirations in ill accord with their depressed

[1] It is only in respect to chap. vii. 21 that any diversity of interpretation prevails. See at the close of this Dissertation, p. 448.

and abject condition. It was therefore the part of Christian wisdom to throw the fence mainly on the more exposed side, and urge them, as their main concern, to the cultivation of those graces and habits which tended to elevate them as rational and immortal beings.

On this side of the question, then, wisdom was manifestly justified of her children; but was it equally so in the reserve practised, on the other side, toward the masters? If the apostles were right in plying the oppressed class with exhortations to virtue and obedience, why should they not have pressed those who had the power to let the oppressed go free? They certainly did not do this. The considerations chiefly urged upon the masters are, that they should remember they had to do with One who is no respecter of persons; who stood to *them* in the relation of a Master, as they to their fellow-creatures; and that they should consequently forbear, not the use of the lash merely, but even threatening, and should give to all under their control what is just and equal. Such injunctions, if properly carried out, would at least secure *practical* freedom to the slave—such freedom as would enable him to serve God faithfully in the humble duties of his station. But we can scarcely say apostolical precept, in its direct and explicit requirements of the slave-owner, goes further; especially as, when the supposition is made of believing servants under the yoke having also believing masters (1 Tim. vi. 2), the latter are spoken of as still retaining their proprietary rights, and the former are enjoined to do their work of service all the more cheerfully that they were under believing masters. If, however, we take into account not the letter merely, but the spirit also of the exhortations given, we shall doubtless see that something further *is* required of the parties in question, and that they could not have *intelligently and cordially* done so much without feeling impelled in ordinary circumstances to do more. For if the master consented, as he was expressly required, to treat his bondmen as rational beings, capable of the same exalted privileges and hopes as himself, how could he desire to have them kept in a position which exposed them to treatment of another kind, treatment from which his own spiritual nature must have recoiled? Plainly he could not with hearty good-will take the one part of a

Christian behaviour, without feeling drawn to do something also in respect to the other. And that the Apostle Paul thought persons in that situation *should* have so felt and acted, is evident from the style of address in his letter to Philemon respecting Onesimus, in which, as already indicated, he did not indeed claim strictly as a right, or demand as by divine authority, yet besought with powerful suasion, the reception of Onesimus, not merely as a forgiven bondman who had wronged his master, but in a higher character —"above a slave (as he expressed himself), a brother beloved." To yield to this affectionate entreaty, and yet re-assert over Onesimus his proprietary rights as a slaveholder, had been impossible; the very attempt to do so would have been justly branded as a pitiful evasion.

But if such were the mind of the apostles, and the certain tendency of their instructions, might it not have been better to go straight to the point, and lay upon every Christian slave-owner the authoritative injunction to enfranchise his slaves? So some have, even in *our* time, been bold enough to assert. But had the course in question been taken, how many enfranchisements might have been expected through its operation? Or what progress was Christianity likely to have made in ameliorating the social evils of the Empire? With this startling demand among its requirements,—in the very front, we may say, of these requirements (for it was sure to be the first that should ever meet the eye of the slave-owner),—persons of this class would with one consent have denounced Christianity as the opponent of their legal interests and hereditary rights; they would have everywhere met it with their determined opposition—would have put it, in fact, under the ban of the Empire, as a system that, under the guise of religion, aimed at unsettling the foundations of society, and kindling the flames of a servile war. It was at once the wiser and the more humane course to make the direct prescriptions of the gospel bear only on the just and equitable treatment of the slave, so that the moment he was placed under the dominion of a believing master he should become practically free to move within the ordinary sphere of Christian duty; and in addition to this, to place the master as well as the slave under motives and considerations of a higher kind, which, in proportion as they were realized and acted on, necessarily led to the readjustment or removal of whatever in their mutual relationship was at variance with the essential principles of rectitude and goodness.

2. This touches, however, upon the second point—the higher influences brought by the gospel to bear on the hearts of slave-owners, and tending indirectly to loose the bonds of slavery. The whole spirit and tendency of the religion of the gospel must have wrought in this direction.

The view given in Scripture of the common origin and natural relationships of mankind—even this, which is implied in the revelations of the gospel, rather than directly announced—could not, if thoughtfully pondered, be without effect in this particular line. That all should be the offspring of one parent,—inheritors of one blood, and partakers of the same rational and immortal nature,—and yet that they should make merchandise of one another, as if some belonged to a different world, or a different order of creation from the rest;—who that justly considers the one can find it in his heart to do the other? How especially could he do so, if he coupled with men's brotherly relation to himself their filial relation to God, though he should only think of that relation as it exists in nature, implying the formation of all alike in God's image, and their calling as such to occupy the earth, and use its means and opportunities of good for Him? To treat a human being so formed, so constituted and destined by the hand of his Maker, as from the mere accidents of position bereft of freedom of will and independent action, were virtually to disown and shamefully dishonour the claims and interests of such a natural relationship.

Yet this is but the preliminary ground or implied basis of Christianity, not its proper substance; and its influence in this direction becomes much greater when its grand central doctrine of the incarnation and death of the Son of God for the salvation of mankind is brought distinctly into view. This, when rightly known and considered by men, could not but be felt to be like the letting in of a new light upon the world, tending by a moral necessity to raise the common platform of humanity to a higher than its former level. It is from hence, most of all, that has sprung the idea of the brotherhood of mankind—of their original equality in God's sight, and of the honour and blessedness of ministering to their wellbeing, apart from all the outward and artificial distinctions which in the heathen world entered so largely into men's estimation of their fellow-men, and threw something like an impassable gulf between race and race, and one condition of life and another. The infinite condescension and glorious example of Christ virtually established for all a claim to the highest offices of kindness, and, wherever practically known, gave such an impulse to the more generous feelings of the heart, and the more active charities of life, that everything like cruel neglect or lordly oppression toward even the humblest grades of society could not fail to be regarded otherwise than as an outrage on humanity.

Then, regard to the interests of salvation must have wrought in the same direction. From the moment that any one became a genuine believer, it was part of his obligations to see that everything of a proper and fitting kind was done to bring all under his influence or control to partake with him in the blessings of salvation. But how could the slave-owner commend to others about him the offers of a love, of which it was but too clear he had not yet received the full impression in his own bosom? How could he desire in earnest to see them rising to the possession and enjoyment of the liberties of God's dear children? The attainment of such a standing in spiritual things, with its high privileges and endowments, he could not but see, would only render them the more deeply conscious of the ignoble chains which rested on their bodily condition; for how could they possess the rank of sons in God's house, and realize their title to the glorious inheritance of the saints in light, without feeling the incongruity and the dishonour of being denied the place of citizens of earth, or of being allowed to take an independent part in the ordinary concerns of a present life? It was obviously impossible that the intelligent Christian slave should have felt otherwise than is now represented; and if not absolutely impossible, at least not very natural or easy, for his master to become a sincere convert to the gospel, and still keep the yoke of bondage riveted on the neck of a Christian brother.

Of the force of these considerations the history of the

subject has yielded two very instructive and convincing illustrations. The first is the reluctance commonly exhibited by slave-owners to let those under their sway enjoy the full benefit of Christian instruction and privilege. How far this was the case in ancient times we can only infer from what has happened among the modern representatives of the class; but in the particular point under consideration, it is likely to have been worse rather than better in the earlier as compared with the later ages. Yet, as regards these later ages, no one in the least acquainted with the history of slavery can be ignorant how commonly slave-owners have been jealous of the diffusion of Christian knowledge and instruction among their slaves—what restraints they have generally laid upon it—how often even they have expressly and by severe penalties interdicted it. Viewed as a whole, it is not too much to say of their conduct, that it has betrayed an unmistakeable conviction that the light and liberties of the gospel carry along with them a certain danger to their proprietary interests, and involve views of truth and duty materially different from their own. The other confirmatory fact consists in the grounds and reasons which have most commonly induced believing slave-owners to grant liberation to their bondmen. It appears that in the actual progress of events the spirit of the gospel, imperfectly as it was too often understood and imbibed, played an important part. While the work of emancipation made slow advances compared with the progressive advancement of an external Christianity, it still was always proceeding, and generally did so within the professing church as a response to the undeserved mercy of Heaven—an act of becoming tenderness and compassion in the recipients of divine grace and blessing. This may be seen by referring to the ancient charters of that description given by Du Cange, or even from the specimens selected out of them by Dr. Robertson (*Charles V.*, note 20). We find there grants of freedom made by sundry persons in favour of their slaves—made "for the love of God," "for the benefit of the soul" of the grantor, or something to that effect. When Pope Gregory the Great bestowed liberty on some slaves that had become his property, he prefaced the deed thus: "The Redeemer made Himself a propitiation to free men from the yoke of bondage, and restore them to their pristine condition; whence it well became men to restore those whom the law of nations, not nature, had brought into servitude, to the freedom which originally and properly belonged to them." Hence also a large number of manumissions appear to have been granted by persons on their death-beds, when their near approach to the judgment-seat rendered their consciences more alive to the great realities of the gospel, and the corresponding obligations: they granted the boon, it is commonly stated, "for the redemption of their soul." And hence also occasions of special favour and blessing were not unfrequently seized for conferring the grant; the benefit received on the one side being naturally felt to call for the bestowal of a like benefit on the other.

Indeed, it is difficult to understand how any one, if he could only divest himself of the perverting bias of habit, or the still more perverting bias of worldly interest, and would calmly look at the matter in the light of gospel truth, could come to another conclusion than that of either abandoning his right of property in his fellow-men, or of disclaiming allegiance to the authority of Christ. I do not see how, even with the kindest and most considerate treatment of his slaves, he could feel that he had discharged his obligations according to the requirements of the gospel without releasing them from their bondage. By one of these requirements he is called to be an imitator of Christ in that very walk of love wherein Christ has at once set so illustrious an example and given so costly a sacrifice. By another, he is enjoined to do to others whatsoever he would that they should do to him. By a third, he is urged to do good to all around him, as he has opportunity—to do it beyond the measure of the heathen, and for the promotion especially of the higher interests of mankind. But, on the supposition of his continuing to be a slave-owner, what honour do such precepts receive at his hands? He deliberately prefers holding men subject to bondage, while it was the special glory of his Master to deliver them from it; he practises upon them a wrong; and if he does not personally inflict, he leaves them in a position in which they may have inflicted upon them, insults and injuries, pains and cruelties, which no man of sane mind would wish another to have the power of inflicting upon himself. And instead of using his opportunities to do the part of a wise benefactor and moral regenerator of the world, he lazily and selfishly contributes to the maintenance of one of the foulest stains on the brotherhood of mankind; he lends his countenance and support to a system of which, as a whole, and as regards its inherent tendency, it has been not more eloquently than justly said: "It darkens and depraves the intellect; it paralyzes the hand of industry; it is the nourisher of agonizing fears and of sullen revenge; it crushes the spirit of the bold; it is the tempter, the murderer, and the tomb of virtue; and either blasts the felicity of those over whom it domineers, or forces them to seek for relief from their sorrows in the gratifications, and the mirth, and the madness of the passing hour."[1]

It is proper to add, however, that there may have been persons in ancient times, as there are known to have been some in later, who were not insensible to the considerations now noticed, and yet refrained from granting liberation to their slaves, out of regard chiefly to the present temporal comfort of the slaves themselves. In those States where slavery has become a widely-extended and compact system, the manners and usages of society so adapt themselves to it, that emancipation in individual cases, or on isolated properties, might have the effect of throwing the emancipated out of one class without being able to secure their introduction into another, better, or even so well, situated for employment and comfort as the one they had. They might, in consequence, if enfranchised, become exposed to neglect and want. There can be no doubt that such was the case, about the gospel era and before it, with many freedmen in certain districts of Italy, where, from the general employment of slaves in the cultivation of the soil, the free part of the population often fell into a very depressed and pitiable condition. The same may have happened, and doubtless did happen, in other provinces of the empire, of which we have less specific information; and it is also known to have happened in particular portions of what but lately were the slave states of the West Indies and of America. So that it

[1] Speech of Dr. Andrew Thomson, Edinburgh.

would not always be simply from the power of the gospel not being felt, or from a deliberate disregard of its claims in this particular direction, that the bondmen of Christian masters did not regain their freedom. A benevolent regard to their present wellbeing, even though possibly a somewhat mistaken or undue regard, may have often contributed to the result.

3. We turn now, lastly, to the practical measures in which, so far as we know, the early teachers and representatives of the gospel gave effect to the direct instructions, and the indirect, the higher considerations under which, in this respect, they were placed by their belief of the truth.

On this point our means of information are very limited and fragmentary, and there is much we should like to know of the earlier periods of church action of which we must be content to be ignorant. Undoubtedly the process of relief within the church would have been quick and satisfactory, compared with what we have reason to believe it was, if all in the position of slave-owners, who professed obedience to the gospel, had risen at once to the proper height of knowledge and attainment in this branch of their calling. But we are not at liberty to suppose that; the pleading alone in the Epistle to Philemon, shows plainly enough how slowly the very best of the early converts grasped here the full results and consequences of their faith. There would doubtless be many who at once felt it their duty to give hearty obedience to the precepts of the gospel, in so far as these required a kind and considerate treatment of their dependants, who yet, from the force of habit or other influences, would never think of bringing the system itself of slavery to the test of the great principles of the gospel. The case of John Newton, in modern times, may be cited in proof, since, after undergoing one of the most remarkable conversions on record, he continued for a time not only insensible to the common evils of slavery, but even actively engaged in the inhuman transactions of the slave-trade, conceiving all his obligations in the matter to be discharged if only he looked after the bodily comfort of the unhappy victims who fell into his hands. The utterly antichristian character of the traffic disclosed itself but gradually to his mind. A bequest may also be noticed in the same connection, which was left by an American gentleman of last century to the Society for the Propagation of the Gospel—"a plantation stocked with slaves." "An odd legacy," says Warburton, in the sermon preached by him for the Society of the same year; "an odd legacy to the promulgators of the law of liberty, but intended, perhaps, as a kind of compensation for these violations of it." Custom had in all probability rendered the individual entirely unconscious of the inconsistence.

It should not therefore surprise us to learn that, in the church of the apostolic and immediately subsequent age, there were Christian slave-owners as well as Christian slaves in her communion, with a relaxation no doubt of the bond, and a tendency begun toward its dissolution, yet still no general movement made for its formal extinction. Slaves and masters alike, on their professing Christianity, came under the discipline of the church, and were amenable to it for their actual behaviour. This was of itself a great security against all harsh treatment, considering what discipline was in those early times—how impartial and how stringent; and it is probably the main reason why so little is said on the subject of slavery in the more ancient Patristic writings, although doubtless the ascetic tendency which so early began to tell on leading men in the church exercised, to some extent, an unfavourable influence also here. The so-called Apostolic Fathers—Justin Martyr, also Irenæus, Tertullian, Cyprian—very rarely refer to the subject of slavery in any way, and give no special instructions concerning it. Even in the voluminous writings of Augustine, we shall scarcely find a more explicit or pointed testimony than the following: "A Christian should not possess a slave after the same manner that he does a horse or a piece of silver" (*De Serm. Dom. in Monte*, L. i. § 590). And when giving a summary of what the church, as the true mother of all Christians, enjoins upon her children, the whole he says in her behalf as to the relation of master and servant is: "Thou teachest servants to cleave to their masters, not so much from the necessity of their condition, as from delight in the duties of their calling. Thou makest masters placable toward their servants, from regard to the great God, their common Lord, and more ready to give counsel than to practise coercion"

(*De Mor. Eccl. Cath.* § 63). Chrysostom failed even more than Augustine to bring out on this point the true spirit of the gospel; and his continuous commentaries on the epistles of the New Testament furnished him also with better opportunities. In his exposition of Philemon, while he speaks strongly enough of the scandal brought on Christianity by slaves running away from their masters, and of Christians abetting and aiding them in their attempts to do so, he does not say a single word on the duty of Christian masters to grant liberty to their slaves; he speaks also quite familiarly of *our* custom of purchasing slaves with money, and of its being esteemed the glory of a master to have many of them. He is somewhat better at Eph. vi. 9, where masters are enjoined to do the same things toward their slaves that the slaves themselves were exhorted to do, and to forbear threatening, as knowing that they had a Master in heaven, with whom there is no respect of persons. Here Chrysostom presses the consideration that masters shall assuredly have their measure meted back to them; that they must do as they hope to be done to; and that they should teach their slaves to be pious and godly, and then all would go well. But emancipation is not once hinted at.

Notwithstanding such comparative failures, however, on the part of the standard-bearers of the church, the mild, beneficent, love-embracing spirit of the gospel made way, first lightening the yoke, and then subverting the existence of slavery. This appears especially in the efforts put forth from time to time to obtain the freedom of Christians who by misfortune had been reduced to slavery, and the fresh facilities that were given to slave emancipation by legal enactment. The barbarous treatment of the servile class was openly condemned by the ministers and councils of the church. Clement of Alexandria absolutely prohibited the acceptance of any oblations from cruel and sanguinary masters; and several councils appointed temporary excommunications to be pronounced against those who, without any judicial sentence, put their slaves to death. Acacius, bishop of Amida, had the gold and silver vessels of his church melted to redeem 7000 captives, whom the Romans had brought from Persia, and sent them back free. Ambrose did something of the same sort at Milan. Cases are even mentioned of persons who sold their whole property to purchase the freedom of their fellow-Christians. One Melania is said to have liberated so many as 8000 slaves; Obidius, a Gaulish Christian, 5000, etc. And so congenial did the work of manumission seem to the spirit of the gospel, that Constantine, while suspending ordinary work on the Lord's day, expressly allowed the manumission of slaves, as having in itself the essential characteristics of a pious and charitable action.[1]

In another respect, also, the ancient church did good service: she guarded the chastity of female slaves, and servile birth formed no disqualification for the sacred offices of the priesthood. The legal statutes, for a considerable time, embarrassed her operations, and made the progress of the work more difficult. The Code of Justinian recognised, indeed, the original equality of mankind, but it admitted the forfeiture of this equality by the casualties which use and wont had allowed to entail the loss of freedom. Still, what was not removed was in several respects alleviated. Masters were forbidden to abandon their slaves when sick or enfeebled with age—they were obliged to have them privately cared for, or sent to the hospitals. In heathen times, slaves could not properly marry; their union was merely concubinage; and for a free person to marry a slave was even held a capital offence. The Christian church struggled long and stedfastly against such things, and at last succeeded in getting legal sanction to the marriage of slaves, and gave to marriages of this kind, as well as others, her benediction. The tendency of the imperial legislation became increasingly favourable to the interests of the slave; and Gibbon says of Justinian's Code, that " the spirit of his laws promoted the extinction of domestic servitude." But the extinction was much retarded, especially by two causes.

The first of these was the growing worldliness and corruption of the church. The salt, to a very large extent, had lost its savour. In process of time, churches themselves came to hold property in slaves, and even had their property in this respect guarded by special enactments.

---

[1] Guizot, *Hist. of Civil. in France*, ii. p. 128; Bingham, *Ant.* B. xx. c. 2, 5.

While churches were constituted asylums for runaway slaves, slaves that belonged to ecclesiastics or sacred foundations, if they became runaways, were denied all right of protection; any one who harboured them became liable to pay a triple fine (Milman's *Lat. Christianity*, i. 365). The other circumstance was the enormous multiplication of slaves consequent upon the irruption of the northern nations. This increased the evil to such an extent that, by its very excess, it helped to work out the remedy. Slaves ceased in a manner to be saleable; they became serfs—labourers attached to the soil; and by this appropriation they had conceded to them a measure of security against the caprice and despotism of the masters. In this state one could not be sold, save as part and parcel of the ground on which he resided; and while thus bound to a kind of hereditary serfdom, his position was regulated by law—guarded, though still but imperfectly, from the freaks of arbitrary violence and oppression. Other changes, mainly effected by trade and commerce, came in to ameliorate their condition; and after centuries of delay, and a step-to-step progress, serfdom itself passed, throughout the different countries of Europe, into personal and social freedom.

Broken, therefore, and chequered as the history is, interrupted by many haltings and even temporary reverses, it has still been an advancement—Christianity has vindicated her title to the character of a friend of the captive and the bond. She would have done so, it is true, far more speedily and extensively if she had herself remained free from the corruptions of the world, and if her grand aims for the good of mankind had been properly carried out. But, as matters actually stood, a gradual rectification took place; a milder and better tone was diffused throughout society; a standard of generosity and loving-kindness was everywhere raised, which might be said to frown on the intolerance and cruelty of slavery, and prepared the world for giving practical effect to the feeling of a common brotherhood. Nothing, indeed, can be more certain, from the struggles and triumphs of the past, than that this horrid institution, which is alike dishonouring to God and injurious to the best interests of society, cannot stand with a healthful and robust Christianity: as the one lives and thrives, the other of necessity gives way; and were there a gospel everywhere triumphant, there would infallibly be a free as well as a righteous and a blessed world.

NOTE TO P. 435, ON I COR. VII. 21.

IN illustration of the general principle that people, on becoming Christians, should abide in the calling wherein they were called, the apostle refers, along with some other cases, to that of bondmen: "Wast thou called, being a slave? Care not for it. But if also (or indeed) thou art able to become free, use it rather." "That is," says Chrysostom, "rather be a slave. And why, then, does he bid *him*, who had it in his power to become free, to continue a slave? He did it to show that slavery no way injures, but rather profits (ὅτι οὐδὲν βλάπτει ἡ δουλεία, ἀλλὰ καὶ ὠφελεί)." Rather strange doctrine, surely, to ascribe to one who in his own case valued so highly, not merely his common liberty, but his special freedom as a Roman citizen, that he would not allow its rights to be trampled on; and who, in respect to his convert Onesimus, showed how well he could distinguish between the disadvantages of a slave's place and the honourable position of a brother! Chrysostom adds that he was aware there were some who understood the *use* recommended of liberty: if you are able to become free, embrace freedom rather. But he rejects this view as against the connection, which (he thinks) requires that even if a believing slave had the option of becoming free, he should prefer his slavery. And the same view is taken by Theodoret, Theophylact, also by various modern commentators of note, in particular by Estius, Wolf, Bengel, Meyer, Alford. Several of them hold it to be the only view grammatically tenable; for when καί succeeds εἰ, it does not belong to εἰ, but to the following clause, which it is spread over and qualifies; so that the meaning (it is alleged) can only be: But if even thou canst be free, use it—namely, slavery—rather. Dean Stanley hesitates between the two modes of explanation. Whether *freedom* or *slavery* is to be supplied to the verb *use*, he conceives to be "one of the most evenly balanced questions in the interpretation of the New Testament." And he goes on to state, with his wonted dexterity, the considerations that appear to make for the two views respectively, but commences with the strange assertion that the verb χρῆσαι "may either be *choose*, or *make use of*, although it leans rather to the former, and thus favours the first interpretation"—that, namely, which would couple it with slavery. He does not, however, produce any passage in the New Testament in support of the sense of *choosing*; nor can a single one *be* produced. In the two Epistles to the Corinthians it occurs, besides the present passage, six times (1 Cor. vii. 31, ix. 12, 15; 2 Cor. i. 17, iii. 12, xiii. 10), but never in the sense of *choosing*—always in that of *using, making use of*. And retaining this as the only allowable meaning, how could the apostle exhort any Christian slave, who had the opportunity of becoming free, to use slavery rather? Slavery is not a gift or talent to be used, but a restraint, a hardship to be borne or submitted to—if necessary—but no more. And with all its tendency to asceticism, and to a foolish self-imposition of outward restraints, the ancient church still had common sense enough, and native instincts remaining, to dispose her members generally so to regard it. The well-known practice of Christians in freely spending of their means to liberate their brethren from servitude, when by some calamity reduced to it, was a virtual protest against the inflated oratory of Chrysostom, and his false exegesis.

As to the grammatical canon, very formally propounded by Alford, that καί after εἰ qualifies the succeeding clause, so as to mark a gradation upward—*if even*,—one has only to look at the passages in which the particles occur to see how far it will carry us. Sometimes, no doubt, the ascensive force is plain enough, as at Phil. ii. 17, " But if I even be offered (ἀλλὰ εἰ καὶ σπένδομαι);" to which may be added 1 Pet. iii. 14. But take other examples—such as 2 Cor. xi. 15, where, speaking of Satan and his instruments of working, the apostle says, "No great wonder, therefore, if also (εἰ καί) his ministers are transformed as ministers of righteousness." Here the particles indicate merely an additional and subordinate fact—if progress at all, a progress downward, not upward. So also at 1 Cor. iv. 7, "What hast thou, that thou didst not receive? But if also (or indeed) thou didst receive it—εἰ δὲ καὶ ἔλαβες" (also 2 Cor. v. 16, vii. 8); on which Alford is himself obliged to let go the ascensive force. It does not appear that for the New Testament usage one can go further with a grammatical principle in the matter than as stated by Winer: "In general, εἰ καί signifies *although, si etiam*, quanquam, indicating something as an actual fact;" or, as Mr. Moulton puts it in a note, indicating either that what the sentence expresses is, in the writer's belief, an actual fact, or a concession on his part that the supposition is correct (*Gr.* § 53, 7, Clark's ed.). Mr. Moulton, however, himself adopts the ascensive force in the passage before us.

The difficulty, as appears to me, in giving a natural and proper explanation of the passage has been aggravated by supposing that either ἐλευθερία, *freedom*, or δουλεία, *bondage*, must be supplied for the verb χρῆσαι. The more natural construction is to supply the noun involved in the preceding verb; the stress lies on it—on δύνασαι. "Wast thou called, being a slave? Care not for it. But if also thou art able (δύνασαι) to become free, use it (the δύναμις, ability) rather;" having the power, turn it rather to account. It is not properly the use of the freedom which the apostle advises (in which case we should certainly, as Alford remarks, have judged ἐλευθερία to be the proper word to be supplied to χρῆσαι), but the use of the *power* to obtain freedom; and either this, or the whole clause, *power to become free*, is the thing to be supplied. Thus viewed, two suppositions are made in the verse: first, slavery without the power of escaping from it—in which case the principle of abiding in one's station holds without any qualification, and under the elevating influence of the gospel a noble indifference is recommended; second, the gospel of acquiring freedom, with an advice to take advantage of the opportunity. Then, in the following verse, a twofold consideration is introduced by γάρ, suited to the two suppositions going before: the bondman, even though remaining such, is the Lord's freeman, and the freeman is the Lord's bondman. Either way a qualifying circumstance—in the one case tending to abate the natural evil, in the other to circumscribe and regulate the natural good. But to leave no doubt that the apostle was not insensible to the superiority of a free over an enslaved condition, and regarded the former as alone properly suited to the place of a believer, he adds, ver. 24, "Ye were bought with a price; do not become slaves of men." Seeing how great a price has been given to raise you into the glorious liberty of the gospel, do not act an unseemly part by becoming bondmen to your fellow-creatures. And of course, if they should not voluntarily become such, neither should they voluntarily continue such, when it was in their power to escape from the anomalous position.

Interpreted in this manner, the exhortation of the apostle is throughout reasonable and consistent. His general direction is that people, on becoming Christians, should continue in the relations which they at the time occupied — the married (though to a heathen spouse) in wedlock, the uncircumcised in uncircumcision, the slave in bondage. But where a change to the better might be found practicable, let it be adopted—the Christian wife drawing over to the faith her unbelieving husband, or, failing in that, and finding domestic peace impracticable, retiring into privacy; the slave having the power to become free, using that power; but the free on no account bartering their freedom for a state of bondage, since that would be unsuitable to their high calling as the redeemed children of God in Christ.

THE END.